St. Louis Community College

Forest Park
Florissant Valley
Meramec

Instructional Resources
St. Louis, Missouri

Legends of the Earth, Sea, and Sky

An Encyclopedia of Nature Myths

Legends of the Earth, Sea, and Sky

An Encyclopedia of Nature Myths

Tamra Andrews

ABC-CLIO

Santa Barbara, California
Denver, Colorado
Oxford, England

Library of Congress Cataloging-in-Publication Data

Andrews, Tamra.
    Legends of earth, sea, and sky : an encyclopedia of nature myths /
Tamra Andrews.
      p.   cm.
    Includes bibliographical references and indexes.
    ISBN 0-87436-963-0 (alk. paper)
    1. Nature—Mythology—Encyclopedias. I. Title.
    BL435.A53   1998
    291.2'12'03—dc21   98-40603

02 01 00 99   10 9 8 7 6 5 4 3 2

ABC-CLIO, Inc.
130 Cremona Drive, P.O. Box 1911
Santa Barbara, California 93116-1911

This book is printed on acid free paper ∞ .
Manufactured in the United States of America

CONTENTS

PREFACE

The world around us has affected the way we think and live from time immemorial. But nowhere do we find such vivid imagery of the physical world as we do in ancient myths. Early people were closer to nature than we today can imagine. *Legends of the Earth, Sea, and Sky* helps us imagine, and it helps us understand our age-old desire to interpret and control the phenomena of the natural world.

Long ago, when the sky was dark and the earth was bare and the sea seemed boundless and endless, people tried to philosophize about those foreboding forces. Mythology was their form of philosophy. The myths and legends the ancients told served a purpose. These stories were thought processes, earlier ways of reasoning what people now theorize though scientific method. So the reader of mythology must look beyond the symbols and metaphors and search for underlying truths.

No one will ever be able to crawl into the mind of ancient skywatchers and take their view of the stars or take the oars of ancient seafarers and see what they saw beneath the waves. But the myths help us try. Readers of these myths internalize the stories and interpret them in their own way. Readers of nature myths learn that in the ancient world, people invested natural phenomena with the same qualities they knew in themselves. They walked, so the sun walked; they breathed, so the wind breathed. For this reason, and because the original sources of myths in many countries are scarce and difficult to interpret in the first place, modern scholars interpret early myths in thousands of ways.

I hope that the readers of *Legends of the Earth, Sea, and Sky* reach beyond the mythical interpretations I have collected and see beyond the metaphors. They only scratch the surface of what scholars have been saying for hundreds of years. Furthermore, I chose entries broad in context, so the information provided can only scratch the surface. I did limit the scope of the encyclopedia to a discussion of natural phenomena, and specifically to nonliving phenomena, such as wind, clouds, meteors, and tides. In the entry for the Aztec deity Quetzalcoatl, for instance, I stressed his role as god of the sky and of wind rather than his role as god of medicine, fertility, and wealth. The references I provide at the end of each entry refer the reader to sources that further discuss the terms in the appropriate context and that provide additional information as well.

The types of entries in the encyclopedia include natural forces, gods and goddesses of natural forces, terms relating to the myths of natural forces, and broad geographical areas. The terms appear in one alphabetical listing, yet I made the attempt to provide some form of cohesiveness. Much information can be gained by making use of the cross-references at the end of each entry and the extensive subject index at the back of the book. I also included an index by culture that categorizes the entries by geographical areas. Under each area I listed the related god and goddess entries, and I included a category that lists cross-cultural entries as well. Alternate names for gods and goddesses appear in parentheses next to their names.

Many of the entries contain retellings of myths and legends about natural phenomena.

Keep in mind that similar myths vary greatly from source to source and that these variations are inevitable. The references at the end of each entry and the bibliography contain both primary and secondary sources. Ancient sources of the myths are not included in the bibliography but in an appendix, divided by culture area. The sources chosen for the appendix represent the best extant sources that I found to include the largest selection of myths of natural phenomena. As for the secondary sources of nature myths, I used as a starting place for many entries classic works on mythology and religion, such as the *Mythology of All Races*, Mircea Eliade's *Encyclopedia of Religion*, Sir James George Frazer's *The Worship of Nature*, and several series written by credible scholars. Fletcher Bassett's *Legends and Superstitions of the Sea and of Sailors in All Lands and at All Times* proved to be an indispensable source of information on sea lore.

Though monotheistic philosophies incorporate nature myths into their literature, they rely on the existence of one being with total control over natural forces. For this reason, I chose to include only those mythologies that relied on specific gods who controlled various aspects of the environment. The forces the ancients revered and feared and the deities who controlled them form the basis of *Legends of the Earth, Sea, and Sky*. Goddesses who raised the waves, shamans who summoned the rain, and great sky gods who hurled lightning bolts come alive in these pages. When I began researching *Legends of the Earth, Sea, and Sky*, I intended to include only beliefs that existed in ancient times. I found this difficult to do. Many groups of people in such areas as Africa, Australia, South America, and North America continue to hold tight to their beliefs and continue to bond with their land. I indicated current beliefs when known. Nature religion is alive in the world today. I hope everyone who reads *Legends of the Earth, Sea, and Sky* gains an understanding of these religions, and emerges with a renewed sense of wonder at the physical world.

ACKNOWLEDGMENTS

Writing a reference work such as *Legends of the Earth, Sea, and Sky* is a lonely task, yet never was I alone. I'd like to thank the many people and institutions that remained by my side and gave me the gift of their knowledge.

This book would not be possible were it not for the many scholars whose works I relied on as standard sources of information. The hard work, dedication, and insights of these people paved the way for many others, like myself, who have grown to know them only through their writings. Joseph Campbell, Mircea Eliade, Sir James George Frazer, and other writers in the field changed my life forever and afforded me what I consider privileged glimpses into the spiritual world that exists in nature. I found myself turning to the reference materials of Arthur Cotterell, Richard Cavendish, and Anthony Mercatante time and time again, and I relied heavily on Marjorie Leach's *Guide to the Gods,* both for its exhaustive list of deities and its extensive bibliography. But I'd like to particularly thank two people whom I did have the opportunity to know outside their writings and whom I grew to rely on for their professional assistance. For the generous gift of their time and knowledge I will always be grateful.

I developed a love of sky legends and nature myths largely from reading the books and articles of Dr. E. C. Krupp, director of the Griffith Observatory in Los Angeles. I began corresponding with him while writing *Legends of the Earth, Sea, and Sky*, and my love of sky legends quickly developed into a passion. Dr. Krupp taught me to look at mythology from a functional standpoint, but he also taught me to read the myths with humor, ardor, and respect for their creators. His books never fail to enchant me, his knowledge never ceases to amaze me, and his insights will live forever in my mind as well as in my writings.

Dr. R. Robert Robbins, archeoastronomer at the University of Texas at Austin, also provided me with the assistance and inspiration I needed to write this book. I began writing about sky legends years ago for *Star Date,* a radio show and magazine produced by McDonald Observatory, and through the years, I often turned to Dr. Robbins with questions. He was always there with answers and encouragement. I feel fortunate to have been the recipient of his knowledge, a treasured book or two from his personal library, and the unselfish gift of his time.

I also feel fortunate to live in Austin, Texas, and to have available to me the wealth of information in the libraries at the University of Texas. It often seemed it would be impossible to conduct such research in nearly any other place. Thanks to the General Libraries and the university, and to the reference librarians and bibliographers who helped me track down sources. I am also grateful for the Austin Public Library and the librarians and services there, for the Austin Community College library, and for the Westbank Community Library, where I spent many hours pouring over myths. Carolyn Foote, the librarian at Westlake High School, also welcomed me into

ACKNOWLEDGMENTS

her library and shared with me her knowledge of mythology in high school curricula.

Several other people were instrumental in answering many of my questions.

I'd like to thank Dr. Mark Cloos, a geologist at the University of Texas upon whom I relied for technical information on geological processes.

I'd like to thank Divya Mehta, my dear friend, who shared with me her knowledge of the Hindu religion and lent me many indispensable books.

I'd like to thank Damond Benningfield, producer of McDonald Observatory's *Star Date* radio show, and Jeff Kanipe, former editor of *Star Date Magazine,* who published my first writings on astronomical mythology, which I believe enabled me to continue publishing in the field.

I'd like to also thank the professors and research scientists at McDonald Observatory and the Astronomy Department at the University of Texas for whom I had the pleasure of working as a librarian. They stimulated my interest in astronomy, helped me gain an understanding of astronomical phenomena, and made me look to the sky with a sense of awe.

Last but not least, I'd like to thank my copyeditor, Susan Brown, and the editors I had the pleasure of working with at ABC-CLIO—Liz Kincaid, who selected the illustrations; Henry Rasof, who got me started on this project and gave me the encouragement I needed to begin; and Todd Hallman and Susan McRory, who continued providing encouragement and guidance until publication of the book.

INTRODUCTION
The Will of the Gods

People long ago created myths to satisfy their curiosity about nature. They recited them to reinforce the bond they shared with the world around them and to win the favor of the gods and spirits who animated it. Some scholars have argued that all myths originally explained natural phenomena and that the gods were originally inseparable from the forces they represented. The natural world moved constantly. The wind blew, the rivers flowed, and the celestial bodies rose and set in the heavens. The natural phenomena the ancients witnessed in the earth, the sea, and the sky appeared to act by a force of will. The clouds poured rain, the earth produced vegetation, and the sun gave light and heat. Movement, to these early thinkers, meant life. Nature worship in this early form assumed that all phenomena had human qualities and characteristics.

In 1871, the anthropologist Sir Edward Tylor, in his book *Primitive Culture*, used the term *animism* to define the belief in spirits that he identified as the core of religion. To animistic societies, every inanimate object and every physical force has a spirit analogous to human spirits, and each is worthy of worship. These spirits are the nature gods, and although polytheistic societies have nature gods as well—rain gods and sea gods and gods of the rocks—animistic societies have one separate spirit for each raindrop, each wave, each pebble. Monotheists have one god who controls all these forces. But because even monotheists see their god manifest himself in the world of nature, it can be argued that they too maintain some degree of devotion to the animated universe. The Great Spirit rules supreme, and it did so as well in cultures commonly identified as polytheistic. But that Great Spirit manifested itself in each ray of sunlight, in each flood of rain, and in each energizing bolt of lightning. So although Christian missionaries attempted to rid the world of spirits, these manifestations were such powerful personages that many of the pagan gods maintained their dominion as Christian saints.

Nature myths compose a large category of literature. It includes astronomical myths, myths of sailors, and myths told by frightened people in the frigid north to explain why their earth died for such long periods of time. In addition, other types of myths masquerade as nature myths, so scholars often interpreted them in that context. They called the golden apples of immortality in the West the immortal setting sun. They called everyone who died and resurrected a sun god. Friedrich Max Muller, a Sanskrit scholar and a professor at Oxford, spearheaded the nature myth movement in the nineteenth century, and he found a solar hero everywhere. But long before Max Muller espoused his theories, scholars recognized that myths reflect universal phenomena, many of them in the physical world. The earth, the sea, and the sky were, at first, deities, and all the phenomena that moved within those realms were born from them and then gained power in the universe.

Myths and legends of the ancient world largely reflected the landscape and climate where the stories originated. The ancients continually had to battle the elements. Those in the cold countries battled frost and ice.

Those in the hot countries battled heat, lightning, and fire. The forces of nature overpowered the world, yet people still tried to control them. Believing that nature powers acted through will made it necessary to placate them. People thought that through worship and sacrifice they could influence the gods to maintain order in their world, to turn the seasons, to regulate the waves and the tides, and to steer the celestials on their proper paths.

From far back in antiquity, people tried to control nature. They tried to help the sun turn around, to scare the eclipse monsters away, and to encourage the rain gods to release water. Nature myths recount these attempts. Early seafarers needed to predict the weather. Hunter-gatherers and agriculturists needed to know the seasons. Because human survival depended on seemingly supernatural forces, people incapable of fighting those forces had to figure out who commanded them. The ancients revered their nature gods because they feared their power and because they feared neglecting any power strong enough to control the destiny of the world.

The worship of nature, then, involved the reverence of natural phenomena as animated, conscious forces. Early nature worshipers considered natural phenomena living beings analogous to people but far, far more powerful. People felt the power of these beings each time the thunder rumbled or the waves crashed. They felt awe each time the sun rose and fear each time the moon disappeared. These phenomena today are readily explained by science, but in the ancient world, they were simply mysteries. So people created myths to solve them, using only human experience and imagination as tools. Because the ancients did endow natural phenomena with will and feeling, they spun a common thread that linked cultures in all areas of the world. Therefore, people from culturally diverse societies created similar myths. Nature was revealed to them in sym-

bols, and early people symbolized everything that appealed to the human mind.

Keep in mind that the ancients weren't consciously creating nature myths. They weren't trying to build allegories and metaphors. They were simply affirming their belief that all forms of natural phenomena acted by will. A person who knew nothing of astronomical phenomena saw the sky darken and believed someone stole the light. A person who knew nothing of geologic phenomena saw a mountain erupt and believed an angry goddess spit fire from the ground. The myths of these early thinkers are so full of such metaphors that it's easy to interpret them as we would the modern poem or the abstract painting. But while artists use the abstract to explain the concrete, ancient mythmakers used the concrete to explain the abstract. Myths cut to the core of the unexplained and expressed the deepest fears of the people who created them.

So what significance does nature mythology have today? Now we have scientific explanations for rain and for thunder. We know why the tide ebbs and flows and why the moon appears to die and resurrect itself. We know, so we take nature's power for granted. We see the sunrise and call it science; the ancients witnessed the same sunrise and called it a miracle. We have long lost touch with miracles. We no longer recognize the sacred. The ancients had an intimate relationship with the sky. They lived close to the land and they respected it, because they learned that given proper respect, the earth fulfilled their needs. The Australians continue to consider themselves part of the sacred landscape. Their bond to the land is so strong that some people still know the locations of sacred landforms that vanished long ago through natural geologic processes. The Australian Aborigines look after the environment to maintain harmony with their world, which they believe was the wish of the earth's creators. Because these Australian groups believe their mythological ancestors created each feature of the earth, they believe they themselves are, in essence, a part of nature.

It is difficult in the modern world to appreciate nature in the sense that these Australian groups do or in the sense that people all over the world did long ago. Because they invested physical phenomena with spirit, they bestowed upon their deities the capability of either reward-ing kindness or taking revenge for mistreatment. Nature could be their greatest enemy or their dearest friend.

Most people are familiar with the phenomenon of the mirage, an illusion that appears when images are displaced or dis-torted under specific atmospheric conditions. The mind's eye takes over. Perhaps such vision is what is necessary to understand nature mythology from a modern perspective. People who behold the mirage see castles in the air and phantom ships on the ocean. They move beyond the mundane to the extraordinary, and they search for what might be possible. The eye can see these things, if only the mind could believe them. Perhaps then people in today's world could understand ancient myth and appreciate the wonderment in nature that led people of the past to create the most captivating legends of the earth, the sea, and the sky.

A

ABSU

In ancient Mesopotamia, the absu, or apsu, was the realm beneath the earth that contained a freshwater ocean. Like many ancient peoples, the Mesopotamians believed the salt sea encircled the earth. But the absu, they believed, contained another ocean, an ocean that had existed long before the creation of mankind and that provided the source of water for all the springs, wells, streams, rivers, and lakes of the world.

The absu was the realm of Enki, a water god who resided there with a host of other primordial creatures long before the creation of mankind. In the Babylonian epic *The Creation of Mankind,* it is said that Absu first existed as a creature who lived in the dark abyss

The ancient Babylonian god Absu was said to have lived under the earth with his mate, Tiamat; they are depicted in this undated woodcut.

under the earth with Tiamat, his mate. With Tiamat, Absu had offspring, among them Anu and Enki. But Absu was resentful of these younger gods whose activity and light opposed his inertia and darkness, and he waged war against them. Enki led the battle and won, casting a spell on Absu that put him to sleep and killed him. The spell did not kill his essence, however. Absu existed from then on as a place—the dark, abysmal realm that housed the subterranean ocean and led to the Underworld.

As primordial creatures, Absu and Tiamat were envisioned as a pair, yet they stood in opposition to one another. Absu represented the inert freshwater, and Tiamat, the salty and tumultuous seawater. In myth, these two forces mingled together to produce Mummu, a representation of mist and clouds. But because of his battle with Enki, Absu was immortalized. Cult centers were dedicated to him, constructed around ponds or basins representing his waters. The House of Absu was one of the oldest sanctuaries in Mesopotamia, erected in the city of Eridu and dedicated to Enki. (Gray 1982, Mackenzie 1996, McCall 1990)

See also Enki, Mesopotamia, Primordial Sea, Tiamat

ACHELOUS

The oldest of the Greek river gods, Achelous was ruler of the river Achelous, the largest river in Greece. He controlled its rise, he controlled its fall, and for many years he was said to live in its waters, sometimes existing as the river itself. The river Achelous is now called Asproptamo, and it flows into the Ionian Sea at the entrance to the Gulf of Patras.

Though some legends say Achelous was the son of Helios and Earth, and others say he was one of the sons of Poseidon, the ancient Greeks generally believed that he and all the other river gods were the offspring of

1

ADAD

Oceanus and Tethys, two of the most powerful sea gods. Achelous became a river by falling into the waters after being fatally wounded with an arrow. From that time on, he was worshipped throughout Greece as a powerful deity.

Achelous's power over the river led to the miraculous formation of the Echinades Islands. When four river nymphs performing a ritual sacrifice to the gods on the riverbanks one day neglected to sacrifice to Achelous, the river god himself, Achelous, got angry. He rose his waters and swept the four nymphs into the sea. From then on, they existed only as islands, lying at the mouth of the river.

In his most common form, Achelous appeared with a horned head and a serpentlike body. But he could change forms. Sometimes he appeared as half bull–half man, and other times as a snake. In his famed contest with Herakles over the river nymph Deianeira, he turned into a bull and wrestled with Herakles until Herakles tore off one of his horns and forced him to surrender. (Graves 1988, Rose 1959)

See also Greece and Rome, Rivers and Lakes

ADAD

Adad was a powerful Mesopotamian rain god and the personification of winter storms. Worshipped in Palestine and Syria from about 1900 to 200 B.C., he was often called upon to destroy enemies, and he quickly obliged, with his forceful winds, his thundering voice, and his weapon—the flashing bolt of lightning.

As storm god, Adad could be terrifying, enveloped in black clouds and carrying thunderbolts in both hands. But part of his power lay in his ability to either produce rain or withhold it. As rain god, he was benevolent and the answer to many a prayer. When drought threatened the survival of the land, Adad caused the river to flood and provide the necessary fertilization for crops.

Adad was often depicted in human form, standing on a bull and wearing a horned headdress and a tiered skirt decorated with stars. In the Babylonian flood myth, Adad was described as a whirlwind, ascending to the heavens from the horizon on a black cloud and obliterating the light with darkness. From the beginning of the second millennium, Adad controlled the storm. He was one of the three supreme gods who, along with Sin, the moon god, and Shamash, the sun god, replaced the earlier Babylonian triad composed of Enlil, Enki, and Anu. Anu was Adad's father, and the two shared a temple in the capital city of Ashur that had one entrance and two shrines. Adad was often symbolized either as a figure with three forks of lightning or as a crouching bull sprouting a two-forked lightning bolt from his back. (Gray 1982, McCall 1990)

See also Cows and Bulls, Mesopotamia, Rain and Rain Gods, Storms and Tempests

ADARO

Among the many sprites said to inhabit the Pacific islands, Melanesian sea adaro came to life during sun showers, when they were said to wriggle about in waterspouts. They lived in the sun until a rainbow appeared, then they traveled down the rainbow to earth where they interacted, often maliciously, with human beings.

Adaro were depicted in wood carvings as having human heads and fishlike bodies with gills. They could be friendly, sometimes appearing in people's dreams to teach them songs and dances. But they could also be harmful and were noted for shooting flying fish at human victims and rendering them unconscious. Like most spirits, however, adaro could be placated with offerings. A flying fox flung into the waters would awaken the human victim from his unconscious state and protect him from otherwise certain death. The islanders had to be careful when canoeing and keep watch for Ngorieru, the chief of these malicious sea sprites, who was said to haunt the seashore off the coast of San Cristobal. (Poignant 1967)

See also Oceania, Water and Water Spirits

AEGIR

An ancient Norse sea god called Lord of the Stormy Seas, Aegir preceded the two races in Norse mythology, the Aesir and Vanir gods. He existed before them, and it was believed he would survive long after they died.

Aegir was a giant, fierce and hostile, and was usually perceived as an old man with long, white hair and fingerlike claws. He lived in the icy waters of the ocean far away from land and was greatly feared by Norse voyagers traveling to his domain. But perhaps more fearful was Aegir's wife, Ran, who lurked behind the ice and captured ships with a net, dragging them down to the bottom of the sea. She stole the gold of the drowned sailors and placed it on her hearth, where it shimmered and sparkled through the waves. Aegir was often depicted surrounded by the stolen treasures of Ran's victims, the sparkle of which the Vikings called "the flame of the sea."

Aegir lived deep below the surface in a great underwater hall surrounded by a fence made of white sea foam. Sailors crossed Aegir's realm, far out in the ocean, with great fear and trepidation. They often sacrificed a member of their crew to the icy waters to appease Ran and to assure safe passage for the rest of their sailors. However, regardless of the sacrifice, Ran captured many ships, with the help of her giantess daughters. These nine wave maidens assumed the form of gigantic waves that destroyed the ships and pulled the sailors to their death. The drowned sailors then surrendered their gold to Ran so they could remain as ghosts under the sea, feasting in Aegir's underwater hall. (Davidson 1964, Guerber 1980)

See also Scandinavia, Sea and Sea Gods, Waves

AEOLUS

Aeolus was the Greek god of winds, often petitioned by sailors who asked for his help in guiding their ships. He had the power to help them, for he controlled all the winds, both gentle and fierce, and he had the ability to either rouse them up or calm them down. He could release helpful trade winds to gently guide the sailors, or he could release harmful storm winds that caused shipwrecks and steered them off course. Aeolus lived on Aeolia, called Lipara, or the Island of Winds, off the coast of Sicily, where he kept all his winds in leather bags, tied with silver strings and locked in a cave.

The best known myth of Aeolus appears in Homer's *Odyssey*. When in his travels Odysseus landed on Aeolia, Aeolus gave Odysseus a goatskin bag containing all the winds that would impede his voyage, warning him to keep them imprisoned in the bag so he could return safely to Ithaca. But while Odysseus was asleep, his traveling companions saw the bag and, out of curiosity, opened it. The winds escaped and caused a storm—a storm that pushed Odysseus's ship straight back to Aeolia.

Legends say Aeolus was married to Eos, the goddess of dawn, and that he fathered the directional winds. He is also credited with inventing the sails on ships. His temple, the Tower of Winds, or the Horologion, still stands in Athens today in the Acropolis. An octagonal marble structure with each side facing one of the eight principal directions, the tower was used as a timekeeping devise by the ancient Greeks, having a sundial, a waterclock, and a weathervane. Each of the eight sides has a flying figure representing one of the winds. (Fox 1964, Watson 1984)

See also Greece and Rome, Winds and Wind Gods

AETNA

Mount Aetna was a volcano in Sicily under which the Titans were buried and the Cyclopes had their workshop. In Greek mythology, the workshop was headed by the metal-worker Hephaestus, the god of volcanoes; in Roman mythology, by Vulcan, the god of fire and metalworking. Classical myths tell that under Aetna, Hephaestus and the Cyclopes created thunderbolts for Zeus and armor for all the gods and heroes.

In classical times, Mount Aetna dominated the city of Catania in East Sicily. The myth of Typhon and Enceladus was one of the few myths that explained the volcano's fiery eruptions. Typhon was a monster created by Gaia, the earth, to attack Zeus in revenge for destroying her children, the Titans. But Zeus waged war against Typhon and slew him with his thunderbolts. Gaia then sent another giant to revenge Typhon's death, Enceladus, whom Zeus defeated as well. Enceladus was bound with chains and buried in a burning cave under Mount Aetna. It was said that Enceladus was restless and resentful, causing earthquakes each time he turned over and volcanic eruptions when he hissed and stuck out his fiery tongue. The smoke from Mount Aetna was explained as a by-product of Hephaestus at work, molding metal into arms in his underground smithy. (Fox 1964, Rose 1959)

See also Cyclopes, Earthquakes, Fire and Fire Gods, Greece and Rome, Hephaestus, Volcanoes

AFRICA

The mythology of Africa is characterized by a diversity of beliefs. In a country with thousands of separate cultures and thousands of languages and dialects, a unified religious philosophy could never have developed. But mythologies reflect individual locales and landscapes, and because most areas of the continent share a similar environment, common themes run through the body of African mythology. Among these themes, a reverence and respect for the natural world is one of the most significant and widespread.

The nature myths of Africa appear in many different forms and in many different places. In ancient times, much of the African continent was isolated. Many early people lived in the open grasslands and tropical forests and settled along the Atlantic and Indian oceans where they established unique local cultures. Different belief systems developed, even in tribes that spoke the same language. Because of this isolation, written culture didn't permeate the tropical forests until the nineteenth century. Still, these ancient tribes recorded their myths. They recorded them in their art—on rock walls, on gourds and calabashes—and later, they told their stories to the Europeans and Americans who recorded them in writing and passed them on.

Most early Africans recognized the existence of a Supreme Being. In the tribes of the west, east, and south, this being was usually the Sky, and the Sky controlled the rain the people so desperately needed. But earth worship was more common in the tribes of the north. Sacrifices to the earth or to the sky were commonplace throughout the continent and believed to be essential appeasement for the Supreme Being, lest he hold back the rejuvenating rains.

Though most African tribes worshipped the sky or the earth as the Supreme Being, they also worshipped many lesser gods and goddesses who controlled natural forces. These deities assumed particular importance because they dominated the physical world. They didn't rule from Heaven like the Supreme Being; they ruled from earth, and they made their presence known in powerful ways. Consider the physical forces at work in ancient Africa. The continent was hot, water was scarce, and the winds swept the open grasslands with devastating force. So the most important nature deities in ancient Africa were those of the storm. These deities delivered the clap of thunder and the bolt of lightning, they drove the winds with power and might, and they never failed to put on an impressive display.

The most constant force at work in ancient Africa was the heat of the sun. Most ancient sun myths around the world addressed the need to bring the sun back after it disappeared for long periods of time. But in Africa there was no need to bring the sun back; it was a constant, driving force. Sun and moon myths were not as prevalent in Africa as they were on other continents, but many did exist, particularly among the San and Khoi Khoi of southern Africa. These people prayed to the sun, moon, and stars, and they spun myths to explain the presence of these celestial bodies in their sky. The San believed the sun and moon were once human beings who lived on earth, then ascended to the sky. The Khoi Khoi prayed to the praying mantis, who they believed owned the moon.

Solar and lunar deities in African stories existed primarily to explain the origin of life. For instance, the sun and the moon often married, and sometimes they begot the stars. These types of myths were also used to explain eclipses, as many groups believed that eclipses occurred either when the sun and moon argued or when they made love. Whereas sun and moon deities appeared in stories simply to explain what the ancients witnessed in their world, storm deities had a more crucial function. Sorcerers and magicians appealed to them in the rainmaking rituals that were commonplace in many African societies. Temples were erected to honor them; cults were established to worship them. The mythology of the storm connected all groups in all parts of the continent.

Animal spirits were another common thread that connected the myths of this vast land, and in many African stories, natural forces took animal forms. In southern Africa, it was widely believed that lightning was a bird and that a gigantic Thunderbird controlled the weather and delivered the storms. In the Congo, it was believed that lightning was a magic dog that gave a sharp bark. But thunder was more often deified than lightning. Like the powerful bolts hurled from the hammers of Zeus and Thor, lightning was seen as a weapon, commonly a thunder-axe that fell to earth with devastating blows.

Among the animals most prevalent in African nature myths, the snake, the chameleon, and the spider formed the basis for many beliefs. Many stories of central and southern Africa feature the spider's web, and particularly a thread from the spider's web, which the gods used to get to and from Heaven. The San prayed to the chameleon, who they believed had the power to bring rain. The serpent or snake probably appeared in myths most frequently, usually as a primal being and the origin of the cosmos. The snake was often associated with the rainbow; to the Dahomey, a great rainbow serpent circled the world with his coils. The python, in some myths, circled the sea.

Animals in African nature myths were often credited with obtaining fire. The mason wasp was said to have brought fire to earth from the celestial regions. The San believed the praying mantis brought them fire, and the Pygmies said fire arrived with a dog or a chimpanzee. Fire held a high place in African culture, not only for its utility in everyday life but also for its power in ritual. Rainmaking, for instance, required building a fire and creating large puffs of black smoke to resemble storm clouds. The fire gods of Africa, like the other gods of natural phenomena, were the spirits driving the force—they created the clouds of smoke, they blew life into the ashes, and they animated the flames.

Scholars argue whether African nature gods were actual personifications of physical forces or simply the ghosts of dead ancestors. In African culture, ancestors were the most recognized spiritual force. But whatever these deities meant to the ancients, the nature gods had powerful control over the natural world. Early Africans worshipped that power, and they worshipped the gods as manifestations of power itself—the power of the sky, the power of the earth, and the power of the storm. Perhaps this natural power was the most crucial thread connecting the myths of Africa, for ancient African thought was centered on power and vital energy. It was natural that the myths the people spun of their world centered on the most powerful forces they witnessed—the mighty winds, the driving rain, and the ravaging storm. (Frazer 1926, Herskovits 1938, Mbiti 1970, Parrinder 1986, Werner 1964)

AGBE

Agbe is the sea god of the Dahomey in Nigeria. He was sent to earth by his mother, the Supreme Goddess Sogbo, who gave him control over the earth and the waters. Sogbo and some of her other children remained to rule from the sky.

Agbe lived in the sea, where he could send water up to the sky when rain was needed. He could not actually cause the rain to fall; Sogbo did that. When Agbe's seawaters rose nearly to the sky, Sogbo would shout, and the rain would come pouring down.

Though god of the seas, Agbe was considered a thunder deity as well, because the Dahomey realized that seawater and rainwater were somehow connected. Sogbo and her sky children controlled the lightning that struck land. However, as thunder deity, Agbe controlled the lightning that struck ships, for he had power over all occurrences that influenced his realm. He gave authority over drowning and ship sinking to Gbeyogbo, the most evil of the Dahomey sea gods. Gbeyogbo represented the receding surf, the most dangerous obstacle met by sailors when launching their boats. (Herskovits 1938)

See also Africa, Sea and Sea Gods

AGNI

Agni, the Hindu fire god, was in ancient, or Vedic, times one of the three supreme deities, along with Surya, the sun god, and Indra, the rain god. Holding his high position in the Hindu pantheon, Agni was one of the guardian deities of the world, called lokapalas. Each of these deities, accompanied by an elephant, presided over one of the eight points of the compass. Agni controlled the southeast, the point where the dawn breaks.

In the hymns of the Rig Veda, the oldest surviving religious document of India, Agni was said to dwell in the two pieces of wood that made fire when rubbed together. He symbolized the vital spark in nature and represented the three forces of lightning, sun, and earthly fire. Perhaps the best known of the fire gods, Agni's powers extended to the home and hearth, where he served as a friend to people and a witness to human events. He was said to be present in every home, and for this reason, he assumed the role of mediator between gods and people.

Agni was associated not only with earthly fire and the hearth, but particularly with sacrificial fire. In fact, in later years, Agni was perceived not so much as a fire god, but as a purifier of sacrificial offerings. An explanation of why fire acts as a purifier is found in the Indian epic, *Mahabharata*. When Bhrigu, the sage, carried away a woman who was engaged to another man, the man summoned Agni to help locate his lover. When Bhrigu learned of Agni's interference, he got angry and sentenced Agni to consume everything, both pure and impure. But Agni argued that his truthfulness was necessary and befitting of a god. So Bhrigu added a blessing. Agni could eat everything, even the impure, yet remain pure. As god of fire, Agni consumed to give life. He was born fully matured, and because his parents could not provide for him, he consumed them. Then he licked up the butter poured on the flames of the sacrificial fire.

Agni was usually clothed in black, with two faces, four hands, seven tongues for licking up the sacrificial butter, and skin as red as fire. He was often depicted wearing a garland of fruit and riding on a ram. Some sources refer to Agni as a Marut, one of the Hindu storm gods, and in this capacity, he carried a flaming spear and rode in a chariot with wind for wheels, drawn by fiery horses.

Though Agni's cult disappeared in India long ago, the importance of fire in Hindu ceremonies remains, so Agni remains an important deity. Because Agni can grant immortality and purify sinners after death, he is often called upon at weddings and funerals and looked upon with great reverence. In the Rig Veda, the number of hymns addressed to Agni numbered over two hundred, second in number only to Indra, the Supreme Being. (Moor 1984, Thomas 1980)

See also Fire and Fire Gods, Sacrifice

AIR AND AIR GODS

Air typifies contemplation, the immaterial, the soul, and the Supreme Deity. It is the motion of the world and the reason we are able to live. Earth, fire, water, and air have been labeled the primal forces of nature; they shaped the world and provided a base from which all matter was formed. Early Greek philosophers placed air above the other three forces. It breathed life into the universe and provided the life force that transferred from this world to the next. It encompassed the sky and the realm of the heavens and was thereby elevated to supreme importance.

Viewing air as the eternal force in nature led to the perception of air as a god with everlasting life. In cultures that associated air with Heaven and the eternal, deities of the air occupied high places in their pantheons. The distinction between air gods and sky gods is difficult to make. The Greeks called the upper air *aither,* and the summit of Mount Olympus was in the aither. Zeus lived on Olympus, so in a sense Zeus was considered an air god. But the true air gods occupied a realm below the vault of Heaven. They occupied the atmosphere, that ethereal place that hovered between Heaven and

earth. Because the air and atmosphere were invisible, air deities often made themselves known as wind.

Aside from the four winds, various air gods populated the myths of the world. The Finns recognized the Virgin of the Air, who lived in a palace with a rainbow roof behind the northern lights and within a wall of mist. The Greeks worshipped Aether as their air god, and the Chinese worshipped How-Chu. The Egyptians considered their air god, Shu, the deification of emptiness. Enlil ruled the air in Mesopotamia, as did the Mayan Kukulcan and his Aztec counterpart, Quetzalcoatl in Mesoamerica.

Aerial beings in many lands were not gods per se, but spirits—the souls of dead ancestors or evil demons of disease. In much of the eastern world, air demons personified epidemics, such as smallpox and cholera, and wandered about the atmosphere spreading death and disease. Evil air spirits were particularly commonplace in Arabia, where storm fiends rode on whirlwinds and mischievous goblins called jinns haunted caves, woodlands, and wells, manifesting themselves as the essence of smoke and fire. The Inuit feared the aurora borealis as an evil air spirit, as well as the souls of dead relatives, who they believed hovered in the air to scare or injure the living. The Plains Indians considered thunder the most evil air spirit of all.

Because the invisible air made its presence known only as wind or some kind of atmospheric phenomenon, many people personified air spirits as atmospheric deities and often considered them evil. The Nuer of Sudan said that people struck by lightning became air spirits called colwics, children of the god Kwoth, who lived in the sky.

Air spirits took the forms of thunder gods, storm gods, and in Brazil, even the moon, who was perceived as an evil force. When these gods made mischief in the forms of storms or eclipses, people shot arrows in the air to prevent any mishap and to scare away the evil demons that hovered in that mysterious place between worlds. (Hastings 1925, Watson 1984)

See also Elements, Shu, Vayu, Winds and Wind Gods

ALA

Earth worship was commonplace in African cultures, and to the Ibo of Nigeria, the earth goddess, Ala, was the most highly revered deity. Ala made life possible through her blessings of fertility. Unlike in many Indo-European lands, in some tribes of West Africa the earth goddess outranked the sky god. Ala was one such goddess. She was both the spirit of the earth and the queen of the Underworld, and she served as moral guardian and dispenser of the laws of the land.

As an earth spirit, Ala controlled fertility, both of the soil and of women. As a goddess of the dead, she received the Ibo ancestors into her womb, then guarded and protected them after death. Ala had the power to punish people with death for offending her by breaking taboos. But death, to the Ibo, was not punishment enough. The offenders were denied a ground burial and thus access to Ala's Underworld.

Worship of the earth, and of Ala, was the integrating force of Ibo society. The people made regular sacrifices to their great goddess to bless their land—at planting time, at the time the first fruits rose from the earth, and again at the time of full harvest. Every Ibo community had shrines and temples to the earth goddess, and, in some areas, houses called Mbari erected for special occasions. These houses contained painted mud figures of major deities, such as the storm god, the water god, and Ala, always at the center like an African Madonna, with child in arms and sometimes with a halo over her head. (Parrinder 1986, Talbot 1967)

See also Africa, Earth and Earth Gods

AMATERASU

One of the world's most illustrious and well-known sun goddesses, Amaterasu was the Supreme Deity of Japanese Shinto and the ancestress of the imperial line. Born from the eye of Izanagi, the creator god, she ruled the sky, while her brother Tsuki-yumi, the moon god, ruled the night, and her brother Susanowo, ruled the sea and storms.

The story of Amaterasu is one of the most popular sun myths and represents the victory of light over darkness. The storm god, Susanowo, was jealous of Amaterasu's beauty and grew hostile, invading his sister's sky realm to cause havoc and destruction. Exercising his powers of chaos, he stirred up violent winds and covered the sky with dark storm clouds. This terrified Amaterasu, and she hid in a cave, dooming the world to total darkness. When darkness demons took over the land, the gods devised a plan to lure Amaterasu out of the cave. They decorated the _entrance with a mirror and strings of glimmering jewels. They summoned Uzume, the dawn goddess, to enchant Amaterasu and dance to beautiful music at the cave's entrance. Believing that a more beautiful sun goddess had taken over her rule and was dancing outside the cave, Amaterasu emerged to see her own reflection in the mirror. The gods then drew her out of the cave completely, chasing away the dark forces and bathing the world in light.

Some scholars believe that the myth of Amaterasu and the cave originated from observation of a solar eclipse. Clearly the sun disappeared, then reappeared from out of the darkness. Most definitely, however, the myth illustrates the importance of the sun goddess in Japanese culture. Most cultures personified the sun as male, and the moon as a goddess. But even in cultures that did worship sun goddesses, nowhere but in Japan did the female deity assume primary importance. Amaterasu was the Supreme Deity, a symbol of light, and her mirror, a representation of brightness and purity. Even today the imperial family regularly visits her shrine in the province of Ise to consult with her on all matters of importance to national life. This shrine, the innermost of the Grand Shrines at Ise, has been sacred for more than 1,300 years. Though now the imperial family visits Amaterasu there in private, up until the nineteenth century, they were accompanied on these visits by thousands of worshippers, all wishing to pay homage to the goddess they believed to be the pillar of their spiritual life. (McCrickard 1990, Mackenzie 1994, Piggott 1983)

See also Caves, Japan, Mirrors, Sun and Sun Gods, Susanowo

AMMA

Amma was the Supreme Deity of the Dogon of western Africa; he was their creator god and their god of rain. Supreme deities in Africa often controlled rain rather than sun, as in other lands, because in the hot, dry African continent, sun was a given, but rain was a precious commodity. Amma first created the heavens and earth, then he fertilized the earth with his life-giving rains.

Amma meant "the one who holds." Amma was the cosmic egg, the seed of the cosmos, and the creator of the sun, the moon, and stars, and of all the life on earth. Amma created the sun and the moon from clay, like pots, surrounding the sun with eight rings of red copper and the moon with eight rings of white copper. He made black people from sunlight, white people from moonlight, and the stars from broken pieces of the sun, which he scattered across the sky. He then created the earth in the shape of a female body, forming her genital organs from a gigantic ant hill, had intercourse with the earth, and fertilized her with rain. (Bonnefoy 1991, Parrinder 1986)

See also Africa, Creation Myths, Rain and Rain Gods, Sky and Sky Gods

AMON

Amon was a sun god of ancient Egypt and one of the most powerful deities worshipped by the people of the Nile valley. At first a local fertility god and patron of the city of Thebes, Amon rose to the position of Supreme God when in the second millennium B.C. he fused with the ancient sun god Ra, the previous Supreme Deity. Some scholars consider the worship of Amon-Ra an early attempt at monotheism. Combining the powers of two of the most venerated gods in the land, Amon-Ra was revered as the source of life and the creator of the universe.

Amon's name meant "the hidden one," an allusion to his mysterious powers and perhaps to the setting sun. The sun god appeared in numerous forms, sometimes with the head of a frog or a serpent and sometimes as an

The sun god of ancient Egypt, Amon, is depicted with a quadruple head, symbolizing the four elements.

ape or a lion. Most commonly, however, he appeared as a bearded man, wearing numerous bracelets and a double-plumed headdress of various colors. From his tunic hung the tail of a lion or a bull, a symbol of his solar attributes and an indication that he was a god of earlier times. References to a "hidden one" in the early *Pyramid Texts* may indicate that Amon was the ancient deity responsible for the creation of the universe. In one myth, Amon assumed the form of a goose and laid the egg from which the world was formed, and in another myth, he appeared as a snake and fertilized the cosmic egg.

When Amon rose from the local god of Thebes to a deity worshipped by the entire nation, those who worshipped Ra considered this new sun god a threat to their cult. Battles broke out in Egypt over which god was greatest, and those battles subsided only by fusing the two deities. The new god, Amon-Ra, rose to power swiftly. As the supreme creator, he took on attributes of the entire Egyptian pantheon, with the exception of Osiris, whose cult could not be rivaled. In a short time, the priesthood of Amon-Ra became the most powerful cult in the land. (Budge 1969, Hart 1990, Rosalie 1980, Spence 1990)

See also Egypt, Ra, Sun and Sun Gods

AMPHITRITE

Amphitrite was a Greek sea goddess, Poseidon's wife, and the feminine personification of the sea. She was the daughter of either Oceanus or Nereus and the mother of Triton, who was half man and half fish and who lived with Amphitrite and Poseidon in the watery depths. At first merely a sea nymph, Amphitrite won the heart of the great god of the oceans and over time rose to prominence in the sea pantheon of the Greeks. Amphitrite took her place next to her husband, helping him rule his kingdom and riding on a pearl shell chariot across the waves.

Poseidon spotted Amphitrite one day dancing at low tide with her sisters on the isle of Naxos. He fell immediately in love with her and asked her to marry him. But fearful of Poseidon's violent nature, Amphitrite refused and fled to the depths of the sea. Poseidon sent her gifts of coral and pearl and sunken treasures, but to no avail. Finally he sent a dolphin to charm her and to urge her to reconsider. When the dolphin returned with Amphitrite and she agreed to become his bride, Poseidon placed the dolphin among the constellations as a reward. That act was said to be the origin of the delphinus constellation.

Amphitrite was depicted as a beautiful woman, wearing only a crown of seaweed adorned with crabs' claws. She usually rode beside Poseidon in her own chariot drawn by dolphins or glided through the waters perched on a dolphin's back. In contrast to Ran, the wicked sea goddess of the Vikings, Amphitrite was gentle and kind and personified the calm, sunlit sea. (Bell 1991, Graves 1988, Guerber 1992)

See also Greece and Rome, Nereids, Poseidon, Sea and Sea Gods

ANDROMEDA

The constellation embodying the Greek myth of Princess Andromeda occupies a large portion of the sky and includes the star groups of Andromeda, Cepheus, Cassiopeia, Perseus, Pegasus, Medusa, and Cetus. Andromeda was the daughter of King Cepheus and the vain Queen Cassiopeia of Ethiopia. The queen took her vanity too far when she bragged that her daughter was lovelier than the Nereids. The Nereids were the sea nymphs, renowned for their beauty, and they complained bitterly when they heard of Cassiopeia's boastful words. They appealed to Poseidon, and the great sea god took revenge. He flooded Ethiopia, then sent a hideous sea monster named Cetus to cause untold further destruction. Cepheus turned to an oracle for help and, to his dismay, was

This fourteenth-century Spanish miniature illustrates the constellations of Perseus and Andromeda.

advised that the only way he could save his land was to sacrifice Andromeda to the sea monster. The king had no choice, and chained her to a rock.

As the king bound his daughter to a rock by the sea, Perseus flew by on Pegasus, his flying horse, and fell in love with the beautiful maiden in chains. He told King Cepheus he would rescue Andromeda if he agreed to let her be his bride. Cepheus agreed. So Perseus slew the sea monster (using the head of Medusa, who he had just defeated and beheaded), and married Andromeda.

Because Perseus defeated Cetus, a monstrous sea force, as well as Medusa, a monstrous creature of the earth, the myth of Andromeda has been said to explain humanity's control over nature. Even the chaining of Andromeda to the rock indicates control, in the sense that the female force represents nature itself. But more commonly this myth explains the placement of many prominent star groups. Athene was supposed to have placed Andromeda in the sky, where she appears, arms outstretched, as positioned when she was chained to the rock. Pegasus appears as a square of stars near the princess, Cepheus and Cassiopeia lie just to the north of her, and in autumn, Cetus, the sea monster, lies low over the southern horizon, separated from Andromeda by Pisces, the fishes. Perseus towers over Andromeda, holding the head of Medusa, with the bright star, Algol, marking her head. Ancient people noticed that Algol changed in brightness every three days, and they attributed this phenomenon to Medusa winking her evil eye. (McDonald 1996, Ridpath 1988, Staal 1988)

See also Constellations, Greece and Rome

ANIMISM

Animism was an early belief that all phenomena of nature were possessed by a spirit or a soul. The term derived from the Latin word *anima,* which means "breath, life, or soul." Ancient cultures in all parts of the world held animistic beliefs. They populated their world with spiritual power, and they believed all natural occurrences in the earth, sea, and sky to be activated by the spirits within them.

Animistic belief held that each wind, each cloud, and each individual phenomenon of nature had its own god or spirit. Animism, at one time, was perhaps the most widely held religious belief. Sir Edward Tylor in his 1871 book, *Primitive Culture,* asserted that animism was the earliest stage in one development of religion, the belief that accounted for the progression of religious thought. But today animists continue to exist, as do polytheists, who believe in one god who controls all winds or one god who controls all clouds, and as do the monotheists, who believe in one Supreme God who controls all. These groups share the common notion that supernatural power moves the physical world.

Early people adhered to animistic beliefs to explain the world around them. To the ancients, movement meant life, so they concluded that forces powerful enough to move the earth, sea, and sky must have powerful life forces themselves. But the permeation of everything by spirits meant that people had to learn the ways of those spirits and how to win their favor. So shamanism developed. Through shamans, people could navigate the complex maze of nature and make direct contact with nature's powers. (Eliade 1987, Tylor 1958)

See also Shamanism, Totemism

ANU

Anu was the Babylonian sky god, the controller of Heaven, storms, winds, and waves. Anu was the Sumerian word for Heaven, and thus a fitting name for the supreme leader of the pantheon. Anu was said to have inherited the realm of Heaven at the beginning of creation when Heaven and earth separated. At this time, Enlil inherited the earth, and Enki inherited the waters.

As sky god, Anu originated as a god of rain and weather, then gradually rose to supreme status. He was credited with creating the universe and all the gods and people, and he was said to personify the creative power of the sun. Although Anu ruled supreme, he never came down to earth but remained in the uppermost region of the heavens in a sky land similar to Mount Olympus, the home of the Greek sky god Zeus. In that part of the sky, on the summit of Heaven, Anu had his palace, though he often walked along the vertical band of stars along the eastern horizon known as Anu's way. Because this great Babylonian god was an abstract deity, he was not worshipped like the other gods. Yet still he was king of the sky. The stars were his soldiers; the sky, his throne. From his palace in the heavens he manifested himself as a warrior sun god, and he controlled the seasons and the atmospheric forces that affected the world below.

Anu was often represented by a tiara placed on a throne or depicted as a bull whose bellowing was likened to the sound of thunder. In Neo-Assyrian art, his symbol was an eighty-horned cap, a headdress denoting divine status. The headdress, like the bull, symbolized the strength and power befitting a sky god. (Jacobsen 1976, Mackenzie 1996)

See also Cows and Bulls, Enki, Enlil, Mesopotamia, Sky and Sky Gods

APEP

Each night as the Egyptian sun god, Ra, sailed his boat through the twelve hours of night, Apep, the demon of darkness, waged war against the forces of light. Apep was a serpent, said to have scales of flint and to measure over fifty feet long. He roared, he hissed, and, together with his army of night serpents, he put up a terrible fight each night, only to be conquered each morning as the sun rose over the horizon. The character of Apep was represented in nearly every ancient mythology. He was the Babylonian chaos dragon Tiamat, the night-dragon of Chinese mythology, the Fenris wolf in Scandinavia, and other darkness demons in many other lands.

Apep was the leader in the perpetual war the darkness waged with the light. He began his battle on the western horizon when the sun descended to the Underworld and continued it until the sun reached the eastern horizon at dawn. During each of the twelve hours of night, Apep's serpent warriors accosted Ra. Ra met his greatest challenge when he encountered Apep himself, in the seventh hour, in the home of Osiris.

Early accounts of Apep fighting his battle for darkness appear in Egyptian mortuary texts, including *The Book of What Is in the Underworld* and *The Book of the Dead*. *The Book of Overthrowing Apep* lists spells to cast when attempting to defeat the demon of darkness. These spells were read each day at the Temple of Amon-Ra at Thebes and told how Apep was to be mutilated and destroyed. (Hart 1990, Krupp 1991a, Spence 1990)

See also Chaos, Darkness and Light, Demons, Egypt, Ra, Serpents and Snakes

APOLLO

Although the Greek god Apollo had multiple functions, he was originally a sun god and a god of light. He was brother to Artemis, the moon goddess, and, like her, he was an archer who shot arrows of light through the sky. Apollo's bow was golden like the sun and his arrows were beams of sunlight that pierced the heavens. In his best-known myth as sun god, he drove the sun's chariot across the firmament, bringing light and heat into the world.

Apollo had various epithets that described his solar nature. He was Chrysocomes, meaning "of the golden locks," and he was Xanthus, "the fair." But, most famously, he was Phoebus, "the brilliant," father of Phaethon and driver of the sun's fiery chariot. It was Phoebus's task to guide the sun through the maze of zodiacal beasts while the sphere of the heavens revolved constantly underneath him. The magnitude of this task was proven in the myth of Phaethon, who asked to drive his father's chariot to prove his divine parentage.

Apollo was a Greek god, adopted by the Romans under the same name. He was often confused with Helios, who was actually a personification of the physical sun. A popular subject of Greek art from the seventh century B.C., Apollo was depicted as a handsome young god, often naked, and often carrying his bow and appearing with his sister, the moon goddess Artemis. The cult of Apollo was widespread, and the most celebrated of Apollo's many sanctuaries was the oracle of Delphi. Many birds were sacred to him, including the hawk, the cock, the crow, the swan, and the vulture, all of them symbols of the sun. (Graves 1988, Rose 1959)

See also Arrows, Artemis, Chariots, Greece and Rome, Helios, Phaethon, Sun and Sun Gods, Sunbeams and Moonbeams

AQUARIUS, THE WATER CARRIER

The eleventh sign of the zodiac, Aquarius, is usually depicted as a boy pouring water from a bucket or an urn. He is a water carrier, a common occupation in the ancient world, and one of the two zodiacal signs not represented as an animal. In classical times, the sun passed into Aquarius during the rainy season, which perhaps led to the connection of Aquarius with water. In dry countries, this water bearer was regarded as a benevolent bringer of rain, and in wet countries, he was feared as an evil bringer of flood waters.

Aquarius was believed to control water and flooding in many lands. One Greek myth says Aquarius caused the Deluge, in the guise of Zeus. The Egyptians believed he caused their annual flood by dipping his pitcher into the waters of the Nile and pouring those waters over the land. No myth explains why, in the sky, Aquarius pours water into the mouth of Piscis Austrinus, the Southern Fish. Most scholars agree that in Greek mythology, Aquarius represents Ganymede, a handsome Trojan boy whom Zeus abducted and carried off to Olympus to carry water for the gods.

The watery sign of Aquarius is found in the part of the sky referred to as the celestial sea. This area contains other water constellations as well, including Pisces, the fishes; Delphinus, the dolphin; and Capricorn, the sea goat. Aquarius has many stars, among them a collection of faint stars that represent drops of water spilling from the water carrier's urn. Among these stars is the bright star Fomalhaut, which marks the stream's end in Piscis Austrinus. (Ridpath 1988, Staal 1988)

See also Constellations, Zodiac

ARCTIC REGIONS
The myths of the Arctic lands reflected the continual battle the Inuit fought with the elements. Like every early culture, the Inuit depended on the goodness of the natural world to survive. But in the arctic regions of North America, in Greenland, in Iceland, and in Siberia, the natural world was particularly cruel. The people who did survive faced the constant threat of starvation, and they believed that only by the goodness of the spirits would they survive the long months until spring.

Because the people relied on these spirits for survival, it became crucial to understand their every whim. For this reason, the religious life of the Inuit revolved around shamanism, a practice whereby designated people communicated with the spiritual world. The shamans alone could visit the nature spirits in visions they achieved during trances. Through the shamans, the world of nature was interpreted, and by the shamans, the powerful spirits of nature granted their favor.

The Inuit found nature full of invisible spirits, and the shamans continually strove to strike a harmonious relationship with them. The Arctic people had spirits of fire, water, mountains, and wind. They had spirits of bears and elk and every animal that populated their world. They called the invisible forces *innua*, which they thought existed in every aspect of nature—from the air, to the stones, to the ever-present sea and all the game animals it harbored.

Because the sea was of crucial importance to the Inuit, many sea spirits populated their myths. Aulanerk caused the waves. Agloolik lived under the ice, and Nootaikok inhabited the icebergs; both these spirits led hunters to seals. But of all the sea spirits, and indeed of all the spirits, that dominated Inuit life, Sedna was the most feared. She was the spirit of the sea itself, and it was by her doing that the sea provided any food at all. Like the sea, Sedna was most often viewed as harsh and cruel and a constant force to be reckoned with.

Although Sedna had a strong hand in controlling the food supply, she did not act alone. The moon had a hand in that as well. The cycles of the moon determined the seasons, and the seasons determined the availability of game. So the Inuit took care to note the moon's behavior. They also noted the movements of the stars, because they too set the calendar. The positions of the stars and their first appearance on the predawn horizon indicated when the land would freeze and when the ice would break. They determined the migration of salmon and caribou. Hunting people like the Inuit relied on their astronomical knowledge to survive. So these people watched the sky closely and spun their myths around the constellations and around spirits like Aningaaq, or Moon Man.

Like many early people, the Inuit believed in a layered universe, with lands in the sky and lands under the surface of the earth. Aningaaq, or Moon Man, represented the male principle of the world, the essence of the sky. He inhabited the Land Above, and was endowed with characteristics much like the people on earth. Moon Man lived in an igloo situated somewhere along the road to the moon, and he often visited the earth, driving his sledge across a sky made of ice and up and down clouds made of drifted snow. He was a hunter, and the Inuit envisioned him in front of his igloo surrounded with seal skins. Moon Man controlled fertility because his motions determined the seasonal cycle. He was kind and helpful, protecting hunters who ventured out in the moonlight and distributing seals along the coast through his link with the tides. Like Sea Woman, however, Moon Man was a moral guardian. He could punish as well as provide, and he often doled out his punishment as retribution from nature for breaking the taboos against all forms of disrespect for the natural world.

The powers of the moon dominated Inuit myths, whereas the powers of the sun played very little part. The sun appeared in some myths as the moon's sister, and the partner with whom the moon had incest, without the sun's knowing his identity. When she discovered his identity, she marked his face with ashes so she would recognize him later, then she ran away. This myth explained why the moon had marks on his face and why the sun and the moon moved continually around the heavens.

While many cultures considered the sun and the moon the primary pair of deities, the Inuit considered the moon and the sea the most important. Moon Man and Sea Woman together balanced the universe be-cause the forces they personified controlled Inuit life. In between them, or perhaps sharing the celestial domain with Moon Man, was another powerful deity, Sila, or the Spirit of the Air. This spirit controlled the rain, the snow, and the wind, and caused storms and blizzards. Like Sea Woman and Moon Man, the Spirit of the Air had great powers—as well as an explosive temper. If the Inuit acted disrespectfully to nature, by harming animals or killing more than could be eaten, for instance, the Spirit of the Air took revenge by bringing harsh weather or withholding food.

Sila, Moon Man, and Sedna all had dual roles as nature deities and moral guardians. They used their control over the physical forces to maintain harmony in the natural world and to guard and protect the animals. Because animals inhabited the North American continent long before humans, this reverence for nature and animals seemed natural. In fact, throughout North America, animals appeared as creator deities and were thus worthy of the utmost respect. Raven was creator in Alaska. He descended from the sky, created the world, and taught men how to make fire. Along with the other important gods in Inuit life, Raven also maintained order, and he too did so by manipulating the forces of nature. Like animal creator deities in other parts of the world, Raven was a trickster, and one of his more popular tricks was stealing light and fire. In lands perpetually plagued by ice and cold, light and heat were highly coveted, and in some myths, Raven maintained order by obtaining these treasures from those who kept them from the world. (Burland 1985, Eliade 1987, Judson 1911, Norman 1990, Rink n.d.)

ARIES, THE RAM
The ram played a large role in the mythologies of many cultures, and was thus a fitting animal to be represented in the heavens. The significance of this constellation lies in its

position in the sky, rather than in its brightness. Aries is a faint constellation and hardly recognizable as a ram. But about two thousand years ago, the sun passed through Aries on the first day of spring, making it a convenient marker of the vernal equinox. Because many ancient people considered spring their year's beginning, they considered Aries leader of the zodiac. Most people today still consider Aries the leader, although due to precession of the equinoxes, or the slow westward movement of the earth's axis, Pisces marks the vernal equinox today.

Though many cultures recognized Aries as a ram, the best known myth came from Greece and centered on the ram with the golden fleece in the story of Jason and the Argonauts. The ram's story began when a goddess named Nephele returned to Mount Olympus and left her mortal husband, King Athamas, and their two children, Phrixos and Helle, on earth. King Athamas took a new wife named Ino who hated the children and schemed to have them sacrificed. But Nephele heard of this plan and sent a ram with wings and golden fleece to fly down to earth and save them. On the day of the sacrifice, the ram swooped over the sacrificial altar and carried the children into the air and over the Black Sea. Helle fell off the ram and drowned, but Phrixos arrived safely in Colchis. To thank the gods for his life, Phrixos sacrificed the ram to Zeus, and gave its golden fleece to King Aeetes. Zeus then placed the ram in the heavens as a constellation.

Jason's quest for the golden fleece, which followed these events, was believed by some to be a solar myth, a metaphorical journey to enlightenment. The golden color of the fleece appeared to symbolize the sun, and the ram's ability to fly appeared to symbolize the sun's movement. The Jason myth also explained the faintness of the constellation, as the ram no longer had its bright golden fleece when Zeus placed it the sky. But perhaps a tale from Homer's *Odyssey* better ex-

plains the constellation's connection to the vernal equinox. In this myth, Odysseus strapped himself to the underside of a ram to escape from the dark cave of Polyphemus, the Cyclops. Polyphemus then let this ram, and unknowingly, Odysseus, out of the dark cave and into the daylight. Some sources say that this was the ram that appears among the stars. Because the ram carried Odysseus from darkness to light, it became a symbol of the vernal equinox, the time when the dark winter months end and spring begins. (Ridpath 1988, Staal 1988)

> *See also* Constellations, Sun and Sun Gods, Zodiac

ARROWS

In myths throughout the world, gods and goddesses possessed arrows, which they used to deliver their gifts of nature to the world. As agents of destruction, these arrows flew from the bows of storm gods and delivered the strike of lightning. As agents of good, they flew from the bows of sun gods and moon goddesses and penetrated the world with light.

The shape and direction of the arrow contributed to its symbolism. Directed upward, the arrow represented the vertical axis and thus the intercommunication between the realm of earth and the realm of heaven. Directed downward, the arrow became a powerful weapon, like the bolt of lightning that struck the earth. Arrows of sun gods like Apollo traveled a straight path through the air, and thus served as a metaphor for the sun's path from east to west. These sunbeams appeared to penetrate the western horizon, just as the sun seemed to disappear there at the end of each day. Moonbeams shot by goddesses like Artemis followed a similar path, piercing the sky like moonlight pierced the darkness. (Biedermann 1992, Chevalier and Gheerbrant 1996)

> *See also* Apollo, Artemis, Sunbeams and Moonbeams

ARTEMIS

The Greek Artemis, or the Roman Diana, was a moon goddess, slender and beautiful, and associated with fertility and light. She rode through the night in a silver chariot drawn by white horses and shot moonbeams through the sky with her silver bow.

Artemis had a wide range of functions, but she primarily served as goddess of the hunt. As huntress, she retained her association with the moon however, with her silver bow a glistening symbol of the lunar crescent. Like the moon, Artemis ruled the tides, swinging them to and fro on a silver leash and causing them to ebb and flow.

In her capacity as moon goddess, Artemis watched over women in childbirth and controlled other critical times in women's lives, such as birth, puberty, and death. Though usually perceived as young and beautiful like the waxing moon, in her role as fertility goddess she symbolized the full moon, and as controller of death she symbolized the waning moon.

Artemis went by other names, including Cynthia, Delia, Hecate, Luna, Phoebe, and Selene. As Artemis, she was most often depicted as a huntress, carrying her silver bow, although she was sometimes depicted on coins with a torch in her hand or with the moon and stars surrounding her head. (Bell 1991, Walker 1983)

See also Apollo, Arrows, Greece and Rome, Moon and Moon Gods, Selene, Sunbeams and Moonbeams

ASTRONOMY

Ancient astronomy was an intermingling of science and myth, an attempt to connect the order of the cosmos to the practical and spiritual needs of everyday life. When the ancients looked at the sky, they saw power. When they recorded what they saw, they believed they were recording not appearances of celestial objects, but visits by great sky gods.

The Greek moon goddess Artemis, who rode through the night on a silver chariot drawn by white horses and shot moonbeams through the sky with her silver bow.

Sky phenomena fascinated people from the beginning of history. The sky marked the passage the time and the rotation of the seasons. It determined the world's directions. It was natural for early people to try to tap into that kind of order. Today's skywatchers build metal domes from which they dissect the heavens, but ancient skywatchers built pyramids and ziggurats with long stairways. Today's astronomers aim their telescopes into the sky realm, but the ancients tried to reach that realm themselves. They climbed stairways to talk to the sky powers, and they recorded the movements of those powers from sacred temples built as high as they could reach.

Early astronomy was more of a spiritual search than a scientific analysis. Even so, early cultures made amazingly precise calculations of celestial movements. The early Babylonians and ancient Mayans recorded detailed observations of the moon and planets and developed systems of predicting eclipses that far surpassed systems of later civilizations. The intent of these early skywatchers was to understand the divine order the sky gods imposed on the heavens. They witnessed that order continuously as day turned to night, the moon waxed and waned, and the sun and the stars underwent seasonal migrations. These regular occurrences were comforting and an affirmation that the sky gods had some divine cosmic plan. Irregular occurrences, such as comets and eclipses, were perceived as threats to that plan and viewed as frightening introductions of chaos.

The attempt to understand cosmic order preoccupied ancient life and fathered the desire to study the heavens. The heavens housed the forces that ordered the universe and powered the world. Deification of those forces was the next logical step. Because only the highest powers in heaven had the ability to transmit their sky power, only the highest powers on earth had the ability to understand it. Skywatching then became the duty of shamans and astronomer-priests, who made their observations from secret chambers and shared their knowledge with only a chosen few. This kind of thinking kept astronomy a pastime of the elite and for centuries perpetuated the belief that the sky was sacred. But it was precisely this kind of thinking that led to the development of astronomy as science. People felt motivated to understand the sacred, so they took pains to watch the sky closely and to develop scientific ways of tapping that power.

The fruits of their labors were transmitted on clay tablets and in ancient codices, on Ice Age animal bones and on the walls of caves. Star charts were recorded on buck skins, and models of the cosmos fashioned on circular gourds. Many cultures combined their astronomical observations with weather phenomena and correlated them with current economic and political happenings in their everyday lives. They used their sky knowledge for divination and included in their

records omens and prodigies. Today scholars label this kind of astronomy astrology and consider it a pseudoscience. In the ancient world, astronomy and astrology were one and the same, synonymous in the same way that power was synonymous with the sky.

From the desire to understand ancient sky knowledge, the fields of archeology and astronomy fused. The new science was called archeoastronomy, and scholars in that field learned to interpret artifacts and remnants of early civilizations to discover what the ancients knew of their heavens. Since the 1970s, the field of archeoastronomy has gained acceptance in the scientific community and burgeoned into the study of science and culture, myth and magic. Archeoastronomers attempt to dissect the sky as early hunters and agricultural people did when they constructed their calendars and fashioned their lives to imitate the order of the heavens; they attempt to understand the cosmos as the ancients understood it, when they looked into the dark night and saw a sky alive with power. (Cornell 1981, Hadingham 1984, Krupp 1991a, 1997b)

See also Clocks and Calendars, Cosmic Order, Sky and Sky Gods

ASWINS

The Aswins, in ancient India, were the twin horsemen of the sun. They were connected to dawn and to celestial light, and they made their appearance just before sunrise, when they rode into the sky in a golden chariot and cleared a path through the clouds for Ushas, the dawn goddess, to ride into the sky in her chariot. Most commonly, the Aswins were identified as the sons of Surya, the sun, and a cloud goddess named Saranyu, but they were sometimes identified as the husbands of the sun, or as the sons of Dyaus, the sky. These twin horsemen have been interpreted as many things—as day and night, as Heaven and earth, as sun and moon, as terrestrial and celestial fire, as Castor and Pollux, or as the two appearances of the planet Venus, the Morning Star and Evening Star.

Considering their crucial role in ushering in the morning light, the Aswins clearly had solar connections. They were golden in color, and they rode in a chariot drawn either by horses or by birds, both animals connected with solar power. These twin horsemen were often called Dasra and Nasatya. They were ancient deities, yet they remained forever young and had the power to bestow youth on human beings as well. The Aswins were handsome and brilliant, like the dawn, and as they made their appearance each morning, they scattered dew with their whips and brought the first light of day into the sky. (Lang 1996, Muller 1897)

See also Dawn, India, Sun and Sun Gods, Surya

ATAR

Fire is the center of Zoroastrian ritual today, as it was in the ancient world. The ancient Persians personified fire as Atar, the son of Ahura Mazda, who rode behind the chariot of Mithra, the god of light and the sun. Atar represented both celestial and terrestrial fire. Like Agni in Vedic India, he was present in the sky as lightning and in the earth in wood from which sparks were kindled.

According to the Persian prophet, Zoroaster, the battle between good and evil brought about world order. Atar fought as a warrior for the good. As the light force, he fought demons of darkness, and as the lightning force, he fought demons of drought. In one ancient text, he fought a dragon-monster named Azhi Dahaka, who personified destruction and tried to extinguish the Divine Fire so revered in Zoroastrian thought. Atar succeeded in stopping Azhi Dahaka by threatening to destroy him with flames. With Atar the defender protecting it, the Divine Fire remained burning, bright and unattainable. (Curtis 1993, Hinnels 1973)

See also Agni, Duality, Fire, Mithra, Persia

ATEN

As a form of the Egyptian sun god Ra or Amon-Ra, Aten was the solar disk, the golden orb worshipped for its light and warmth. Originally, Aten was perceived as simply the home of Ra, but during the reign of Amenhetep IV, later called Akhenaten, the disk itself rose to cult status as the creator god. During the early years of the fourteenth century B.C., worship of Aten became the primary religion of Egypt.

Like Ra and Horus, Aten was all-powerful and perceived as the giver of life. But there the similarities end. Aten had none of the customary adornments of sun gods—no boat to sail the heavens and no gods or goddesses to accompany him in his perpetual sky journey. In fact, Aten was not personified at all but represented only as a red disk, with rays emanating downward and terminating in human hands that accepted offerings and bestowed blessings on his worshippers.

Perhaps because of the simplicity of this religion, Aten's cult lasted only during the reign of Amenhetep IV; the Egyptians then went on to worship their more elaborate sun gods. Yet still, the cult of Aten left an indelible stamp on the religious history of Egypt: Aten was immortalized in his temple, the Palace of the Obelisk, and in numerous hymns addressed to him that glorified the solar disk. (Budge 1969, Rosalie 1980)

See also Amon, Egypt, Ra, Sun and Sun Gods

AURORA

An aurora is a diffuse glow seen most commonly in the night skies of the earth's polar regions. In the Southern Hemisphere, the glow is called the aurora australis, or the southern lights, and in the northern hemisphere, the aurora borealis, or the northern lights.

The northern lights can take a variety of shapes and forms, often hanging like a curtain over a large part of the sky and at other times forming a horizontal arc spanning a much smaller area. Some say the Chinese got the image of their dragon by viewing the northern lights. When it appeared in an arc, it may have resembled the mythological dragon that permeated Chinese myths.

The name aurora stems from classical mythology, from the Greek Eos or the Roman Aurora, goddess of dawn and mother of winds. With a star sparkling on her forehead and the morning dew dripping from her fingers, Aurora announced Helios, the sun god, just as dawn broke each morning. Such myths attest to the ancients' knowledge of the aurora's connection to sunlight. In Norse myths as well, the northern lights appeared when sunlight reflected off the armor of the Valkyrie, warrior daughters of the gods.

In the northern countries, particularly in Alaska, Scandinavia, and northern Siberia, the aurora borealis lit the skies up to 243 nights a year—and lit it brilliantly in ancient times when no city lights obscured its appearance. To the ancients, the glow often seemed to precede bad weather, and for this reason early people sometimes used it as a predictor.

They also considered the aurora mysterious and somewhat frightening and wove it into their myths as a bad omen. Some cultures associated the glow with war and pestilence, and many others believed it to be the apparition of the dead. The Inuit of Hudson Bay thought the light came from the lanterns of demons searching for lost souls. In Alaska, some tribes thought the glow occurred when spirits of the dead played a ballgame using the skull of a walrus as a ball. Plains Indian tribes believed the glow came from fires the northern tribes built when they boiled their enemies in large pots. But the Estonian tribes had a pleasant view. They told a folktale in which the glow appeared when shining sleighs and horses carried guests to an enormous wedding in the sky. (Dennis 1992, Lockhart 1988, Watson 1984)

AUSZRINE

In Baltic mythology, Auszrine was Venus, the radiant Morning Star, the daughter of the sun goddess Saule, and the sister of the Evening Star, Wakarine. Auszrine was beautiful and powerful; so much so, in fact, that when she was born she so transfixed the moon god, Meness, that he did not rise for two nights. The love of Meness for Auszrine led to the moon god's decline. Though married to the sun goddess, Meness seduced her lovely daughter, and Perkons, the storm god, sliced him up to avenge the betrayal of Saule. Auszrine patched him up again. The myth of the adultery between Auszrine and Meness not only explained why the moon waxed and waned, but it emphasized the importance the ancient Balts placed on the brightness of Venus. They saw Venus, the Morning Star, as a rival of the sun.

Several variations of this Baltic sky myth dealt with the rivalry between these two bright celestials. In one version of the myth, it was the sun, not the moon, who did not rise for two days. The sun goddess remained below the horizon because when Auszrine rose from the sea, she appeared more radiant and beautiful than the sun goddess herself. In another version of the myth, the birth of Auszrine was the reason the sun set. Because Auszrine outshone her, the sun goddess was forced to descend to the sea. Auszrine, in all her beauty, was goddess of dawn and of spring as well as of Venus as the Morning Star. She and her sister, Wakarine, the Evening Star, tended Saule's sun palace and cared for the horses that guided her golden chariot. (Greimas 1992, McCrickard 1990)

See also Baltic and Slavic Lands, Morning Star/Evening Star, Saule

AYERS ROCK

The Aborigines of Australia invest their land with spirit and energy, and they assign specific landforms, such as Ayers Rock, a special place in their mythological history. This particular landform is made of red sandstone and sits 2,820 feet above sea level. At two and a third miles long and one and two-thirds miles wide, it's the largest individual rock in the world. To the Aborigines it is also one of their most sacred sites. The Aborigines call this monumental structure Uluru, and they say it was created in the primordial creation period called Dreamtime by mythological ancestors who gave the rock, and all the features in and around it, their creative energy and spiritual power.

Uluru is only one example of a geographical landform with mythological significance, but because it dominates the landscape, the Aborigines assigned to this structure particularly colorful myths. One myth explained how Uluru was formed by two young boys who shaped a mound out of mud after a rainstorm. Additional myths account for particular features of the rock. A lizard digging for a boomerang made grooves in the mound and created the caves. The Carpet Snake People and the Snake Warriors engaged in battle, and their spilled blood formed the pools and streams. Blue Tongue Lizard stole some emu meat from two hunters and buried it, creating the slabs of rock, and the brothers, in revenge, turned the Lizard into the large boulder that currently sits at the base of the Uluru. People who believe they are descendants of these mythical beings keep these myths alive by repeating them to their people. They also appoint themselves caretakers of their ancestor's spirit forms. A descendant of Blue Tongue Lizard, for example, looks after the boulder at the base of Ayers Rock, and by doing so he shows respect for the land and his mythological ancestor who infused the land with spirit. (Bernbaum 1990, Mountford 1970)

See also Dreamtime, Oceania, Rainbow Snake, Taniwha, Wondjina

AZTEC CALENDAR STONE

The Aztec, among other groups in Mesoamerica, believed in a succession of world

The four larger glyphs inside the Aztec Calendar Stone represent the world ages, each linked to a primal element of nature.

ages, and they depicted those ages on a massive stone scholars have labeled the Aztec Calendar Stone. The structure got its name because twenty glyphs on the outer edge of the stone represent the days in one of the ancient Aztec calendrical systems. But the meat of this ancient relic lies inside the calendar, where four larger glyphs represent the world ages, or "suns," each linked to a primal element of nature. With Tonatiuh, the present sun, at the center of these glyphs, the Aztec Calendar Stone symbolizes the whole of the Aztec universe.

In the Aztec belief system, the primal element of each world age related both to the composition of the world and to its destruction. In the first age, depicted on the stone by the jaguar, the world was populated by giants, and the age ended when the jaguar, who may have symbolized earth, devoured them. In the second age, depicted by Ehecatl, the wind god, the world ended when a hurricane carried away all of earth's inhabitants. In the third age, depicted by Tlaloc, the rain god, a fiery rain destroyed the world, perhaps representative of a volcanic eruption. Then in the fourth age, depicted by Chalchihuitlicue, the water goddess, the world ended in deluge. In each age, the god or goddess in control of the world was defeated by the destructive side of his or her own element. Earth became devourer, air or wind became hurricane, fire became lightning or volcanic ash, and water became flood. Each of these four ages existed in prehistory. According to myth, Tonatiuh ruled the current age, or the fifth sun, which the Aztec believed would end in an earthquake. (Aveni 1980, Brundage 1979, Campbell 1974, Krupp 1981, Taube 1993)

See also Chalchihuitlicue, Ehecatl, Elements, Jaguar, Mesoamerica, Quetzalcoatl, Tezcatlipoca, Tlaloc, Tonatiuh

BALDER

Balder was the Norse god of light, of spring, and of peace. Kind, gentle, and wise, he was looked upon with love and admiration by all the gods as he sat on his throne in a hall that glimmered with light so bright and radiant that it shone to the farthest corners of the world. There he studied the laws of the land and passed judgment and gave advice to all those who turned to him.

The son of Odin and Frigg, Balder was handsome and fair, with white-hair and white eyebrows. He was born at the winter solstice, the day the sun's light began its journey to maximum brightness, and he died at the summer solstice, the day the sun shone with the greatest power but from which it then slowly began to fade.

The death of Balder was the light god's most famous myth, a myth that symbolized the seasonal cycle of death and rebirth marked by the solstices. Balder dreamt of someone or something wanting to kill him and take away the light and the springtime. So he asked his mother, Frigg, for help. Frigg went to all the gods, all the plants, all the animals, all the diseases, and all the forces of nature to ask for their protection. They all pledged not to harm Balder. But Frigg neglected to speak with one small but deadly plant, mistletoe, and it was that plant that caused Balder's death. Annoyed that Balder could not be harmed, Loki, the mischievous and sometimes malevolent trickster, tricked the blind god Hodur into throwing mistletoe at Balder's heart. The poison killed him immediately, on the day of the summer solstice when the sun's light began to fade.

The death of Balder at the summer solstice symbolized the beginning of the sun's descent into winter. In many lands, the time when the sun reached the high point of its yearly path and began its descent was likened to a death and was illustrated by seasonally slain gods like Balder. But whereas the sun

BACABS

Among the ancient Maya, the Bacabs were four wind gods who held up the sky at the corners of the earth. To the Maya, the universe was multilayered, and the Bacabs supported the thirteen heavens. Equivalent to the four Tezcatlipocas of the Aztecs, the Bacabs were the spirits of the cardinal points. The Bacabs assumed the task of supporting the thirteen heavens when a great flood poured down from the waters of the firmament, ended the rule of Chalchihuitlicue, the water goddess, and collapsed the sky.

Bacab was in theory a singular deity, the son of Itzamna, who, like many gods of Mesoamerica, manifested himself in four parts. Each of the four Bacabs was associated with a color to identify him with the direction over which he presided. Hobnil, god of the east, was red, a color the Maya identified with the rising sun. Zac Cimi, god of the west, was black, representative of the sun's descent into darkness below the western horizon. Can Tzional, god of the north, was white like the cold northern lands, and Hozanek, god of the south, was yellow like the southern sun that shone on the yellow maize fields.

The Bacabs appear frequently in an ancient text called *Ritual of the Bacabs* and as figures with upraised arms supporting many altars constructed by the Olmecs during the Toltec period at Chichen Itza. (Bunson and Bunson 1996, Nicholson 1967, Thompson 1970)

See also Cardinal Points or Directions, Mesoamerica, Winds and Wind Gods

was immortal and returned to full power each year, Balder was not. When Frigg asked the goddess of the dead to restore her son to life, the death goddess agreed to grant that wish if everyone on the earth would weep for Balder (symbolic of a thaw after a frost). Everyone wept except for Loki, disguised as a giantess. It was believed that Balder would return from the Underworld only after Ragnarok, or the Twilight of the Gods, when the world was made new. (Crossley-Holland 1980, Dumezil 1973, Guerber 1992, Page 1990)

See also Darkness and Light, Death, Scandinavia, Solstices

BALLGAME

Throughout Mesoamerica, the ancients played a ballgame believed to have been a symbolic reenactment of the play of cosmic forces. The game was played extensively, in all parts of Mexico and Central America, and archeologists have found ballcourts throughout the land near ancient temples. Scholars have suggested that these ballcourts, either enclosed in masonry or underground, represented the Underworld and that the ball often represented the sun, the moon, Venus, or the Maize God.

The players of the ballgame took their sport seriously, sometimes playing simply for sport, but often reenacting myths by putting on masks of gods and playing the game as if they were the gods themselves. The players, be they human or god, played for high stakes. The object of the game was to keep the ball in play, suggestive of the need to keep the sun in the sky and out of the Underworld. If the players failed to keep the ball in play, the "sun" sank below the metaphorical horizon and died—and the player or team of players representing the sun then had to die as well.

While the ball symbolized the sun in the hands of one team, it often symbolized the moon or Venus in the hands of the other. In another version, the ball symbolized the Maize God. There were other variations in the game. There were two teams, usually with two or three players on each side. In one version, one team attempted to guard the sun as it passed through the Underworld, and the other side attempted to destroy it, as Venus, the Evening Star, extinguished the sun's light. In another version, players assumed the guises of Huitzilopochtli and Coyolxauhqui and reenacted the mythic battle in which the sun god slew the moon goddess. Following the myth closely, the game ended when the player representing Coyolxauhqui, the moon, was beheaded, and the players representing the night stars were slain. In each of the games, the losing team experienced a metaphorical descent into the Underworld. When the ball fell to the ground, it was Venus, or the sun, or the moon sinking below the horizon, or sometimes, the hero twins descending to the Underworld to rescue First Father who died, then emerged as the Maize God and renewed life in the world.

Carved relief panels along ballcourts throughout Mesoamerica tell the stories of the myths reenacted in legendary ballgames. A mural at El Tajin on the Gulf coast tells how Quetzalcoatl was tricked into incest by Tezcatlipoca and executed, his heart then rising into the sky and becoming the sun. The ballgame, called thlachli, was considered a cult, and the ballcourt, the thlachlo, a temple of the night sky. The cult was macabre, the game brutal, but the mystery and intrigue of the play attracted attention and inspired awe, as did the celestial bodies. The message the game conveyed was not of death but of renewal. The sun renewed itself each day after it was slain by Evening Star, the moon renewed itself each night as it reappeared in the heavens, and the Maize God returned each year after his descent into the Underworld. (Brundage 1979, 1985, Markman and Markman 1992, Miller and Taube 1993)

See also Death, Morning Star/Evening Star, Quetzalcoatl, Sacrifice

BALTIC AND SLAVIC LANDS

The area of the world that encompasses Russia, Siberia, and the countries of northern Europe bordering the Baltic Sea is characterized by ice, snow, and frigid weather. In times of old, when people had little recourse against the elements, they saw themselves fighting for survival in a land full of evil nature spirits. The nature myths of this area varied greatly because they encompassed the beliefs of a large number of ethnic groups. But the bitter cold rendered a common thread. These people shared a preoccupation with warmth, and they revered the deities who could return fertility to their world, as if by magically unlocking the chains of ice that kept the sun goddess imprisoned deep within the earth.

The Lithuanians actually did use the metaphor of unlocking the earth to describe the return of the sun in the spring. The sun was female in this part of the world, and the spring sun was described as a young maiden who had been imprisoned in a mountain or a cave all winter long. Sometimes she was freed by the star gods, and in Lithuanian myth, specifically by her daughter, Auszrine, the Morning Star, who obtained a key from the goddess of the Underworld, liberated her mother from death, and then returned with her to the morning sky. In Russian myth, Perun, the storm god, unlocked the prison doors. He liberated the earth and let warmth and light into its dark recesses. Some say this key symbolized the lightning. He opened the earth with his storm power, and, in essence, freed the sun that had been trapped and rendered powerless during the long, cold winter.

Perhaps Perun's greatest feat was freeing the sun from its winter prison, for which he achieved high status—some say supreme status—in the pantheon. In a similar manner, he freed the rains imprisoned in the castles of clouds. Farther south, Yegory, the sun god of Bulgaria, was likewise imprisoned, and in his myth as well, the thunder and wind unlocked the dungeon doors that kept him trapped in darkness. The sun god emerged, battled the winter demon, and won. Perun and Yegory were refreshing presences after the evil ice gods had ruled for so long. During the winter months, gods of the winds and the frosts not only locked up the sun, but they took every opportunity to ravage the earth and to destroy as much as possible before the sun and storm gods arose to defeat them.

The pagan Balts and Slavs deified the wind and the frost, the ice and the cold, because they venerated everything in nature that held powerful influence on their land and their lives. Although Perun and the sun goddess are no longer worshipped, their roles were usurped by Christian saints. However, the lesser deities held their places much longer, possibly into the present day. The earth in this area was covered with vast forests and pockmarked by rivers, lakes, pools, and streams. The types of spirits that inhabited these natural areas varied from place to place, but most of them were evil, or at least mischievous, because their natural world was a dangerous place. Hunters ventured into the forests and found themselves at the mercy of the Leshy, or forest spirits. Fishermen traveled over lakes and often fell prey to the evil Vodyanoi, who dragged them down and made them slaves in their underwater kingdoms. The winds roared and wailed in these countries, and when they did, it often meant death to the earth. The people of these cold lands, in fact, envisioned paradise as a place where no winds blew at all.

The natural phenomena that these early Europeans feared and revered were powerful forces, but the most powerful and the most precious, was, of course, the sun. Sun worship prevailed in these northern lands, and the people developed elaborate seasonal festivals to carry out their worship. The death of winter was clearly a time for rejoicing, so at the winter solstice, the villagers gathered together to celebrate the rebirth of their solar

goddess. In pagan Russia, the solstice ceremony featured a young girl dressed in white
who traveled through the village on a sled.
The villagers sang songs to her and urged her
on her way. The girl, representative of
Kolyada, the goddess of the newborn sun,
moved from house to house, just as the sun
itself moved from the southernmost point it
reached at the solstice back on its northward
path across the sky.

The solstices were celebrated in many
lands, and people conducted ceremonies particularly at the winter solstice when the
turning of the sun was most crucial. In the
Baltic lands, the summer solstice also war-
ranted a special festival. The summer solstice
was again a time to celebrate the sun goddess, and in Lithuanian tradition, worshippers
stayed up all night to watch the sun rise in
the morning. Their sun goddess, they believed, had married the moon god, and on
midsummer morning she left her sky palace
in her horse-drawn chariot and performed a
beautiful dance on her way to visit him. The
summer solstice was the day the sun shone at
its brightest, and the ancients eagerly awaited
the arrival of their goddess. The peasants
built a bonfire and waited for her to appear,
whirling about and emitting sparks of fire as
she danced in her colorful clothes. (Gimbutas 1971, Harva 1964, McCrickard 1990,
Ralston 1872, Simonov 1997)

BAST

The Egyptian cat-headed goddess Bast or
Bastet was the goddess of flame and fire, a
personification of the sun's heat. Bast was a
complex solar deity; she was originally worshipped as simply a cat who symbolized the
mild fertilizing heat of the sun in spring and
early summer. Bast was often confused with
her lion-headed counterpart, Sekmet, who
symbolized the fierce heat of noon and the
sun's destructive power.

Bast has been identified with the moon as
well as the sun, perhaps because of her connection to fertility, a common lunar trait.
However, identifying Bast as a moon goddess
appears to be a Greek interpretation of her
character, and not what the Egyptians intended. Bast was the daughter of Ra, the sun
god, and in Egyptian writings, she represented the morning sun rays. She usually appeared as a cat, or as a woman with a cat's
head, dressed in a red patterned robe. In the
tradition of sun goddesses from the Baltic
lands and Australia, Bast's red robe symbolized
the rising sun. (Budge 1969, Spence 1986)

See also Egypt, Sun and Sun Gods

BEARS

Bears have appeared in myths throughout
the world as symbols of nature's capacity for
rebirth. Bears die a metaphorical death each
winter when they retreat into their caves,
much like Mother Nature dies each winter
when the land becomes dry and cold. When
Mother Nature awakens to a new world each
spring, so too does the bear. Its annual awak-
ening is an affirmation of seasonal renewal,
because each year the animal emerges from
its cave, often bringing bear cubs, and thus
new life, into the world.

Bears were popular figures in the myths of
Asia, North America, and the Arctic lands,
where they were highly respected, and
among many people, highly venerated for
their strength and power. Bears were almost
always connected in some way to the female
life force, either being female themselves and
giving birth or being the offspring of a
human female. This quality reinforced the
bears' intimate connection with fertility, renewal, and, often, the moon. Mother Earth
and the bear vanish and reappear, as does the
moon. The cyclical nature of the bear's habits
thus link the animal with the annual cycle of
vegetation and the order of the seasons, controlled by the phases of the moon.

A famous representation of the bear in the
earth mother image is a stone carving by the
Haida Indians of Canada, now on display at

the Smithsonian Institution. The carving is known as Bear Mother, and it illustrates a legend of a woman who bore a child who was half woman and half bear. (Campbell 1988a, Mercatante 1974, Shepard 1985)

See also Caves, Earth and Earth Gods, Moon and Moon Gods

BENTEN

Benten was the sea goddess of Japan, the daughter of the dragon-king, and the only female among the seven Gods of Good Luck. She was worshipped along the seacoast and had numerous shrines near the water, in caverns, and on islands. The most famous of Benten's temples is a group of buildings that stands on Enoshima. During low tide, Enoshima is a peninsula, but during high tide it looks more like an island. When the tide rises, Benten's temples become nearly immersed in water and they appear to be floating on top of the sea like a dragon's palace.

The island of Enoshima was the site of one of Benten's most popular myths. Once, a malicious dragon lived in a cave on the mainland close by Enoshima, and he was eating all the children. Enoshima was undersea at that time and remained so until an earthquake in the sixth century. After the earthquake, Benten appeared in a cloud in the sky and the island appeared out of the water, rising up as if by magic so that Benten could descend to earth and restore order. Benten stepped down onto Enoshima, which after the earthquake connected to the mainland with a strip of sand, married the dragon, and ended his rampage.

The worship of Benten extended to the worship of rivers and of water in general, and, perhaps, to the connection of water and wisdom. Benten, in her role as goddess of wisdom, was the equivalent of the goddess Sarasvati of Hindu India. Both rose from the sea on a lotus. Benten was usually portrayed emerging from the waves riding a dragon or in the company of a white snake named Hakuja. Both the snake and the dragon are symbols for the sea and the waters. (Getty 1962, Knappert 1995c, Piggott 1983)

See also Dragon-Kings, Dragons, Japan, Sarasvati, Sea and Sea Gods

BIFROST

In Norse legend, Bifrost was a rainbow bridge made of water, fire, and air that led from Midgard, the home of mortals, to Asgard, the home of the gods. Bifrost was the strongest of bridges, presided over by the light god, Heimdall, whose name meant "rainbow" or "he who casts light." Heimdall stood guard night and day at the rainbow bridge and alerted the gods when he heard the approach of the trolls and frost giants that plagued the land.

Rainbows often served as a path for gods in the mythic literature, and Bifrost was a classic example. The gods in the world above traveled down the rainbow to interact with the people on earth. But the rainbow bridge shook and trembled when mortals tried to cross it, and the red part was made of fire. It scorched the feet of the trolls and frost giants and prevented them from crossing and reaching Asgard. Despite Heimdall's efforts and the strength of the bridge, Bifrost broke under the weight of the frost giants at Ragnarok, or the Twilight of the Gods. Heimdall sounded his warning horn too late. The forces of evil trampled across Bifrost into Asgard and defeated the gods. (Crossley-Holland 1980, Guerber 1992)

See also Bridges, Rainbows and Rainbow Gods, Scandinavia

BIRDS

Birds of all forms appeared in myths as symbols of celestial power. Their ability to fly enabled them to transcend the realm of the earth and disappear into the realm of the sky. The birds' wings were the key to their power. They could beat them to cause thunder and wind, or spread them out and soar into the heavens to reach the highest powers of all—the sun and the sky gods.

Myths relating birds to the sun appeared in many lands. In China, the sun was once a cock, and in Japan, cocks helped lure the sun goddess, Amaterasu, out of her cave. The fire-bird of Russian legend was also a type of cock, colored red like the sun, and in Celtic lands, a wren with similar red markings brought fire from the sun to the earth. The bird's coloring reinforced its solar symbolism. A golden warbler accompanied the Chinese warrior Shen I on his visits to the sun because this bird was believed to know the sun's behavior. With plumage of gold and red that fanned out like sun rays and represented flames, colorful birds of many species symbolized fire and heat and solar energy.

Many types of birds appeared in legends as solar symbols. Eagles and hawks were commonly associated with the sun, perhaps because of their ability to soar high into the heavens. The Egyptian sun gods Horus and Ra were both hawk headed, and so throughout Egypt the hawk was worshipped and the winged disk was representative of the sun's power. In many North American tribes, the eagle represented the sun, and in Peru, the condor did. In the Nahuatl language of ancient Mexico, the terms for ascending eagle and descending eagle were used to refer to the rising and setting sun, and Huitzilopochtli, the Aztec sun god, considered the appearance of an eagle on a cactus an omen for the founding of their capital city, Tenochtitlan.

Because birds appeared able to tap into the power of the sun, they presumably could tap into other sky powers as well. In China, birds were deemed incarnations not only of fire and sun but also of clouds and thunderbolts. They were wind deities, as was the Garuda Bird of India and the Thunderbird of North America, believed by most every North American culture to flap its wings and cause wind and storms. The appearance of birds in the spring led to the notion that

these winged creatures had the power to deliver the spring and, thus, the wind and rains that came with it. For this reason, shamans often impersonated birds in springtime rain dances in an attempt to lure the water from the heavens. The ancients theorized that if the sky powers could reach people in the likeness of birds, then in the likeness of birds, people could similarly reach the sky powers.

Because birds could transverse heaven and earth, they often served as messengers between gods and people. In the Celtic world, birds were highly venerated as assistants of the gods. Many cultures entrusted birds with the task of proclaiming omens and revealing secrets of high deities. Some messengers, if not actual birds, were birdlike, such as Iris, the Greek rainbow goddess, who delivered news from celestial regions by flying swiftly back and forth with her wings of gold.

As the bird became a symbol of high power, the mythmakers put these winged creatures to use. They carried messages and pulled sky chariots, and in some myths they even created the world. Birds were so convincing as sun deities that they sometimes tricked the world with their powers, like when Vucub Caquix, the celestial bird of the Maya, rose as a false sun, or when the nine birds of Chinese myth blew fire into the sky and created nine false suns. Even mythological birds like the phoenix symbolized the sun. The phoenix died in its own fires every night and rose from them each morning, a convincing symbol of solar power. (Biedermann 1992, Chevalier and Gheerbrant 1996, Ingersoll 1923, Mercatante 1974)

See also Garuda Bird, Lightning Bird, Phoenix, Sun and Sun Gods, Thunderbirds, Winds and Wind Gods

BOGS

Bogs are treacherous; they appear innocuous but can catch people unaware and suck them down into the watery mud. Throughout the Celtic world, particularly in the Iron Age,

Bogs represented the ancient dwelling places of evil spirits. Grendel, the archetype of natural evil in the epic of Beowulf, *makes his home in a bog.*

bogs were the centers of cult and ritual. People believed they were the abodes of evil spirits, and they commonly made offerings and sacrifices to the bog spirits, burying coins, metalwork, and even human beings deep into the marshy water.

Throughout Celtic Europe, and indeed throughout the world, people found spirit in water. Water had the ability to cleanse and purify, so the spirit in water, particularly in running water, was revered for its curative powers. Bog water did not appear to have curative powers, however. The waters were murky and still and the powers seemed evil. So the Celts felt the need to propitiate the evil spirits, in many cases through human sacrifice. Bog burials appear to have been common Iron Age rituals. Archeologists have

found mummies in bogs throughout Europe, particularly in Germany and Denmark, many weighted down with sticks and heavy branches or with ropes tied around their necks. No one knows for sure whether these people were criminals and their bog burials a form of punishment, or whether the people were simply sacrificed to appease the gods. Some scholars believe the ancient Celts made bog sacrifices in winter or early spring to ask the bog gods for a good growing season. (Coles and Coles 1989, Green 1992)

See also Celtic Lands, Marshes and Swamps, Water and Water Spirits

BRAHMA

Brahma is the creator god of Hindu mythology and, along with Vishnu and Shiva, one of the three aspects of the Supreme Being. Brahma is the lord of light, and as such he is thought to be guardian of the world. This creator deity sprang from the lotus flower out of the ocean of milk, connecting him to the realms of both earth and sky. When he opened his eyes, the first world came into existence, and the light that sustained the world emanated from his four faces and permeated all four corners of the universe.

A day of Brahma corresponds to the Hindu perception of world ages. When Brahma opens his eyes, an age begins, and when he closes them, it ends—and it ends in cataclysm. In the course of one day of Brahma, the world is annihilated using the same forces that characterize the weather of India. The scorching sun turns to fire, and the torrential rains turn to flood. Then, finally, all is still and nothing exists but, once again, the primordial sea. This is the night of Brahma. One day of Brahma is called the kalpa, which in Hindu mythology is the cosmic unit of time. Each day of Brahma is one world age, comparable to 4,320 million earth years. (Campbell 1974, Zimmer 1962)

See also India, Lotus, Primordial Sea, Shiva, Vishnu

BREEZES

The ancients told many myths of the wind, and they personified it in its different aspects, sometimes as the furious tempest and other times as the soft, gentle breeze. Winds moved, and when they moved gently, particularly in spring and summer, they breathed life into the earth. Mythmakers who deified the breeze sometimes said the deities stirred the leaves on the trees and awakened the flowers after their winter sleep. Whereas the wind gods who personified tempests and hurricanes had violent tempers, those who personified the breezes were kind, though often mischievous.

The Greeks had many deities who personified the breeze, and so did the Indo-Iranians. The Ribhus perhaps embodied the breezes in ancient India. They played a large role in creation, made the grass and the herbs, and were said to sleep in the winter, then awaken in spring. Aura was the Greek goddess of breezes, one of the winged air nymphs. The easy-going forest god, Pan, personified the breeze when he blew gently on his reed pipe; he was the son Hermes, who some say was the deified wind. Also in Greek myth, the West Wind, Zephyrus, personified the breeze, though he was not always so gentle. Zephyrus, it was said, was once wild and savage like the North Wind, Boreas, his brother. But Zephyrus fell in love with Flora, the goddess of spring, and her gentle love settled him down. From then on, Zephyrus was kind and gentle and left the howling and raving to his brother. (Baring-Gould 1897, Watson 1984)

See also Winds and Wind Gods

BRIDGES

In the cultures of many lands, bridges symbolized transition or passage, commonly from one realm to the next. They linked the ordinary with the extraordinary, the tangible with the intangible. For this reason bridges provided a handy path for the gods. Deities throughout the world crossed metaphorical bridges as they traveled to and from earth and their home in the sky.

The rainbow and the Milky Way were the two most common metaphorical bridges, and Bifrost, the well-known bridge of the gods in Norse mythology, likely represented both. The rainbow appeared to touch the earth and extend to the sky. The Milky Way spanned the length of the sky and again appeared to bridge two worlds. Souls of the deceased commonly took the Milky Way path as they passed from the world of the living to the world of the dead. (Biedermann 1992, Chevalier and Gheerbrant 1996)

See also Bifrost, Milky Way, Rainbow and Rainbow Gods

BRIGIT

Brigit was the great earth goddess of the Celts, often called "mother of the Irish gods." Born at dawn in a pillar of fire, she was worshipped throughout the Celtic world as a fertility goddess, mother of the Tuatha De Danann, the ancient gods of Ireland who possessed all the skills known to humanity. Brigit was goddess of healing, fire, poetry, and wisdom and was intimately connected with fertility and childbirth. As nurturer and sustainer, she epitomized the great goddess from which all life flowed and to which all life returned.

As fertility goddess, Brigit presided over the ale harvest and protected the fields and the flocks. She was often depicted in triplicate, with two sisters considered to be part of her persona, carrying babies and other fertility symbols, such as fruit, grains, or bread. From her land, Brigit could supply limitless food, and from her cows, an endless supply of milk. Venerated in all of Ireland, she ensured the fertility of women as well as the fecundity of the soil, and was often invoked by women in childbirth who wished her to protect them.

Brigit was such a popular goddess that she was adopted by the Christians and was made a saint, retaining her same fertility aspects. St. Brigit, or St. Bride of Kildare, protected flocks, guarded the family hearth, and presided over childbirth, in addition to serving as the foster mother of Christ. Saint Brigit was honored in one of the four great Celtic festivals, a pastoral celebration, connected with the lactation of wolves and of ewes. Held every year on February first, the festival of Saint Brigit was a celebration of continuity and renewal and was a tribute to Mother Earth, the great goddess and saint responsible for the maintenance of daily life. (Green 1993, Stewart 1990)

See also Celtic Lands, Earth and Earth Gods

CANCER, THE CRAB

Cancer is the fourth sign of the zodiac and the hardest to see in the night sky. In ancient Greece, the sun passed through this constellation on the summer solstice, the day the sun shone the longest. This event gave the crab a connection with the sun. The Egyptians saw in this star group their scarab beetle, a common symbol of solar birth. But other peoples saw a crab, and they found another solar connection. At the summer solstice, the sun appeared to hesitate, then to move backward across the ecliptic, its path across the sky. The crab exhibited a similar peculiarity of movement. It too appeared to hesitate, then walk backward across the earth like the sun walked backward across the sky.

In Greek mythology, Cancer the crab figured into one of the twelve labors Hercules had to perform to achieve immortality. During his second labor, the battle with the Hydra, Hercules encountered the crab; Hera had sent the gigantic creature to bite Hercules and prevent him from completing his task. The crab emerged from a swamp and bit Hercules on the heel, but Hercules crushed the crab, then went on to kill the Hydra. Because Hercules was the illegitimate son of Zeus, Hera's husband, she had hated him from his birth and felt gratitude to the crab for helping her try to destroy her enemy, even if he failed. As a reward for his services, Hera raised the crab into the sky as a constellation.

The Tropic of Cancer was named after this star group. At noon on the day of the summer solstice in ancient Greece, the sun appeared directly over the crab. (Ridpath 1988, Staal 1988)

See also Constellations, Scarab Beetle, Zodiac

CANYONS, GORGES, AND RIVER VALLEYS

Any landform of great size inspires awe in those who behold it, and large cavities in the land are no exception. People searched for explanations of these depressions long before scientists explained the geologic processes that created them. The contrast between mountains and valleys inspired wonderment. This wonderment inspired myths. When early people beheld large depressions in the land, they surmised that only giants could dig such enormous holes.

In the minds of many early people, monsters and giants existed side by side with people at one time. In life, these giants caused large-scale natural phenomena, such as hurricanes, earthquakes, canyons, and rivers, and in death they became mountains and rocks. These giants existed in both human and animal form. In Australia, giant serpents slithered through wet earth to form valleys, and in Scandinavia, humanlike giants stomped out canyons and river valleys, then their goddesses filled them with the water of their giant tears. A gorge in Iceland called Asbyrgi looks like an impression made by a galloping horse, so in myth, that's exactly what it was. Odin's giant horse, Sleipnir, was said to have created the landform when he struck the land with one of his eight hooves.

Some of the most colorful explanations of canyons come from Australia, where some tribes continue to attribute these features to mythical ancestors. These ancestors roamed the earth in Dreamtime, a primordial creation period, and, among other things, they gouged out canyons and valleys as they traipsed over the earth. In one legend, crocodiles created the Narran River valley by thrashing through the earth, and in another legend, a giant fish created the Murray River valley by burrowing in the ground then widening his path by swishing his tail back and forth. Kamapua'a, the pig god of Hawaii, performed similar feats by digging up the earth with his snout. According to a legend from Borneo, a gigantic crab hollowed out the valleys when he dug up the earth with his pinchers. Another myth from Oceania tells how Maui, a character credited with creating many phenomena of nature, pulled the entire island of New Zealand out of the sea. The island emerged in the form of an enormous fish. When Maui began to cut up the fish, the slices he made with his knife formed the river valleys.

Maui was a trickster, and tricksters in myths were often culture heroes as well. In that role they performed all kinds of creative deeds. The North American trickster, Coyote, created Hell's Canyon, the large gorge at the base of the Blue Mountains in Oregon. According to legend, seven vile giants once lived in the Blue Mountains, and they continually tormented people and ate their children. Coyote instructed the animals to dig holes in the ground, so the giants would fall into them when they stomped around in search of their meals. The giants did fall into the gorges, as planned, and they stuck fast, thrashing and struggling in the boiling liquid the animals used to disguise the holes. Coyote turned the giants into mountains and the boiling liquid into copper. Then, to ensure no other giants could cross there, he beat the ground below and created Hell's Canyon— the deep gorge at the foot of the mountains. (Vitaliano 1973)

See also Dreamtime, Giants, Kamapua'a, Rivers and Lakes, Tricksters

CAPRICORN, THE GOAT

Capricorn, like Sagittarius, is an ancient constellation that scholars have traced to Babylonian times. The Arabs, Persians, Turks, and

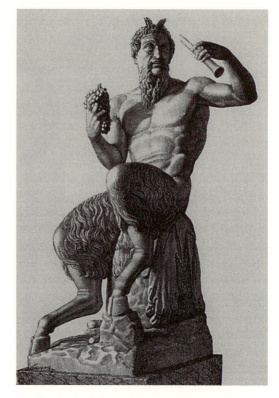

In Greek mythology, Capricorn is generally associated with Pan, who has the front quarters of a goat.

Syrians recognized this star group as a goat, but in Babylonian zodiacs, Capricorn appeared close to his modern form of half fish and half goat. In Greek times, Capricorn marked the winter solstice, and even though the constellation originated long before it served this function, most scholars find the symbolism of the winter solstice significant. Because a goat climbed as the sun did when it began its journey north on the first day of winter, the goat symbolized the climbing motion of the sun in Capricorn. Because the first day of winter marked the start of rains and floods, the fish tail symbolized the watery nature of the winter season.

In Greek mythology, Capricorn was generally connected with Pan, who jumped into the river to escape the monster Typhon and attempted to change himself into a fish. Pan moved so quickly when the monster came, however, that only his hind quarters changed into a fish; his front quarters remained a goat. The arrival of Typhon on the riverbanks that day led to his celebrated battle with Zeus, who eventually bested the monster and buried him under Mount Aetna, where he moans and writhes and causes earthquakes. But during this battle, Typhon pulled the muscles out of Zeus's legs, and, with the aid of Hermes, Pan replaced them. As a reward, Zeus placed Pan in the sky as Capricorn.

Like several other of the zodiacal constellations, Capricorn has only faint stars, so its distinction likely stems from its function as solstice marker. The sun keeps moving through the zodiac, but because the earth's axis wobbles, over two thousand years, the sun's position at the solstice changes from one constellation to the next. This phenomenon is called precession, and due to precession, Sagittarius serves the same function today that Capricorn did about two thousands year ago. Because Capricorn held this position years ago, the Tropic of Capricorn was named after this character. In ancient Greek times, the sun appeared directly overhead at noon on the winter solstice, when the sun passed through Capricorn. (Ridpath 1988, Staal 1988)

See also Constellations, Zodiac

CARDINAL POINTS OR DIRECTIONS

Direction is an attempt to inject order into the world and to organize undifferentiated space. It is a natural progression from the state of chaos to a structured and ordered cosmos. In Norse mythology, for instance, the beginning of the world was characterized only by Ginunngagap, the gaping abyss of darkness, and in many other cultures, by only a primordial sea or some great expanse of boundless and undifferentiated matter. But there was order and direction in the cosmos. So when the primordial gods created the sky,

they created a model for determining directions. The spinning sky, or rather the illusion of the spinning sky, established them.

Much of ancient life involved organizing the world to mirror the structure of the cosmos. Through myth and ritual, ancient people found ways to turn chaos to order. The first step in creating order was to define a cosmic center and four directions in respect to that center. Because the earth rotates on its axis, the sky appears to spin, and the spinning sky appears to revolve on some stable pole the ancients believed marked the center of the universe. So using that pole, the north celestial pole, as a vantage point, early people mapped order onto their world.

This cosmic center was many things to many different people. Scholars labeled it the world axis, or the Axis Mundi, but in reality it was likely a sacred mountain, or perhaps a cosmic tree that traversed the universe because its roots extended into the earth and its branches extended into the heavens. Before long, every culture began to define a cosmic center. Palaces were placed there, aligned to the cardinal directions, as well as temples, burial sites, homes, and entire villages. To the Italians, Rome marked the center; to the Vikings, Yggdrasil; to the Hindus, Mount Meru; and to the Inca, the Coricancha, or the Temple of the Sun. But whatever the center, be it mountain or temple, that place became sacred, and like magic, natural directions flowed from it and became sacred as well.

In many ancient religions, the magic of the cardinal directions was conveyed by atmospheric phenomena connected with each point, particularly by the winds and the rains. The Greeks believed four gods blew winds from these stations, and the Aztecs believed four gods sat there and cried tears that brought the rains from each area of the world. Early agriculturists discovered that the winds and rains that emanated from each direction related to the changing seasons, so for this reason, many myths connected north with winter, east with spring, south with summer, and west with autumn. Gods, the ancients believed, had to control those seasons, to drive the winds and the rain, and, perhaps more importantly, to remain stationed at each of the four corners of the world to support the sky.

Almost every culture had cardinal guardians who propped up the universe, controlled the seasons, and sent wind and rain or sunshine and fair weather from their respective stations. In northern Europe, four dwarfs, Nordri, Sudri, Austri, and Westri, held up the heavens on their shoulders, and in the Mayan lands, the Bacabs performed that task. These guardians enforced the cosmic order and guarded the four quadrants of Heaven. By holding up the sky at the four crucial points, they anchored the world and upheld the laws of the universe. (Eliade 1958, Krupp 1997b, Mackenzie 1970)

See also Bacabs, Cosmic Order, Seasons, Winds and Wind Gods, World Axis

CAVES

Dark and mysterious to ancient people, caves represented a world hidden from view, a world that fired imaginations and conjured up images of invisible forces much like those in the realms of Heaven and the Underworld. Magic or natural energy was said to exist in caves. In myth and legend, they housed winds and waters, sheltered dragons and earth gods, and provided access to the supernatural Underworld and the realm of the dead. Like the spirits that inhabited them, caves harbored sources of power.

The symbolism of caves spanned the three realms; caves served as passageways from sky to earth, and from earth to the Underworld and the waters beneath the earth. Gods themselves emerged from caves, as well as lightning and thunder, wind and rain, and in some cases, even the celestial bodies. Because caves served as places of emergence, they were perceived as centers of the world and

symbols of fertility. They were the wombs of the earth goddess, manifestations of her interior space. As the womb of Mother Earth, the power that existed in caves was tremendous. People throughout history and in cultures around the globe decorated caves with images of their gods and symbols of divine forces, and they retreated to caves to perform sacred rituals and conduct secret ceremonies. (Biedermann 1992, Eliade 1959, Krupp 1997b)

See also Bears, Earth and Earth Gods, Mountains

CELTIC LANDS

Much of Celtic mythology involved the veneration of natural phenomena. The Celts perceived divine forces in all aspects of nature, from the sun that powered the heavens to the marshes and bogs that delved deep into the earth. The early people who settled the British Isles were farmers; they depended on the land for sustenance and maintenance of everyday life. They found in their earth the spiritual essence that carried them through the seasons; in their waters, the curative powers that healed diseases; and in their sky, the comforting rhythms that brought about guidance and cyclic renewal.

The body of Celtic myths encompassed the cultures of Ireland, Gaul, and Great Britain. The early settlers were Druids, a group of people preoccupied with controlling supernatural forces through divination and ritual. Druidism lost influence in the Christian era, but in earlier times it defined a culture grounded on the reverence of natural phenomena. The Druids worshipped the earth. They worshipped the ground and the stones and the trees. The early concepts they formed of the great earth goddess as a symbol of fertility and abundance laid the foundation for many other primal nature cults based on reverence of specific landforms.

The earth goddess encompassed birth and rebirth, and in this role she was frequently associated with trees, another form of regenerative imagery. Reverence for trees was one of the most widespread forms of earth worship. It was believed by some that the first man and first woman were trees and that the gods transformed them into human beings. Tree cults thrived in the Celtic world because the forests that covered ancient Europe dominated, and in fact overpowered, the land. Many studies of Druidic culture mention oak worship, and it is believed that the first sanctuaries in the Celtic world were probably in oak groves. The tree symbolized fruitfulness, both of Heaven and of earth. The sky fertilized the earth with rain and the trees grew in abundance.

The reverence the Celts had for trees exemplified their concept of sacredness and tied together the nature powers they worshipped in all three realms. Sacred trees usually grew over wells or springs, thus connecting the powers of the earth with the powers of the waters. Both tree and well were sacred sources of power because they dug deep into the earth and provided a link to mysterious earth energy connected to the Underworld. Water cults as well as tree cults thrived in this part of the world. Because the Celts believed that life and power came from beneath the ground, they constructed many of their temples and shrines over springs, wells, and caves. From the middle of the Bronze Age through the Celtic period, worshippers cast all types of metals, weapons, cauldrons, jewelry, and coins into the waters to appease the water spirits and to activate their supernatural powers.

Rivers, springs, wells, and bogs permeated the Celtic lands, so water cults became imbedded in the mythological traditions of these countries. The powers of the water gods, together with the powers of the sun god, constituted a crucial aspect of Celtic worship. Springs and wells, it was believed, were receptacles for solar powers and stopping places for the nighttime sun. The sun's light and heat had obvious curative power,

and so did water. The Celts believed that each night the sun god descended from the sky into the waters beneath the earth and heated them. Apollo was a Roman sun god adopted into the Celtic pantheon under the epithet Apollo Belenus, meaning "bright" or "brilliant." Apollo Belenus was venerated at many curative spring shrines where miniature sun wheels were sometimes cast into the waters to placate the gods who had the power to heal. There were various epithets added to the sun god's name, in fact. Apollo Grannos was an important healing spring deity as well and was widely venerated along with his consort, Sirona.

The strong Roman influence in the Celtic world is one of the problems in identifying true Celtic myths. When Julius Caesar invaded the area, he brought with him many of the Roman gods, among them Apollo and the sky god Jupiter, both of whom were likely worshipped in solar cults. The wheel symbol was taken as evidence that these solar cults existed, and miniature sun wheels were cast into Apollo's hot springs, as well as depicted on stone monuments and altars dedicated to Jupiter. The wheels appeared together with Jupiter's thunderbolt, most likely in acknowledgment of the sky god's power over all celestial activities. Jupiter became the Celts most popular deity. Clearly, he controlled the rain, the sun, and all aspects of storms. He directed the lightning, commanded the floods and the droughts, and was specifically worshipped in connection with the oak. His power over thunder and lightning manifested itself in the forests and trees when they moved and often split open with storm power.

Because the Druids and the later Celts were agriculturists, they naturally revered forces like sun and rain and storm that worked to renew their earth. The Druids lived by a seasonal calendar and learned to interpret the cycles of the celestial bodies that controlled the seasons. They were diviners as well as farmers, and they most likely needed calendars to calculate appropriate times for ritual. The Druids worshipped stones, and they also used stones to build fascinating edifices. Researchers have determined that the gigantic megaliths found throughout the British Isles were aligned to coincide with important seasonal events, such as the rising of the sun at the summer solstice and the rising of certain stars that marked important dates in the calendrical year.

Perhaps the most famous of all ancient archeological ruins, Stonehenge, was believed to have been erected by the Druids. This mysterious configuration of standing stones was probably built over a long period of time, beginning as early as 4000 B.C. Many scholars agree that Stonehenge was an ancient astronomical site. Alignment of the stones to certain sky events attests to the significance the Celts placed on the rising and setting sun, the solstices, and the predawn risings of certain stars that would have helped early farmers establish agricultural cycles. But though the megaliths represented an attempt to understand celestial movements, it is not clear they weren't erected primarily for ceremonial purposes. The early Druids and the later Celts placed their faith in the spiritual forces that empowered the earth, the sky, and the waters. They probably made sanctuaries out of stone just as they did over sources of underground water and in the vast forests that covered their land. (Green 1986, 1992, 1993, MacCana 1985, Stewart 1990)

CHAC(S)

The most frequently mentioned god in the Mayan codices, Chac was the four-part god of lightning, thunder, and rain. Chac was a kind god who served as the patron of agriculture. The four Chacs that composed his persona were often associated with the moist coastal winds of the Yucatan and with the fertilizing rains that they brought from the four corners of the world.

Chac was usually depicted as an old man with a long nose and whiskers like a catfish. In the classic period he looked reptilian, his long nose snoutlike and his body covered with scales. The Chac of the later period appeared more human. Chac often carried weapons—flames and torches and a hafted stone axe or a serpent, Mesoamerican symbols of thunder and lightning. In Mayan iconography, Chac was associated with the muan owl, or screech owl, a bird identified with rain, clouds, and mist.

Each of the four parts of Chac were identified with a cardinal point and color and corresponded to the Bacabs, the supporters of the sky at the four corners of the earth. Chac determined the colors of the cardinal points by sending white maize down from Heaven in one of his thunderbolts. The thunderbolt scorched the maize, turning it the colors sacred to each of the earth's corners, where the four warrior Chacs cried streams of tears and caused the rains. The red Chac Xib Chac brought rain from the east, the white Sac Xib Chac brought rain from the north, the black Ek Xib Chac brought rain from the west, and the yellow Kan Xib Chac brought rain from the south.

To ensure that rain fell on the Mayan lands, the people often offered sacrifices to Chac and impersonated him in rituals. In one ritual, a priest performed the sacrifices, assisted by four old men who impersonated the Chacs and held the sacrifice victim at the four corners, his arms and legs, while the priest sliced open his chest. In another ritual, held in late summer, four young boys were tied to four corners of an altar, where they were made to croak like frogs to summon Chac and bring the rain. The Mayans considered frogs heralds of their rain god because the sound of their croaking generally preceded the rains.

Chac was one of the longest continuously worshipped gods of ancient Mesoamerica, considered by some to be a manifestation of Itzamna, the Mayan moon god. The Maya were agricultural people, and they relied on Chac, as rain bringer, to bring them the maize that formed the basis of their civilization. Worship of Chac was widespread and continues to this day. Pyramids were erected in his honor with Chac masks incorporated into the designs, some of them eight feet wide and six and a half feet tall. (Bunson and Bunson 1996, Markman and Markman 1992)

See also Bacabs, Mesoamerica, Rain and Rain Gods, Tlaloc

CHALCHIHUITLICUE

Chalchihuitlicue was the Aztec goddess of water, particularly of rivers, lakes, and streams. As the wife and female counterpart of the rain god, Tlaloc, she was often held responsible for floods and for raising storms on the seas. But as goddess, her female aspect connected her with the watery nature of the womb, and she played an important role in birth and baptismal ceremonies.

Translated as She of the Jade Skirt or Petticoat, the goddess' name came from the word *Chalchuitl,* which in Nahuatl, meant "jade." Her name was therefore a metaphorical allusion to the blue-green waters of the tropical ocean, which shined like the colors in the precious stone. Perhaps because of its association with water, jade was the most valued rock in Mesoamerica, and because agricultural societies like the Aztecs depended so heavily on water for survival, Chalchihuitlicue was worshipped as a fertility goddess throughout the land.

In iconography, the water goddess appeared to glisten, with turquoise eyebrows and a skirt painted blue-green like seawater and ornamented with water lilies. A green stone necklace dangled from her neck and a blue cap with a spray of quetzal feathers adorned her head. She wore turquoise earplugs and clappers, always a symbol of water deities, and she carried a vase in her right hand with a cross, a symbol of the four corners of the world from whence the rains came.

To illustrate her connection with birth and fertility, Chalchihuitlicue sometimes appeared in the codices with two infants, one male and one female, both floating in a stream that issued from the goddess. She was other times portrayed as a river from which a pear tree grew, laden with fruit. Sometimes the water goddess was symbolized by a frog, a denizen of water and symbol of fertility because its croaking preceded the rains.

Because of her crucial importance to Aztec life, Chalchihuitlicue was honored in ceremonies connected to Tlaloc that often involved sacrifice to guarantee favorable treatment from the rain gods. Chalchihuitlicue was also venerated in her own movable feast, the fourteenth of the Aztec feasts, celebrated by people in occupations connected with water, such as reed gatherers, canoeists, fishermen, and water carriers. (Markman and Markman 1992, Nicholson 1967, Spence 1977)

See also Floods and Flood Gods, Mesoamerica, Tlaloc, Water and Water Spirits

CHAOS

In myths around the globe, creation was preceded by an original state of chaos. Chaos meant darkness and formlessness; it defined a state where nothing existed except a gaping void or abyss and where nothing lived except forms of primordial sea serpents that held the seeds of life within them. The Nordic people called this chaotic void Ginunngagap, the Polynesians called it Po, and the Egyptians called it Nu or Nun. Creator deities had to emerge from the darkness and introduce light and order. Then they had to fight the forces of darkness, who struggled to return the world to its original chaotic state.

The duality of light and dark, order and chaos, is perhaps the most fundamental concept of myth. In the Persian account of creation, Ahura Mazda, the god of light, opposed Angra Mainyu, the god of darkness, and their battles characterized the constant struggle between order and chaos. Nature myths in other lands as well featured this struggle when they pitted sun against storm, rain against drought, and fertility against barrenness. But before any of these dualities could exist, before any of their battles could occur, light had to break up the darkness of the original chaotic state. Only after light entered the picture could the gods establish order. They ordered the sky, they layered the universe, and they divided their powers between three realms.

The gods who ruled the earth, the sea, and the sky were the most powerful gods around. They had the ability to manipulate nature, and they used the forces of nature to maintain order in the world. But in nature myths, these high gods constantly met with demons who could also manipulate nature and who constantly tapped into nature's destructiveness. The gods guaranteed rain and the demons threatened drought. The gods calmed the seas and the demons stirred up tidal waves. These demons personified the natural phenomena most feared by the mythmakers. They uprooted the earth and exploded mountains. They fell from the sky as shooting stars; they chased after the sun and the moon and took big bites out of them. When these demons introduced chaos, the gods had to restore order. They had to slay the drought demon to release the rain, and they had to return the summer sun after the demons froze the earth with their icy grips.

Because sunlight was crucial to survival, one way the gods maintained order was to ensure the proper functioning of the sun. They had to keep it on its path, and they had to make sure it turned northward at the winter solstice and didn't disappear from the world completely. But the monsters and giants who embodied the force of chaos desired to restore the world to darkness; one of their favorite tricks was to fiddle with the sun's power. When the North American trickster deity, Coyote, carried the sun's torch, he let it

fall from his hands and nearly burned up the world. Each time Rahu, the Hindu eclipse monster, swallowed the sun, he nearly plunged the earth into eternal darkness. In the Norse myth of the building of Asgard's wall, one of the giants tried to accomplish something similar. He offered to build a wall to separate his race from the race of the gods, but in return, he demanded the sun, the moon, and Freya, the fertility goddess. He did not succeed, but if he had, the giants would have won their battle. Without sun or moon, they would have returned the world to its original state of chaos, darkness, and cold.

World mythology is full of stories that illustrate the battles between chaos and order. Order was essential, but the constant intrusion of chaos was essential, too, for cyclic renewal. In Norse mythology, the world tree, Yggdrasil, stood at the center of the world and served as the model of an ordered universe. In Iran, the Tree of All Seeds stood as a similar model in the Vourakasha Sea. But at the bottom of both of these trees, something gnawed at the roots. The Nidhogg serpent gnawed continually on Yggdrasil, and a frog gnawed on the Tree of All Seeds. In a universe structured and supported by world trees, the creatures attempting to destroy the trees continually attempted to reintroduce chaos. (Campbell 1974, Krupp 1983)

See also Astronomy, Cosmic Order, Darkness and Light, Duality, Persia, Primordial Sea, Tiamat, Tricksters, Yggdrasil

CHARIOTS

Since the invention of the wheel in early antiquity, sky gods of many lands drove chariots across the heavens. Commonly called Chariots of the Sun, the vehicles represented the passage of the sun as it traveled from east to west. Perhaps the most popular myth of the sun chariot involves Phaethon, the mortal son of Apollo who drove his father's chariot and nearly destroyed the world. Chariots of Apollo and of many other sun gods across the globe flashed through the heavens, wheels aflame, while their spokes of fire shot sparks of light in all directions.

The mythmakers used chariots as symbols for movement, and the use of chariots as sun symbols stemmed from the ancients' need to understand the movement of the sun. In Norse mythology, the gods created the sun, moon, and stars and placed them in the sky, but they somehow had to make these celestial objects move. So they created chariots, one for the moon and one for the sun. Two horses named Aarvak and Alsvid drove the sun's chariot, and it moved continuously as the horses raced around and around the sky, thus explaining noon, dusk, darkness, and dawn.

The chariot as a sun symbol appeared in mythologies throughout the world. The chariot's wheels were circular, like the sun, and the spokes emanated outward, like the sun's rays. But as the wheels turned and the chariot moved, it produced a rumbling noise that resembled thunder. So thunder gods drove chariots as well. The Norse god Thor, the Greek god Zeus, and weather gods from many other lands produced thunderous booms as they rumbled their chariots across the firmament. (Biedermann 1992, Chevalier and Gheerbrant 1996, Gelling 1969, Green 1991)

See also Horses, Phaethon, Sun and Sun Gods, Thunder and Thunder Gods

CHHIH SUNG-TZU
Chhih Sung-tzu was the Master of Rain who lived on a mythical mountain in China called Khun-lun. He was reputed to be magic and to have the ability to float through air and pass though water and fire without getting wet or burned. During a terrible drought in the third millennium B.C., the mythical emperor Shen Nung called upon Chhih Sung-tzu to use his magic to summon the rain. Chhih Sung-tzu did not disappoint him. He ended the drought and was thus given the title of Master, or Lord, of the Rain.

Chhih Sung-tzu proved himself an effective rainmaker by using his magical powers. He asked the emperor to pour water into an earthenware bowl and bring it to him. The emperor did so. The magical Chhih Sung-tzu then took a branch from the mountainside, dipped the branch into the bowl, and sprinkled the earth with rain. Quickly, the drought ended. Clouds covered the sky, rain fell in torrents, and rivers flooded over the land.

In art, Chhih Sung-tzu was often depicted standing on a cloud and wearing yellow scale armor and a yellow and blue headdress. He was sometimes shown pouring rain from a watering can or a pot and other times holding the earthenware bowl that held the water or a plate that held a tiny dragon, the Chinese symbol of rain. In some myths, Chhih Sung-tzu appeared as a silkworm chrysalis accompanied by a black-faced concubine and a bird called a shang yang who could suck in water through its beak and blow it out like rain. The appearance of this bird meant that Chhih Sung-tzu was on his mountain, summoning the rains that would soon fall from the sky. (Christie 1985, Werner 1995)

See also China, Mountains, Rain and Rain Gods

CHINA
The ancient Chinese believed the structure of the heavens paralleled the structure of the earth, a philosophy that trickled down to many aspects of their myths and legends. What distinguishes the nature myths of China from those of other countries, even other Asian countries, is the control of natural phenomena by Celestial Bureaus of Ministries similar to the bureaus of ministries on earth. Many officials in these ministries once held high government positions, and after their deaths, they transferred their power to control of the sun, moon, and stars, as well as the many forces that moved the earth and powered the waters.

Because most Chinese gods were once

A Chinese dragon from an old lantern silhouette.

human, an extremely large number of deities populated the Chinese pantheon. There were gods of the Buddhists, gods of the Confucians, and many, many gods of the Taoists. In a mingling of Taoist and Buddhist traditions, each of the sky gods was said to live in a separate palace in a Heaven composed of levels that mirrored the levels of the Chinese government. The gods with the most power lived at the top, so that the topmost level housed the Jade Emperor and his assistants and the layers below housed the officials of the Ministry of Thunder and Storms and the Ministry of the Waters.

Chinese storm officials compared with the Buddhist Asuras and Hindu storm demons, the Maruts. These deities made the thunder roar and the lightning flash. They blew winds across the land and determined the distribution of clouds and rain. The Chinese did not personify these atmospheric elements, but simply assigned gods to control them. The same held true for the sea and the freshwaters. They were full of spirits but had no spirit of their own.

The most popular figures in Chinese myths were sea spirits, colorful dragons who had tremendous powers over the waters they inhabited. The Chinese dragons governed waters throughout the land, not simply the seas. In fact, the waters housed so many dragons that only sacred numerals could be used to count them. Within the Ministry of Water, five dragon-kings resided in the seas and controlled the Department of Salt Waters, and other dragon spirits guarded the freshwaters and controlled the Department of Sweet Waters.

Unlike the dragons of other lands, the dragons of Chinese lore were beneficent, and their importance in Chinese mythology can not be overestimated. Some believed the dragons to be the fathers of great emperors, and others believed that celestial dragons provided the strength that supported the palaces of the sky gods. Dragons guarded pools and wells and mapped out the courses of rivers and streams. They produced rain and represented the fecundating power of nature. The dragons of China were held in highest esteem because they appeared everywhere and in every realm, sleeping in the waters, guarding treasures beneath the earth, and floating in the sky as strange cloud formations, ready to burst into rain and nourish the land.

Though dragons were worshipped throughout China, perhaps most revered were the celestial deities, the gods of the sun, the moon, and the stars. Numerous star gods populated the Chinese pantheon, among them, the God of Literature, the Goddess of the North Star, the God of Happiness and a star god who presided over each sixty-year cycle. The Chinese considered the sun and the moon to be stars as well. They revered them as such and sun worship was a common practice. But the Chinese had a particular affinity for the moon.

Lunar symbolism dominates Chinese myths and legends, and moon worship continues to this day. The Festival of the Moon in mid–August occurs each year, and at this time people pay homage to the orb of the night by baking mooncakes, which they share with friends and neighbors. The timing of this festival coincides with the harvest moon, the brightest full moon of the year, believed to have the most influence. It was said that Buddha became enlightened under the full moon, and that other Zen masters followed in his footsteps. Perhaps that explains the moon's influence. The moon was connected to spirit and enlightenment and for that reason was the object of worship and sacrifice for centuries.

Worship of the spirits of the earth persists in China as well. The Emperor Shun was said to have offered sacrifices to the hills, and sacrifices were also made to the four corners of the earth, to rain, to Heaven at the winter solstice, and to earth at the summer solstice. In the spring and fall, ancient emperors performed sacrifices to the earth and sky gods to ensure plentiful harvests and fertile soil. The ultimate task of Chinese rulers was to strike a harmonious relationship with nature and the heavenly powers. If an emperor performed this task sufficiently, good things came about. But if the emperor failed, bad things, such as earthquakes and droughts, occurred.

This concept of harmony permeates Chinese thought and has its basis in the dualistic principle of yin and yang, the opposite and complimentary extremes of nature. Yang represents day, sun, fire, light, and heat, whereas yin represents night, moon, water, darkness, and cold. In early Chinese philosophies, yin and yang, along with wood, metal, water, fire, and earth, the five basic elements of nature, explained almost everything in existence. They formed the basis for the myths of natural phenomena, and perpetuated the basic idea of Chinese religion, that human beings come from nature, grow in nature, and will ultimately return to nature. (Christie 1985, Mackenzie 1994, Staal 1984, Werner 1995)

CHURNING THE OCEAN

In Hindu epic literature, the myth of Churning the Ocean explained the struggle between the gods and the demons over Soma, the elixir of immortality and the Water of Life. In a world locked in a continual battle of good and evil, the gods needed Soma to come out ahead. In ancient, or Vedic, India Indra ruled as Supreme Deity, and he began

to lose strength as the demons waged their battles. Indra and the other gods turned to Vishnu for help, and Vishnu told them that they could gain control of the universe if they churned the ocean of milk and obtained the magical Soma.

Churning the Ocean was no small task; to accomplish it, the gods and the demons had to join forces. Using Mount Mandara as a churning pole and the serpent Vasuki as a rope, the gods and demons set to work. As they churned, vapors escaped from Vasuki's mouth, causing lightning-charged clouds that released rain. Fire encased the mountain and destroyed many plants and animals. But eventually, the workers made progress. The moon emerged from the sea of milk, and with him, the sun, many other gods and goddesses, and a golden cup brimming with Soma.

When the elixir appeared in a cup, the demons snatched it up, but Vishnu tricked them by turning into an enchantress and bewitching them with her charms. He then gave the elixir to the gods. As the Water of Life, the milky liquid was said to symbolize semen, the life-giving fluid responsible for fertilization, and thus the continuation and immortality of the world. But the liquid was also identified with the moon, as Chandra, the moon god, emerged from the sea of milk and henceforth controlled fertility and regulated the earthly waters. In time, Chandra became fused with the god Soma, a deification of the immortal moon and a symbol of fertility and the life-giving power of the waters. (Ions 1984, Willis 1993)

See also India, Moon and Moon Gods, Sea Foam, Soma, Storms and Tempests

CIRCUMPOLAR STARS

In the northern hemisphere six constellations are called circumpolar because they never rise or set, but revolve constantly around the North Star. These six constellations are Cepheus, Cassiopeia, Ursa Minor, Ursa Major, Draco, and Camelopardalis. Fourteen constellations lie equally close to the South Star and are thus considered circumpolar from the southern hemisphere. The Greeks told myths of these constellations to explain their circumpolar movement.

Most people know Ursa Major, or the Big Bear, as the Big Dipper. This familiar ladle lights up the night skies almost all over the world, and is actually just a part of the Big Bear. The star group dates back five or so millennia to ancient Mesopotamia but has been known throughout history to people across the globe, almost always as a bear. That most ancient cultures likened the constellation to a bear is rather remarkable because the arrangement of stars doesn't resemble a bear at all. But one classical myth explains the translation of a big bear to the heavens, and it explains why this big bear, or Ursa Major, never sets. In the *Metamorphoses*, Ovid told the story of Jupiter's love for a nymph named Callisto with whom he had secret trysts behind Juno's back. Juno learned of their affair, and turned Callisto into a bear, sentencing her to live out her life wandering alone in the forest. When Jupiter finally found Callisto, he discovered that she had a son, the young bear cub that became known as the Little Bear, or Ursa Minor. Jupiter swept Callisto and her cub up to the sky in a whirlwind to live among the stars, as retribution for their suffering. But Juno became enraged that her husband placed his mistress and her son in the heavens, and a deal was struck to appease her. It was agreed that Ursa Major would never enter the realm the other constellations do when they set but stay well above it, revolving constantly around the North Star.

Cassiopeia lies opposite the Big Dipper. In classical myths, she was the vain queen of Ethiopia who bragged that her daughter, Andromeda, was lovelier than the Nereids. One myth explains that the Nereids took revenge on Cassiopeia and tied her to a chair then placed her high in the sky. There she remains, chained and stationary, never rising, and never setting.

The Roman myth of Draco the dragon also explained the notion of circumpolar movement. This story began with the battle between the Titans and the Olympians, with the dragon fighting as one of the monsters among the Titans. The dragon battled with Minerva, but Minerva overpowered him by grabbing his tail and hurling him into the heavens, close to the North Pole. The dragon spun around and got tangled up in knots. Before he had time to untangle himself, he froze, and there he remains. Although today Polaris serves as the pole star, in the ancient world, it was alpha Draconis, a star in the dragon's tail. The myth of the frozen dragon explained why the star remained fixed. (Allen 1963, Krupp 1991a, Olcott 1911, Ridpath 1988)

See also Andromeda, Horus, North Star, Shang di, Stars and Star Gods

CLOCKS AND CALENDARS

The ancients built calendars based on the rhythms they saw in nature. They patterned their lives after the behavior of the sky gods, and they incorporated those patterns into their ceremonies and festivals, their myths and rituals. The creation of calendars meant that the ancients relied on natural phenomena to set the stage for an ordered world. The first calendars were more than practical tools to time the availability of food, they were spiritual tools and sacred methods ancient people employed to relate to the sky.

Early calendrics was based on the knowledge of the sky as a model of order and rhythm. The moon and the sun made convenient clocks and calendars because they exhibited the most obvious rhythms. Calendars based on the moon came first, possibly as early as the Ice Age. Scientists studying animal bones and antlers from the Ice Age found peculiar markings on the bones, and they saw patterns in the markings that appeared to represent a calendric system based on lunar phases. The markings, called notations, appeared as a series of notches made with different instruments, which indicated they were made over time. In some of the Ice Age specimens, serpentine figures wound along a horizontal edge and appeared to represent two months of moons, with numbers signifying the different phases in the cycle of waxing and waning. Later calendars in Greece, Rome, Scandinavia, Siberia, England, and pre-Columbian America also showed markings juxtaposed with symbols, which indicated significant rites, myths, and seasonal changes.

The waxing and waning moon offered the simplest of rhythms, but the sun had a rhythm of its own. As soon as people learned to compare the rhythms of these two celestials, solar calendars emerged. But people had yet to learn that the earth revolved around the sun, and that that movement made the seasons change. So calendar makers had difficulty with accurate timekeeping for centuries. The ancient Egyptians developed an accurate solar calendar as early as 4200 B.C., which was adopted by other cultures and used as an astronomical reference throughout the Middle Ages. The Egyptians had figured out a way to correct the discrepancies between the number of lunar months and the days in a solar year—at least temporarily. This problem was not truly solved until 1582 when the Gregorian calendar in use today was developed. The Egyptian calendar, though quite accurate for a time, eventually drifted out of synch with the seasons. But these early calendar keepers clearly tackled the problem. In myth, Thoth, the moon god, controlled the calendar, and he won a game of draughts against the moon and received as his prize five extra days of the moon's light. He added them to the calendar at the end of the year.

Aside from the sun and moon, other celestial bodies exhibited traceable rhythms, and the ancients learned to use them, too, as timekeepers. The Egyptians based their calendar not only on the sun but also on the motions of Sirius, the star that appeared brightest in the night sky. Stars like Sirius appeared close to the ecliptic, the sun's path across the sky, so they made perfect calendar stars because each spot along this path divided the year in some way. Because of its brightness, Sirius was easy to track. Sirius appeared in the eastern sky just before sunrise after a period of invisibility, and the Nile river rose just after that. So the Egyptians combined the motions of the sun, of Sirius, and of the Nile to make their calendar. They came up with a year of 365 days.

The fact that the ancient Egyptians had no knowledge of the earth's rotation yet developed a calendar based on celestial movements meant they were shrewd observers. The fact that they connected calendar making with mythmaking meant that they respected the celestial gods for their role in maintaining cosmic order. People in other cultures made calendars using the celestial bodies as well, and scholars learned much about early calendrics by studying artifacts from these civilizations. They found that many puzzling structures appeared to have alignments to celestial events. The medicine wheels of the Plains Indians, the pyramids of the Maya, and Stonehenge and other stone circles throughout the British Isles indicated that early people used the sky for a clock. Peoples in Latin America used the Pleiades because, in the Tropics, it appeared close to the ecliptic. The Maya, for instance, used the Pleiades to track the seasons.

Skywatchers among the Maya used their celestial observations to make calendars as early as the sixth century B.C., and the planetary and eclipse calendars they developed were unknown in other cultures of the new world. The Maya learned that eclipses occurred in regular patterns, and they recorded those patterns in hieroglyphics, in the Dresden Codex, which remains the best source of information on Mayan astronomy. The elaborate tables in the codex indicated that the Maya had advanced concepts of time and of the movement of planets. They also illustrated the close connection between science and myth. Their skywatchers took care to record detailed observations not only of eclipses but also of lunar phases and of the movements of Venus, the great sky god they personified as Kukulcan, the feathered serpent.

Among the Maya and in other groups throughout the world, calendrics played an essential role in mythology as well as in daily life. The early Mesoamericans named their gods and their world epochs in the calendrical cycle, as evidenced in one of the most definitive examples of connecting myth with calendrics, the Aztec Calendar Stone. The occupation of calendar making dominated the minds of the ancients. They needed their sky calendars to survive, but they also needed them to get in touch with the spirits. Because early people felt at the mercy of natural forces, they had a prevailing urge to create order. They found that order in the natural rhythms of the sky. (Aveni 1989, Hadingham 1984, Krupp 1983, O'Neill 1975, Williamson 1992)

> *See also* Astronomy, Aztec Calendar Stone, Cosmic Order, Mama Kilya, Medicine Wheels, Mesoamerica, Solstices, Thoth

CLOUD PEOPLE

The Pueblo of the Southwest worship a class of supernatural beings called Cloud People, who live in the Underworld and bring rain and moisture to earth. These Cloud People are actually spirits of the dead who lived as good people on earth and then embodied clouds in the afterlife, some say by forming them with their breath. The Pueblo are agricultural people, so they place primary emphasis on the sun as the source of light and heat and on clouds as the source of moisture. The belief in Cloud People reflects the connection the Pueblo draw between death and clouds. They associate the Kachinas, another class of mythical ancestors, with death as

well, and they call upon both the Kachinas and the Cloud People to bring rain. The Pueblo believe that if they pay proper respect to the dead, the spirits will return the kindness and bring the rain and moisture necessary for life to the people on earth. (Green 1996, Parsons 1996)

> *See also* Clouds, Kachinas, North America, Rain and Rain Gods

CLOUDS

Like nature itself, clouds can be soft and gentle or fierce and menacing. They change size, shape, and color and form a myriad of patterns as they shift and move across the sky. In nature, clouds serve as protectors against the sun's heat and indicators of upcoming weather changes. In myth they take on a supernatural quality. They materialize in odd shapes, like celestial gods, and they help predict nature's moods.

In ancient times, people in many areas of the world watched the clouds meticulously. Polynesian navigators paid particular attention to the peculiarities of individual cloud formations and assigned special significance to the colors the clouds turned at sunset. The Maori used the clouds to predict birth and death, the comings and goings of great chiefs, and imminent attacks from rival tribes. They worshipped Ao, the God of the Clouds and the first ancestor of the Maoris, connected with light and enlightenment. As was true of many of the Polynesian deities, epithets to Ao's name distinguished various aspects of his character. The many Aos were the children of Tawhiri-matea, the storm god. There was the god of dense clouds, of dark clouds, of fiery clouds, of massy clouds, of gloomy thick clouds, of wildly blowing clouds, of clouds of thunderstorms, of clouds preceding hurricanes, and of clouds reflecting glowing red light.

Though the Polynesians associated clouds with light, they also, quite logically, associated them with rain and storm. Equipping cloud deities with powers to regulate the weather was common practice in the ancient world. The cloud deities likely to possess these powers were animals, often those whose color or appearance resembled the floating puffs of vapor. Clouds have been likened to celestial cattle, sheep, horses, and mules, particularly those clouds reflected in the waves of the sea, which the ancient Romans called the herds of Neptune. Because the Chinese thought dragons brought rain, they also thought dragons materialized as clouds, particularly those clouds that assumed odd shapes or floated through the sky trailing serpentine tails. Many early mythmakers equated birds with clouds: the fluffy white cirrus clouds in ancient India were swans, and the threatening black clouds in Scandinavia were ravens. If early people perceived the clouds as birds, they sometimes perceived the lightning that flashed from the clouds as worms or serpents wriggling in the bird's beaks. Their wriggling movements made the lightning flash and their hissing made the sound of thunder.

The ancient Hindus thought elephants brought rain, their bodies representative of clouds and their trunks the vertical paths the rain took from the sky to the earth. The Hindus believed clouds were the celestial relatives of the white elephants that roamed the earth. But all elephants, they said, could at one time fly and change shapes like clouds. One day, the flying elephants landed in a tree and the tree's heavy branches fell on some students underneath who were studying with a yogi. The yogi condemned all elephants to walk the earth, and from then on they could no longer fly or change shape like clouds.

The ancients had other symbols for the clouds that covered their heavens, tied to explanations of how the clouds formed. In Polynesian myth, the clouds formed when Hina, the moon goddess, stretched her white tapa-cloth across the heavens. In Greek myth, the clouds, represented as the Symplegades Mountains, parted for the flying ship Argo when Orpheus played his harp. Rocks and mountains frequently symbolized clouds, and so did ships. The ancient Aryans connected their use of ships as cloud symbols to the notion of a cosmic sea and the belief that the clouds floated over the cosmic sea like sailing vessels. Skidbladnir, the magic ship of the Norse god Frey, symbolized the clouds, and the notion of cloud vessels persisted into the Middle Ages. But other myths offered more precise explanations on the formation of clouds. The Navajo said a great white swan conjured them up when he flapped his wings. The Polynesians said Maui, the trickster, pushed up the sky with a poker and the dark marks he made now remain as rain-bearing clouds. The people of Papua New Guinea told the story of Dudugera, who became the scorching sun and who was gradually destroying the plant and animal life and all of humanity. Dudugera's mother threw lime in his face and formed the clouds. From then on the clouds protected the earth from Dudugera's intense heat. (Bassett 1971, Cox 1887, Dennis 1992, Fiske 1996)

See also Cloud People, Cosmic Sea, Frigg, Hina, Rain and Rain Gods, Sheep and Cattle, Ships, Skidbladnir, Swan Maidens, Thunderbirds

COATLICUE

Coatlicue was an earth goddess of the ancient Aztecs and an embodiment of Mother Earth. Like most earth goddesses, she symbolized the contradictory notions of birth and death, womb and tomb. All life came forth from Coatlicue and all life returned to her, and her earth, in the end. Coatlicue was a fertility goddess. She ensured seasonal renewal and guaranteed a staple harvest with her powers over the earth and the soil. Perhaps most famously, she mothered the sun, Huitzilopochtli, the moon, Coyolxauhqui, and four hundred warrior sons said to be the stars of the Milky Way.

A popular myth of Coatlicue involved her conception, without intercourse, of Huitzilopochtli, the sun god, and the subsequent slaying of darkness by daylight. Coatlicue was praying one day in a field when a ball of feathers, brilliant like the sun, fell to her from the sky. Miraculously, the feathers impregnated her. But her daughter Coyolxauhqui and her four hundred sons, a tribe of Indians called Centzon Huitznahua or the Four Hundred Southerners, were enraged by their mother's conception and planned to kill her. Huitzilopochtli came to his mother's defense. He emerged from her womb fully armed and wielding a flaming fire-serpent. With lightning from his serpentine spear, he shattered his brothers, the stars, and sliced up Coyolxauhqui's body as, metaphorically, the sun slices up the moon when it wanes. Huitzilopochtli then cut off Coyolxauhqui's head and tossed it into the heavens, where it became the glowing orb of the night sky.

The slaying of Coyolxauhqui and the Four Hundred Southerners not only represented the defeat of the moon and stars by the sunrise, but also guaranteed the rebirth of the sun and the continuation of the cycle of life. Coatlicue herself, as Great Mother, was an agent of death and rebirth, and in that capacity, she represented the entirety of the earth, the sky, and the cosmic process. Depictions of Coatlicue are fearsome and savage, adorning her with sharp claws, a skirt of snakes, and a necklace made from hearts and hands of the sacrifice victims required to satisfy her lust for blood and flesh. But as Mother Goddess, Coatlicue represented love as well as destruction.

Perhaps the best example of the earth goddess's influence was a sculpture unearthed beneath Mexico City (once the ancient Aztec city of Tenochtitlan) and now exhibited at the National Anthropology Museum of Mexico City. This massive stone sculpture from the fifteenth century appears to describe the entire cosmic process in one complex representation of Coatlicue. Like the deity herself, the statue is believed to express the complexity of existence. It has been interpreted to symbolize all that encompasses the earth and the sky and all the forces and rituals inherent in maintaining the life cycle. (Markman and Markman 1992, Nicholson 1967, Spence 1977)

See also Earth and Earth Gods, Huitzilopochtli, Mesoamerica

COMETS

A strange star lighting up the heavens, an intruder in familiar skies—to ancient people, the appearance of a comet meant trouble. Ancient skywatchers knew the stars that lit their world. They relied on their regular appearance. The stars in the night sky offered regularity and provided a sense of comfort. But when a comet appeared out of nowhere and with no warning, the frightened people imagined chaos descending on their world. Flaming, bright, and infrequent, a comet broke all the rules.

For centuries people dreaded comets as chaotic intruders; no one understood them for a long time. Until the 1500s, comets were thought to be atmospheric rather than celestial phenomena, and into the 1600s they were still considered bad omens. This kind of thinking led to many misconceptions and delayed the scientific study of comets. Hippocrates believed a comet acquired its tail by drawing moisture from the earth. Pliny and Aristotle both said comets caused winds. But most early people simply considered these mysterious strangers signs, to some signs of war and pestilence, to others signs of imbalance in the upper world, and to many others signs of divine wrath, fiery and violent, like the thunderbolts of angry gods.

Many people in antiquity connected the passage of a comet to the death of kings or powerful rulers. When a comet appeared over Rome in 44 B.C., many of the Romans believed it to be the soul of Julius Caesar, ascending to heaven. The emperor Augustus, Caesar's adopted son, apparently believed this too, and he dedicated a temple to the comet and used a comet emblem on coins to honor the dead ruler who had passed on to his son the power of the land. A similar legend appeared in Peru. Two comets that appeared over the sacred Mount Aausangate reputedly shot forth from the mountain to announce the death of the father of Pachacuti, the founder of the Incan Empire. Linking comets to government rulers was common practice, but not always were they linked to death. Ancient Mayan skywatchers may have linked them to birth. Scholars believe the Maya timed the intervals between appearances of Halley's comet and used their calculations to predict the birth of their gods and leaders. In China and Babylon, the government was blamed for a comet's appearance. Only an unstable ruler could allow such chaos to occur. (Krupp 1977, 1991a, Yeomans 1991)

See also Astronomy, Chaos, Eclipses, Meteors and Meteorites

CONSTELLATIONS

When the ancients looked up into their dark night sky they saw more stars than skywatchers today can imagine. There are about 400 billion stars in the Milky Way alone and possibly 100 billion billion in the entire visible sky. But the ancients had no conception of how many stars there were, nor were they aware that those points of light had no connection to one another. Many scholars have maintained that Egypt was the first to give shapes and names to the star groups, and many other scholars have said India was the first. But people of almost every culture felt the need to organize the stars into some kind of arrangement. From this need, the constellations were born.

The constellations have been referred to as "a picture book" in the days before writing. The pictures the ancients drew in the heavens told the stories of their myths—myths in which the stars and the patterns they formed represented some divine cosmic order. Early people learned that they could use the order of the heavens to make sense of their lives. So they paid close attention to interpreting the stories written in the heavens and to creating a celestial picture book that made the night sky a familiar place.

When the early Mesopotamians organized their sky patterns, they charted the heavens using thirty-six stars that rose reliably at certain times of year in the predawn sky. These stars represented the paths of their primary gods, Enlil, Anu, and Ea. But the stars were more than lights along celestial roads. They fit into a larger scheme of patterns that served as calendar markers, and those patterns formed the basis for calendars around the world. But the ancients used the rising of stars and constellations for many purposes, not just for calendar making. Sailors used the lights in their sky as navigational aids, and these sailors gave names to many of the southern constellations. Most of the constellations in the northern sky grew from a list of forty-eight constellations published by Ptolemy in his *Almagest* in A.D. 150. These constellations were popularized in Greek myths, and the patterns were then accepted and adopted by the Persians, the Hindus, the Arabs, the Romans, the peoples of western Asia, and then the people of the New World.

Constellation myths were plentiful in early cultures and a preoccupation with stars and their patterns was pervasive, particularly in North America. The Pawnee of the Central Plains made detailed star charts of their constellations, believing that those charts were transmitted by star gods to impose divine order on earth. Many North American tribes had an extensive collection of constellation myths, stories in which people projected on the sky images of things that dominated their world on earth. Most of the constellations recognized by North American peoples were animals, animals believed to be ancient, deified after death, then transferred to the sky.

In today's world, every star in the night sky lies within the limits of one of the constellations. But long ago, this was not the case. The Navajo had a myth to explain why some of the stars appeared outside the constellations and why those stars had no names. The primary deity of the Navajo, Black God, or Fire God, planned to create one constellation to represent each animal on earth, and he began the task by carefully and methodically placing crystals in the sky in patterns, moving from east to west. But Coyote, the trickster, intervened. He got into Black God's crystals and threw some randomly into the heavens, creating many unnamed stars lying outside the constellations Black God planned.

The Navajo had an extensive constellation mythology and believed that each constellation represented a law for them to follow. The stars were powerful and harsh deities, and they set important rules. The Navajo believed that when they stopped obeying the rules written in the stars, their tribes would come to an end. Perceiving the constellations as agents of cosmic order was common thinking among ancient groups. Arranging the stars in patterns was their attempt to understand that cosmic order and to interpret the powers of the heavens. (Allen 1963, Gallant 1979, McDonald 1996, Olcott 1911, Ridpath 1988, Staal 1988)

See also Astronomy, Stars and Star Gods, Zodiac

COSMIC ORDER

The ancients told myths to reflect meaningful universal issues, and one of the most meaningful universal issues was the order of the cosmos. Stories that told how the gods ordered the cosmos were creation myths, but stories that told how the gods maintained that order could more accurately be labeled nature myths. The ancients witnessed order in the earth, the sea, and the sky. They saw the most obvious order in the sky, so usually, the mythmakers entrusted the gods who ruled the sky with defending the order. In the myths, the sky gods ensured that the seasons kept turning and the world kept renewing itself in each of the three realms.

Early mythmakers in tune with the movements of nature decided that certain natural phenomena served as models for order. The sky as a whole served as a model, and so did the tree and the mountain, which appeared to reach into the sky, to traverse the entire universe, and to delve deep into the earth. Because the tree and the mountain extended from the Underworld to the sky, mythmakers used these landforms to mark the center of the universe, to symbolize the world axis or the north celestial pole around which the sky objects appeared to spin. Certain objects in the sky moved around the world axis in recognizable patterns. The Pleiades star group appeared in nature myths all over the world because its seasonable rise and set made it a reliable weather predictor. Venus and Mars alternated between Morning Star and Evening Star. Four bright stars glistening in different parts of the sky appeared to mark the cardinal points. The North Star never moved, and in most areas of the world, the circumpolar stars circled around it and never set below the horizon. The sun and the moon, of course, exhibited the most obvious patterns of all.

To recognize the patterns in the heavens, the ancients had to take skywatching seriously. It was easy to see that the sun rose and set, but to find patterns in the stars and planets, people had to watch and track the movement of these celestials over long periods of time. The ancient Maya tracked the movements of Venus, for instance, and they compiled detailed tables that wove together their astronomical observations with their recognition of the gods. The Maya may have considered Venus, who they identified as the feathered serpent, Kukulcan, a kind of defender of world order. He moved through the sky with unwavering regularity, so he ensured stability in the cosmos.

Because many ancient peoples believed the sky served as a model of order, they tried to replicate celestial patterns in their everyday lives. Some people planned homes to imitate the structure of the cosmos. The Pawnee of the Central Plains patterned their homes after the arrangement of the stars; their earth lodges looked like miniature replicas of the heavens. They had an eastern door as a shrine for Morning Star, which they identified as Mars. The sun entered this door and illuminated a western alter, for Evening Star, or Venus. A circular floor represented the earth, a domed roof represented the heavens, and a central fire in the earth lodge represented the sun. According to Pawnee thought, four stars they called the world quarter stars held the sky away from the earth. The Pawnee represented them with four posts, which they used to hold up the roofs of their earth lodges, each aligned to a semicardinal position.

The Pawnee fashioned not only their individual lodges after the heavenly arrangement, but also each village and the placement of the villages composing the entire Skidi band. Other tribes did something similar. The Algonquin tribes patterned their shaman's conjuring lodge after the Pleiades, with seven poles to represent the seven stars. The early Mexicans constructed the entire city of Teotihuacan to mirror the cosmos, aligning avenues, streets, temples, and even individual dwellings to significant celestial objects. The Navajo also built their hogans to reflect the sky order. The central fire in the hogan represented Polaris, or the Pole Star, and the married couple who circled the fire represented Ursa Major and Cassiopeia. The married couple never left the fire, just as these star groups never left Polaris. Ursa Major and Cassiopeia are circumpolar star groups. They continually circle the Pole Star, and thus in most areas of the world never set below the horizon.

These attempts to maintain cosmic order demonstrate that the ancients considered that order crucial. The fact that they told disturbing myths of cosmic disruption meant that they feared any natural forces they believed threatened the order they strove to understand. The ancients knew that the sun rose and set, they knew that the tide ebbed and flowed, and they knew that the moon disappeared, then filled up again like magic. But when a comet flashed across the sky or a fiery meteor fell from it, that frightened them. When during an eclipse the moon looked like something had taken a bite out of it, that frightened them too. To the ancients, these events proved the existence of demons, and in the myths the people told of these events, the demons were bent on reintroducing chaos into an ordered world.

Another way the ancients conveyed their fear of cosmic disruption was by creating myths of false suns. Early people knew that in an ordered universe only one sun could rule the heavens. In a tale from the Arctic lands, there were originally two moons and two suns, and a titmouse had to kill the extra sun and the extra moon to make things right with the world. In a tale from China, nine false suns appeared in the sky when nine birds blew fire out of their mouths and threatened to singe the land. But Shen I, the divine archer, saved the land. He shot arrows at the suns, which turned into red clouds and then melted away.

False suns and other symbols of chaos continually cropped up in world myths, because chaos was essential to order. The two were interdependent, like light and dark, night and day, yin and yang. Duality defined the structure of the world. A common notion in world myths was that the universe consisted of layers, and in each layer, gods controlled the natural forces and worked to balance the world.

Often times, people believed they had to sacrifice to these gods to maintain the balance. They did this under the premise that from death comes rebirth. Without death, there could be no renewal, just as without chaos, there could be no order. (Campbell 1974, Griffin-Pierce 1992, Krupp 1991a)

> *See also* Astronomy, Cardinal Points or Directions, Chaos, Clocks and Calendars, Duality, Sacrifice, Sky and Sky Gods, World Axis

COSMIC SEA

The belief in a heavenly ocean existed in many lands. Perhaps this belief stemmed from the notion of a primordial sea, though more likely it simply explained what the ancients appeared to witness in their environment. They saw the coastline and the horizon as boundaries between the finite and the infinite. Beyond the coastline lay boundless waters, and beyond the horizon lay something similar and equally boundless, the great expanse of sky.

The belief in waters of the firmament became a common notion as the ancients searched for links between what they witnessed on the earth and what they imagined in the heavens. There appeared to be an exchange of water between the two realms, a liquid that flowed on the earth in rivers and ocean currents and a liquid that fell from the sky as rain. Because the ancients thought that the order of the earth paralleled that of the cosmos, it was natural for them to find celestial counterparts to what they saw on earth. They saw fluid in earthly waters and fluid in the air, so they conceptualized the waters of the firmament.

Many cultures subscribed to the notion of these waters and visualized a cosmic sea. The early Aryans equated the sea with the sky and so did some tribes of the Pacific islands who believed their ancestors came from heaven in a boat. In the myths of many lands, gods and heroes embarked on metaphorical sea voyages that took place in the celestial sphere. They had to cross the horizon and transcend the finite. They had to locate that realm of boundlessness that they perceived as Heaven, when the only boundlessness they ever witnessed was the sea. (Bassett 1971, Zimmer 1962)

> *See also* Primordial Sea, Sea and Sea Gods, Ships, Swan Maidens

COWS AND BULLS

The cow and the bull were common images in world myths, and they often served as symbols of gods of the sky and the earth. The cow typically represented the earth mother, nurturing the world with her milk, and the bull typically represented the sky or weather god, fertilizing the earth with his potent strength and his seed.

The notion of the bull as sky god stemmed from the bull's connection with the roaring thunder and the fertilizing powers of the storm. The bull symbolized power and masculine virility, and his bellowing represented the roaring thunder or the winds of a hurricane. Sky gods in Persia, India, Africa, Egypt, and other lands were often likened to bulls, and as bulls, they inseminated their cow goddesses and brought the earth to fruition. These cow goddesses wove together the notions of fluid and life, as was evidenced in the earth and the moon. The Egyptian Hathor and other popular cow goddesses had lunar attributes and their horns represented the horns of the crescent moon. Together with their bull mates, they represented duality in the universe—the nurturing earth goddess, passive and lunar, and the active, virile, fecundating power of the sky. (Biedermann 1992, Eliade 1958)

> *See also* Adad, Anu, Hathor, Mithra, Sky and Sky Gods, Thunder and Thunder Gods

CREATION MYTHS

Creation myths are cosmogonies, stories that explain how the world came into being. The word *cosmogony* has its roots in the Greek word *kosmos,* which meant "order"—so creation myths attempt to explain the order of the universe. Cosmogonies generally include the creation of the world and the creation of mankind, and they often include the order in which all forms of life and matter in the earth, sea, and sky developed. Early cultures lacked the knowledge to explain the order of the universe scientifically, so they explained it symbolically. They exploded the bodies of primordial dragons to form the sea, they pulled mud out of the waters to form the earth, and they pushed celestial gods and goddesses away from their earthly spouses to form the sky.

In many cosmogonies, the world began with the primordial sea, a large expanse of undifferentiated water, often embodied by a serpent or dragon. This water was unformed, dark and still, both a model for the chaos that existed before life formed and a metaphor for the waters of the womb. In Inuit and Norse mythology, the primordial sea was a frozen ocean. It was Absu to the Mesopotamians and Nun or Nu to the Egyptians, a great abyss, and within it, tremendous energy. Often times, that energy was contained in a cosmic egg floating on the primeval waters. Creator deities tapped into the powers hidden in the great abyss. They hatched the cosmic egg. Then from those powers within the egg and the waters they created the earth and sky.

The exact way the earth formed reflected the peculiarities of each society's landscape. In Iceland it formed from the mingling of ice and fire. In one Oceanic myth, it formed from part of a clamshell. In cultures where the sea came first, the earth was commonly made from the mud of the waters. In some myths, a creator deity called an earth diver plunged into the waters, symbolically washing away the old so that new creation could begin. He then retrieved mud from the sea floor and used it to form the land. In other myths, creator deities remained outside the waters and fished up land from underneath.

The physical features of the earth were sometimes believed to form from the broken parts of some androgynous being like the Babylonian chaos dragon, Tiamat, or the Norse Frost Giant, Ymir. Sometimes certain landforms developed from his bodily secretions or the secretions of an earth god like Geb, the Egyptian earth god, who cried tears that filled the rivers and seas. Many people subscribed to the notion of a female earth, a mother goddess and the embodiment of the creative principle. The notion of the earth as a Mother Goddess was so widespread that in many traditions, human beings formed from the earth. They were molded from mud or clay or formed from rock or stone. This female earth embodied all the physical features of the landscape, with the caves and hollows her womb. In those recesses of her earthly body was water, filled with creative energy. And from those recesses, too, the winds emerged and breathed life into the universe.

The earth as Mother Goddess, however, needed a mate to help her produce, a great sky god who could fertilize her with his rains and make her vegetation grow. Complementary opposition defined the cosmos in world myths, and the most basic opposition was that of earth and sky. In most creation myths, the world began when light entered the picture, when the sky god separated from the earth goddess. Only then did the opposition of earth and sky exist. Before light, there was oneness, earth and sky together as two primordial lovers locked in an embrace. Light separated them, and suddenly there was sky above and earth below. When the earth goddess looked up, she saw the canopy of heaven spread above her, lit by the moon and the sun and shimmering with stars.

In myths around the world, creation and world order came about in one of five ways: from the separation of earth and sky, from a cosmic egg or earth mound, from the process of earth diving, from emergence from other worlds, or from an original state of chaos.

There were similar themes, yet each culture embellished those themes with its own myths and symbols. Almost all creation myths explained the origin of the earth, sea, and sky, and almost all those myths drew connections between them. Each of the three realms existed only in relation to the others. Creation myths from the most ancient times told us that human beings perceived of, and needed to perceive of, a unified cosmos. (Bierlin 1994, Freund 1965, Leeming 1994, Van Over 1980)

See also Darkness and Light, Duality, Earth and Earth Gods, Primordial Sea, Sky and Sky Gods

CROCODILE

The crocodile appeared as a solar symbol in many countries because it rose from the darkness like the sun each morning and sank below the darkness like the sun each night. A common belief in the ancient world was that when the sun set, it sank into a watery realm, that great sea that was supposed to exist under the earth. So the behavior of the crocodile mimicked that of the sun. It retreated into the water at night and walked the land during the day.

The ancient Egyptians not only incorporated the crocodile into their solar symbolism but also went so far as to create a crocodile cult. They believed the crocodile to be an incarnation of the god Sebek, the great crocodile god of lakes and rivers, and in some areas the people kept real crocodiles and adorned them with bracelets and shimmering jewels and fed them delicacies by hand, in reverence to the god. Sebek wore a solar disk on his head, and in his beneficent aspect was associated with Ra, the primary solar deity. But he had a dark aspect as well. His greed was like the night that devoured the sun each evening. The crocodile itself represented the conflicting notion of light and dark, its eyes a symbol of the dawn and its tail a symbol of the darkness. (Budge 1969, Mercatante 1974)

See also Sun and Sun Gods

CUYCHA

To the Inca, Cuycha was the deified rainbow, a name derived from the term in Quechua, the Inca language, for rainbow, halo, and other forms of glowing phenomena. This rainbow god was revered along with the other principal deities in the Coricancha compound, the magnificent Inca Sun Temple, and Cuycha rated a temple of his own within the compound, one with a golden arc painted with the seven colors of the rainbow. The Inca considered Cuycha an important deity because rainbows appeared often in the Peruvian sky during the long rainy season.

Because of the prominence of rainbows, the Inca developed many beliefs about the colorful god who arched across the heavens. They determined the sex of each glow by noting its predominant color, for instance. Blue rainbows were male and red were female. Rainbows, in Incan belief, were serpents with two heads who rose out of springs, arched into the sky, and buried themselves either in another spring or somewhere within the earth. Rainbows moved—that much could be witnessed—and because the ancients deified rainbows, they believed that they moved willfully and often for malevolent reasons. They could steal from men or enter women and cause stomach pains. If a rainbow did enter a person and that person got sick, however, there was a cure. The Inca believed the sick person would get well if he unraveled a ball of yarn made of the seven colors of Cuycha, the rainbow. (Urton 1981)

See also Rainbows and Rainbow Gods, South America

CYCLOPES

The original Cyclopes were Greek storm demons, one of the first races of giants born from the union of Gaia (earth) and Ouranos (sky). Hesiod named three of them: Brontes,

The Cyclops Polyphemus of Homer's Odyssey *was a descendant of the original Cyclopes, who were Greek storm demons. To the ancient Greeks, the single eye represented the fiery sun, which in turn attests to the Cyclopes' nature.*

CYCLOPES

who personified thunder; Steropes, who personified lightning; and Arges, who personified the thunderbolt or sheet lightning. This first race of Cyclopes (as well as their descendants that appeared in later Greek myths, such as Polyphemus of the *Odyssey*) had one blazing eye in the middle of their foreheads, said to represent the fiery sun. Upon their birth, Ouranos considered them so hideous that he threw them from his starry heaven into Tartarus, the lower region of the Underworld, just as the sky hurled thunder and lightning down to earth.

The Cyclopes lived in Tartarus for a long time. After the castration of Ouranos, the Titans released them, but later, Kronos, Ouranos's supplanter, banished them there once more. When Zeus supplanted Kronus, the new sky god had to fight the Titans before he and the other Olympian gods could gain control of the world. He released the Cyclopes from Tartarus again, on the condition that they work for him forging thunderbolts. The Cyclopes are perhaps best known for their role as master smiths and the spirits of volcanoes, working for Hephaestus, the fire god, under Mount Aetna and forging thunderbolts for Zeus. (Graves 1988, Guerber 1992)

See also Aetna, Greece and Rome, Hephaestus, Storms and Tempests

DARK CLOUD CONSTELLATIONS

When the people of the Peruvian highlands look into the night sky, they see clusters of dark shadows in the southern portion of the Milky Way that scholars have labeled dark cloud constellations. These dense star clusters appear as silhouettes against the brighter band of light, and people throughout the southern hemisphere recognized them. The Quechua of Peru saw animals in these dark cloud formations, and they wove many fanciful myths about these animals rising to the sky and dwelling in the clouds. These animal myths left vital clues to ancient beliefs about the cosmos.

Early Quechua tribes believed the dark cloud constellations played an active part in the circulation of water. They saw the Milky Way as a celestial river and the route by which water was transported from the cosmic sea, to the sky, and then to the earth. When the Milky Way set below the horizon, the Quechua envisioned the cloud animals dipping into the cosmic sea and drinking water before passing to the Underworld. When the Milky Way rose above the horizon, they envisioned the animals transporting the water into the atmosphere and releasing it as rain.

Myths of the dark cloud animals were simply explanations for what the people witnessed in their world. The cloud animals appeared to contribute to the water cycle because they stayed below the horizon during the dry summer months and rose above it during the rainy season. The Quechua called these star clusters Yana Phuyu or Pachatira and described them as representations of the animals and birds that populated their world.

Ancient South American sky-watchers built intricate relationships between earthly events and each one of the dark cloud constellations. Celestial equivalents of the llama, the rainbow serpent, and many other animals were thought to be responsible for the survival of their equivalents on earth and were believed to play an important role in continuing the life cycle. (Urton 1985, Willis 1993)

See also Astronomy, Cosmic Sea, Milky Way, South America

DARKNESS AND LIGHT

In the dualistic perception of the universe, the most fundamental opposition was the notion of darkness and light. From the beginning of time the alteration of these forces was the most obvious of nature's rhythms; it served as a clock and a calendar and divided the world into intervals that made sense. This basic rhythm injected structure into life and defined the nature of the world. In the myths of many cultures, gods of light and demons of darkness fought battles that symbolized the battle of good and evil, and combined strengths to create a polarity in which each force depended on the other.

Most creation myths began with the opposition of light and darkness, and usually darkness came first. Darkness was primeval, a force equated with the chaos that defined the world before the birth of light. The emergence of light from darkness triggered the process of creation. Bright light characterized the beginning of the world. Conversely, perpetual darkness characterized the end. Many mythologies described the world's end as a time when darkness engulfed everything and the world returned to its original chaotic state.

The battles between light and darkness took many forms. In Egypt, the sun god Ra battled nightly with Apep, the serpent of darkness who accosted the sun god as he sailed his barque through the Underworld. In the Celtic lands, Lugh and Balor fought it out, with Lugh finally slaying Balor with his spear and sling. Absu, the force of darkness that existed under the earth in Mesopotamia, dueled with the younger gods of light and happiness who planned to take over the world and who succeeded. In myths throughout the world, someone stole the sun or the moon and imprisoned it, then some kind of culture hero retrieved it and returned it to mankind. But though many myths stressed the need for light and many rituals and ceremonies emphasized light's significance by the use of candles and fire, other myths stressed the need for darkness. In some of these stories, light came first, and someone had to obtain darkness to achieve balance in the world. In Melanesia, a creator spirit named Qat set out to obtain the nighttime to combat the endless daylight in the beginning of the world. The African Kono of Sierra Leone had a similar myth. In their story, there was no darkness and no cold at the beginning. The sun lit the day, and the moon lit the night. But God gave the bat darkness in a basket to carry to the moon. The bat got tired on the way and set the basket down while he went off to get food. Some animals opened the basket searching for food, and the darkness escaped. Now the bat flies at night trying to catch the dark and take it to the moon.

Because light made all things apparent, it symbolized wisdom and indicated divine presence. Light was usually personified as an all-seeing, all-knowing sky god and often as a sun god, the most obvious source of light that appeared in the sky every day. Like Balder in Scandinavia or Mithra in Persia, light gods were wise. They emanated light and glowed with inner energy. Light symbolism dominated religious iconography from

ancient times through the Christian era, when saints and divine figures were depicted surrounded by glows or crowned with halos of brightness.

While light was generally personified as a beautiful god or saint who radiated wisdom and kindness, darkness was generally personified as a serpent or other slithery creature connected with the Underworld. Darkness demons were chthonic deities, inhabitants of the earth and the Underworld, just as light gods were celestial, inhabitants of the sky. In Zoroastrianism, the battle between light and dark took the form of a continual struggle that began when Angra Mainyu rose from the dark abyss and invaded Ahura Mazda's kingdom of light. Their dual became the basis of the Zoroastrian religion and a metaphor for the perpetual contest between good and evil. Light and darkness were not always portrayed as hostile principles, however. They were often seen as complimentary. The Chinese principle of yin and yang emphasized the interdependence of opposites like light and dark. Yang originally meant sun or light, and yin originally meant shadow or darkness. The coexistence of the two forces created harmony in the world and produced all the phenomena of nature. Light and dark, day and night, sun and moon, yin and yang were complimentary and mutually dependent. (Eliade 1987)

See also Balder, Chaos, Duality, Mithra, Night, Solstices, Sun and Sun Gods

DAWN

In creation myths of many lands, darkness preceded light, with dawn the force that lured the light out of darkness. The ancients viewed dawn as a beginning, the beginning of light, the beginning of enlightenment, and the beginning of the sun's journey across the heavens. The myths of dawn involved the act of introducing light into the world, and the gods and goddesses who personified dawn announced the arrival of the sun gods by opening the gates of heaven and preceding them into the daytime sky.

As night and day were often perceived as realms, so too was dawn, a transitional realm that connected the kingdom of day with the kingdom of night. Dawn emerged from the Underworld ahead of the sun, and paved the way for the brighter light. As transitional deities, the gods and goddesses of dawn had intimate connections both to sun gods and to gods of night and darkness. In Iceland, Dawn was one of Night's husbands. In the Baltic lands, dusk and dawn were daughters of the sun. The Greek Eos was the wife of Astraeus, god of the starry night, and the Hindu Ushas was the daughter of Dyaus the sky god, the sister of the sun and of the night, and the mother of the sun's rays.

Dawn deities were most often goddesses, bright and kind and the epitome of youth and loveliness. Ushas was always young because she was reborn each morning. The hymns of the ancient Indian text, the Rig Veda, refer to Ushas as the fairest of lights. She poured light over her body and rode a white mare through the gates of heaven to make a path for Surya, the sun god. Dawn goddesses wore bright-colored clothes, and Ushas was no exception with her crimson sari and golden veil. She had rosy fingers, symbols of the sun rays that extended into the sky during the pale morning sunrise. In myths of many lands, dawn goddesses had rosy fingers, and in Baltic myths, they adorned them with rings—rings that were perpetually stolen by the Evening Star as twilight stole the light from day. (Cox 1887, Krupp 1991a)

See also Darkness and Light, Sun and Sun Gods

DEATH

In the context of nature mythology, the notion of death relates to the cycles of the sun, the moon, the earth, and the tides. The theme of death and the realm of the Under-

world makes up an entire subfield of mythology, and literature in this subfield is abundant, especially in Egypt and Africa. But the process of death is evidenced everywhere in the natural rhythms of the earth, sea, and sky. A death occurs each night as the sun sets, each month as the moon wanes, each year as the earth shuts down for the winter, and each time the ocean waters recede with the tide.

The concept of death in nature was a promise of hope. With each death, there was a resurrection. Nature had the capacity for renewal. Myths of dying and rising gods illustrated this capacity as the gods perished at the summer solstice as the sun began its descent into winter and were resurrected at the winter solstice with the return of the sun and the promise of new life. The immortality of these gods paralleled the behavior of the sun, traveling through the Underworld then reemerging into the sky.

Because the setting sun disappeared in the west, its death made the western horizon a door to the Underworld. Through the door was a place of darkness, a place where serpents and snakes fought battles to retain the dying gods and extinguish the light of the sun. They never succeeded, for the dying gods and the sun were immortal. The god rose each winter when the sun began its journey south, and the sun rose each morning to take over the world.

In the phenomenon of the sunrise, nature underwent another death, that of the moon. Like Huitzilopochtli, the Aztec sun god who slew his sister, the moon, the sun itself slew the moon each day and sliced it up bit by bit, causing it to get smaller and smaller over its monthly cycle until it finally disappeared. The ancients viewed the disappearance of the moon as the death of a silvery goddess. But this goddess, too, was immortal. She perpetually died but perpetually regained strength and returned to her full, round self again.

The sun and the moon resided in the celestial realm, so were immortal like most celestial deities. But the earth was not. It died a true death each winter when its vegetation died and frost and snow covered the land. Yet still the earth had the capacity for renewal. Like a great Mother Goddess, it gave birth to a new generation each year. The ancients witnessed these births and deaths and structured their lives by these rhythms of nature. They saw death in their world everywhere, from the sky above to the sea below. The sun sank below the horizon, the moon disappeared completely, the animals hibernated and shut down for the winter, and the cycle of vegetation stopped. Life receded into death like the ebbing tide receded into the sea. But like the tide, life reliably returned. (Eliade 1959, Krupp 1997b)

> See also Cosmic Order, Demeter, Moon and Moon Gods, Morning Star/Evening Star, Sacrifice, Seasons

DELUGE
See Floods and Flood Gods

DEMETER
Demeter was a widely worshipped earth goddess in ancient Greece, and she specifically represented the cultivated soil. The name Demeter meant "Mother Earth," but unlike Gaia, the goddess who personified the physical land, Demeter presided over the harvest, and her worshippers appealed to her to restore the earth to fruitfulness after the winter months. Demeter's most famous myth involved her descent to the Underworld to recover her daughter, Persephone, who had been kidnapped by Hades, the ruler of the dark abode of the dead. Persephone too represented the harvest, and with both her and her mother buried beneath the ground, the earth withered away and died.

Demeter's descent to the Underworld metaphorically represented the corn seed that got buried underground. Demeter died as the earth died but returned as the corn sprouted up again each spring. Though Hades wanted Persephone to remain beneath the earth with him and be his wife, he made a deal with Demeter and allowed the young maiden to return to the earth with her mother for part of each year. Like all earth goddesses, Demeter and Persephone had links to death, but also to resurrection. Demeter's myth, then, emphasized the earth goddess' role in birth, death, and the cycle of seasons.

Demeter was usually depicted wearing a long robe and a veil that trailed down the back of her head. Sometimes she wore a crown of corn or carried corn in her hand, along with a scepter or a torch. The myth of Demeter and her trip to the Underworld provided the base for the most famous mystery cult of antiquity, called the Eleusinian Mysteries. Because Demeter's myth emphasized rebirth of the land, worshippers in this cult drew parallels to human rebirth through Demeter's promise of life through death. (Burn 1990, Frazer 1950, Graves 1988, Guerber 1992)

> See also Death, Earth and Earth Gods, Greece and Rome, Ishtar, Seasons

DEMONS
Demons in myth and legend embodied humanity's deepest fears. In nature myths, they controlled or personified destructive forces in the natural environment that ancient people considered a constant threat to survival. Many forms of demonic creatures populated nature myths, including monsters, giants, serpents, and dwarves. Demons of the earth wreaked havoc by shaking the ground and erupting volcanoes, demons of the sky hustled clouds and caused tornadoes, and demons of the sea pulled ships and sailors into the dark depths of the waters and drowned them.

Some of the most fearsome demons in nature myths caused violent storms, either on land or on sea. For this reason, many myths portrayed the winds as incarnations of

An Arabic conception of the demons that haunt the sea.

the middle of their foreheads. Often, these monsters ruled the world at the creation of mankind, and a new race of gods had to defeat them to make the world habitable. In many mythologies, demons ruled the world first because they symbolized the primordial chaos that existed before the creation of the universe. They slithered around in that chaos like snakes and embodied darkness and evil. But tremendous amounts of energy existed in the primordial chaos, enough energy to create a world. For this reason, demons had enormous powers. They emerged from the darkness and caused storms and floods, avalanches and eclipses, famines and droughts. Demons personified the harsh forces of nature, and the myths pitted them in a balancing act with the gods. In nature myths, sun gods slew darkness demons, rain gods conquered drought demons, and sea gods calmed evil giants who roused the waves. Demons were as essential to the myths as were gods, because good and evil existed in all three realms: earth, sea, and sky. (Bonnefoy 1991)

See also Apep, Chaos, Darkness and Light, Duality, Giants, Rahu, Serpents and Snakes, Water and Water Spirits, Winds and Wind Gods

demonic forces. On land the winds often resided in mountain caves, where they swirled about in captivity then emerged to terrorize the earth. Sailors have connected demons with winds since ancient times. Because they often flared up over the waters and caused tempests and tidal waves, sailors perceived the winds not as natural phenomena but as devils with mysterious powers. These unforeseen sea hazards led to beliefs of demons residing deep under the surface and pulling people down into the darkness with them. Many people never dared to rescue a drowning man for fear of angering the sea demons, and other people even sacrificed to the sea demons to placate them.

Demons were usually portrayed as misshapen and enormous, like the gigantic frost giants in the Norse myths or the evil Cyclopes in the Greek myths, with one eye in

DENG

The Dinka of Sudan associated their deity, Deng, with rain, thunder, and lightning. He was an important sky god, to some clans an ancestor and creator god of the Dinka people, and he manifested himself in the fertilizing water that fell from the heavens. The word *deng* meant "rain," and the phenomenon was itself revered as a creative force. Deng, as the rain, promised new life and ended famine and drought.

The personified Deng ensured fertility, but he also had the power to cause death and destruction. He used lightning as his club. When people were struck by lightning, the Dinka said Deng hit them on the head. Deng had no erected temple, but trees hit by lightning were worshipped as his shrines. Sacrifices were made to him in the homestead, usually animals with black and white body markings to represent the white sky full of dark clouds or the dark sky full of white lightning. (Lienhardt 1961, Parrinder 1986)

> *See also* Africa, Hammers, Lightning, Rain and Rain Gods, Storms and Tempests

DESERTS

Travelers across the desert encountered a harsh world, one of blinding sandstorms, racing whirlwinds, and suffocating heat. People who lived in desert lands needed gods to protect them while crossing the desert and spirits to help them cope with the demons that seemed to materialize before their eyes. Some desert myths explained how those barren expanses of land got there in the first place, as did the Greek myth of Phaethon who parched these areas when he steered the sun's chariot off course. But most desert myths involved images of what people thought they saw—castles glittering in the distance, pools of water that appeared then disappeared, and horrifying demons masquerading as gigantic whirls of sand.

The largest desert in the world is the Sahara in North Africa, so many desert myths came from the people of this area. The Egyptians associated the desert with barrenness and with any area of land outside the fertile Nile valley. The great contrast in the Egyptian landscape gave credence to the myth of Seth and Osiris; Seth was the personification of the dark, barren desert, and Osiris was the personification of the fertile Nile river valley. Seth appeared as a red god to represent the hostile desert, and in one of his most hostile moments, he shut his brother, Osiris, in a coffin and sent him floating down the Nile to his death. Osiris was resurrected, but the incident with Seth represented a horrifying, though temporary, victory of barrenness over

fruitfulness. Seth's consort, Nephthys, added to the desert imagery. Nephthys personified the dry desert edge. She was barren, yet she longed for a child. Nephthys married Seth, but got his brother Osiris drunk one night and conceived his child. Osiris represented the Nile and his drunkenness, in this myth, represented the high flood waters. When the Nile waters got especially high, the desert edge became fruitful, even though it was usually barren.

The Egyptians had other desert deities who personified the arid landscape: the lion-headed goddess Sekmet, whose hot breath represented the hot desert winds; Ha, the god of the western desert, an area the Egyptians believed led to the Underworld; and Min, the god of the eastern desert, who protected people from hostile desert forces and whom travelers frequently invoked before they began their journeys. But often in myth and legend the hostile desert forces assumed the form of some sort of monster or demon who dwelt underneath the sand or in some oasis, then emerged unexpected to harm or devour people. Many African demons lived in the desert areas and often took the forms of snakes, scorpions, owls, leopards, or whirlwinds. Often people thought these demons were sent to punish people for their sins, as was the Dahomey god Tinggfame, who sent blinding sandstorms. In Arabic and Islamic mythology, demons called ahl-ah-trab manifested themselves as the sandstorms themselves. They lived beneath the Sahara, drank pools of water before travelers could reach them, and whipped up sand in camels' eyes. The Khoi Khoi believed in man-eating monsters called Alamaguza who crawled around on their hands and feet and trapped people underneath them. Fortunately, however, the Alamaguzas had eyes set on the insides of their feet, and because they had to lift up one foot to see, many victims escaped unharmed.

Desert travelers faced long monotonous journeys, and the unique climactic conditions in the desert led to an optical phenomenon called the mirage. Due to temperature gradients over still land and the nature of reflection and refraction, it looked as if large pools of water, walled cities, or orchards and castles lay just ahead. This phenomenon gave rise to many stories of desert demons who deluded travelers using seductive voices or creating visions of grass and flowers, lakes and treasures, and distant palaces shining in the moonlight. The travelers followed these visions to find nothing but sand and sometimes manifestations of the demons themselves, disguised as gigantic whirlwinds sweeping across barren land. (Knappert 1995a, Lurker 1980)

See also Demons, Mirage, Osiris,
   Whirlwinds

DEW

Dew is moisture that renews the earth. Condensed from the air, it falls in droplets and covers the grass and plant life, seemingly like magic, during the night. Perhaps for this reason, many early people believed dew of celestial origin. It healed like rain, cooled like snow, and therefore represented water from some heavenly force.

Many early people attributed dew to the sky forces; some to the moon, others to the stars, and still others to the night or the thunder. The ancient belief that the moon was cold and watery led to the common notion of moon dew, a silvery liquid sent by a lunar deity to nourish the crops. In Chinese and Japanese myths, dew dripped from the stars, and in some Scandinavian myths, dew dripped in foamy droplets from the bit of Hrimfaxi, the horse who brought night. In Iroquois legend, dew fell from the wings of Oshadagea, the Big Eagle of Dew, who worked as the assistant to the thunder god Hino and who carried a lake of dew on his back. When fire destroyed the earth and obliterated the earth's vegetation, Oshadegea spread his wings and let the moisture from his lake of dew fall from his back and heal the land.

Some myths attributed dew to specific deities of the heavens, often to a god or goddess crying tears of grief. In New Zealand, Rangi, the sky, shed those tears after his separation from Papa, the earth. In some classical myths, the dawn goddess Aurora shed them every morning as she lamented the death of her brother, Memnon, who was slain by Achilles. These gods and goddesses lamented their loved ones daily, so their tears continually watered the earth. This made sense, symbolically. Dew was water from the heavens, permeated with the power of the Immortals. It renewed life and restored youth. Like the celestial dew in Norse myth that fell in silver droplets on Yggdrasil, the world tree, the water of heaven healed the earth and gave it perpetual life. (Brueton 1991, Larousse 1968)

See also Moon and Moon Gods, Water
   and Water Spirits, Well of Life

DRAGON SLAYING

Tales of gods slaying dragons commonly appeared in the myths of Indo-European nations. The gods generally had solar attributes (some were bona fide sun gods), and the dragons represented the darkness or some destructive force of nature that threatened to obscure the sun's light. The type of battle that arose and the type of dragon that fought the sun god varied from place to place because each dragon embodied the threatening force peculiar to his area of the world. But in general, mythological dragon fights pitted good against evil, darkness against light, and sun against earth.

Of course, in the myths, dragons were not always dragons per se but some kind of dragonlike creature, a serpent, perhaps, or a sea monster. Serpents symbolized earth energies, darkness, and evil, and some sea monsters, it was said, symbolized the dark storm clouds that drifted over the ocean and blocked out the solar light. In Scandinavia, Sigurd killed Fafnir, the dragon son of a magician named Hredimar and the spirit of the cold earth. In India, Indra killed the drought dragon Vritra, who according to some symbolized not only drought but also the dark storm clouds. In Persia, Mithra fought Angra Mainyu, the spirit of darkness, and in Greece and the Celtic world, solar heroes fought dragons of all sorts. When these heroes slew their dragons, they restored the balance of nature. The solar force rose victorious, and the solar heroes continued the cycle of life. (Baring-Gould 1897, Howey 1955)

> *See also* Darkness and Light, Dragons, Indra, Sea Monsters, Serpents and Snakes, Sun and Sun Gods

DRAGON-KINGS

In Chinese mythology, five dragon-kings served as rainmakers and rulers of the waters. Four of them were stationed at the cardinal points and ruled the seas, and their chief resided in the center. The dragon-kings were enormous and could stretch over the sea to control the entire expanse of the waters. Lung Wang was often the name given to these five dragons, who were perceived as five parts of one deity. As king of the waters, Lung Wang remained coiled up under the sea during droughts and flew up to the sky during the rainy season when he caused his waters to fall on the land.

The dragon-kings of China lived in crystal palaces under the sea, where they fed on pearls and opals and were attended by a large array of fishes, crabs, and crayfish. These palaces were part of the Underworld, that elusive realm beneath the ocean that could only be reached through an underground mountain cave or well. The dragon-kings had tremendous powers, including fiery breath that could boil fish. When they rose to the surface, they caused waterspouts and typhoons, and when they flew through the air with miraculous speed, they caused rain to

fall in torrents and hurricanes to sweep over the oceans.

Though the dragon-kings were often petitioned during drought and flooding, they were not worshipped directly. They took their orders from the Jade Emperor, and it was he who determined how much rain these kings would distribute and to which areas. Perhaps more respected by the people were the lesser dragon-kings, who the Chinese believed controlled each inland watercourse and well in the land. These dragon-kings were assigned to their posts by Lung Wang himself, who had little contact with living creatures but stayed confined to his underwater palace where he could control the seas. The dragon-kings were bearded, with hairy legs and a hairy tail. They had five feet that each had five claws, yellow scales, a long snout, a long tongue, and sharp teeth. (Bonnefoy 1991, Werner 1995)

> *See also* China, Dragons, Drought, Rain and Rain Gods, Ryujin, Water and Water Spirits

DRAGONS

The ancients believed dragons to be weathermakers, forms of winged lizards or serpents who controlled the waters beneath the earth and the rains that fell from the heavens. Because dragons had the ability to either rejuvenate the earth or destroy it, they were both worshipped for their power and feared for their potential for destruction.

Most commonly, dragons inhabited pools, lakes, rivers, or seas, where they hibernated in the winter during drought season in their underwater palaces, coiled up like gigantic sea serpents. In the spring, when rains were imminent, the dragons rose up to the clouds in the spiral paths of whirlpools and waterspouts. As the dragons ascended, the pressure of their feet on the clouds caused rain. Storms were said to occur when the dragons were angry and battled with each other in the clouds. If they battled too long, floods occurred. If they flew too high, the land remained dry.

Dragons appeared in the myths of many lands as enemies of humanity and as symbols of destruction. They caused floods and storms and great tidal waves, and they spouted fire and fury from their mouths. But the dragons of Chinese mythology were originally benevolent, preservers and sustainers as water was a preserver and sustainer. However, the Nagas, the Buddhist dragons who inhabited the mountains of India, were noted for their destruction, as was Tiamat, the Mesopotamian chaos dragon of the subterranean saltwater ocean.

Dragons were divided into categories, and the most common kind controlled rain and water. Celestial dragons supported the heavens. Subterranean dragons guarded treasure beneath the earth. The Chinese categorized dragons by color. Blue dragons were the chief spirits of water and rain and presided during the springtime when their dragon magic sustained the earth. Red and black dragons were fierce and destructive, the ones that waged battles in the clouds and caused violent storms.

Aside from bringing rain, sky dragons performed other important functions. When the Chinese monster, Kung Kung, battled with the Emperor Yao and tore a hole in the sky, a dragon replaced the hole, causing daylight when it opened its eyes and nighttime when it closed them. When the great sky dragon inhaled, it brought forth summer, and when it exhaled, winter. Sea dragons controlled the ebb and flow of the tides. In many lands, dragons existed as controllers of weather. Their eyes flashed streaks of lightning, their flight caused the winds, and their breath condensed to rain when they ascended to the clouds. (Allen 1963, Baring-Gould 1897, Huxley 1979, Ingersoll 1928, Mackenzie 1994)

See also China, Dragon-Kings, Rain and Rain Gods, Serpents and Snakes, Water and Water Spirits, Waterspouts

A relief sculpture of a dragon on a pagoda in Hanoi, Vietnam.

DREAMTIME

The mythology of the Australian Aborigines has its base in a mythological creation period called Dreamtime when supernatural beings roamed the earth and formed the physical features of the land. The term *Dreamtime* is a translation of aboriginal words, and the concept is difficult to grasp because it defines both a primordial time and a state of mind. As a time, Dreamtime occurred in the distant past when only mythological beings existed, built the earth, and deposited the seeds for future human beings. As a state of mind Dreamtime defines the intimate connection the Aborigines have with the earth, as well as their profound understanding of nature's sacredness.

Because the supernaturals in Dreamtime created the physical landforms, the Australian Aborigines believe they should have an intimate connection with the earth. These creator beings were mythological ancestors.

They formed the rock country, the rivers, the valleys, and the plains, then they disappeared back into their spirit homes and became the creatures they created, the plants and animals and natural forces. For this reason, Aborigines today take living off the land seriously. They believe they have a duty to guard and maintain it. The spirits of their ancestors remain in the earth, so the modern Aborigines who adhere to the concept of Dreamtime believe themselves to be an integral part of nature. (Breeden 1988, Eliade 1973, Mountford 1970)

See also Ayers Rock, Oceania, Rainbow Snake, Taniwha, Wondjina

DROUGHT

The power of water was never so evident as in times of drought. In the ancient world, drought times meant death times, and because people greatly feared drought, they reflected their fear in myth and ritual. Often, these myths and rituals involved demons who kept the water or those who controlled the waters captive. Often the myths conveyed a reverence for storm gods. To ensure that the storm gods slew the demons and released the waters, people propitiated them with offerings and sacrifice. In times of dire need, the ancients believed these offerings to be their only recourse. If they showed the gods their reverence, they might influence the course of nature.

Storm gods were the most likely recipients of drought-time sacrifices because they had the power to send the rain. Tlaloc, the Aztec god of storm and rain, received thousands of sacrifices when rain was needed, and so did the dragon-kings of China. The dragon-kings lived at the bottom of pools or the sea, and during the winter drought season, they stayed there, asleep, keeping the water the people needed on earth down with them. But spring brought relief from winter drought: The dragons began to stir in their underwater beds, then rose up to the sky to fight with

one another in the clouds. These dragon fights were not terrifying, as it would seem. They were welcomed. As the dragons clawed and roared and thrashed their monstrous tails, they caused thunderstorms and torrential downpours and ended the drought.

The dragons of China may have kept the waters from falling when they remained asleep in their lairs, but creatures in other lands caused drought by swallowing the waters. In a popular Indian myth, Vritra, the drought demon, imprisoned the cloud cattle in a mountain cave, but in another version of the myth, Vritra swallowed the waters. Indra, the storm god, saved the land when he sliced open Vritra's belly. In Mesoamerica, a sky serpent and companion of Tlaloc or Ix Chel kept all the waters contained in his belly. In India, Agastya, the ocean drinker, drank all the seawater to help the gods discover that their enemies lived and thrived in the ocean realm. In North America and Australia, a gigantic frog commonly swallowed all the waters. The Australian Aborigines told a story about how the animals tried to make the frog laugh. Each animal tried, but the eel finally succeeded when he danced on his tail. The frog spit his sides, literally, and the water came gushing out. Though the frog's action certainly ended the drought, it also caused the Deluge. With rain, there is a delicate balance between too little and too much. The dragons of China also flooded the earth when their cloud battles lasted too long.

The rush of waters that often followed periods of drought were both welcomed and feared. In India, the drought season ended when monsoon rains rushed across the North China Sea, and in Mesopotamia, when the Tigris and Euphrates flooded their banks. Among the Pueblo of North America, the drought ended when the Kachinas, the spirits of rainclouds, returned to their mountain homes. In Peru, the season of drought occurred in the first place because Con, a Peruvian thunder god, lost a battle with his brother, Pachacamac, and left Peru in defeat. When he left, he took the rain with him. (Donnan 1977)

See also Dragon-Kings, Dragons, Indra, Ix Chel, Kachinas, Rain and Rain Gods, Tlaloc

DUALITY

Myths often expressed conflicts between opposing forces. Gods with creative powers fought gods with destructive powers; gods of light fought gods of darkness. The mythmakers recognized polarity in their world, but they also recognized an interdependence of opposites. Their myths reflected their observations. A world with rain and no drought destroyed the earth with flood, and a world with sun and no moon reduced the earth to ashes. In a world with day and no night, time didn't move at all.

The ancient Greeks surmised that four elements made up the world: earth, air, fire, and water. Earth was the opposite of air, and fire was the opposite of water. The concept of pairing these opposites formed the basis of many nature myths. Earth was female; air, male. The wind blew seeds of life into the female earth. Water was female and fire, male. The fiery sun married the watery moon. In North America, the Navajo divided most aspects of their world into male and female beings, and so did the Pawnee. The Aztecs embodied this same concept—that of complementary opposition—in their creator god, Ometeotl, the god of duality, who possessed both the female and the male creative principle.

The Mesoamerican perception of Ometeotl divided the world of nature into two parts. The Chinese adhered to the same belief when they embraced the principle of yin and yang. Yang was male; yin, female. Yang was day; yin, night. Yang was sun; yin, moon. Yang was the essence of fire and air, whereas yin was the essence of earth and water. Maintaining a balance between these two parts of nature kept the universe moving in recurrent cycles. When one of the two forces overcame the other, the cycle stopped and the world ended in cataclysm. In Aztec myth this happened four times, and in each case, the same element responsible for life caused the death of the world. Recognizing the necessity of opposition in the world formed the basis for polarity in myths. The marriage of yin and yang guaranteed life in the world. (Campbell 1974, Krupp 1991a, Teich 1994)

See also Aztec Calendar Stone, Chaos, Cosmic Order, Darkness and Light, Elements, Persia

Earth and Earth Gods

EARTH AND EARTH GODS

Earth is the foundation of human existence, the womb that gives life and the tomb that receives the dead. Many individual gods and goddesses qualified as earth deities, and these spirits empowered trees and mountains, protected crops, and ensured the fertility of the land. But almost every ancient culture deified the earth itself as a single animating power—a power that represented the cycle of life and death and the process of cosmic renewal.

Most early people deified the earth as female, the great fertility goddess and creator of all life. This earth mother existed since prehistory and appeared to embody both the earth and nature itself. She was Mother Earth and Mother Nature, the Great Goddess and the spouse and counterpart of the sky. She lay down over the land and received semen from the sky god in the form of rain. She gave birth continually. Plant and animal life alike emerged from her womb and thrived in her world.

The earth goddess spanned all cultures and assumed many guises. To the Sumerians, she was Ninhursag, and to the Akkadians, Ishtar or Inanna. Ala was one of the most important earth goddesses of Africa, the Great Mother and fertility goddess of the Ibo of Nigeria. The Hindus had Prithvi, the Polynesians Papa, and the Greeks had Gaia, who formed herself out of chaos then gave birth to her partner, Ouranos, the starry heaven, then created the mountains and seas. The worship of earth goddesses like Gaia took a backseat to the worship of popular sky gods like Zeus,

yet Gaia played an integral role in creation. Gaia and Ouranos together created the first races of mankind, but the earth goddess accomplished the initial acts of creation alone. Gaia, like many other earth goddesses, was not visualized in human form but rather perceived as a personification of the material earth. The earth's waters were her fluids; the mountains, her breasts; the caves, her womb.

While the earth mother embodied life as a creator goddess, she also embodied death and took the form of death goddess. In this aspect, she was terrifying. She demanded life in order to give life and required blood sacrifice in order to thrive. In the Aztec world, Coatlicue represented this terrifying Mother Earth, and in the Hindu world, Devi. These goddesses took life but then sprang forth new growth, and their myths were metaphors for the regenerative power of nature. Snakes too symbolized this regenerative power, and Coatlicue wore a skirt of snakes that added to her earth goddess imagery. Snakes shed their skin and emerged anew, and thus illustrated that death, as well as birth, was necessary for cosmic renewal. They coiled their bodies in gigantic circles and thus embodied the life cycle, as did the earth goddess as she turned the seasons.

People saw evidence of cosmic renewal and the cyclic nature of the universe in many places in the ancient world because early people kept attuned to the movements of their cosmos. They saw the earth grow and die and the tide ebb and flow, and they looked into the sky and witnessed the same immortality in the heavenly bodies. The moon died each month, then filled up again with what the ancients perceived as the Water of Life. So early people outfitted many of their earth goddesses with lunar attributes. The Egyptian goddess Isis, the Babylonian goddess Ishtar, and the Polynesian goddess Hina all combined lunar and chthonic qualities.

No matter what forces the earth goddesses controlled, or what processes they regulated, these women embodied creation. The earth had energy and spirit and could sustain the forces of fire, flood, earthquake, and storm yet still emerge anew. Plants sprang from the earth each spring, food issued from her body, and, in many mythologies, creator deities molded the world's first human beings from the earth's clay. In Sudan it was believed that people of different colored skin came from different types of earth. White people came from white loam, brown people from desert sand, and black people from the fertile riverside clay.

Worship of the earth and the earth goddess was one the earliest forms of religion. The earliest depictions of the earth goddess were found in caves, which the ancients perceived as the womb of their goddess. An actual Mother Goddess cult arose in the seventh or sixth millennium B.C. and spread over the Near and Middle East, the central Mediterranean, and other places in Europe and Asia, its advent coinciding with the agricultural revolution. The connection was easy to make. Farming communities relied on Mother Earth to maintain the land, and she did not disappoint. They worshipped and revered her as creator and nurturer. Though natural forces continually worked to destroy the land, Mother Earth remained forever fertile. (Campbell 1998a, Frazer 1926, Michell 1975)

See also Death, Elements, Gaia, Geb, Moon and Moon Gods, Serpents and Snakes

EARTHQUAKES

In the ancient world, people attempted to assign responsibility for any force strong enough to affect the earth. Rumblings of the earth certainly did not happen by themselves, but rather someone caused them to happen—and for good reason. Such powerful movements, they believed, could only

The Japanese attributed earthquakes to the wriggling of a giant catfish, usually kept under control by the god Kashima, who held the catfish down with a large stone.

come from something alive and powerful enough itself to cause the earth to shake and tremble. They attributed earthquakes to the writhing and twisting of either a god or some sort of creature, either one trapped beneath the earth or one responsible for supporting it.

The type of creature that caused earthquakes varied from country to country. In India, it was the burrowing of a gigantic mole. In other lands it was the heavy stamping of a giant. In Maori myth, Ruau-moko, the youngest child of the sky god Rangi and the earth goddess Papa, was never born but remained trapped inside Papa's womb even after the separation of sky and earth. His wriggling and writhing caused earthquakes. Some Asian tribes attributed earthquakes to the movements of Shie-Ou, a god imprisoned in the earth by the sun god, and other Asian tribes attributed the rumblings to an entire race of people who lived under the earth and who shook the ground to find out whether anyone lived on top. The Japanese attributed earthquakes to the wriggling of a giant catfish, usually kept under control by the god Kashima, who held the catfish down with a large stone. When Kashima left his post, however, the movements of the catfish caused the earth to shake and rumble.

Many ancient stories attributed the rumblings to someone imprisoned in the earth. Aristotle attributed earthquakes to the winds, struggling to escape from underground caves. In Greek myths, the earth shook when the giant Typhon, or in some stories, Enceladus, moaned and groaned from his prison under Mount Aetna. In the Norse myths, the trickster Loki caused the quakes, imprisoned by the gods and forced to lie under the earth on sharp stones while the venom of a poisonous snake dripped constantly on his face. Usually, his wife, Sigyn, caught the venom in a bowl. But when the bowl filled up and she left to empty it, the poison hit Loki's face, causing him to shake violently enough to move the earth.

Earthquakes were most commonly attributed to the creatures who supported the earth. The Algonquin Indians thought that the earth was supported by a giant tortoise and that his movements caused the quakes. In Mongolia, the creature was a frog, and in Persia, a crab. Two tales came from India. In one, seven serpents took turns supporting the earth, and quakes occurred each time they changed shifts. In the other, eight elephants held the earth on their backs and caused tremors when they shook their heads. A myth from the Philippines told a similar story of a python writhing around the earth's pillars. In many myths, whoever supported the earth got tired and had to change hands, thereby causing the earth to shift and rumble.

Natural forces like earthquakes had untold potential for destruction, and the people had no way of predicting or preventing them and no scientific knowledge of what caused them. The earth rumbled like the angry voice of some hidden god, and then the land split apart in what appeared to be a manifestation of the god's fury. Often, people believed the gods caused earthquakes to punish mortals for wrongdoings, and they envi-

sioned such deities as the evil Kisin of Mexico, who dwelled in the Underworld and took charge of punishing sinners. But even though earthquakes were always terrifying, not all earthquake gods meant harm. In Peru, the people thought the quakes occurred when their earthquake god kicked up his heels and danced. (Vitaliano 1973)

See also Aetna, Giants, Volcanoes

ECLIPSES

Eclipses of the sun or the moon had a powerful impact on the minds of the ancients. During a lunar eclipse, they watched a dark shadow move slowly and silently over their moon, often changing it to an eerie red color. During a solar eclipse, they saw their sun disappear completely. To ancient people who knew nothing of the science behind eclipses, it appeared that something sinister was attacking the celestial forces, forces the people knew needed to remain intact for their world to survive.

A common belief among many cultures was that during an eclipse, the sun or moon was being devoured by some sort of beast. To the Chinese, it was a dragon. To the Vikings, it was two wolves named Skoll and Hat. In many lands, it was a serpent. There were eclipse tales of birds, frogs, dogs, and even vampires taking bites out of the sun or the moon, eventually swallowing it, then spitting it out. The event was terrifying to watch. Each time an eclipse occurred, the people feared for their lives. But they didn't plan to surrender easily. They banded together, shot arrows at the sky, and made a lot of noise—in a frantic attempt to scare the eclipse monsters away.

People continued these scare tactics for centuries, because after all, it appeared their methods worked. The sun or the moon always emerged unscathed. In the northern countries, when the people banged their pots and beat their drums, Skoll and Hat dropped their treat. In China, the great sky dragon surrendered his prize. Triumphant, the people

This depiction of Columbus and horrified islanders in the New World viewing a solar eclipse illustrates the European view of nonscientific beliefs.

then retired their pots and drums and resumed their daily activities. They had exercised their control over the sky.

Because people viewed eclipses with such terror, even those people who made no attempt to explain why they occurred tried to predict when they occurred. The Chinese and the Babylonians were among the first to recognize that these sky events occurred in regular patterns. As early as 750 B.C. Babylonian scribes began to keep meticulous records of eclipses, timing the events with water clocks and making calculations using an advanced system of mathematics. The ancient Maya did something similar. Paying close attention to the movements of the heavens, they composed eclipse warning tables and recorded them in the Dresden Codex, the most detailed hieroglyphic document of ancient Mayan civilization.

Though some Australian tribes described an eclipse as the moon and sun kissing or making love, most ancient cultures feared any unusual appearance or event they witnessed in their sky. The heavens were supposed to act in an orderly fashion, and an eclipse was an introduction of chaos. The Chinese legend of Hsi and Ho illustrated how deep the fear of eclipses ran. Hsi and Ho were two court astronomers appointed by Emperor Yao and entrusted with the official duty of skywatching. These astronomers were not only expected to understand the heavens, but were held responsible when things went wrong. When Hsi and Ho failed to predict a solar eclipse in time to warn the people that the sun was being swallowed by a dragon, the astronomers were put to death. Never mind the fact that the sun escaped unharmed. Hsi and Ho's failure to predict the eclipse in time exposed their land to the angers of the heavens. (Hadingham 1984, Krupp 1991a, McCrickard 1990, Moore 1968, Wright 1968)

See also Astronomy, Chaos, Rahu

EGYPT

The nature myths of the Egyptians reflected the dependence these people had on two natural features of their land—the Nile River and the Sahara Desert. These two landforms stood in opposition to each other, the promise of life against the threat of death. The dry heat and barrenness of the Sahara justified to ancient mythmakers the identification of the desert with fearsome gods of death and destruction. The life-giving waters of the Nile justified the identification of the river with fertility gods and gods who helped keep the water pulsing through cataracts and overflowing its banks.

The importance of the Nile to the ancient Egyptians can not be overestimated; it was the lifeblood of the country and its symbolism permeated Egyptian myths. Little rain fell in ancient Egypt, so the water that brought life and fertility came from the river and from the annual floodwaters that washed over the Nile valley. For this reason, the Egyptians saw the earth, rather than the sky, as fertilizer. Geb, the earth god, lay prone on the earth with his sky goddess, Nut, arched above him. Vegetation sprouted from Geb's body, nourished by his life fluids. The Nile, it seemed, was the magic elixir. It gave human beings the gift of life and gods the gift of immortality. To the Egyptians, the Nile was the earth, the sea, and the sky. These people did not travel the seas, but sailed only on their beloved river. Even the sun gods sailed their solar barques along the celestial Nile, through the heavens by day and through the Underworld by night.

The Egyptian pantheon consisted of gods who personified all the elements of nature. It included gods of the Nile and gods of the Sahara. It included gods who ruled from heaven and gods who ruled from earth. The first gods belonged to the Ennead, a group of nine deities who personified the primal forces of nature: earth, air, fire, and water. Atum, or Ra-Atum, was the first of these

gods, the sun god and the sole creator. He rose from the primordial sea and stood upon a mound of earth representative of the islands that arose every year after the flood waters receded. Atum stood on this primeval island and created the other eight gods, in pairs. Shu and Tefnut personified air and moisture, Geb and Nut personified earth and sky, Isis and Osiris personified the fertile waters of the Nile, and Seth and Nephthys personified drought, darkness, the parched earth, and the barrenness of the desert.

Atum, as the creator deity, affirmed the Egyptian belief in the power of the sun. The ever-present heat characterized their land as profoundly as the Nile did, so sun worship predominated in Egypt more than in any other land. Atum represented the primordial sun, but as time went on, different sun gods arose to personify various aspects of solar power. Sun symbols abounded. Then during the reign of Amenhetep IV, sun worship reached its extreme. This pharaoh decreed that the people of Egypt worship only the solar disk. The Supreme Deity of Egypt then became simply a golden orb with rays emanating outward like hands.

The worship of Aten, the solar disk, lasted only as long as Amenhetep's reign. When Tutankhamen succeeded him, he reinstated the old ways of worshipping; once again Ra, the personified sun god, ruled supreme. The Egyptian pharaohs had an intimate connection with Ra and were believed to join the sun god in his sky world after death and accompany him on his daily journeys across the firmament in his solar barque. The pharaohs thus received the utmost respect and reverence, both in life and in death. They were buried in elaborate tombs, within temples in the magnificent pyramids. These pyramids connected the pharaohs to the sun god and their afterlife in the heavens. They probably served as ramps to give the pharaohs access to the gods.

The people made sure to prepare their

pharaohs for their immortal life in the heavens. In decorating their pharaohs' tombs, they included any food and personal items they might need in the afterlife and spiritual items as well. These spiritual items included elaborate zodiacs and star charts etched onto the ceilings, charts that indicated the early Egyptians considered the heavenly arrangement sacred and that they revered the celestial deities as models of order. The people of the Nile River valley watched the sky closely, and they took note of the order they witnessed. They designed their calendars and their lives using thirty-six stars they labeled decans, prominent stars of the night sky whose rise and set dates could be used to record the date and time of year. Sirius was the most important of the decan stars, because it rose at the time of the Nile flood. The Egyptians personified Sirius as their beloved fertility goddess, Isis. In myth, the goddess Isis rose in the sky, and the water flooded the land.

Isis was a model of order, and as a star goddess she ensured stability in the cosmos. Her husband, Osiris, ensured stability as well, because as god of the Nile and of vegetation he resurrected the earth after it died each year. The resurrection of the sun, of Sirius, of the Nile, and of the earth reliably occurred; however, the Egyptians still feared the consequences should they fail. They were preoccupied with death, so they pitted good against evil. Osiris conquered his demonic brother, Seth. Ra conquered the darkness demons. Both Osiris and Ra traveled through death and then were resurrected. Their battles represented the contrasting states of life and death inherent in the Egyptian landscape. The people witnessed death under the scorching sun and the heat of the desert. But they witnessed life when the river flooded and turned their valley into fertile land. Because ancient Egyptians experienced nature's power as both annihilating and merciful, they developed a profound belief in life after death. They seemed to view death as simply a stage in an ongoing life process. (Hart 1990, Ions 1983, Rosalie 1980, Spence 1986)

EHECATL

Ehecatl was the Aztec wind god, the most important aspect of the snake-bird deity and god of air, Quetzalcoatl. As a manifestation of the wind, Ehecatl symbolized fertility and human breath, and because movement indicated life force, he took on the larger role of creator, blowing life into the earth as he stirred the winds.

As creator god, Ehecatl was credited with creating the present race of human beings, the earth, and the heavens and with raising the sky. In one of his most popular myths, he introduced sexual love to mankind as well by stirring the passions of Mayahuel, a maiden he brought from the Underworld and made love to on earth. Where the two made love, a tree grew, and from that time forward, the Aztecs believed the sound of the wind in the trees represented Ehecatl's desire.

In the Aztec codices, Ehecatl was black with a conical head and wore shell jewelry and a red bird mask that covered his mouth. His most prominent piece of jewelry was a "wind jewel" that dangled from his neck and was cut from the cross section of a conch shell. Through this jewel came the living voice of the wind, which led the Aztecs to view the conch shell as a god itself as well as a symbol of wind and a talisman of power. Through the beak on his mask, Ehecatl blew the winds and was said to "sweep the way" for Tlaloc, the rain god, who brought the rain and storms.

Ehecatl was a popular Aztec deity, sometimes conceived in four parts and associated with the winds of the four cardinal directions. Because the Aztecs both feared and respected the powers of wind, they offered sacrifices to Ehecatl and built temples to honor him. The temples were circular with conical roofs and appeared to symbolize caves to the

Underworld. As a circle is endless and round, the rounded corners on these temples likely represented the wind god's limitless powers. (Brundage 1982, Markman and Markman 1992)

   See also Mesoamerica, Quetzalcoatl, Winds and Wind Gods

ELEMENTS

The people of ancient Greece recognized four distinct elements of the natural world—earth, air, fire, and water—and they used combinations of these elements to explain all natural phenomena. Each of these elements energized the universe, but each acted differently from the others. Water was the source of life; air, its breath and soul. Earth was the womb and the tomb of existence, and fire the source of light and warmth and the all-powerful sun.

   The notion of four elements permeated the thinking of classical mythmakers and led them to make the gods of earth, air, fire, and water star figures in their myths and legends. In the earliest myths, people emerged from the earth, earth emerged from the water, fire took the form of the sun and brought light to the darkness, and air took the form of wind and breathed life into the universe. As ancient mythologies developed beyond the creation stories, each of the elements became associated with a color, a season, an animal, a celestial object, and a cardinal point.

   People in other cultures identified primal elements, but they conceptualized them differently. The Greeks used their four elements to define the character of matter. The Chinese identified five elements and considered them the active forces in nature. They grouped different kinds of natural phenomena into one of the five classes. Wang Mu was the spirit of metal, Mu Kung the spirit of wood, Shui Ching-tzu the spirit of water, Ch'ih Ching-tzu the spirit of fire, and Huang Lao, the spirit of earth. The Aztec assigned a talismanic function to the same four ele-

ments recognized by the Greeks. Each of the Aztec elements defined a world age, and each destroyed the universe as the mighty gods who embodied the elements engaged in perilous battles.

   Stories of many lands told of both marriages and battles between the elements. In Greek myth, the fire god Hephaestus battled Scamander, the river deity. In Polynesia, Ke Ahi, the embodiment of fire, opposed his father, Pa'eva, the sea god. In Mesopotamia, water battled earth when Enki angered Ninhursag. Each time a sun god fought a storm god, it affirmed the mythmakers' recognition of the opposition of fire and water. Each time a bird fought a serpent, it affirmed their recognition of the opposition of air and earth. Not only did these myths and events reflect local climactic conditions, but they also reaffirmed ancient beliefs about the basic structure of the universe. (Campbell 1974, *Parabola* Spring 1995)

   See also Air and Air Gods, Aztec Calendar Stone, Dragon Slaying, Duality, Earth and Earth Gods, Feng Shui, Fire and Fire Gods, Water and Water Spirits

ENKI

Enki was the Sumerian water god and god of the Absu, the primordial freshwater ocean that lay beneath the earth. Always kind and benevolent, Enki was a helper to humanity, serving as a purifier (as water was a purifier) and rendering his assistance in times of flood. Though Enki resided in the Absu, he was considered the god of all waters. From the waters of the Absu he filled the irrigation channels. He controlled the rise and fall of the Tigris and Euphrates, arranged the pattern of the coastline, distributed the marshes around the land, and organized the fall of rain.

   Enki was often portrayed in the Absu, or in his shrine called the Absu House or E-Absu, surrounded by channels of water. He was often represented as part man and part fish or as a goat with a fish tail. In some depictions he appeared human, a man with a long beard, a horned cap, and a long, pleated robe. Sometimes he carried a vase and had streams of water running down his arms or waves springing from his shoulders.

Enki was considered a god of wisdom and magic, perhaps through his connection with the depth and mystery of the waters. His Babylonian name, Ea, meant "house of water," but the Sumerian name Enki meant "lord of the earth." His crucial connection with the earth was illustrated in the myth of Enki and Ninhursag, in which the union of the two gods, water and earth, led to the growth of vegetation. Enki's crucial role as a sustainer of life make him a primary deity, one of the principal trio of ancient gods, along with Enlil and Anu. In the Babylonian poem *Enuma Elish* he was given credit for creation, and in the Gilgamesh epic he helped humanity escape the great flood. (Black and Green 1992, Gray 1982, Mackenzie 1996)

> *See also* Absu, Mesopotamia, Ninhursag, Water and Water Spirits

ENLIL

Enlil was the Sumerian god of the earth and one of the triad of principal deities, along with Anu, the sky god, and Enki, the water god. Originally a local god of Nippur, the religious center of ancient Babylon, Enlil rose to power as supreme ruler of the earth and atmosphere. He was known as Lord of the Land, and he appeared to be the embodiment of energy and force. He was benevolent when he fought and conquered the chaos dragon, Tiamat, and destructive when he ordered the flood that destroyed humanity.

Enlil was a Sumerian deity, though his power and attributes were usurped by the Babylonian god Bel, or Marduk, as the political power of Mesopotamia shifted northward. In Sumerian, Enlil meant "Lord of the Wind or Storm," which stressed his connec-

tion with the air as well as the earth. As Lord of the Air, Enlil had total control over atmospheric forces and was said to personify the wind and the hurricane.

Enlil was worshipped along with his wife, Ninlil, a fertility goddess and a form of Ninhursag, the great earth goddess and mother of the gods. Ninhursag went by many names in different regions, and as Ninki she mated with Enki, the water god, to produce all the vegetation in the land. As Ninlil, Enlil's queen, her powers were eclipsed by her husband, however, who was worshipped throughout Mesopotamia as king of the land. Like Zeus, Enlil symbolized the forces of nature and controlled human fate. He owned the earth rather than personified it, having separated the earth from the sky and then taken possession of his realm.

Mesopotamian clay figures depict Enlil in human form with long hair, a beard, and a horned headdress, a symbol of divinity. His temple at Nippur, called E-Kur, or "House of the Mountain," was erected in the center of the city and built on an artificial mound to protect it from flood. (Black and Green 1992, Gray 1982, Mackenzie 1996)

> *See also* Earth and Earth Gods, Hurricanes and Tornadoes, Mesopotamia, Winds and Wind Gods

EYE

The eye was the most ancient and widespread sun symbol, perhaps stemming from the belief that the sun was a god who saw everything in existence as he gazed down upon the earth. All-seeing, all-knowing, that bright circular disk was the eye of the heavens, the most powerful attribute of the most venerated gods. To the Greeks, the sun was the eye of Zeus; to the Hindus, the eye of Varuna. In Egypt, entire cults developed around the eyes of Horus and Ra. To the Egyptians, that burning ball of fire characterized the solar cult and meant light, knowledge, and universal fertility.

In this ancient Egyptian hieroglyph, the sun is propelled on a boat with two watchful eyes guarding it.

Similar myths in other cultures identified the sun and the moon with the eyes of their most important gods. Such was the case with the Chinese god, P'an ku, whose body became the universe. His left eye became the sun and his right eye, the moon. The Hindu god Shiva had a third eye in the middle of his forehead, and, like the eye of Ra, it represented fire. The burning eyes of these high gods attested to their fiery nature, but they also connected the light of fire and the sun with wisdom and power. (Biedermann 1992, Chevalier and Gheerbrant 1996)

See also Mirrors, Moon and Moon Gods, Sun and Sun Gods

FENG PO

Feng Po was the Chinese wind god, called the Wind Earl or Count of the Wind. The ancient Chinese perceived wind as the breath or the soul of life, so they equipped Feng Po with tremendous powers. He proved his power when as a minister on earth he walked from place to place with enormous speed. He was thus deified after death as Lord of the Wind and became an official in the Ministry of Thunder. From thenceforth, he took his orders directly from the thunder god.

Some myths identified the wind god as a kind of monster or dragon named Fei Lein, and it was this dragon, they said, who walked so swiftly. In these stories, the wind dragon worked as a wicked minister in the tyrannical Chou dynasty. In the guise of this dragon, Feng Po had the body of a stag, the head of a bird, and the tail of a serpent. In human form, he appeared as an old man with a white beard, a yellow coat, and a blue and red cap. Feng Po held in his hands a large sack that contained the winds, and he had the power to blow them out of the sack at will, in any direction he pleased.

The dragon guise of the wind god emphasized his destructive aspect. Because in China strong winds swept over the land and dried out the vegetation, Feng Po was often associated with drought. One myth explained how Feng Po was transformed into the monster-dragon when he rebelled against the mythical emperor Huang Ti and stirred up tremendous storms. In this myth,

Yi the Archer rode on the wind to a mountaintop, where he shot an arrow at Feng Po. The arrow subdued the blustery wind god and ensured that he would no longer misuse his powers but conduct the winds in an orderly fashion.

Feng Po controlled the winds in early myths, but in later ones, a woman named Feng Pho-po played an increasingly important role. Reputed to be Feng Po's wife, she was commonly called Mrs. Wind and could often be seen riding through the clouds on her tiger. (Christie 1985, Werner 1995)

See also China, Feng Shui, Winds and Wind Gods

FENG SHUI

Feng shui is an ancient Chinese doctrine based on the notion that every part of the earth is pervaded by spirit. Feng means "wind" and shui means "water," specifically water from clouds that the wind distributes over the earth. The Chinese regard wind as the breath or the soul of life and water as the source, and they believe the two work together to create invisible currents that pulse through the earth and energize the earth spirit. But the two invisible currents do not act alone. They are continually modified by the positions of the celestial bodies, particularly the sun and the moon, as they vary their positions and set up tides and currents within the earth's magnetic field. The essence of feng shui, then, is that the patterns of the earth follow the patterns in the heavens and that the activating spirit of nature requires a balance of forces in the earth, sea, and sky.

Feng shui has been practiced from antiquity in China and throughout the Asian world and has recently become a sensation in the western world, where people now apply the principles of feng shui to the design of homes and offices. The practice involves manipulating the earth's energies, channeling the earth's forces to influence the fate and prosperity of people. In ancient times, feng shui determined how to build graves, temples, and houses to ensure a balance between the forces of nature and to allow for the free flow of "breaths," or winds. Successful manipulation of the earth's energies ensured harmony between the yin and the yang.

The principle of yin and yang asserts that opposition is essential to harmony. In ancient thought, yin was the earth spirit, represented by a serpent who glided through channels in the earth's crust. Yang was the sun, whose movement through the sky created the appropriate conditions in the earth to activate the yin. Ancient myths cast yin and yang in these roles and pitted them against each other in tales of solar dragon-slayers, such as the myth of Apollo killing Python, the serpent of the earth goddess, or Zeus killing Typhon, the spirit of the typhoon or hurricane winds and the offspring of Gaia, the earth. Because the dragon or serpent represented the earth's energies, these sun gods fixed the earth's energies in one spot when they slew the dragons. (Mackenzie 1994, Michell 1975)

> **See also** China, Dragon Slaying, Duality,
> Earth and Earth Gods, Elements,
> Serpents and Snakes, Water and Water
> Spirits, Winds and Wind Gods

FENRIR

In Norse mythology, Fenrir embodied the chaotic, destructive power of nature. He represented subterranean forces like volcanic fire. Fenrir was a gigantic wolf, so huge that his jaw stretched from the earth to the sky. He was nature in its wildest form. When wolves surfaced in the myths, and Fenrir in particular, mythmakers were attempting to portray the environment as the enemy.

One of the most popular Norse myths told of the binding of Fenrir. The dwarves forged a chain made from secret world powers, such as the roots of mountains, the noise of moving cats, and the breath of fishes. Then the gods bound Fenrir in a metaphorical at-

tempt to control nature's destructiveness. Eventually, Fenrir broke through his chains with such force he shook the world tree. The gods had tamed nature for a while, then once again it became unleashed and uncontrolled. In a land of ice and fire, of explosive volcanoes and chilling cold, the ancient Norse people seemed to believe that they could only ensure cosmic order by "binding" or somehow subduing the destructive natural forces. (Crossley-Holland 1980, Davidson 1964)

> **See also** Chaos, Scandinavia

FIRE AND FIRE GODS

Ancient people worshipped fire as they did the sun. Fire gave warmth, enabled people to have hot food, and separated people from the foreboding darkness and the enemies who lurked within it. Fire myths throughout the world emphasized the importance the ancients placed on the element while at the same time attempted to account for its origin. Because fire represented heat and light, ancient people usually traced it to the natural sources of heat and light they witnessed in their world. In some myths, fire came from the sun, in others it came from the moon or the stars, and in still others it descended from Heaven in great arrows of lightning or exploded from subterranean crevices in volcanic eruptions.

Many cultures believed their ancestors had to obtain their first fire through some act of trickery. Often they obtained fire by stealing it from someone who selfishly guarded it in some far away place. In a Tlingit myth, Raven obtained it from the sea, perhaps as an explanation for the phenomenon called phosphorescence, in which the waters appear ablaze in light. But more commonly someone stole fire from Heaven. Because fire was thought to exist in Heaven, the ability to fly made birds primary candidates for these fire missions. These types of myths served the dual purpose of explaining the origin of fire

A 102-year-old Tlingit headdress representing Raven. According to legend, Raven brought fire to the earth by stealing it from the sea.

and also the birds' bright colors. The animals generally outwitted the original fire owner but were burned, and thus colored by, the bright flames while stealing away with their treasure. During their trips home with the stolen fire, they frequently endured other hardships as their flames were nearly extinguished by wind and rain.

Many ancient fire rituals involved the use of fire to stop the rain, just as many myths told of fights between the deities of fire and water. A Melanesian legend of such a fight explained why fire will not burn in water. Ke Ahi was the embodiment of fire and the son of Pa'eva, the sea god. Ke Ahi got angry with his father and ran away to the surface, but everything Ke Ahi touched burst into flames. An old woman then killed Ke Ahi to protect her island from being destroyed by the fires. Pa'eva went looking for his son and followed his ashes to the woman's house. When Pa'eva embraced the stick that the woman used to kill his son, Ke Ahi magically returned to life.

His father took him back to the ocean, but Ke Ahi, who did not want to return, let himself die again, just as fire dies when it touches the water.

Some fire myths used fights between fire and water to explain the kindling of fire by rubbing two sticks together. In a Maori myth, fire escaped from the water by hiding in a tree. Hiding fire in trees occurred frequently in these nature myths and served as a explanation of why friction caused the sparks. People who made fire from flint often hid their fire in stone for similar reasons. A California tribe who believed lightning to be the source of fire also believed that the primordial bolt deposited the fire in wood. Because the fire lived in the wood, it could be aroused when rubbing the wood together.

Whereas many myths attributed the origin of fire to lightning, surprisingly few attributed the origin to volcanoes. In Polynesia, Maui obtained fire from the subterranean region, and in Hawaii, the fire goddess Pele was clearly connected with volcanoes. But these myths were the exception. The Greeks associated volcanoes with fire, and they put their fire gods, Hephaestus and the Cyclopes, inside volcanoes to forge metals. According to one tradition, Prometheus, the original Greek fire god, stole the fire from Hephaestus's forge, suggesting that fire originally came from volcanic forces. But more widely accepted was the belief that Prometheus stole fire from the sun. Many cultures considered fire a celestial phenomenon. Certainly the Celts did, for in both their myths and their rituals earthly fire was thought to be of the solar kind, a precious gift to humanity from the sun god.

People venerated fire all over the world, but particularly in the Celtic lands and other cold areas of Europe. Because the pagan Europeans considered fire the terrestrial counterpart of the sun in the heavens, they held fire festivals to acknowledge the power of the sun and to replicate its heat and light on earth. Bonfires lit at the Celtic festival of Beltane on the first day of May, for instance, encouraged the sun to warm the earth after a long, frozen winter. Pagan fire festivals in the Celtic world involved rolling a flaming wheel down a hillside and re-erecting it in the temple of the sky god, a ritual later adapted by Christians in the area.

Because people recognized the consequence of fire, fire rituals assumed primary importance in certain cultures. In ancient India and Persia, fire existed everywhere. Agni, the Indian fire god, was born from the wood and the sticks, from the sun, and from water in the clouds, because Agni, like fire itself, had its origin in all three spheres—in the earth, in the sky, and in the waters. Agni was the primary deity in Vedic rituals, and like the Iranian Atar, the object of a prominent fire cult. Worshippers of fire in these lands and others venerated fire as both creator and destroyer. In Norse mythology, the end of the world came when Surt, the fire demon, re-

duced the nine worlds to flame, then smoke, then nothing but ashes. But flame and fire, in Norse myths, played a role in creating the world as well. In Aztec myth, the diseased god Nanahuatzin threw himself into a bonfire and rose as a new sun. Fire was rejuvenating. Many legends dealt with the theme of renewal or rejuvenation through fire, as did the legend of the phoenix. The phoenix burned himself in his own fires, then arose, renewed, from the ashes. (Bellamy 1959, Frazer 1996)

See also Agni, Atar, Elements, Lightning, Mason–Wasp, Phoenix, Sun and Sun Gods, Volcanoes

FLOODS AND FLOOD GODS

Most people probably associate the flood myth with the biblical story of Noah and the ark, but flood myths occurred in cultures in just about every part of the world. These stories occurred worldwide because in most geographical areas, people knew firsthand of the destructive power of water. When torrential rains poured from the heavens and annihilated most of humanity in these myths, they clearly dissolved the established order of the cosmos. Deities who controlled the world's waters could show their strength and their destructive power by unleashing their fury on earth and temporarily restoring the world to its original chaotic state.

This dissolution of order was pervasive yet temporary—temporary because in most flood myths, at least two people survived to rebuild the world and continue the human race. Flood, therefore, was both an end and a beginning. It was a re-creation myth. Because in most creation myths the world began as a limitless expanse of water, in most flood myths the established world ended with that same water. When the gods inundated the land, they recreated the primordial sea. Their water abolished form and order, but, as in the beginning, it sprang forth new life.

Everyone understood the power of water. It permeated the world and nurtured the seeds necessary for growth. The ancients knew that rain fell from the sky and that rivers and streams flowed underground, so in their myths, water existed both beneath the earth and above it. Flood waters originated from either place. In Maori myth, the god Tawaki caused the flood when he cracked the crystal floor of Heaven and sent the sky waters cascading downward. Some myths attributed the great flood to the overflowing of subterranean wells; in South America, it followed the destruction of the world tree, which was connected to underground springs. In the South American myth, the flood occurred when water gushed up from the severed stem. Cutting down the world tree, or destroying the foundation of Heaven, meant the dissolution of order. The act thrust the world right back where it started, with only the formlessness associated with water.

In the story of Noah's ark, God supposedly flooded the entire world, obliterated the wickedness of humanity, and left remaining only the people who could begin a better world. But people in the biblical land of Palestine were not acquainted with natural disaster in the entire world, and neither were the tellers of other flood myths. Each group of people knew only that flood occurred in their own limited area, and they knew only that when it occurred, the survivors of their own land restored order. With flood, fire, or any natural disaster, the mythmakers experienced these events, and then they generalized them. To the Utes in the American West, the worldwide flood occurred when the Colorado River overflowed, and to the Babylonians, when the Tigris and Euphrates overflowed violently and inundated the alluvial plain. To the Hawaiians the flood occurred when the Pacific Ocean rose over their land, an event which in the myth was the work of a malevolent sea goddess.

The story of the Deluge is an ancient one.

In fact, the oldest known myth is the Sumerian Deluge story, which dates from 2400 B.C. It was likely this story that formed the basis for similar myths in surrounding areas, perhaps even for the flood myths of Greece. When the Greeks told the story, only Deucalon and Pyrrah survived and only Parnassus remained above water. When the Hindus told the story, Manu survived the flood and went on to father the current race of Indians. In myths of the Maya, Ix Chel, the water goddess, poured the torrential rains of a tropical cloudburst from her jug, and in Aztec myth, Chalchihuitlicue, the water goddess, destroyed the fourth world. In each of these places, flood waters at one time or another caused devastating destruction, so the people feared water's strength. They considered the unleashing of that strength the work of angry deities. The mythmakers used flood not only to reflect real occurrences but also to demonstrate the gods' ability to use natural disaster as a punishment for humanity's wickedness.

As mentioned before, the obliteration of form that occurred after the flood was only temporary. It was assumed that the new forms that emerged were purified and free of sin. The chosen people, such as Deucalon and Pyrrah, survived and then repopulated the world with a better, more deserving race. Among peoples of the northwest coast of America, one good man and his family survived the flood by climbing a rope to Heaven before the Great Spirit released the rains. Then when the water subsided, the man and his family climbed down from the sky to the summit of what is now Mount Rainier and repopulated the earth. Most commonly, however, people remained on the earth and survived in some type of ark or boat. The most popular of the Chinese flood myths, however, took a different slant to the story. It involved Yu, a legendary engineer, who used his ingenuity to put the water to good use. When during the reign of the Emperor Shun floodwaters threatened to destroy northern China, Yu channeled the water to the sea by making passages for streams and rivers. He stopped the flood, saved the people, and irrigated the land. As a reward for this, the people allowed Yu to found the first dynasty of China. Yu, too, recreated the world.

In the story of Yu, or in any of the flood myths that involved the death of humanity, re-creation arose as a primary theme. These stories obviously reflected an awareness of the cyclic patterns of nature. Sometimes, the mythmakers reflected nature's cycles by combining lunar myths with themes of the Deluge. When the moon was full, they said, the water was contained. But when it waned, the water drained. It poured from the heavens; it inundated the earth. The moon, once drained, emerged in new form, just as people did who came into existence after the flood. In most flood myths, it appeared that the water both destroyed and purified. The newly emerged were given a second chance. Flood myths then, involved destruction, resurrection, and purification. Humanity returned to the water from whence it came, then began again. (Bellamy 1959, Bierlin 1994, Dundes 1988, Graves 1966, Leeming 1990)

> **See also** Drought, Primordial Sea, Rain and Rain Gods, Water and Water Spirits

FOG AND MIST

When fogs and mists emerged in myths, they usually accompanied the appearance of spirits. On land they hovered over valleys or enshrouded mountaintops, and at sea they floated mysteriously above the waters. Many unusual images seemed to materialize in fogs. Human faces took shape, specter ships popped out of nowhere, and magnificent castles or entire islands suddenly glistened like magic in an ethereal, undefined realm. Fogs and mists, like clouds, drifted, and as they moved, they conjured up images and reflections in what is commonly called a mirage.

The illusive shapes formed out of floating vapors gave rise to stories of mythical lands beyond the sea. They led to fabrications of the elusive Otherworld. In Celtic myth, fog covered the area leading to the Islands of the Blessed, that mysterious paradise and home of the Immortals. The Chinese told of palaces in the sea mist, and the Japanese too believed they saw palaces in the fog, the undersea palaces of sea gods. In Norse myth, Nifflheim was the home of fog and mist, a region of darkness inhabited by frost giants. The mirage or fog bank revealed all sorts of reflections readily perceived as magical—mountain paradises, submerged cities, phantom ships, or elusive realms of immortal beings that could only be reached by crossing the water and penetrating the fog.

The mythology that developed around fog and mist was similar to that which developed around clouds. Just as people imagined forms in the floating clouds, they imagined forms in the hovering fogs and mists. Sometimes mists, like clouds, appeared to resemble sheep or cattle, so Huaillepenyi, the god of fog to the Araucanians of Chile, took the form of a sheep with a calf's head and a seal's tail. Sometimes, the forms appeared human. In Wales, the mist rising above a river was thought to be a spirit of the dead. In Iceland, the fog was thought to be the king's daughter under some magic spell. The way mists appeared and disappeared did seem magical; in Finland, it was thought that mists were brewed by wizards, and in Germany, by witches, elves, or dwarfs. To the Finns, an air deity named Udutan or Terhenetar caused the mist by holding a sieve and siphoning moisture from the sky to the earth. To the peoples of the northeast coast of America, the billowing fog that floated around Martha's Vineyard was thought to be the pipe smoke of Maushope, the giant who inhabited the island. To the Maori, the mists that frequently rose over the islands were the grievous sighs of Papa, the earth, rising to the sky and to her sky god, Rangi, for whom she forever mourned after their separation in the early stages of the universe. The Maori had another myth that explained both the appearance and disappearance of mists. Hine-pukohu-rangi was Sky Mist Woman and Hine-wai, her sister, was the rain, specifically the rain that falls in foggy weather. At night, Sky Mist Woman descended to earth to visit her lover in secrecy, and at dawn, her sister called out to warn them that daylight was coming. Sky Mist Woman and her sister returned to the sky. But because Sky Mist Woman had warned her human lover never to tell of their trysts and he did, she never returned to him. He searched and searched for her until, finally, he died. After his death, he became the rainbow that accompanies the mist. (Bassett 1971, Orbell 1996)

See also Clouds, Mirage, Sheep and Cattle

FORESTS

In ancient times, vast forests covered much of the earth, so naturally the people who lived close to the land felt a certain reverence for the majesty and mystery of their dense, dark world. Massive trees towered high into the sky and blocked out the light as they canopied the earth in a tangled mass of leaves and branches. Underneath the trees in the darkness, nature seemed wild and uncontrolled. People had to fight the forest creatures to survive, so the forest itself represented nature in its wildest form.

Life in the forest was dangerous, and the place itself, a foreboding force. When early hunters ventured into the secluded darkness, they feared for their lives, and many lost them to wolves and bears and other wild animals. But in myths and legends, not only wild animals inhabited forests but also elves, dwarves, giants, and fairies. No one knew exactly what forces might dwell there in the darkness, so mythmakers conjured up the most mysterious creatures imaginable. The Leshy inhabited the forests of Russia and perhaps embodied the forest itself. The Leshy disappeared every autumn when the leaves fell from the trees and reappeared in the spring acting wild and untamable. This creature was not evil unless provoked, but was mischievous, like a trickster, and changeable, like the forest itself. The Leshy hated hibernating in winter, and when he stirred to action in the spring, he often caused travelers in the forest to get lost in the quickly sprouting underbrush.

The Leshy and many of the creatures who inhabited forests were threatening, and some of them were dangerous. Forests in myths became symbols of human fear. Ancient stories were full of evil forest demons who caused disease or death and often did so to punish hunters for overkilling the animals who lived within the forest walls. But benevolent forest creatures existed too, and often times they protected hunters. Forests were among the first places dedicated to the gods for this reason. Sacrifices were performed there and offerings were hung from trees to propitiate the forest gods. In a place that represented nature in its most chaotic and destructive form, it seemed wise, even essential, to call upon the earth deities for protection against demons and help in taming the land. The forest after all, provided food plants and game animals, so the benevolent forest gods had the power to help in hunting and gathering. (Frazer 1950, Harva 1964, Porteous 1968)

See also Celtic Lands, Trees

FREY

The Norse god of sun and rain, Frey was the embodiment of springtime showers, summer warmth, and bountiful harvests. He was young and beautiful and traveled either on a boar with golden bristles that symbolized sunbeams, or, in some myths, in a boar-drawn chariot similar to the Greek Apollo's chariot of the sun. Frey's boars traveled through the sky and under the earth, like the sun, and represented the golden light that graced the northern lands only during the summer months. His magic ship, Skidbladnir, traveled on earth, sea, and sky and represented the bright summer clouds.

One of the most popular myths of Frey involved his marriage to Gerd, an enchanting Norse frost giantess whose radiant beauty lit up the earth and the heavens. Some mythologists believed this meant Gerd personified the aurora borealis, or the northern lights, but others believed that first and foremost she personified the frozen earth. In a myth called *Skirnismal* or *Skymir's Journey*, Frey fell madly in love with the icy giantess and tried desperately to win her favor. Frey sent his servant, Skymir, to help plead with Gerd and offer her apples and a golden ring. But only when Skymir resorted to threats did she relent and agree to marry the sun god. Because she finally yielded to his love, the marriage of Frey and Gerd likely represented the conquering of winter by the summer sun.

Several elements of this seasonal myth lent credence to this interpretation. Gerd refused Frey for a long time before she finally accepted his marriage offer. She resisted his offer of apples, a symbol of fruitfulness, and gave in to him only under fierce threats, perhaps representing the fierce heat of the summer sun. Skymir threatened Gerd with barrenness and eternal marriage to a cold, icy frost giant. But she still made Frey wait— nine long months, the length of a frozen northern winter—while she remained with Gymil, the frost giant, in a home safely guarded by watchdogs said to personify winter winds. Frey's threats likely symbolized the threat of the sun's heat to the stubborn ice of winter, and his love likely symbolized the warmth of the summer sun that melted the frozen fields. The ice giantess, however, like the fields, reluctantly yielded to the sun's embrace. (Crossley-Holland 1980, Page 1990)

See also Freya, Frost and Ice, Frost Giants, Njord, Scandinavia, Seasons, Sun and Sun Gods

FREYA

In the Norse myths, Freya was a beautiful goddess of love, a Vanir deity, the daughter of Njord and Skadi and the twin sister of Frey. Mythologists have called her both an earth goddess and a sky goddess, for she had qualities and possessions that identified her with both realms. First and foremost, however, Freya was a fertility goddess noted for her promiscuity, her tears, her plumed headdress, and her sparkling necklace. She was incredibly beautiful, and all the gods, giants, and dwarfs tried to possess her, just as the icy frost of winter tried to overpower the earth's fruitfulness.

Freya shunned the icy giants just as the summer warmth shunned the winter cold. But she did engage in trysts with many gods, among them Odin, Frey, and Odur, all of them associated with sun and fertility. Freya's husband, Odur, was a god of the summer sun and Freya loved him dearly. Unfortunately, however, Odur liked to roam, and Freya cried many tears of grief. The tears that fell in the seas turned to amber and the tears that fell on the land penetrated the rocks and turned to gold. Freya's tears connected her to both the sky and the earth, as they were said to symbolize both the golden corn seeds and the fertilizing summer rains.

Freya's tears identified her as a fertility goddess, and her two most prized possessions strengthened that identification. Freya loved jewels and all sorts of bodily adornment, and she often wore falcon plumes that enabled her to fly and were thought to symbolize the summer clouds. When Freya saw the dwarfs making a necklace one day, she found the piece of jewelry so beautiful she gave herself to each of the craftsmen in order to own it. The necklace, called Brisinga-men or Brisling's necklace, became, along with her plumed headdress, her most popular attribute. Some said it was an emblem of the stars; others called it a symbol of the earth's fruitfulness. The necklace has been alternately identified as the rainbow, the moon, the Morning or Evening Star, the Milky Way, the red dawn, or the sun setting in the sea.

Freya was often depicted riding a chariot drawn by cats and sometimes as riding along in the boar-drawn chariot of her brother, Frey, scattering fruits and flowers on the land. In Germanic myths, Freya was often confused with Frigg, perhaps in part because the feather headdress Freya wore as she sailed through the sky signified the clouds. (Guerber 1980, MacCullough 1964)

See also Frey, Frigg, Scandinavia, Seasons, Tears

FRIGG

Frigg was a Norse fertility goddess and the embodiment of both the earth and the sky and clouds. Like most fertility goddesses, Frigg was likened to Mother Earth, though more accurately she exerted influence over the atmosphere. Like the Greek goddess Hera, Frigg controlled the clouds, married the high god of the pantheon, and mothered many of the gods and goddesses of the land. Frigg lived with the high god, Odin, in the sky but spent most of her time in Fensalir, her palace of mists. In Fensalir she sat at her spinning wheel along with eleven hand-maidens, spinning strands of golden thread into brightly colored clouds.

Frigg was known for her elaborate weaving ability, and her spinning wheel was immortalized in the heavens. Norse mythmakers called the constellation Orion Frigg's Distaff, a distaff being the part of the spinning wheel that holds the fiber from which the thread is drawn. As a weaver, Frigg perhaps served a similar function to the Greek Fates, who were also weavers and who controlled time by measuring lengths of fiber through their spinning wheels. Frigg, too, was considered a mistress of time because she knew the future but never disclosed it. Frigg worked diligently on her jewel-studded spinning wheel, and each night as she spun,

The Norse fertility goddess Frigg being pulled in her chariot by two catlike beasts.

the wheel turned. Like the stars spinning around the polar axis, the glittering jewels rotated and sparkled on the gigantic spindle and lit up the heavens.

Frigg was tall and beautiful and often had plumes crowning her head and keys hanging from a golden girdle around her waist. The heron plumes, it was thought, were symbols of the feathery clouds, and the keys were symbols of the northern housewives whom she guarded and protected. As goddess of clouds, Frigg wore either white or dark clothes, depending on her moods. (Guerber 1980, Krupp 1996a)

See also Clouds, Freya, Scandinavia, Spinning and Weaving

FROST AND ICE

Myths of frost and ice commonly appeared in lands where the numbing cold posed a continual threat to survival. People created these myths when they had little protection against the cold; they feared it, so they made frost and ice hostile beings who materialized as summer gave way to winter and the earth became dead and cold. During this time of year, sparkling crystals encrusted the land, beautiful crystals, yet deadly. So when the ancients saw icy magic cover the earth, they often considered it the work of malevolent deities.

Because frost and ice were both lovely and deadly, both aspects appeared in the myths. In Norse mythology, the frost giantesses looked beautiful and alluring, yet the entire race personified the harsh, destructive forces of winter. Winter spirits typically controlled the weather and had the power to bring severe storms that ravaged the earth. In Finland, Frost Woman and Frost Man had these powers, Frost Man bringing the frost that covered the fields in the morning, and Frost Woman bringing the frost that covered the fields at night. Moroz, the Russian Father Frost, a blacksmith, used his chains of ice to bind the earth and sea. People attempted to placate these gods with offerings and sacrifices to prevent them from causing blizzards, death, and destruction.

The threat of freezing to death in the ancient world permeated ancient thought. It was a giant concern, so the mythmakers made the deities who personified cold giants themselves. Throughout the cold months, these winter giants waged war against the summer and won battle after battle. They lived in the frigid north and they cast icy death spells on victims struggling to recapture the warmth of summer and to protect the fields from the giants' death grip. The Norsemen believed that a plumed giant named Hraesvelgr sat at the extreme north of the heavens and raised his arms to send icy north winds over the earth. Some North American tribes envisioned the winter giant as an old man with a beard of icicles who also lived in the north, in a teepee on a snowy mountaintop. When people visited

him and smoked a pipe with him in his teepee, the Winter Giant cast his freezing spell on his visitor and froze him to death.

Ice, frost, and freezing winds generally emanated from the north, so harsh, cruel winter giants of all sorts lived there. Many of them personified the North Wind, the wind that brought the frost and stilled the world with its icy breath. The cruel giant Waziya of the Lakota personified the North Wind. He dressed in wolf skins, controlled the snow and the ice, and delighted in causing winter deaths. Waziya lived in an ice-covered teepee in the sky, and he guarded the entrance to the aurora borealis, or the northern lights. Early skywatchers often associated the aurora and other northern sky phenomena with ice and frost. In Australian aboriginal myths, frost originated with the seven stars of the Pleiades. According to these stories, the stars were once seven sisters who lived on earth, and they sparkled with icicles because they were so cold. They took refuge in the sky, where once a year they pulled icicles from their bodies and threw them to earth. The Pleiades, in the southern hemisphere, rose in the sky in the winter months and heralded the cold weather, frost, and ice. (Dennis 1992)

See also Aurora, Frost Giants, Giants, Moroz, Pleiades, Snow

FROST GIANTS
In Norse mythology, frost giants, or Jotuns, personified the cold northern European winters dominated by snow and ice. They lived in the frozen, glacial land of Jotunheim beneath the ground underneath the roots of the world ash tree, Yggdrasil. The early settlers of Iceland and the Germanic lands fought a constant battle with the elements; their world was dominated by icy waters, crashing waves, monstrous glaciers, and bitter cold. Somehow, the settlers had to defeat these elements, and they symbolized that challenge by creating frost giants, the first living beings. Like

the wild, destructive forces of nature, the giants had to be defeated before Aesir, the land of the gods, could be created.

Frost giants dominated the Norse myths, and the gods intermingled with them constantly. The giants in general were hostile and destructive, but some of their women, like the snow-covered cliffs, were exceptionally beautiful. In several stories, sun gods married ice giantesses, and the union of the two symbolized the penetration of the frozen earth by the summer sun. These myths came primarily from Iceland, and the Vikings told them to signify the seemingly miraculous, though temporary, melting of the ice that occurred each year. During these brief summer months, the land turned from ice to stone. Some frost giants, too, turned to stone when touched by the sun's rays. The Germanic race of frost giants remained locked in the earth, because they could only thrive in darkness and fog. (Crossley-Holland 1980, Guerber 1980, Time-Life 1985)

See also Frey, Frost and Ice, Giants,
Moroz, Njord, Scandinavia

FUJIYAMA

Mount Fuji, or Fujiyama, the most sacred mountain in Japan, was revered by people of both Shinto and Buddhist faiths as an abode of the Immortals. The gods who lived there had to be powerful, the people surmised, because the mountain arose so suddenly, in just one night, after a fiery eruption during the earthquake of A.D. 286. Fujiyama is the youngest of the Japanese mountains, but it is also the tallest. In Buddhist myth, another mountain, Mt. Haku, was said to be higher than Fuji at one time, but Fuji, personified as a goddess, beat the god of Haku on the head. She cracked his skull into eight pieces, the mountain's eight peaks, and reduced his height. Fujiyama then stood as the loftiest and most magnificent mountain in Japan.

The Japanese considered Mount Fuji the center of the world. They considered it the source of the Water of Life, which in Buddhist myth flowed from a stream on the slopes guarded by Sengen, the goddess whom some believed to be the daughter of the mountain god. The Shinto worshiped Sengen as Sakuyu Hime. They said that a childless couple found her in a bamboo grove at the foot of the mountain one day, and when she grew up, she returned to the mountain. She had grown into a lovely woman, and her husband loved her desperately. But Sakuyu Hime left him to return to the Palace of the Immortals on the summit, leaving him only a mirror in which he could see her image. Her husband chased after her but never found her, and in desperation he jumped from the peak of Fujiyama, clutching the mirror in his hand. His burning love for his mountain goddess set fire to the mirror, and the smoke from that fire could be seen for many years as the smoke that rose from the volcanic Mount Fuji. Sakuyu Hime remained on the mountain and was believed to protect people from the eruptions. (Bernbaum 1990, Davis 1992, Piggott 1983)

See also Japan, Meru, Mountains,
Olympus, Volcanoes, Well of Life

GAIA

Gaia was the Greek Mother Earth, the most ancient divinity born out of chaos. She was the female creative principle and the personification of the physical earth. The earth goddess was the object of a widespread cult but was gradually displaced by more humanized goddesses who embodied the same creative principle. Though Gaia embodied the entire planet, to the Greeks she more likely personified their particular area of earth and the fertile power of the land. The mountains were her breasts, the caves her womb, the earth's waters her female fluids. She gave birth to Ouranos, the sky, then mated with him to create the first races of mankind.

As Mother Earth, Gaia compared with similar personages in myths of almost every culture. She was Prithvi in India, Papa in Polynesia, and Ki or Ninhursag in Mesopotamia. In the beginning, when Gaia existed alone, she was barren and needed a mate to become fertile. So she created Ouranos, the sky, and the two joined together. His rain fertilized her like semen and she became fruitful, growing trees and flowers and fruits and vegetables and laying the foundation for future life. (Bell 1991, Leeming 1990, Rose 1959)

See also Earth and Earth Gods, Greece and Rome, Ouranos

GANGES RIVER

Like the Nile in Egypt, the Ganges is the lifeblood of India. It flows down from the Himalayan Mountains and winds through the middle of the country to irrigate the fields and provide sustenance to the Indian people. Hindu mythmakers personified their sacred river as the great goddess, Ganga, who rose from the ocean of milk when the gods and demons churned it to obtain the elixir of immortality and many other treasures of the waters. When Ganga rose from the milk ocean, the great god Shiva placed her in the turban on his head and kept her all to himself.

Shiva's abode was high in the Himalayas, and Ganga lived there with him, keeping her moisture confined to the mountains. At the beginning Ganga was small, and Shiva kept her contained. But as time progressed, she grew larger and more abundant. It was then that the sage Bhagarathi prayed to the gods to release Ganga and allow her to flow down the mountains and water the lands. According to some sources, Ganga did not desire to leave her mountain home with the gods, so she threatened to rush down the mountain with great force and drown all the people. Shiva stopped her. He allowed her to flow through his hair, which acted like a dense forest and siphoned her into rivulets. The Ganges today flows gently down the mountains, through the forests, and then splits up into tributaries.

The Hindus created Ganga to explain their river's origin in the Himalayas. As god of the Himalayas and Ganga's protector, Shiva assumed the name of Ganga-dhara, which meant "upholder of the Ganges." But the myth of Ganga's fall assumed greater significance viewed in light of the people's reverence of the river water. The Himalayas was the abode of Heaven, an elusive realm above the high peaks, obscured by mist and clouds and endowed with all the mystery and majesty of the sacred mountain. Before the Ganges reached earth, it had to flow through the abode of Heaven, where it was believed to form the Milky Way in the sky. It then coursed down the mountains, through the earth, and penetrated the Underworld. The great goddess Ganga then watered the entire world. (Ions 1984, Thomas 1980, Zimmer 1962)

See also Churning the Ocean, India, Mountains, Rivers and Lakes, Shiva

GA-OH

The Iroquois of northeastern America worshipped Ga-oh as the spirit of the winds. He was a giant and, like the wind itself, benevolent but restless and sometimes violent. Ga-oh lived in the sky in a house or, some say, in a mountain cave called "The House of Winds." From his home, Ga-oh turned the seasons and sent the winds blustering down to earth.

Some mythologists say the wind giant of the Iroquois kept the winds locked up in his house, trapped inside the cave until he received orders from the Great Spirit to release them. Others say the four winds prowled outside the House of Winds and guarded it. Each of Ga-oh's winds were personified as animals and assigned specific duties. A bear sent the north wind, a panther sent the west wind, a moose sent the east wind, and a fawn sent the south wind. (Burland 1985)

See also North America, Tate, Winds and Wind Gods

GARUDA BIRD

In Hindu mythology, Garuda was a gigantic bird with the wings and talons of an eagle and the body and limbs of a man. He was Vishnu's bird, a sacred bird, a demigod, and a symbol of wind. As king of birds and a vehicle for Vishnu as the sun, Garuda appeared to be not only a manifestation of the wind but also a personification of the sky.

Garuda gained his reputation for "mocking the wind" when he stole a moon goblet of the magic elixir, Soma, from the gods to

In Hindu mythology, Garuda was Vishnu's bird, a sacred bird, a demigod, and a symbol of wind.

give to the demons. He did this because the demons had imprisoned his mother, Diti, and demanded the Soma for her release. The Soma was trapped inside a mountain cave surrounded by roaring flames and violent winds. To save his mother, Garuda drank up rivers and put out the fire that flamed up around the mountain. Then swiftly, he flew inside the mountain, stole the Soma, and delivered it to the demons. The demons, in return, released Diti. From that day forward, Garuda was said to "mock the wind with his fleetness."

Garuda appeared in many pictures, usually carrying Vishnu and sometimes Vishnu's consort, Lakshmi, on his back. Usually described as a kind of eagle, the Garuda bird had a long beak and brightly colored feathers, predominantly of red, green, and blue. Sometimes he was represented as a peacock with a long tail and a golden body. He glowed like the blazing sun. Because of his brightness, and perhaps because of his swiftness, some sources identify him with lightning and with Agni, the fire god. Just after his birth, he was said to have been worshipped as an incarnation of Agni because he glowed so beautifully when he was born. (Knappert 1995b, Mackenzie 1971, Moor 1984)

See also Agni, Birds, India, Lightning, Thunderbirds, Winds and Wind Gods

GEB

In ancient Egypt, Geb personified the earth. He represented the earth as an element and he embodied the earth's surface. Geb stretched out over the land and was usually seen raised on his elbows and with one knee bent, to signify the mountains and valleys. With plants, trees, and herbs sprouting from his body and a erect phallus extending to the sky, he presented himself as a vegetation god and represented the earth's fertilizing power.

Like earth deities from other cultures, Geb embodied the creative power of the land. Though he differed from the traditional female earth goddess in Indo-European myths, he retained some of her aspects. Geb was the male creative principle, the phallic power of the universe, and his erection signified the earth's ability to procreate. The reason the Egyptians personified their earth as a god rather than a goddess reflected the unique climactic conditions of Egypt. In most cultures, semen from sky gods fell to the earth like fertilizing rain. But in ancient Egypt, it hardly ever rained. To them, the fertilizing water came from the Nile River, and the Nile River dominated the earth. Geb's tears filled the seas and his semen fertilized the sky goddess, Nut, who produced Isis, Osiris, Seth, and Nephthys. (Frazer 1926, Ions 1983)

See also Earth and Earth Gods, Egypt, Nile River, Nut, Tears

GEMINI, THE TWINS

Castor and Pollux, the two stars that dominate the constellation of Gemini, gave the third sign of the zodiac its label as heavenly twins. People have recognized these stars as twins from antiquity, and they wove the story of this celestial duo into their sky legends. In India, the stars were twin horsemen, in Egypt they were the twin gods Horus the Elder and Younger. The Eskimos called them two door-stones of an igloo, the Arabs called them twin peacocks, and other ancient cultures believed them to be two young goats.

But the Greeks named the twins Castor and Pollux, twin brothers immortalized and placed in the sky by Zeus as a reward for their brotherly love.

In the classical myth, Castor and Pollux were the sons of Zeus and Leda, hero warriors in the tale of *Jason and the Argonauts*. The brothers joined Jason in his quest for the golden fleece as protectors of his ship. Castor died in battle and was destined to be separated from Pollux forever, because Pollux was immortal. But the two brothers never wished to be separated, and they begged Zeus to help them. Zeus obliged and let Castor share Pollux's immortality. He placed the brothers in the sky as stars but stipulated that they change shifts, one occupying the realm of Heaven while the other occupied the Underworld. This alternation of life and death explained the celestial movement of the two stars. When Castor set in the west or rose in the east, Pollux followed him immediately afterward.

The movement of Castor and Pollux also symbolized the alternation of day and night. Six thousand years ago, the two stars served as indicators of the first new moon of the year. They marked the equinox, the time of year when day and night were of equal length. Castor and Pollux appeared equally bright and rose and set at equal intervals. Today, thousands of years after these heavenly twins ceased to mark the equinox, Castor and Pollux still symbolize the season of equal day and night over which they presided in ancient times. These two conspicuous stars, the closest two stars in the northern hemisphere, mark the heads of the warrior brothers of Gemini, standing together forever, arm and arm in the sky. (Krupp 1995b, Ridpath 1988, Staal 1988)

See also Constellations, St. Elmo's Fire, Zodiac

GEYSERS

In lands where underground water comes in contact with hot volcanic rock, the water boils and bubbles, and in the case of geysers, periodically erupts. The underground pressure builds up, as if the heated water were in a gigantic steam cooker. It bursts, and the steaming water spurts up into the air. Before science explained this phenomenon, it seemed that only some supernatural force could cause water to boil without fire.

Geysers are commonly found in Iceland, New Zealand, and in parts of North America, particularly in Wyoming in what is now Yellowstone National Park and in certain areas along the west coast, including an area in the Cascade Mountains north of San Francisco. Long ago, when people discovered the perplexing phenomena, they believed spirits empowered the water, spirits they believed to be evil. The peoples who lived around Yellowstone feared these spirits, apparently so much so that they rarely mentioned them, and thus they left little mythological material about the geysers. But some of the peoples prayed to the geysers. Some thought the water made them invisible. Others thought the noise that accompanied the geysers came from spirits underground, forging weapons. It appeared that everyone who encountered these phenomena recognized spirit within them, and they knew that that spirit must have moved and heated the water for a reason.

According to one legend, the peoples in the San Francisco area attributed the geysers to the spirit of a bear. Two young hunters shot a grizzly bear one day, but the bear escaped, and the hunters followed the wounded animal up a canyon to ensure their kill. When they finally spotted the grizzly at the bottom of a gorge, they found him dead, and to their amazement, they also found steaming water spouting from the hills all around him. The water smelled like sulfur, and the earth trembled beneath them. The frightened hunters witnessed what they believed to be a manifestation of the bear's evil spirit. But in myths and legends, early people

believed spirits heated underground water for curative purposes, and the tribal Medicine Man said the grizzly likely brought the steam to heal his wounds. From then on, the people took their sick to the geysers there so the water might heal them too. (Edmonds and Clark 1989, Hultkrantz 1981)

See also Springs and Wells, Volcanoes, Water and Water Spirits

GIANTS

Giants appeared in myths and legends as races of colossal beings with superhuman powers. Most likely, mythmakers created giants to explain giant forces that moved their world. Often these beings arose as the first races of people, such as the Titans of Greek lore and the frost giants, or Jotuns, of Scandinavia. When people of average size inherited the land, they had to battle these giants and defeat them, just as they had to battle the forces of nature that seemed monstrous, evil, and uncontrollable.

Giants probably originated as personifications of gigantic landforms, earthquakes and volcanoes, glaciers, and violent storms and cyclones. The ancients could not explain these natural phenomena scientifically, but they recognized them as enemies and perceived them as destructive. So early people created large creatures made of frost and ice to explain glaciers. They created men of superhuman strength racing across the sky to explain storm clouds. They attributed the thunder to a giant's booming voice and the earthquakes to the stomping of his feet, and they envisioned giants gouging out river valleys, then crying gigantic tears to fill them up.

Many legends told of giants either creating or becoming such landforms as mountains, boulders, islands, and large bodies of water. In Scandinavia, the giants survived only in darkness and fog, and as soon as the sunlight touched them, they turned to stone. One of the most popular mythological giants was Atlas, the Greek Titan, whose myths explained the creation of the Atlas Mountains that the Greeks believed held up the sky. In the most famous myth relating to Atlas, the giant was sentenced to support the sky on his shoulders when Zeus and the Olympians wrested power from the Titans. Another myth recounted the story of Perseus showing Atlas the head of the gorgon whom he had killed in one of his famous battles. Atlas was petrified, literally, and turned into the mountain bearing his name. His beard and hair became the forests, his arms and shoulders the cliffs, his bones the rocks, and his head the summit. Each part increased in size until he finally became large enough to support the sky. (Heller 1979, Time-Life 1985, Vitaliano 1973)

See also Canyons, Earthquakes, Frost and Ice, Frost Giants

GIBIL

Gibil was the fire god of ancient Babylon, and he represented fire in both its creative and destructive aspects. The Babylonians used fire for magical purposes, and they called upon Gibil for help in driving away demons. Because Gibil succeeded in burning the demons of disease, his fire served as a purifier. He destroyed evil, or the effects of evil, and his worshippers considered him a healing deity.

That the Mesopotamians practiced this type of magic indicates that they peopled the world both with good spirits and with demons. It means that they knew the power of fire and considered it a supernatural force. Some scholars believe that Gibil, the fire god, was assimilated into the fire god Nusku during a later period. Both deities were frequently invoked during burning rituals, and both then used their powers to burn the offending demons or evil sorcerers. Nusku personified the light of fire and the sun. Because the Mesopotamian fire god embodied the full strength of his element, his powers were as creative as the light that dispelled the evils

of darkness and as destructive as the scorching sun during the heat of summer. (Jayne 1962)

See also Agni, Fire and Fire Gods, Mesopotamia

GLACIERS

Huge masses of ice inspired myths and legends, as did every other impressive show of nature's strength. Enormous sheets of ice floating in the polar regions gave rise to legends of floating islands and legends that identified these frozen lands as the homes of evil spirits, malevolent sea demons, or wicked goblins and trolls. The polar ice caps break up around the edges with huge cracking sounds the Norse mythmakers explained as the cracking of a cauldron or Thor's hammer on the heads of the frost giants. Despite such breaking at the edges, glaciers remain as rivers of ice. They expand and contract, but they usually remain frozen solid and unbreakable for centuries.

Glaciers form in the polar regions and in areas of high altitude where more snow falls in the winter than melts in the summer. The snow compacts and turns to ice, a process that, in the case of mountainous glaciers, begins on the peaks. New Zealand's Franz Joseph Glacier, according to myth, formed from a young girl's tears that streamed down the snow-capped mountains when she cried hard and long after her lover fell to his death on the rocks. Her hapless lover lived on the plains and was not accustomed to climbing mountains, but he wanted to be with his lover. When he fell, the girl collapsed sobbing on the peaks. Her flood of tears eventually formed a river of ice, which the gods hardened and turned into a glacier—the Franz Joseph Glacier, which now stands beneath the Southern Alps.

In myth, the formation of glaciers occurred when the chill of winter overpowered the earth. When the winter gods cast their icy spells, plant life died, the ground froze solid, and rivers and streams stopped flowing to the sea. In a myth from Alaska that explained the formation of an enormous glacier on the Stickeen River, the ice god got angry when the river refused to fall to his powers. While the other waters froze, the Stickeen continued flowing. The ice god had an icicle spear and a voice as strong as the winter wind, so strong that it shook the snow out of the clouds. He gathered up the snow and threw it into the river. He covered the river with a bridge of ice so the people could no longer fish there. Then the vengeful god demanded two human lives to remedy the situation. When two people volunteered for the sacrifice, the elated ice god stamped on the bridge and broke it, opening up the water, but leaving one large chunk of ice behind. (Ferguson 1996, Skinner 1899, Vitaliano 1973)

See also Frost and Ice, Frost Giants, Tears

GLOOSKAP

Glooskap was a culture hero of the American Northeast, a character who manipulated the environment for the good of mankind. He existed at the beginning of the world and would exist at the end. Glooskap was a trickster, but he was also a demiurge, creating the sky and earth out of his mother's body and embodying the benevolent creative force in nature. The Algonquin Indians and neighboring tribes told many stories of Glooskap's controlling the land and taming the natural forces.

Whereas Glooskap symbolized the good in nature, his twin brother, Malsum, symbolized the evil. After Glooskap made the earth and sky, Malsum made the mountains and valleys, the thickets and rocks, and all the poisonous animals and snakes that harmed the people and caused problems for mankind. Malsum eventually killed Glooskap with the feather of an owl. But like Balder of Norse myth, Glooskap was resurrected. He then killed Malsum, who went to live in the Underworld as a wolf while Glooskap remained on earth and continued to help mankind by driving away evil.

Glooskap softened the harsh forces of nature in many ways. He tamed the wind bird, killed the Stone Giants, and saved the country from drought by releasing waters from a monster frog who swallowed up all the rivers and lakes. Perhaps the most popular legend of Glooskap told how he melted the Winter Giant and returned summer to the earth. Glooskap wandered far into the freezing north, where he met the Winter Giant and shared a pipe with him in his teepee while the giant told him captivating tales. But all the while the Winter Giant was casting his freezing winter spell on Glooskap, and soon the hero fell asleep, much like in hibernation. When Glooskap awoke, he started toward home and met a tiny fairy with green garlands on her hair who he recognized as the embodiment of summer. He tucked her away in his coat and took her back to the Winter Giant's teepee. Her heat radiated from Glooskap's coat and overpowered the giant's spell. He began to sweat, and finally he melted away. The sun came out, the grass grew, and the flowers bloomed. Glooskap had captured summer and could then return her to the elves and fairies. (Hardin 1993, Spence 1989)

See also North America, Seasons, Tricksters

GRANNOS

Grannos was an important healing deity among the Celts, associated with the sun god Apollo and connected with the curative powers the sun instilled in the waters when it descended beneath the earth at night. In Celtic thought, the sun made nighttime stops in underground waters when it fell below the horizon. Grannos, or Apollo Grannos, was known as the patron deity of thermal springs. Together with his consort Sirona, he presided over many curative springs in the

Celtic world and was widely worshipped as a healing power.

The Celtic Apollo surfaced in the myths with various surnames and various partners. Sirona was worshipped as a fertility goddess, as were other of Apollo's consorts, and all of them had connections to underground water, hot springs, and healing. Throughout the Celtic world, people took pilgrimages to thermal springs. It was there they evoked the power of Apollo Grannos, left him coins and other offerings, and purified themselves in his waters. Sometimes the people remained by the springs and went into "healing sleeps" in hopes that the great sun god would appear to them in a vision. (Green 1986, 1992, Jayne 1962)

See also Apollo, Celtic Lands, Springs and Wells, Sulis

GREAT SPIRIT

People have always tried to comprehend the power that moves the universe. That power they personify as the Great Spirit, the all-seeing and all-knowing creator who remains untouchable and unseen, somewhere in the sky. Native Americans commonly refer to their Supreme Being as the Great Spirit, but this personified power exists in the minds of people in many other parts of the world as well. In polytheistic societies, the Great Spirit dictates his orders to the lesser gods who manifest themselves in the natural forces that affect people on earth.

Though many people regard all natural phenomena as emanations of the Great Spirit, he himself remains invisible. Numerous myths and legends mention him, but he does not play a leading role in these stories, as do the sun gods who drive chariots, the storm gods who hurl lightning bolts, or the sea gods who rouse the waves. The Great Spirit exists in the sky realm, and he never crosses the boundaries to the earth or the sea. However, he acts as caretaker for the universe he created. He established the laws of

nature and he achieved cosmic balance. So he continues to act as divine judge. When people are worthy, he rewards them, but when they challenge the laws he established, he uses his power over nature to set things right. He sends rain as a blessing, for instance, and flood as a punishment.

Societies who believe in a Great Spirit often say they hear his voice when the thunder roars or they recognize his presence when they behold a mountain. They often say this great sky power is surrounded by light. For this reason, the Great Spirits or Supreme Beings in many lands are the sun gods, or, perhaps more commonly, the sky gods associated not only with light but also with any forces that emanate from the celestial realm. People who live close to nature today recognize the Great Spirit just as early people did long ago. Overwhelmed by the magnificence and incomprehensibility of the natural forces, people of all times and places seemed to know that only something equally magnificent and incomprehensible could explain them. (Hultkrantz 1967, Mbiti 1970)

See also North America, Sky and Sky Gods

GREECE AND ROME

The gods of the Greeks and Romans commanded the elements. In all that has been theorized and written about these deities, on that issue, scholars agree. Possibly the gods originally personified the natural forces, but clearly their powers permeated the world. Supernaturals existed everywhere, from the heights of Mount Olympus to the depths of the Underworld. They inhabited trees, rocks, rivers, and springs. They all mingled in human affairs. The highest gods had control over the strongest physical forces, and they either helped or hindered mortals by manipulating nature's powers.

The gods of Greece maintained their influence and their appeal for centuries. The Romans had no pantheon of their own but

This statue of the Greek sea god Poseidon in a fountain at the Library of Congress in Washington, D.C., exemplifies the enduring influence of Greek mythology.

adopted the deities from the Greeks and as- similated them into their own culture. The classical mythmakers created some of the most colorful and memorable characters in the world. When thunder gods in other lands rode chariots across the sky, people often en- visioned the robust, bearded Zeus. When sea gods in other lands roused the waves, people envisioned the tempestuous Poseidon. The Greek gods had human characteristics, and people recognized in them human foibles. Because these gods controlled the phenom- ena of nature and yet had identifiable traits, they made the physical world a less frighten- ing place.

The ancients created nature myths by combining imagination with experience. They felt the wind move through the air, so they imagined a bird in flight. They heard the thunder rumble in the sky, so they imagined something they actually saw when they heard a similar rumble—the wheels of a chariot. The weather of ancient Greece had much to do with the creation of nature myths. Though the summers were hot and dry, it rained often in the winter months, usually in heavy but brief thunderstorms. The numer- ous arms of the Aegean Sea made indenta- tions in the land and caused wayward and unpredictable winds, particularly in winter.

Because the winds rolled in from every direction, they appeared to have minds of their own. The mountain hurricanes seemed like demons, and the trade winds seemed like benevolent gods. Some scholars say Hermes, the messenger god, represented the winds in the way he flitted back and forth through the air. Winged wind spirits were numerous. Among the most prevalent were the winds of the four directions: Boreas, Zephyrus, Notus, and Euros, the sons of Eos, the dawn, and As- traeus, god of the night sky. Each of these gods had characteristics that identified him with a particular season. Boreas, the winter wind of the North, was wild and cruel, and Zephyrus, the summer wind of the West, was gentle and kind. Some scholars identified numerous winds, and, as if to illustrate the er- ratic wind pattern of ancient Greece, not one of them maintained control. In the *Odyssey*, Aeolus controlled the winds from his island home. There he kept all the winds of the world confined in bags and could release them at will. He tried to help Odysseus by confining the storm winds and releasing only the gentle trade winds, but Odysseus's com- panions let the bad winds loose. The luckless travelers wound up tossing and turning in the sea and battling all sorts of sea monsters for twenty years.

The journey of Odysseus and other sea legends were the first myths created by the Greeks because the sea dominated their lives. Greece is on the Balkan peninsula, and it in- cludes numerous islands in the Aegean and Mediterranean seas. The people depended on these seas, yet they felt continually at their mercy. The water often appeared calm and silent then suddenly erupted in violent storms. So Poseidon, the sea god, had a vi- cious temper. Gods and spirits abounded in Greek myths who represented the sea's every characteristic. Scylla and Charybdis and the Sirens represented the monstrous sea and the dangers that awaited in the rocks and whirl- pools. Nereus represented the calm, beautiful sea, and his daughters, the Nereids, the sun- light dancing on the waves. Every experience Odysseus encountered portrayed a different aspect of the water and reinforced the per- ception of the sea as a changeable realm. Nereus had the ability to change shape, and Proteus was noted for it. This shape-changing ability was a characteristic common to ocean deities in other lands as well because of the variable nature of the sea itself.

The Greeks knew the Aegean well, and they knew Poseidon controlled it, as he did all the arms of the sea that cut into their land. There were so many of these arms that mythmakers created the hundred-armed Briareus to personify them. But they also knew of an outer ocean. They called it Oceanus, and they envisioned it as a river that encircled the earth. The god Oceanus and his wife, Tethys, gave birth to three thousand rivers, each one represented as a vigorous male with a long flowing beard. Mythmakers told numerous tales of these rivers uniting with human maidens, a concept that possibly stemmed from the ancient practice of women bathing in rivers to absorb their fecundating powers. The river Asopus mated with Merope and had two sons and twelve daughters. Achelous, the largest of the river gods, fought with Herakles over the maiden, Deianeira. The river Alpheius, once a hunter, fell in love with a nymph named Arethusa, who, to his dismay, rebuffed his advances. She crossed over the sea and became a fountain on the island of Ortygia. Alpheius followed her. He flowed beneath the sea to Ortygia until he reached the outflow of Arethusa's spring, and there their waters mingled together.

It has been said that the mythmakers recognized spirit in springs first, then soon after infused similar spirit in other physical features of the earth. Oreads inhabited the mountains, Dryads inhabited the trees, Limniads inhabited the lakes, and Potomeids inhabited the rivers. These nymphs infused the world with spirit, but, of course, recognition of an all-encompassing earth spirit came long before that. In Hesiod's *Theogony*, the earth goddess Gaia was the first being born from Chaos. She created the sky and the sea and the first race of beings, the Titans. But worship of this earth goddess took a backseat to worship of the goddess Demeter, who represented the corn and the cultivated soil. Demeter made the land fertile, so she served a more immediate function. Goddesses like Demeter, nymphs of all sorts, and great gods like Zeus and Poseidon and the other Olympians animated the world and made nature a familiar place.

The classical gods and goddesses epitomized the divinity of nature. The ancient Greeks looked at the physical world with awe, so they created nature deities who inspired awe themselves. Zeus infused all the forces that emanated from his sky realm with power. Poseidon and the other sea gods animated the realm the seafarers strove to understand. The feeling of reverence ancient people experienced when they beheld their physical world led to the deification of the earth, the sea, and the sky and all phenomena within them. But the deities the Greeks created dominated every aspect of their lives and controlled their destinies. The classical gods were not the first deities to command the elements, but they were arguably the most impressive. They set the stage for scholars who, for years to come, compared their colorful personalities and captivating tales to other deities who commanded the forces of nature all over the world. (Burn 1990, Fox 1964, Graves 1988, Guerber 1992, Guthrie 1950, Rose 1959)

HAIL

Hail has always posed a threat to creatures and crops exposed to the open land. Hail could devastate farmers' fields in seconds, and early agriculturists knew all too well of its strength. When hailstorms ravage the earth, some people even today consider them a show of the Great Spirit's wrath. The destruction upsets the balance of nature, and people find themselves humbled and at the mercy of nature's powers.

People today have specific beliefs about hail, just as they did in earlier times. According to some Bantu tribes, the Great Spirit created air and cold air. The cold air makes the rain that the Great Spirit then puts into the clouds and forms into hailstones. In Africa, as in other parts of the world, the gods' hurl those hailstones for punishment. They use them as weapons, arming themselves with an artillery of ice pellets that they then unleash on earth like shooting darts.

Hail may come from the clouds, the same place as rain, but whereas rain is taken as a blessing from the gods, hail is clearly an expression of their anger. In some cultures, the Great Spirit's anger causes the hailstorms, and in other cultures evil storm spirits or demons cause them. The Maori had many gods of hail, including Au-Whatu, the god of rain that turned into hail. Vritra, the drought demon from India also caused hail, and so did the storm deity Mundur-Tengri in Siberia and a malevolent spirit who lived on an island in Lake Titicaca in Peru. The Quechua of Peru prayed to their hail god,

Santiago, for mercy and protection, and the Chinese prayed to Hu-shen, who was one of several deities who could avert the hail and protect the fields.

Throughout history people attempted to stop hailstorms from occurring. As early as the first century A.D. in Corinth, guards were appointed to watch for hail and to warn the people so they could immediately make sacrifices to the cloud gods. In the 1800s in Austria, farmers fired cannons at the clouds, believing that the large rings of smoke and gas broke up the pellets. It has been said that in the Andes region, people still sacrifice after hailstorms to correct the balance of nature and to appease the Great Spirit's wrath. Hail-stopping rituals are performed among the Navajo and in Mexico, where weather charms are believed to aid the magic, much as they do in rain-stopping rituals performed to stop the water from flooding the land. (Donnan 1977, Reichard 1983)

See also Rain and Rain Gods

HALOS

Rings that appear around the sun or the moon are called halos, or parhelia, and in antiquity, people assigned myths to them because they believed their appearance indicated the coming of storm gods. Halos around the sun, or sundogs, occurred more commonly yet were not easily seen, but halos around the moon, or moondogs, were noticed. They occurred when moonlight passed through clouds of ice crystals, usually high in the atmosphere and usually at the edges of storm centers.

Ancient skywatchers did not know that a lunar halo appeared at the edges of a storm center, but they did believe that this odd appearance of the moon meant the moon god was trying to tell them something. Sailors used the moon to guide them on their night journeys, and the Maori, for instance, appealed to the halos that surrounded the moon to guide them as well. These circles, they thought, were portents of rain, double circles of violent storms and triple circles of tremendous gales. The Blackfoot Indians also associated sundogs with the weather. They said that sundogs occurred when Father Sun painted both his cheeks to warn the people of snowstorms. Rainbows were considered similar portents. The Maori called the lunar halo Hina-ko rako or Pale Woman, who sometimes appeared as a pale rainbow.

Other people had different ideas about halos around the moon and the sun. People in the Arctic commonly believed that the male moon and the female sun hated each other, and not only each other but all members of the opposite sex. These people explained eclipses as the time when the full moon gained on the sun and raped her. They extended this myth to explain the appearance of halos around the sun or the moon: The halos appeared when the moon or the sun dressed up in earrings and side curls to celebrate when someone of the opposite sex died. The Dagomba of Togo interpreted the phenomenon differently. They considered the solar halo evidence of the sun's marketplace, where he kept a ram responsible for all sorts of natural phenomena. When the ram stomped his feet, the thunder roared. When he shook his tail, the lightning flashed. When the ram rushed around the marketplace, the wind blew, and when hair fell off the ram's tail, it fell to the ground as rain. (Bassett 1971, Graham 1979)

See also Rainbows and Rainbow Gods

HAMMERS

In symbology, hammers represented power and might, and in nature myths, celestial power, particularly lightning and thunder. In myths of many lands, high gods, such as the Scandinavian Thor and the Slavic Perun, used hammers to hurl thunderbolts from Heaven to earth. Fire and smith gods used hammers too, to forge the thunderbolts; and artisan gods used them to hammer out the sky and make other weapons and implements for the gods. Ancient people almost everywhere connected the power of the hammer to the power of the storm and the forceful impact the sky gods had when they manifested that power in electrifying strikes.

In Africa, the Ashanti used the term thunder-axe for thunderbolt, and they believed these axes fell to the ground during storms. Ashanti storm priests often carried symbolic thunder-axes with wooden handles and metal blades, but they associated the true thunder-axes, the thunderbolts, with their Supreme Deity, Nyame, who controlled storm activity from the heavens. The Norse god Thor owned the most famous hammer in nature mythology, Mjollnir, a name that meant "crusher." It was double headed like an axe and represented thunder on one hand and lightning on the other. The symbolism of the hammer in general and Mjollnir in particular included not only destruction but also life, fertility, and resurrection. Thunderbolts accompanied the rain showers that fertilized the earth. In some myths, they were used to release the sun after it had been imprisoned in a dark cave, just as the thunder and spring storms renewed life and released the warmth that had been imprisoned all winter. (Cavendish 1994, Chevalier and Gheerbrant 1996, Davidson 1986)

See also Deng, Lightning, Perun/ Perkunas, Thor, Thunder and Thunder Gods

HARPIES

In Greek mythology, the Harpies were winged storm genii, fierce and grotesque, with the faces of women and the bodies of vultures. They were originally orphan girls, believed to be either the daughters of Gaia and Poseidon or of Thaumas and Electra, an ocean nymph. They were raised by the goddess Aphrodite, however, who saw them to maturity, then left to find them husbands.

The Harpies swooped from the sky to carry off food, children, and the souls of the dead.

While she was gone, the Harpyiai, or storm winds, snatched them away, and from then on, some say, the orphan girls too became storm winds, snatching food, spreading filth and noise, and carrying off anything in their path.

The Harpies of Greek myth numbered three: Aello, meaning "wind squall or storm wind"; Ocypete, meaning "fast flier or swiftwing"; and Celaeno, meaning "obscure or dark," like the sky during a roaring thunderstorm. Homer named one of them Podarge, or fleetfoot, married her off to Zephyrus, the West Wind, and made her the mother of a horse. Clearly, the names of the Harpies referred to the winds, and in the Argonautic journey, they were pursued, and some say captured, by Kalais and Zetes, the winged sons of Boreas, the North Wind. The term Harpy derived from the Greek word *harpazein,* which meant "to snatch or to carry away," just as strong winds lifted things into the air. In myths, the Harpies swooped from the sky and carried off food and children and sometimes the souls of the dead. Some say the Harpies themselves may have been dead souls. Their birdlike form was similar to the form the mythmakers used to portray dead souls in flight, swooping up in the sky and rushing through the air like fearsome winds. (Graves 1988, Grimal 1986)

See also Greece and Rome, Hurricanes and Tornadoes, Storms and Tempests, Whirlwinds, Winds and Wind Gods

HARVEST MOON

The harvest moon is the full moon that occurs each year nearest to the autumn equinox, which in ancient times occurred in mid–August. This moon appeared bigger and brighter that any other moon, and more mystical, so early people assigned it special significance. The harvest moon is the most celebrated moon of the year, even today. It is not really bigger and brighter at this time than at any other time, but it appears so because it is closer to the horizon, where the thicker air contributes to its brilliant color and shine. This effect continues for several nights in a row. The moon appears on the horizon just as the sun sets and awards the world with continued bright light.

In agricultural communities of times past, farmers used the extra hours of light to harvest their crops, and they considered the autumn moon a sign from the gods and a blessing for a fruitful season. For centuries and in many different cultures, people celebrated the harvest moon with lavish festivals. The Chinese even today hold a harvest moon festival every August fifteenth, and at this time they honor their moon goddess, Heng O, who ascended to her lunar palace after swallowing a pill of immortality. The Chinese honor her by moon gazing and by baking round cakes with an image of Heng O stamped on them. The Chinese call their harvest moon festival Yue Ping, which means "mooncake," and they exchange their mooncakes with friends and relatives to reward their moon goddess for her influence on the year's crops. (Krupp 1993a)

See also China, Heng O, Moon and Moon Gods

HATHOR

The popular Egyptian goddess Hathor has been labeled a sky goddess, a moon goddess, a sun goddess, a goddess of agriculture, a goddess of moisture, and a universal Mother Goddess and creator of the universe. Originally, she was said to be the daughter of Ra, the sun, and was later said to be his mother and, similarly, his wife. Sometimes Hathor was represented as a cow, and at other times, as a woman with a cow's head. She stood arched over the earth, her feet the pillars of the sky and her star-studded belly the firmament, nursing the world with her heavenly milk.

Although Hathor in many ways served a function similar to the function of Nut, the sky goddess, Hathor was probably primarily a moon goddess. Like the moon, she personified the female principle—primitive, fruitful, creative, and nourishing. Hathor was a fertility goddess and, in that sense, also a goddess of love, much like Isis, the Greek Aphrodite, the Babylonian Ishtar, and the Sumerian Inanna—all of them goddesses with lunar attributes. Hathor was born black, like the new moon, then grew brighter and brighter each day. In some myths, she appeared as the daughter of Nut, and in others, as the mother, wife, and daughter of Ra. These relationships, too, likened Hathor to the moon. The moon rose in the heavens before the sun as the sun's mother, appeared in the sky alongside the sun as the sun's wife, and then rose after the sun set as the sun's daughter.

Hathor was the sacred cow goddess of Egypt, identified with the moon, as was the cow itself, perhaps because of the connection between cows, the lunar phases, and agricultural fertility. Hathor's connection to fertility also associated her with the rise of the Nile River and the corresponding rise of the star Sirius, whose first yearly appearance signified the water's rise. In representations of the great goddess, Hathor was often depicted in a horned headdress with the disk of the moon or Sirius between her horns. (Ions 1983, Spence 1990)

See also Cows and Bulls, Egypt, Moon and Moon Gods, Nut, Sirius

HELIOS

Helios, the Greek sun god, was generally considered the personification of the physical sun. He was often confused with Apollo, the god of solar light, and, like Apollo, he was often said to have driven the sun's chariot across the heavens. Apollo appeared to have usurped the functions of Helios in later myths, as the cult of Helios as sun god retreated deeper into antiquity. Helios was born of Euryphaessa, the moon goddess, and the Titan Hyperion, who also fathered the moon goddess Selene and the dawn goddess Eos.

One myth says that the Titans drowned Helios in the sea, but he rose out of the sea and ascended to the sky to become the all-seeing, all-knowing sun. Helios had a magnificent palace in the eastern sky that he left every morning to cross the heavens in his horse-drawn chariot. Helios arrived in another palace in the western sky every night, a palace in a utopian land often referred to as the Islands of the Blessed. There his horses grazed in the pastures and Helios rested and bathed in the western sea. The sun god then boarded a golden ferry fashioned by Hephaestus, the smith god, and sailed through the river Oceanus back to the east, where the next morning, like the sun, he traveled westward once more. (Graves 1988, Rose 1959)

See also Apollo, Greece and Rome, Horses, Phaethon, Sun and Sun Gods

HENG O

Heng O was the Chinese moon goddess who took up residence in her lunar palace after swallowing a pill of immortality. On earth, she was the sister of a water sprite, and Shen I, the archer, fell in love with her and married her. The story of Heng O and her husband illustrates the interdependence of sun and moon, yin and yang, as well as explains the concept of lunar renewal. The beautiful moon goddess became immortal, growing dimmer and dimmer the closer her husband, the sun, got to his sun palace, but growing fuller and more brilliant as her husband headed back her way to visit her each month in her palace on the moon.

The story of Heng O began when the gods gave Shen I a pill of immortality as a reward for shooting down the nine false suns that rose in the sky beside the real sun and threatened to shrivel up the world. Shen I was to swallow the pill and then rise to the Palace of the Sun, where he would enjoy immortal life in the celestial sphere. But Shen I hid the pill in the rafters of his house for awhile, and Heng O discovered it. She followed a bright light wafting down from the roof, swallowed the pill, and immediately began floating up to the sky. Heng O continued to float upward until she reached the full moon, a silvery land full of cinnamon trees, which became her new home. She vomited up the pill, and the coating became a rabbit, the ancestor of yin, the female principle. Shen I followed his wife into the sky on a golden bird and took up residence in the sun, where he became the sun god. His golden bird, the essence of yang, became the male principle.

The marriage of sun and moon represents the union of yin and yang, but it also explains the moon's immortality. When Shen I flew to the sun, the gods gave him both a mooncake to protect him from the sun's heat and a lunar talisman so he could visit the moon and the two could unite as man and wife. However, the talisman only allowed him to travel to the moon; the moon could never travel to him. So on the fifteenth of each month, Shen I rode to the moon on a sunbeam and united with Heng O in a palace he built out of cinnamon trees. As Shen I got closer and closer to her palace, Heng O shone brighter and brighter in anticipation of him. By the time Shen I arrived on the moon, the goddess was full and brilliant. Yin and yang united. This myth explained how the moon's light comes from the sun and how the moon gets brighter and brighter as the sun approaches. (Krupp 1993a, Werner 1995)

See also China, Duality, Moon and Moon Gods

HEPHAESTUS

The Greek Hephaestus, or the Roman Vulcan, was the god of fire, particularly the natural fire of volcanoes. People in antiquity revered fire not only as one of the primal elements but also for its utility in crafts and metalworking. Hephaestus and many other fire gods from different lands were blacksmiths. They used the heat and the flames of natural fire to mold metal and to create palaces, armor, and fiery thunderbolts for the gods.

Hephaestus molded metals in his sooty forge under Mount Aetna, a volcano in Sicily given to frequent eruptions. He was particularly noted for making thunderbolts for Zeus, aided by his assistants, the Cyclopes. When people saw smoke coming from Mount Aetna, they believed it was Hephaestus lighting his forge. When they heard the rumblings that accompanied volcanic eruptions, they believed them to be the sound of the smith god's hammer as he pounded his metal into shape.

Hephaestus was generally depicted as a large, ugly man with a red beard and a hairy chest. He was practically lame, with a crippled leg that had twisted out of shape when Zeus threw him off Mount Olympus for interfering in his marital affairs. Hephaestus was the child of Zeus and Hera, and Hera had once thrown him from Mount Olympus as well. Upset by the looks of her dwarfish infant son, she tossed him into the sea, where he would have drowned had the sea nymphs not saved him. They carried Hephaestus off to a cave, where they raised him and taught him the art of metalworking. Some say the fall of Hephaestus represented the lightning bolt that came from the sky and kindled fire on earth. On earth, Hephaestus grew from a tiny dwarf to a powerful man, like the fire that grows from spark to flame. (Graves 1988, Grimal 1986, Guerber 1992)

See also Aetna, Cyclopes, Fire and Fire Gods, Greece and Rome, Volcanoes

HINA

Hina was a moon goddess of the Pacific Islands; she was called Hina in Hawaii, but Hine in Polynesia, and Ina or Sina in some of the other island groups. This moon goddess had many aspects, expressed by epithets that identified her with the moon's various aspects and phases. Hina-keha (Pale Hina), for instance, identified her as the moon in its bright phases, and Hina-uri (Dark Hina), as the moon in its dark phases.

Numerous myths of Hina are found throughout the Pacific Islands, and in many of them, she rose from the sea. In this sense, Hina was a water goddess, as were many lunar deities because of the moon's influence over the tides. In Tahiti, some believed that this moon goddess first lived on earth as the daughter of Tangaroa and that she ruled the moon after she died and ascended to the sky. Hina was beating tapa-cloth on earth with a mallet and making so much noise that Tangaroa sent Pani, a messenger, to ask her to stop. But she refused to stop, even though Pani asked her to time and time again. Enraged by her stubbornness, Pani beat her with her own mallet, killed her, and sent her spirit floating up to the sky. There she remained in the moon, forever beating her white tapa-cloth. When she stretched it over the heavens to dry, it formed the clouds. When she removed the gigantic stones that held the cloth in place, they rumbled down the sky and made the crashing sound of thunder. Then when she swiftly rolled up the layers of cloth, glistening in the sunlight, the shimmers of light flashed from the heavens as the lightning bolts. (Andersen 1995, Makemson 1941, Poignant 1967, Williamson 1933)

See also Moon and Moon Gods, Oceania

HINO

Hino was the thunder god of the Iroquois and one of their three most revered gods, along with Wind and Echo. The Iroquois believed Hino lived in the clouds of the far west, had the rainbow for a wife, and served as guardian of the sky. Armed with his bow and arrow, Hino worked to protect his people from harmful natural forces. He had two eagles to help him: Keunu, a golden eagle, and Oshadagea, who carried a lake of dew on his back so he could sprinkle the earth and save it after fire spirits attacked the land.

Usually Hino was peaceful and benevolent; however, like the thunder gods in Indo-European myths, he used thunder and lightning as weapons to deal with threats against his people. In myths the Iroquois told of Hino, he descended to earth two times, once to shoot flaming arrows at the water serpent of the Great Lakes and once to shatter the Stone Giants and end their rule. When Hino killed the water serpent, the broken pieces of his body became the floating islands. When he killed the Stone Giants, he shattered them to bits and changed them into the small pebbles found on the land. (Alexander 1964b, McLeish 1996)

See also North America, Thunder and Thunder Gods

HJUKI AND BIL

In Sweden, Hjuki and Bil were two mortal children who lived in a farmhouse on earth, then ascended to the sky and became personifications of the waxing and waning moon. Most people know these children as Jack and Jill of the familiar nursery rhyme, though few people know the story behind them. In northern Europe, the movement of the moon and sun were controlled by two other children, Mani and Sol, the offspring of a human father named Mundilfari. In some myths they drove the chariots of these celestial orbs, and in others they personified the orbs themselves. Mani, who controlled the moon, had been gazing down on Hjuki and Bil every night for quite some time as they climbed the steep hill from their farmhouse to fetch water from a well. Then one night, he swept them up to the moon and made them his captives.

Many people still see the faces of Hjuki and Bil in the moon today; they disappear and then reappear every month. People have always visualized faces silhouetted on the moon's surface, either a man, some sort of an animal, or, in this case, two children, still carrying their pail of water. Each month as the moon wanes, Hjuki falls off the face of the moon and Bil comes tumbling after. When the moon waxes, they reappear. The pail of water they carry denotes the watery nature of the moon and signifies the moon's control over the tides. (Harley 1969, Time-Life 1986)

See also Dew, Moon and Moon Gods, Moon Spots, Scandinavia

HORAE

In Greek mythology, the Horae ordered the seasons. They regulated weather changes, controlled nature's growth, and maintained stability in the natural world. Most mythologists name three Horae, all kind and graceful young maidens: one who represented spring, one who represented summer, and one who represented autumn. Because winter is the season of nature's death, no one represented winter at all.

The role the Horae played in turning the seasons illustrated how they maintained world order. Each of the three maidens ensured that her season behaved properly. The Athenians named the goddess of spring Thallo. She controlled budding and blossoming. Karpo, the goddess of fall, controlled ripening, and Auxo, the goddess of summer, controlled nature's growth. The Greeks called these same deities Eunomia, Dike, and Eirene, and by extension, they took on the function of maintaining stability in society just as they did in nature. Dike was the most noted of the three Horae; she was represented in the heavens as the zodiacal constellation Virgo, the earth goddess who in ancient times rose in the sky just as spring began and who held a sheaf of grain in her hand. In art, the three Horae are usually de-

picted holding flowers and plants. (Graves 1988, Rose 1959)

See also Cosmic Order, Greece and Rome, Seasons, Virgo

HORSES

Horses appeared in the myths as symbols of power, speed, and vitality. They pulled chariots of mighty gods across the skies and across the seas, and they moved powerfully and with the fleetness of the wind. Horses pulled the sea chariot of Poseidon in Greece, the moon chariot of Mani in Scandinavia, and the chariot of the Indian storm gods, the Maruts. Most commonly, however, horses pulled the chariots of sun gods. Solar deities, such as Surya of India, Dazhbog of Russia, and Apollo or Helios, the sun god of Greece, completed their daily journeys across the firmament only by virtue of their fiery equine companions.

Because of their connection with chariots of the sun, horses figured prominently in solar rituals. Horse sacrifice was common in India, in Scandinavia and the Celtic lands, and in Greece, where horses consecrated to the solar powers were believed to replace the old horses when they got tired. Because of their connection to the sea and the waves, people in many lands also sacrificed horses to the water gods. The Japanese sacrificed white and black horses to bring rain and red horses to stop rain. People throughout the Indo-European lands sacrificed horses to river gods to ensure safe passage across the water. In Scandinavia and the British Isles, worshippers commonly cast horses over cliffs to the sea gods. Because horses sprang up quickly and forcefully, the ancients connected them with waves. The Celts, for instance, called the breakers that rose during a tempest the white horses of Manannan. For this reason, early nature worshippers considered horses fitting sacrifices for gods who had the power to either still the waves or rouse them to fury.

The metaphorical portrayal of horses rising from the depths during storms indicated

A Scottish kelpie, who jumped from the depths to entice people to mount them, then rushed back under water.

their likeness to waves and also to wind. These horses moved swiftly, like the kelpies of Scotland, who jumped from the depths, enticed people to mount them, then rushed back under the water. The North Wind, Boreas, took the form of a horse in Greek myth. Pegasus, the winged horse, and Hofvarpir, the horse of the Norse goddess Frigg have also been likened to wind. In some myths, impregnation by wind led to the birth of horses. Podarge, the Harpy, and the West Wind begat two horses known for their fleetness, Xanthos and Balios, the horses of Achilles. (Howey 1923)

> ***See also*** Chariots, Sea and Sea Gods, Sun and Sun Gods, Water Horses, Waves, Winds and Wind Gods

HORUS

Horus was one of the many solar deities in the Egyptian pantheon, the son of Isis and Osiris, conceived after Osiris's death. Horus was first a sky god, a great falcon with his right eye the sun and his left eye the moon. There were actually many Horuses in the Egyptian pantheon, which has led to confusion over roles and attributes. But primarily in the myths, Horus emerged as the challenger of Seth, the killer of his father, Osiris, over the throne of Egypt.

The battle of Horus and Seth symbolized the battle of light and darkness. Horus was a solar deity identified with Apollo, and he challenged and defeated Seth, the spirit of darkness, in a ruthless fight. Seth tore out the left eye of Horus, the lunar eye, in a possible explanation of a lunar eclipse. Thoth made the eye whole again. Horus tore off Seth's leg, a symbol, it has been said, for the Big Dipper, or the undying circumpolar stars of Heaven. When Horus tore off Seth's leg, he gained a symbol of immortality and a talisman he could use to bring Osiris back to life. The stars of the Dipper never died and neither would Osiris. Osiris threatened to send demons to challenge the gods unless the sun god made Horus king. So Horus was crowned king, and Seth was sent to the sky to become the god of storms.

Horus was usually depicted with a human body and the head of a hawk or a falcon. The falcon symbolized the sun, particularly the flight of the sun as it soured into the heavens, and it also symbolized the sky, because the falcon was worshipped in Egypt as the sky. The name of the cow-headed sky goddess, Hathor, meant "house of Horus"; as sun god, Horus flew into her mouth each night when the sun set then emerged the next morning when the sun brightened the heavens. (Griffiths 1960, Hart 1990, Krupp 1983, 1991a)

> ***See also*** Birds, Circumpolar Stars, Egypt, Hathor, Isis, Osiris, Sky and Sky Gods, Sun and Sun Gods

HUACAS

To the Inca of the Peruvian Andes, huaca is a generic term for any material object believed to contain a supernatural force. Huacas are sacred shrines and include many forms of natural phenomena, including mountains, trees, lakes, caves, springs, fountains, and many rock and stone formations, some made to resemble human beings. Huacas also include the mummified dead, ancient battlefields, and many places identified in Incan myths and legends. These sacred shrines pockmark the Peruvian Andes, and scholars believe them to have had significance in many areas of Incan life. Not only did the Inca use the huacas as ceremonial centers and religious shrines, but they also likely used them to build their calendar and as convenient places to observe celestial events that took place on or near the horizon.

There are nearly five hundred huacas in the vicinity of Cuzco alone, arranged along lines called ceques that radiate outward like sun rays from the Coricancha, or the Temple of the Sun. The ceque system is unique to Incan mythology. Some say that long ago it was a type of religion associated with animism, practiced by early highland farmers who conducted religious ceremonies around huacas connected to the agricultural cycle. Some huacas were placed close to irrigation canals and ensured proper watering of the maize fields. To agricultural people, this type of planning was crucial, so scholars concluded that the huacas played a crucial role in insuring an adequate food supply and were thus deified.

The ceques and huacas of Peru were presumably organized by the Incan emperor Pachacuti sometime in the 1400s. Many of the sacred landforms were stones. In Incan belief, early myths formed the basis for establishing huacas, and the myth of Pachacuti's battle explained the deification of one of these natural landforms. During Pachacuti's battle, an Indian appeared in the air above him and helped him defeat his enemies. Pachacuti took the Indian with him to Cuzco, sat down at the window of a monastery, and turned to stone. Ever since, the stone has been worshipped and sacrificed to in hopes of enlisting the spirit's help in winning wars. (Cobo 1990, Krupp 1983, Morrison 1978, Tierney 1990)

See also Rocks and Stones, South America, Totemism

HUITZILOPOCHTLI

Huitzilopochtli was an Aztec war god who had links to the sun, to storms, to rain, and to fire. Some scholars called him a sun god, and as a warrior, he did have a fierce, solar nature, fighting the darkness as the fiery sun did when it rose into the morning sky. In the myth of Huitzilopochtli's birth, he emerged from the womb of the earth goddess and immediately slew his sister and his four hundred brothers, just as the rising sun slew the moon and the stars. He wielded a fire serpent as a weapon, a common symbol in Mesoamerica of the lightning bolt and the powerful rays of the summer sun.

Huitzilopochtli's metaphorical slaying of the moon and stars stemmed from the Aztec ideology of sacrifice. It represented a reenactment of the perpetual war between the darkness and light. The purpose of Aztec sacrifice was to guarantee rain and abundant harvests and to ensure proper movement of the sun and cosmic renewal. As a solar warrior, Huitzilopochtli fought this cosmic battle. The Aztecs believed that sacrifice victims offered to Huitzilopochtli fed the sun for a time, then went on to live inside the bodies of hummingbirds. The same was true of warriors who died in battle. Without sacrificing to the sun, the world would wither away in darkness. So Huitzilopochtli, as a cosmic warrior, renewed the world through war and sacrifice, and his victims provided the required nourishment for the sun.

The story of Huitzilopochtli's birth had great mythical significance not only as a metaphorical battle of light and darkness but also as a reenactment of how the sun god gained control of the world. In Huitzilopochtli's myth, the Aztecs used the warrior sun as a champion of their own race. In addition to contributing to the perpetual war between the sun and the moon, Huitzilopochtli's battles were metaphors for the Aztecs' own battles. The name Huitzilopochtli meant "Hummingbird on the left"; he was a plumed sky warrior, which further connected him to the battle of light and darkness. Huitzilopochtli was depicted as a blue man, fully armed, as he was at birth, and decorated with hummingbird feathers. (Brundage 1979, Taube 1993)

See also Coatlicue, Mesoamerica, Sacrifice, Sun and Sun Gods, Tonatiuh

HURAKAN

In the Popul Vuh, the sacred book of the ancient Maya, Hurakan existed as a primordial sky force, as the three components of lightning, which manifested itself as the bolt, the thunder, and the illumination. The name Hurakan was a curious utterance in Central America and eventually became the base for the word *hurricane*. Though the deity started out as a demiurgical form of celestial fire, he became over time an embodiment of nature unleashed, a deity of rain and tempest and a sender of cyclones, whirlwinds, and hurricanes.

In the Popul Vuh, the Quiche Maya asserted that the world began when Hurakan, the force of the sky, and Gucumatz, the force of the sea, talked the earth into existence. Their talk stimulated mountains to rise out of the water and vegetation to sprout over the land. These two deities created human beings out of maize and then needed a sun to keep them warm. So Hurakan rubbed his sandals together and created fire.

Hurakan was a creator deity in the same vein as the sky gods of Indo-European myths. In the Popul Vuh, the Quiche called him "Heart of the Sky," so in all likelihood he represented sun and wind and rain and all the other forces connected with celestial power. Hurakan created the earth as he blew over the sea, but he also destroyed the first beings with flood. Some time later, Hurakan made four new beings he considered perfect, and they became the ancestors of the Quiche. (Brinton 1976)

See also Mesoamerica, Sky and Sky Gods

HURRICANES AND TORNADOES

Only a fine line separates strong forces of wind. Hurricanes, tornadoes, whirlwinds, and waterspouts all move violently and have the potential for untold destruction. The distinction between these storm winds is primarily a matter of scale. Tornadoes are much bigger and potentially much more violent than whirlwinds, and hurricanes are much bigger and potentially much more violent than tornadoes.

Witnessing the fury with which these winds manifest themselves, early people who personified the phenomena of nature naturally gave the tornado and the hurricane violent temperaments. These characters were demons, monsters, dragons, and fearsome giants, some that grew bigger and bigger as the winds themselves grew. Otus and Ephialtes, the giant sons of Poseidon, personified the winds and the hurricanes. They started out small but grew nine inches every month. Then finally, Apollo slew them with his golden arrows. The sun god, once again, arose victorious. He defeated the storm giants, who, as embodiments of the wind's destructive potential, had assumed monstrous proportions to wage war against the gods.

The fact that hurricanes and tornadoes grew in size was often incorporated into myths and legends. Some African tribes likened tornadoes to snakes, enormous deified snakes who writhed and twisted as they reached from the earth to the sky. The Zulu called the tornado god Inkanyamba, and they believed that he grew larger and larger as he rose out of his pool and then grew smaller and smaller when he retreated back into it.

The behavior of Inkanyamba paralleled the behavior of a tornado when it swept over the water. It sucked up the water and swirled and twisted it into a column of air and spray, then as the tornado winds dissipated, the column shrank and disappeared back into the body of water from which it came.

The African serpent god Inkanyamba caused waterspouts, just as dragons did in the Asian lands when high winds in those countries blasted over the waters. When tornadoes swept fiercely over land, they often became whirlwinds of another sort: dust devils, a phenomenon that occurred when dirt or sand, rather that water, combined with the air to form the rising column. In Greek myth, the chimera and the Harpies may have personified these raging storm winds. The chimera had the head of a lion, the body of a goat, and the tail of a dragon, and it pounced, twisting its serpentine tail around like a spiraling whirlwind. The Harpies rushed through the air fiercely, with all the fury storm genii could muster, and then they swooped down, touched ground, and snatched up with them anything in their path.

One of the most fearsome personifications of the hurricane or tornado was Seth, the Egyptian god of the storm winds. He and his Greek counterpart, Typhon, personified evil, and they looked like hideous beasts. Both of them roared and screamed as funnel clouds do when they wreak their havoc over the earth. Tornadoes sound like monsters. They breathe like monsters. Typhon had a hundred heads and the tail of a snake. His fiery eyes flashed like lightning. Though Typhon later became known as a volcano spirit, at first he likely represented the hurricane winds that blew down from the mountains. The battles the winds waged as they sweep furiously over land and sea was but one example of the war between the primal forces of nature. Air battled earth during tornadoes, and air battled water during hurricanes. Until Zeus succeeded in defeating Typhon and confining him under Mount Aetna, this monster terrorized everyone, on earth and sea—then like the hurricane, he waged war against Zeus himself, the personification of the sky. (Guerber 1992, Rappoport 1995)

See also Adad, Dragon-Kings, Dragons, Elements, Harpies, Rudra, Storms and Tempests, Typhoons, Waterspouts, Whirlwinds, Winds and Wind Gods

HYADES

The Hyades is the group of stars in the constellation Taurus that forms the V shape of the bull's face. Because this celebrated star group rises with the sun in the springtime, people of the past considered it a symbol of rain. The ancients believed the Hyades brought the rain with them when they appeared in the sky. Because their appearance often presaged heavy storms, some ancient groups also perceived them as dangerous.

The Greeks connected the Hyades with the spring rains in a myth of seven (some say five or six) sisters who cried tears of grief over the death of their brother, Hyas. The Hyades were the daughters of Atlas and an ocean nymph named Aethra and the half-sisters of the Pleiades, an even more celebrated group of stars in the constellation Taurus. When a lion killed Hyas one day while he was out hunting, his sisters, the Hyades, mourned uncontrollably. Some say they were placed among the stars after they died of grief. Others say they were placed there as a reward for nursing the god Dionysus as an infant. In either case, each spring when the rain fell from the heavens, it was said to be tears of grief shed by the Hyades from their home in the sky. (Allen 1963, Bell 1991, Staal 1988)

See also Pleiades, Stars and Star Gods

I

ICE

See Frost and Ice, Glaciers

ILLAPA

Thunder held a high place in the pantheon of the Inca, and Illapa was the god responsible for causing it. Although he was sometimes labeled more generally a weather god, Illapa was best known for carrying a slingshot that he cracked from the sky to cause the thundering noise. Some say Illapa used his sling to shatter a rain jug carried by his sister, thus releasing the rains she gathered from the Milky Way, which was believed to be a celestial river. Illapa used his sling just as thunder gods from Indo-European myths used their hammers—as a mighty weapon that delivered storms the ancients considered supernatural manifestations of sky power.

Though the Inca commonly referred to their thunder god as Illapa, he had other names as well. Some called him Chuqui Illa, Catu Illa, Catequil, or Apocatequil. Illapa was made of stars and wore bright shining clothing that flashed when he spun his sling through the sky. These flashes, the Inca believed, were the lightning bolts. When Illapa decided to release the rain and storm, he would then crack the sling to hurl stones, which sometimes fell to earth. These small round stones were thought to be his children, and each village kept one as protection from lightning and to ensure fertile soil.

The great thunder god was represented in images and shrines throughout Peru, as well as in a temple of his own that housed a gold statue of the god. He was revered in the Coricancha compound, or the Temple of the Sun, where he was depicted with his face veiled by a headdress to symbolize the veiling of the thunder by the clouds. (Brinton 1976, Cobo 1990, Spence 1977)
See also Hammers, Lightning, Meteors and Meteorites, Thunder and Thunder Gods

IMDUGUD

Monstrous birds who caused raging storms appeared often in world myths, and in Mesopotamia, the howling lion-headed bird Imdugud, or Anzu, performed this function. Imdugud was the son of Anu, the sky god, and he personified the rainstorm as he stretched out his wings and covered the heavens with clouds. It has been said that Imdugud probably originated as the embodiment of fog or mist or some other singular force. Whirlwinds and sandstorms were common hazards in this part of the world, and Imdugud caused those forces when he flapped his wings.

In the early years of Mesopotamian civilization, the mythmakers used animal forms such as Imdugud to represent the nature powers. Later, when these gods took human forms, Imdugud became Ninurta, the god of rain. Ninurta was a warrior, and he battled Imdugud or Anzu when he took over the beast's mythological functions. Both Ninurta and Imdugud had threatening appearances to emphasize their connection with the spring flood. As part lion, Imdugud was usually depicted with his mouth wide open to represent the howling noise that accompanied the destruction. As part serpent, he represented the kind of chaotic disturbance in world order the people feared they could not control. (Black and Green 1992, Jacobsen 1976, McCall 1990)
See also Adad, Birds, Chaos, Deserts, Garuda Bird, Mesopotamia, Rain and Rain Gods, Storms and Tempests, Thunderbirds, Whirlwinds

113

INDIA

Hindu India has a long and diverse mythological tradition. It has its roots in southern Russia and ancient Persia, and the mythmakers have assimilated myths and legends of these lands and carried them into the modern world. The earliest myths of Hinduism began in what scholars call the Vedic period, a period named for the production of hymns called Vedas, addressed to the deities. Modern Hindus built their religion on elements borrowed and modified from this time—a time when nature seemed alive with power and when hosts of demons, nymphs, gods, and goddesses represented individual phenomenon that worked together to infuse the world with one universal animating spirit.

The religion of the Vedic Indians grew from their awe of the natural world. These people lived in a land of striking beauty, and they deified the forces that most impressed them. The sun shone down from Heaven and illuminated the land. The Himalayas stretched over a large area of earth and housed the sacred sources of rivers. Then the water flowed down the mountains and renewed the earth. Some scholars said that sanctifying the phenomena of nature formed the basis for the Hindu religion. The people in this land recognized energy in the fiery sun and the cool, refreshing rivers. They formed a wealth of traditions on the belief that the world drew its power from the fire that characterized the sun and the water that enabled life to continue.

Ancient India was not immune to the destructive force of nature by any means. Intense heat and drought characterized the climate, and the Indian people naturally sanctified the waters that renewed their world. It appeared that whoever controlled the water ruled supreme. That's what gave Varuna his power. He ruled the universe in the early Vedic years and was full of creative energy. He caused the rain to fall and the winds to blow. He moved the world and upheld nature's laws. But in later years, the storm god Indra usurped Varuna's creative power by fighting the drought demon Vritra and releasing the waters. This act made him the creator of life and a fertility god. As Supreme Deity, Indra rearranged the world. He built the world like a house with the sky as the roof. He propped up the heavens. He regulated time and the seasons.

The Indians venerated water in many forms. Indra gained supremacy because rain was precious and scarce and he provided it. The fertility goddesses Ganga, Yamuna, and Sarasvati were highly venerated as embodiments of the three major rivers. Behind this worship was a recognition of water as the elixir of life. In the Vedic period, Soma embodied this magic elixir. He represented the nectar that gave the gods their immortality. In later years, Soma became the moon god and retained his association with water. The Indians knew the moon as the source of dew, so, in myth, they entrusted the moon god with amrita, or Soma, the life-renewing fluid both gods and demons coveted. When the gods and demons churned the ocean of milk to obtain the magic elixir, the moon god rose from the waters. So did Lakshmi, the goddess of love and wealth, seated on a lotus. Lakshmi and the lotus both represented the wealth and fertility the Hindus associated with water.

The current Hindus include in their rituals representations of natural forces or elements believed to power the world. Water is one of them, and earth, air, fire, and space are the others. Hindus today do not directly worship these elements or the original gods who embodied them. But they continue to recognize their symbolic significance. In Vedic times, Agni represented fire, Vayu represented air, and Surya represented sun. These were some of the most venerated of the ancient gods. Worship of natural phenomena was the mainstay of Vedic religion, but as the world changed, the nature of worship changed as well.

Agni, Vayu, and Surya made up but one of

the divine triads that characterized Hindu mythology. Indra later replaced Vayu in the triad, and the three of them moved the universe, aided by numerous gods and goddesses of individual forces. Modern Hindus worship the triad of Vishnu, Shiva, and Brahma as three aspects of one divine presence, molded and modified from the original Vedic gods. Brahma is the universal spirit, the creator. Vishnu is the preserver, present in the Vedic age as a kind of sun god. Shiva is the destroyer, a new form of the destructive Vedic storm god Rudra. The three modern deities also move the universe, but they control natural phenomena only in a metaphorical sense. The original nature powers of the three gods have been eclipsed by a more pervasive, all-encompassing power, one that constitutes one unifying deity who manifests himself in numerous forms.

One of the central themes of Hindu mythology today is an alternation between creation and destruction. In the Vedic period, the gods continually battled demons, and the current gods do as well. Vishnu manifests himself each time he is needed to restore order to the world, and Shiva destroys demonic forces with his fiery eye. Underneath these myths lies an underlying tension between order and chaos. In current Hindu thought, the cycle of chaos and order forms the basis of universal time. The Hindus identify each cycle as one hundred years in the life of Brahma. At the end of each cycle, they say, everything dissolves. Destruction consists of a hundred-year drought. Seven suns appear in the sky and drink up all the water. Then waters flood the earth for twelve years. The mythmakers modeled this destruction from the climactic cycle they witnessed in their world. Their land suffered from drought and heat, then from monsoon rains. But after that, the land revived. In myth, Brahma created another world. When this new world started, flood waters covered the earth. Life began again from the water, continued for a

time, then submitted to nature's destructive force once again. (Cox 1887, Ions 1984, Moor 1984, Thomas 1980, Zimmer 1962)

INDRA
Indra was the Hindu storm god, one of the three most important deities in Vedic India along with Surya, the sun god, and Agni, the fire god. The Hindu cosmos was threefold, with a sky realm above, an earth realm below, and a realm of atmosphere in between. The atmosphere belonged to Indra, and he controlled all phenomena thought to originate in his realm. Though over time Indra faded in importance, for much of the Vedic period he held the highest place in the pantheon and was invoked frequently to bring rain to the parched lands. Most Vedic myths centered on Indra, whose strength and power alone could save the country from drought.

Indra ascended to high god by slaying Vritra, the demon who had swallowed the cosmic waters and plunged the land into drought. At this time, Indra had a rivalry with Varuna, the Supreme Deity, and he set out to best him and usurp his position. He accomplished this by attacking Vritra and releasing the cloud-cattle the demon had imprisoned in the mountains. The people pleaded with the gods for help, and Indra answered their prayers. Fortifying himself with Soma, the elixir of immortality, Indra set off in his chariot followed by the Maruts, his companion storm deities. They descended on the serpent Vritra, who lay in coils around the mountains, guarding his prisoners. The Maruts shouted, and Vritra roared his dragon roar when he saw his enemies approaching. Using his thunderbolt as his weapon, Indra split open the dragon's stomach, and the Maruts dashed toward the imprisoned cows and released them. Indra saved the land. Rain fell in a torrential downpour and ended the drought. After Indra's heroic act, he supplanted Varuna and gained recognition as the highest god. Some sources credit Indra with repeating this act every year and ending the drought at the end of each summer.

Indra had a violent nature, which served him well in fighting demons. The demon Vritra personified drought and the harsh aspects of nature, but there were other demons that were equally threatening. Before his heroic battles, Indra always strengthened himself by drinking large quantities of Soma, for which he had an insatiable thirst. Soma gave him the strength necessary to fight demonic forces like the Daityas and Danavas, who he banished to the ocean depths. These demons upset the balance of good and evil in the world, and Indra took it upon himself to restore the balance.

In the myths of Indra, many types of atmospheric phenomena surfaced to aid him in his battles. Vajra, the thunderbolt, served as his weapon, and Sakradharus, the rainbow, appeared as a symbol of his mighty bow. In Vedic myths, Indra rode to battle on a horse or in a golden chariot drawn by two tawny horses, thought to symbolize the sun. In later Hindu myths, he rode on a white elephant, whose full, lumpy body symbolized the raincloud. Many elephants, in fact, were in Indra's employ, with names such as "lightning sender" and "thunder-bearer," which revealed their raincloud nature. Indra's elephant was Irivat, a name that meant "watery," like a cloud. In many artistic representations of Indra, the storm god is seen mounted on Irivat's back.

When Indra assumed his position as king of the Hindu gods, he became associated with the sky rather than simply the atmosphere. Some sources equate him with Zeus and cast him in the role of fertility god and creator god. Like the other high gods of India, Indra resided in his own Heaven, a place devoid of sorrow or fear and adorned with celestial trees, flowers, and singing birds. Indra's Heaven was on the mythical Mount Meru, the cosmic mountain, although it was said that this Heaven could be moved any-

where, like a chariot. Saints and sages populated Indra's Heaven, along with spirits of wind, thunder, fire, water, clouds, plants, stars, and planets. Indra sat among them wearing white robes, a garland of flowers, shimmering bracelets, and a crown. He was accompanied by his queen, Indrani, and attended by the Maruts and many of the other gods, saints, and sages. (Ions 1984, Mackenzie 1971, Moor 1984)

See also Drought, India, Maruts, Rain and Rain Gods, Storms and Tempests

INTI

Sun worship was the official religion of the Inca in Pre-Columbian Peru, and Inti, the sun god, held primary status among the Inca people. The Inca believed that they descended from the sun and that Inti was a divine ancestor of the royal family. With the greatest power of the heavens in their direct lineage, the Inca people believed they too had divine power and ultimate sovereignty as a ruling class.

Some scholars regarded Inti as the highest deity. Viracocha, they believed, ruled supreme, but he was more an impersonal presence than the sun god; Inti was an active force in everyday life. Because the Inca were agriculturists, they worshipped Inti for his regenerative powers. When Inti was pleased, he fertilized the crops, and when he was angry, he caused solar eclipses.

People throughout the community revered Inti, and they erected for him a magnificent temple in the capital of Cuzco, called the Coricancha, or the Temple of the Sun. The Coricancha is arguably the most renowned structure in South America, which indicates Inti's prominence. Inti was represented in the Coricancha and throughout Peru as a shimmering gold disk with a human face surrounded by solar rays. His consort, Mama Kilya, the moon, appeared with him in the great temple, as well as other prominent deities in the Inca pantheon. Inti has also been called Apu-Panchau or P'oncaw, which means "the daylight," or "head of the day." He was believed to rise each day in the eastern sky to rule and then to set each night in the western sea, where his intense heat partially dried up the waters. (Cobo 1990, Larousse 1968)

See also Mama Kilya, South America, Sun and Sun Gods

INYAN

According to myths of the Lakota Sioux, Inyan was the Spirit of the Rock and the creator of the world. He existed as a primordial force and had all the powers of the world within his blood. Soft and shapeless in the beginning, Inyan created Maka, the earth, from his blue blood. However, the creation of Maka took too much of this precious fluid, and Inyan became hard and powerless. He then let the rest of his blood flow out of his veins and thus created the waters of the earth.

The Lakota worship of Inyan illustrates the connection numerous peoples made between reverence for rocks and reverence for the earth. The rock was an immutable force, solid and indestructible and thus representative of the creator of all things. Inyan was the spirit of the earth that lived in the rocks, and the Lakota invoked him more than any other deity. They made sacrifices to him, which usually consisted of pieces of skin left for their great god on oddly shaped stones. (Gill and Sullivan 1992, Walker 1980)

See also Earth and Earth Gods, North America, Rocks and Stones

IRIS

Iris was the Greek goddess of the rainbow and the granddaughter of Oceanus, the ocean, and the daughter of Thaumas, the god of wonder. Characterized by her swift movement, she flashed through the sky and vanished as quickly as the rainbow itself vanishes after a summer storm.

The escapades of Iris appear in many Greek myths, including Homer's *Iliad,* where her appearance foreshadowed war and turbulence, and in Virgil's *Aeneid,* where her appearance preceded the fateful tempest. She was the messenger of the Greek gods, clothed in bright colors and equipped with wings of gold. Compared by Homer to a serpent, Iris was often malevolent, sent to cause trouble or to give warnings of impending storms. But she could also use her powers to help people. As goddess of the elements and meteorological phenomena in general, she filled the clouds with water and released replenishing rains on the earth. (Bell 1991, Graham 1979)

See also Greece and Rome, Rainbows and Rainbow Gods

ISHTAR

The Babylonian Ishtar, or the Sumerian Inanna, was identified as a goddess of love and fertility and of war, classifications consistent with her role as the embodiment of Venus, the Morning Star and Evening Star. Ishtar had many connections to the celestial sphere, and some mythologists identified her with the moon, the rain and the rainclouds, the thunderstorm and the tempest, and with several stars that shone brightly in the night sky. The worship of Ishtar was widespread, and her role as Venus widely recognized. As queen of Heaven, she fulfilled her role as war goddess when she rose as the Morning Star and battled the sun. She fulfilled her role as love and fertility goddess when she rose as the Evening Star as a harlot, lighting the skies and beckoning for gentlemen to come and keep her company through the dark night.

Ishtar featured in many Babylonian nature myths, in those that explained rain and storms and even eclipses. But the myth of her descent to the Underworld illustrated her role as the illustrious planet so revered by the ancients. The Sumerians and Babylonians watched and tracked Venus, and they noticed that the bright celestial object disappeared beneath the horizon in the west and then reappeared some time later in the east. They decided that this celestial event had significance in the cosmic scheme of things, so they immortalized the occurrence in myth. They sent Ishtar into the Underworld for a time, then revived her and sent her back to the earth and the heavens. Ishtar's descent and return has been likened to the Greek myth of Demeter, who similarly traveled to the Underworld and then returned to earth with her daughter, Persephone. Ishtar thus had another identity, that of an earth goddess. Most importantly, she played an essential role in cosmic renewal. Like the earth, she sprouted; like the rain, she fertilized; and like the planet Venus, she arose anew in the daytime sky. Ishtar, as queen of Heaven, embodied the immortal cosmos, and her descent to the Underworld and back revealed that the ancients recognized immortality in objects like Venus, who they believed had the power to die and come back to life. (Jacobsen 1976, Krupp 1991a, McCall 1990)

See also Death, Demeter, Mesopotamia, Morning Star/Evening Star

ISIS

The ancient Egyptians revered the goddess Isis as the Great Mother and guardian of the earth. She was the most widely worshipped goddess in the land, and scholars have connected her to many kinds of natural phenomena, including the earth, the moon, the wind, and the star Sirius. Isis was most famous for her marriage to Osiris and her role in restoring him to life after his brother Seth murdered him and chopped him into pieces. She moaned like the wind when she mourned his death. She reassembled his broken body and made it whole again. Then each spring, she rose into the sky as the star Sirius and signaled Osiris, as the Nile, to rise, or to resurrect. In all her actions, she guaranteed cyclic renewal and fecundity of the earth.

Isis served as a counterpart to the great Osiris, who represented the same concept of cyclic renewal. Because Isis reassembled the god's body, she restored him to life, and because she restored him to life, she played a significant part in his resurrection. Isis was an enchantress and a sorceress, and with help from the moon god Thoth, her powers of magic enabled her to perform this miraculous feat. These two lunar deities renewed the body of Osiris just as the moon renewed its own body every month when it returned from "death" to its full phase once more.

The lunar attributes of Isis corresponded to her role as earth goddess. She guaranteed the fertility of the earth when she replenished the fecundating waters. Isis was a spinner, like many lunar goddesses, and she wove together the threads of life that moved the moon through its phases and the earth through the cycle of seasons. Like Demeter in Greek myth, Isis represented not the earth in general but the cultivated land, the fertile Egyptian river valley made fruitful by the annual inundation of the Nile. The Nile, it has been said, was Osiris, her husband, who fertilized her even after his death. She conceived and gave birth to Horus. Then she transformed into a sparrow and fanned him with her wings, like the wind, and gave him breath. She also blew life into her husband's body.

Osiris was resurrected, never to die again. He became the Nile River and an embodiment of the water that fertilized the land. Metaphorically, Osiris was restored to life each year when the Nile waters rose, and, metaphorically, Isis stimulated the resurrection. The ancient Egyptians used the annual return of the star Sirius to mark the time of the annual flood; when Sirius appeared on the horizon for the first time each year, they believed the star brought the flooding with it. So the Egyptians equated Isis with the bright star. Both as star and as goddess, she stimulated Osiris to rise and to renew the world with his fertilizing power. (Budge 1969, Hart 1990, Spence 1990)

See also Demeter, Earth and Earth Gods, Egypt, Moon and Moon Gods, Nile River, Osiris, Sirius, Spinning and Weaving, Winds and Wind Gods

ISLANDS

People have long viewed islands as strange and mysterious. Sometimes they appeared out of the fog, floated amid the waves, and then vanished beneath the waters as mysteriously as they appeared. Since sailors began navigating the open seas, people have spun myths and legends about islands. Some of these stories explained the formation of real islands, some told fabulous tales of mythical ones, and many legends attempted to identify the kinds of inhabitants who might populate these extraordinary ocean worlds.

Sailors in antiquity, as well as those today, knew the phenomenon of the mirage—an image of fabulous lands glistening amid the waves, somewhere off in the distance. Stories of these floating and vanishing islands appeared in myths and legends everywhere, but particularly among those who sailed the North Sea and who conjured up images of floating islands from polar ice blocks. Norse seafarers based these stories on genuine observations, but other islands never existed in any form. They hid in the fog, glistened between the clouds, and then showed tips of green to bleary-eyed sailors longing for land. Then they sank down into the dark waters and disappeared from sight.

Sometimes mythical islands appeared and vanished in the minds of sailors because during life at sea, they thought land to be unattainable. So islands in general came to symbolize paradise, an unattainable paradise with unattainable treasures, such as a Well of Life and immortality. Such was the case in Scottish-Gaelic legends of floating and vanishing islands and in Chinese legends of mythical paradises that housed the Immortals. In

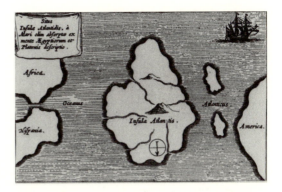

This seventeenth-century map by Athanatius Kircher claims to show the exact location of the probably mythical island of Atlantis.

Mesopotamian legend, Gilgamesh reached these lands by crossing the mythical sea.

In reality, these islands were only imagined, never reached. So islands were associated with death and the afterlife. Classical mythmakers made many references to the Islands of the Blessed, supposedly located in western Oceanus and believed to be some kind of heaven. Celtic mythology had similar places. People labeled these perfect lands utopias, and the search for them led many a sailor to create more and more fantastical tales.

Perhaps of all the mythical islands, Atlantis achieved the most fame. It was awarded to Poseidon early on when the universe was divided among the great sea god and his brothers, Zeus and Hades. Poseidon married on Atlantis and had children, the sea nymphs, who were often seen romping in the waves around the island shores. The Atlantic Ocean was like a spell. It terrorized; it mesmerized. Sailors began to see things under the waves and couldn't tell if they were real or imagined. Mermaids looked real in the shimmering sunlight, but they vanished when the sun set. Islands looked real in the fog, but they disappeared when the fog lifted. Sometimes it looked like plants moved beneath the waves, and sunshine dancing on the water often created images of steeples and peaked roofs of houses just under the surface. Some people even believed they heard church bells. One of Poseidon's children, Atlas, inherited the island of Atlantis. Most scholars today believe that the island was strictly mythical, but others continue to speculate. Like many real islands of antiquity that were created by the movements of wind, wave, and ice and destroyed by the same processes, Atlantis, they say, may have existed and then sank into the sea.

But real islands had their legends too, and people created myths to explain their existence. In the Pacific lands, demiurges continually created islands by fishing them out of the sea. Izanagi and Izanami created the island nation of Japan this way; they stood on a rainbow in the clouds and fished the country out of the seawater. The Polynesians said Maui fished New Zealand out of the sea as well, using the jaw of his grandmother as a hook. Another myth from Oceania explained how five of the South Pacific Islands were once five moons cast with a malevolent spell and hurled by the gods from Heaven into the sea. A similar tale from Tahiti detailed the creation of islands from one moon, hurled down by the gods and broken into pieces. Tales from Greece and Sweden tell of islands created from clumps of earth, a tale from India tells how Sri Lanka was formed when Vayu, the wind god, broke off the top of Mount Meru and threw it in the sea, and another tale tells how Hawaii was formed when the sun hatched it from the egg of a gigantic bird.

All these myths explain the creation of islands, but far more legends embellish the myths. Easter Island has a rich island lore, and so do the islands known to the Native Americans. The Native Americans told tale after tale about the islands seen off of their coasts and even about lone rocks, considered miniature islands. The peoples on the northeast coast said Martha's Vineyard was once inhabited by a giant named Maushope, who waded across to land with the water only reaching his ankles. The rocks that jut out from the waters, they said, were the remnants of a bridge Maushope started building, and the lignite around the area were the coals from his campfires. Maushope found the island by following a bird, a common way for people to find islands in myths of other lands as well.

The tale of Maushope illustrates a common theme in island lore—that mysterious islands housed mysterious beings. In many cases, the most mysterious islands existed off the familiar ship routes and were difficult to reach. So who might live there but giants, fairies, gods and goddesses, or malevolent spirits? People around the world populated their islands with all kinds of strange beings, including phantoms, Gorgons, Amazons, and in Arab legend, even women without arms or legs hanging from trees. All these beings added to the notion of the island as a place of mystery and magic. (Bassett 1971, Mackenzie 1994, Manley 1970, Rappoport 1995)

See also Mirage

ITZAMNA

The powerful and benevolent Itzamna was one of the most important deities to the ancient Maya, connected to rain and dew and considered a fertility god. He was Lord of the Heavens, yet was connected to the sky and the earth as well as the moon. As the sky, Itzamna took the form of Vucub Caquix, a monster bird who claimed to be both the sun and the moon. As the earth, he presided over the cardinal points. Itzamna was a creator deity and a sustainer of life. The "Itz" in Itzamna meant "raindrops" or "teardrops." He was said to have risen from the sea and arrived in the Yucatan when the land was without moisture. By bringing the moisture with him, he guaranteed that adequate rain fell on the fields.

In his human aspect, Itzamna was usually depicted as a toothless old man with sunken cheeks and a prominent nose. However, he sometimes appeared as Vucub Caquix, the Principal Bird Deity, and at other times as four iguanas standing together at the cardinal points with their heads pushed together at the middle. Itzamna held the highest place in the pantheon and was credited with ensuring the fecundity of the earth. His consort, Ix Chel, the water goddess, controlled rain in its destructive aspect, constantly holding the deluge in a jug as a threat to the world. (Alexander 1964a, Markman and Markman 1992)

> See also Ix Chel, Mesoamerica, Rain and Rain Gods

IX CHEL

Ix Chel, also called Lady Rainbow, was the Mayan moon and water goddess who presided over flood and the rainbow. In her benevolent aspect, she was a fertility goddess who controlled pregnancy, childbirth, and weaving. But her destructive aspect predominated, and Ix Chel was greatly feared as the malevolent moon deity responsible for all destruction through water.

Ix Chel was the most important moon deity of the Maya and was often identified as the wife of Itzamna, the chief god of the pantheon. In some myths, she appeared as the sister and wife of the sun, who was perhaps a manifestation of Itzamna. As moon goddess, Ix Chel once shone as brightly as her husband, but one Mayan myth explained why her husband ultimately outshone her. Ix Chel was married to the sun, and together they shared the job of brightening the skies. But the sun discovered Ix Chel having an affair with his brother. Ix Chel fled, but her husband eventually found her and convinced her to come home where again, she shone as brightly as her husband. Then, because the people could not sleep with so much light in their skies, the sun took out one of Ix Chel's eyes, and since then, her light, the light of the moon, has been softer than the light of the sun.

Ix Chel's lunar aspect connected her with the world's waters. She was the Mayan equiv-alent to the Aztec water goddess Chalchihuitlicue. Ix Chel caused cloudbursts and floods and sometimes appeared with a malevolent sky serpent who caused tropical storms. Ix Chel had clawed hands and a skirt decorated with crossbones, and she held a jug containing the deluge as a constant threat against her people. (Brundage 1985, Markman and Markman 1992)

> See also Chalchihuitlicue, Floods and Flood Gods, Itzamna, Mesoamerica, Rain and Rain Gods, Water and Water Spirits

IZANAGI AND IZANAMI

In the Japanese Shinto creation myth, the world began when Izanagi and Izanami formed the islands from a primordial ocean. The world began with only this ocean, a watery abyss and a reedlike substance within it from which three supreme deities formed. These first deities gave birth to Izanagi and Izanami, a brother and sister who descended from the sky and stood on a rainbow, the Bridge of Heaven, floating above the water. Izanagi stirred the ocean with a jeweled spear, and drops of water on the tip of his spear coagulated and formed the first island, Okonoro. Then he and his sister-wife gave birth to eight children, the eight islands of Japan, then created the other natural land features: the waterfalls, the mountains, the trees, and the winds.

Izanagi created the winds from his breath, and they blew away the mists and revealed the newly formed land. When he and Izanami descended to the land and mated, Izanami gave birth to the gods and all sorts of dragonlike creatures who inhabited the sea. But their last child, the fire god Kagutsuchi, destroyed his mother during the birth process and sent her to Yomi, the Underworld. Izanagi, in anger, cut off Kagutsuchi's head. From his drops of blood, eight mountain deities formed.

In Japanese Shinto mythology, Amaterasu was the Supreme Goddess, the sun goddess, and the ancestress to the imperial line.

Susanowo, the storm god, and Tsuki-yumi, the moon god, were her brothers. But Izanagi created them all. When Izanami descended to the Underworld, Izanagi followed her, but the eight gods of thunder chased him back up to earth. Izanagi then washed the impurities of the Underworld from his body and in the process created Amaterasu, Susanowo, Tsuki-yumi, and many sea gods. (Picken 1980, Piggott 1983, Werner 1995)

See also Amaterasu, Bridges, Creation Myths, Japan, Kagutsuchi, Primordial Sea, Rainbows and Rainbow Gods, Susanowo, Tsuki-yumi

JAGUAR

The jaguar was a common image in myths of the Americas, a symbol, it has been said, for both the dark earth and the night sky. The jaguar had nocturnal habits, prowling the earth at night and sneaking around dark crags and mountain caves and roaring ferocious roars that rumbled like thunder. The animal represented earth because it preferred to remain hidden, and it represented the night sky because its spotted coat resembled the starry heavens.

In Aztec symbolism, Tezcatlipoca, the first of the five suns, was called "Jaguar Sun," and in one version of the myth, the sun god became a jaguar and devoured the entire race of giants that populated the earth. Both Tezcatlipoca and the jaguar were dark, frightful creatures capable of inflicting death at a moment's notice. They were both reputed to have magic powers. Tezcatlipoca as the jaguar sun was the darkest of all suns and the ruler of the night, yet still of a solar nature. Other cultures also likened the jaguar to the sun. According to the Desana of Colombia, the sun created the jaguar and placed him on earth to act as his agent. The Desana were among many groups in the Americas whose shamans turned into jaguars in order to use the jaguar's powers. The jaguar, it was said, represented the fertile energy present in the sun, the thunder, and the earth. (Brundage 1982, Burland 1967, Osbourne 1986)

See also Aztec Calendar Stone, Earth and Earth Gods, Shamanism, Sky and Sky Gods, Tezcatlipoca

JAPAN

From the early years of Japan, the Japanese recognized the good in nature. Unlike people in the western world, they strove to become one with nature's forces rather than to overcome them. The Shinto religion pervaded the country from as far back as scholars recognize, and according to Shinto philosophy, nature was benevolent and awe inspiring. Everything that was awe-inspiring the Japanese called *kami,* and kami, they said, existed everywhere, from the depths of the sea to the heights of the sky.

During the fourth century A.D., Buddhism came to Japan from China and Korea, and people adopted different views and worshipped different nature gods. But Shinto and kami survived and thrived. *Kami* was a general term used to mean "god" or "spirit." Most kami were nature spirits, not spirits of the Otherworld but of this world—close by and recognizable in the rush of clear waters, in the whistling of the wind, and on the glistening snow-covered peaks of Fujiyama, or Mount Fuji. The Japanese deified nature because nature's beauty overwhelmed them. So despite the typhoons and the earthquakes common to their volcanic island, those of Shinto faith recognized no struggle between good and evil but had simply a reverence for the divine. With every aspect of nature animated by its own god or spirit, the world became a wondrous, sacred place.

Some of the most popular Japanese myths reflected the Shinto philosophy of nature. The world was divided into two realms, with kami existing in each realm. Kunitsu-kami were the earth spirits who lived in the islands. They inhabited the rocks and the waterfalls, the trees and the plants, the mountains and the rivers. River gods inhabited every river. The god of wells caused water to flow from the earth. Mountain worship was prominent in Japan, ingrained in Japanese history, and often connected to the worship of watersheds or streams. In a volcanic coun-

123

try like Japan, the people recognized numerous mountain deities and revered many mountains themselves as sacred. Fujiyama was the most sacred mountain, but the people constructed shrines on the summits of many other mountains as well to worship other mountain deities. When Izanagi, the creator god, cut off the fire god's head, O-Yama-Tsu-Mi, the lord of the mountains, was born, as well as four other mountain gods who inhabited the slopes. These deities date far back in the country's history. Nai-no-Kami, Japan's only earthquake god, appeared to join the pantheon later, after a violent earthquake in A.D. 599.

The Shinto pantheon consisted of literally millions of deities. The Japanese depended on the sea for food, so Izanagi created gods to rule the sea bottom, the middle waters, the surface, and the tides. The Japanese dragon-king dominated the pantheon of sea gods; they were called Wata-tsumi and were most likely serpents or dragons themselves. Amatsu-kami were the sky gods, and Amaterasu, the sun goddess, dominated all the gods, in the earth and the sea as well as the sky. The storm god, Susanowo, held a high position among the celestials, and so did Tsuki-yumi, the moon god. But the sun goddess ruled. The worship of Amaterasu revealed that the Japanese traced their origin to the kami of nature. They believed that the imperial family of Japan directly descended from the sun goddess. As the deity responsible for life and light, she deserved the highest respect and reverence.

The sky world, in Japanese myth, mirrored the earth world. It had a celestial river, Ama no Gawa, covered with pebbles, just like the rivers on earth, and the two realms had similar landscapes. At the time of creation, a rainbow bridge connected the earth world and the sky world, a bridge similar to Bifrost in Norse mythology. The Shinto bridge had once floated above the water of the primordial sea. In the creation myth, the two creator deities, Izanagi and Izanami, stood on this rainbow bridge and formed the islands. Then they climbed down the bridge to earth. According to myth, the gods used to travel back and forth between earth and sky before the bridge fell into the sea while the gods were sleeping. When the bridge fell, it formed the isthmus west of Kyoto.

The creation of landforms played a large role in Japanese myth. Each time the people discovered new territory, they created new myths to explain the outstanding features, such as the hills, the rocks, the trees, and the freshwaters. Often, the myths involved battles between such land features, most likely to explain battles the people themselves experienced with rival clans. Landforms were sometimes formed as a refuge for gods or heroes. The island Enoshima was created as a reward for Benten, the sea goddess, who stopped an evil dragon from eating all the children. Some myths involved legendary people creating the landforms using ingenious methods. Omi-tsu-mi, who ruled the province of Izumo, enlarged his land using a rope. Izumo sat on a narrow strip of land separated from Japan by a mountain range. Omi-tsu-mi tied one end of his rope to a mountain in this range, and the other to numerous land masses in the Sea of Japan. His people pulled hard on the rope and were able to pull off pieces of land from the islands and attach them to the coast of Izumo.

Shinto meant "way of kami," or the way of the gods or spirits, and practicing the "way of kami" meant adhering to an animistic view of the world. Because everything, all of nature, contained spirit, everything had power and vitality. The Japanese had a close relationship with their nature gods and believed them to be ancient ancestors. The Japanese built shrines to their ancestor gods throughout the land—to the spirits of waterfalls and fountains, to the spirits of trees and mountains, and to the sun goddess Amaterasu and the moon god Tsuki-yumi. (Anesaki 1964, Davis 1992, Picken 1980, Piggott 1983)

124

KACHINAS

In Pueblo Indian society, the Kachinas were mythical ancestors who became the spirits of rain and of rainclouds. The Pueblos are agricultural people, so they depend on the annual return of the rain to plant their corn. In a sense then, the Kachinas are the spirits, too, of corn. Corn is their gift to the people. When they leave their spirit homes on the San Francisco peaks at the winter solstice, they enter the bodies of costumed dancers and stay until midsummer, bringing rain and fertility to the land. The ceremonies and the myths of the Pueblo center on this annual return of rain and on the Kachinas. In myth, the Kachinas once appeared in human form at the foot of the San Francisco peaks, then when the people prayed to them, they formed rain-bearing clouds. In ceremony, members of the Kachina cult impersonate the rain spirits by donning wooden masks and lavish costumes and dancing in underground chambers called kivas. By doing this, the Kachina spirits enter the bodies of the dancers, and the dancers gain the power to make the rain fall.

Though Kachinas most commonly embody rainclouds, they may actually be one of many forces of nature, of sun, thunder, wind, mist, clouds, or snow. Usually, the Kachinas are associated with moisture, and they live in places of moisture, in springs, for instance, or on the San Francisco peaks, which the Hopi Pueblos consider the source of clouds and rain. Nuva, the snow Kachinas, live on the peaks, and they send nourishment in the form of winter snows that melt in the spring, trickle down the mountains, and water the earth. Because the Kachinas bring moisture, it is by their will that the seasons turn and the Pueblo people continue to survive. (Bernbaum 1990, Marriott and Rachlin 1968, Tyler 1964, Wright 1973)

See also Cloud People, North America, Rain and Rain Gods

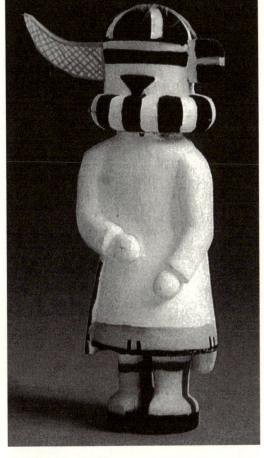

A Hopi rain Kachina.

KAGUTSUCHI

Kagutsuchi was the fire god of Japan. Izanami, the creator goddess, gave birth to him as she did the other deities of natural forces, including the winds, the mountains, and the trees. Izanami gave birth to Kagutsuchi last,

125

and during the process, the fire god burned her so badly she descended into the Underworld and entered the world of death.

Izanagi, Izanami's brother/husband, got mad and cut off Kagutsuchi's head, from which eight mountain gods emerged. Japan was a volcanic island, and the Japanese apparently recognized that subterranean fire existed in their world. They represented the Underworld as a place where gods of earth, fire, mountains, and thunder existed as demonic forces.

Kagutsuchi was both the god of fire and the physical fire. He caused the phenomenon and he also protected against it. The Japanese greatly feared Kagutsuchi because when the high winds blew, fire destroyed their houses. So the priests had rituals to placate him. During those rituals, they lit fires in their palaces and related the myth of the god's birth. (Herbert 1967, Kato 1926)

See also Fire and Fire Gods, Japan

KAMAPUA'A

In Hawaiian mythology, Kamapua'a was a pig god whose adventures explained the formation of many natural features of the land. As a warrior, Kamapua'a was fierce and menacing, charging viciously at his enemies and making loud snorting noises. But as a creator deity, Kamapua'a was helpful to mankind. Using his enormous snout, he created the earth by pushing it up from the bottom of the sea, then he continued to raise up hills, root up springs, dig out wells, and create many other landforms.

The myths of Kamapua'a explained how he controlled nature by cultivating the land as he dug up the earth with his snout. His snout was a phallic symbol, and his digging a metaphor for tilling the female earth. Not surprisingly, most of the myths of Kamapua'a involved his amorous adventures. In one myth, the pig god pursued two women who ran from him and disappeared into the earth. When he dug them up, they turned into springs. But his most popular adventure was his pursuit of the fire goddess, Pele, the legend of which explained the interplay of fertile growth and volcanism and the ultimate separation of earth and sea. Kamapua'a lived in one of the rainiest valleys on Oahu and thus represented the rain and the power of the water to both erode and to fertilize the land. Pele lived in the active crater of Kilauea and represented the wild forces of nature. The stormy relationship between these two nature deities showed how Kamapua'a battled nature's wildness, as the rain battled the volcanoes. At first, Pele wanted nothing to do with the pig god. But Kamapua'a advanced to Pele's crater and the two got into a fighting match. Kamapua'a sent his supporters, fresh green sprouts, to invade Pele's land and pop up through cracks in her lava. Pele attacked them with fire, and the battles waged on. When Kamapua'a and his supporters flooded her volcano with rain and extinguished her fires with mud, Pele finally yielded to Kamapua'a, and the two made love, then agreed to separate forever. Kamapua'a then controlled the rainy island lands, and Pele, the dry lands and active volcanoes. (Beckwith 1970, Frierson 1991, Knipe 1989)

See also Canyons, Oceania, Pele, Rain and Rain Gods, Volcanoes

LEI KUNG

Lei Kung was the Chinese Duke of Thunder, a deity that can be traced back to the first century B.C. In ancient times, he was called simply "the thunderer," but after Buddhism came to China he assumed the name Lei Kung and became an official in the Ministry of Thunder. The Chinese believed thunderstorms were a form of divine punishment, and Lei Kung was one of the primary deities responsible for meting it out. But because he only made the noise of thunder, he enlisted help from the other gods to carry out the storms. Lei Kung often worked in tandem with T'ien Mu, who flashed the lightning, Yu Shih, who poured the rains from a watering can, Yun't'ung, who piled up the clouds, and Feng Po, who released the winds from his goatskin bottle.

Lei Kung, the Chinese god of thunder.

Lei Kung was originally thought to be a bird, similar to the Indian Garuda bird, but in most representations he was depicted as an ugly man with a blue body, batlike wings, and clawed feet. He carried a mallet and chisel, and he wore only a loincloth with drums hanging at his side. Lei Kung produced the claps of thunder when he beat on his drums with the mallet, a function he performed in the ancient world as well as after the advent of Buddhism. Because the most popular gods in China brought wealth, health, and happiness, this horrendous thunder god had few temples and was invoked only by those wishing to hurt their enemies. He complied by striking them with his chisel, which he did in any situation outside the jurisdiction of human laws. (Larousse 1968, Werner 1995)

See also Chhih Sung-tzu, China, Feng Po, Garuda Bird, Thunder and Thunder Gods, Thunderbirds, T'ien Mu

LEO, THE LION

The lion is the fifth sign of the zodiac, and as king of beasts, a fitting animal to appear in the sky. This constellation can be traced back to Sumerian times and on to Babylonia, Greece, Rome, and many other lands. Some mythologists believe that in Sumeria, Leo represented the monster Khumbaba, who was killed by Gilgamesh. Other mythologists speculate that in Egypt, the lion represented the sphinx. But it is generally agreed that the zodiacal lion had some connection with the sun. About 4,000 years ago, the sun entered Leo at the summer solstice, so this constellation marked the day the sun's heat shone at maximum strength.

In Greek mythology, Leo likely represented the Nemean lion slain by Herakles in the first of his twelve labors. One Greek myth says that this lion was the offspring of Selene, the moon goddess, and that the lion descended from his home on the moon as a shooting star and landed in Corinth. There

Herakles found him in his cave, and, unable to shoot him with his arrows because the lion's skin was so tough, Herakles entered the cave and strangled him. Herakles then skinned the lion and wore his skin over his body like a coat. After its death, Zeus returned the lion to the sky as the constellation Leo. (Ridpath 1988, Staal 1988)

See also Constellations, Zodiac

LIBRA, THE SCALES

Libra is the seventh sign of the zodiac, the celestial scales that in ancient times were sometimes depicted in the hands of the neighboring constellation, Virgo, in her role as goddess of justice. Few ancient myths identified the scales as a separate star group. The Sumerians called this area the "balance of heaven," and the Egyptians called it Tula, meaning "a balance." But the Greeks didn't recognize the constellation at all. They called the area Chelae, which meant "claws," and considered it the claws of Scorpio. It was not until Roman times that Libra regained significance as scales, and the Romans assigned particular significance to this constellation because the moon was in Libra during the founding of Rome.

Using scales as a symbol for this portion of the sky made sense astronomically. In the first millennium B.C., the sun passed through Libra on the autumn equinox, the time when day and night are of equal length. For this reason, mythologists have assigned significance to this constellation not only as the weighing of justice, but also as the weighing of day and night and the seasons. Libra is the only one of the zodiacal constellations that is not living but is simply represented as an inanimate object—a set of scales. (Ridpath 1988, Staal 1988)

See also Constellations, Scorpio, Virgo, Zodiac

LIGHT
See Darkness and Light

LIGHTNING

As one of the most powerful forces of nature, lightning has an incredible capacity for destruction. It can split trees, shatter stones, and set flames sweeping across woodlands and grasslands with savage speed. Ancient people viewed lightning as fire from Heaven, and they equipped their most powerful sky gods with this fire as both a tool of creation and a weapon of destruction. In anger, the gods shot arrows of fire to punish sinners, and in kindness they shot them to energize the earth in life-engendering storms.

Ancient people entrusted lightning to their storm gods because they both feared and revered the phenomenon. Early people viewed lightning not as an electrical phenomenon but as a supernatural one, and they often perceived it as a weapon. In Greek mythology, Hephaestus forged the lightning bolts in his smithy under Mount Aetna and was believed to return to his smithy each spring, when lightning storms were imminent, to craft a new supply. Then he gave the weapons to Zeus, who hurled them from the sky. Perun hurled them in Russia, as Adad did in Mesopotamia. Indra used his thunderbolt, Vajra, to slay the drought demon Vritra. These were the storm gods, and the lightning bolts were their symbols. Adad was represented on cylinder seals with a jagged line, and the Scandinavian Thor was most always depicted with his hammer, Mjollnir, that delivered the punishing jolts then shot back to his hand like a boomerang. Lightning clearly belonged to the gods, so the powers of lightning were held sacred. In Greece, people often built fences around an area burned by lightning and turned it into a religious shrine. Guards at the shrine made sure that passersby paid their respects to the great powers of Zeus.

Hephaestus may have forged the lightning in his underground smithy, but in most traditions, lightning originated in what the ancients perceived as the celestial sphere.

ENCELADE PRÉCIPITÉ SOUS LE MONT ETHNA.
Enceladus buried under Mount Æthna.

Enceladus unter dem Berg Æthna bedeckt.
Enceladus onder den Berg Ethna bedekt.

Ancient peoples viewed lightning as fire from Heaven, and they endowed their most powerful sky gods with it. Here, a painting depicts Zeus hurling a bolt of lightning at the giant Enceladus, who was subsequently struck deaf and buried under Mount Aetna.

Because the ancient Greeks saw lightning as fire from Heaven, similar to the fire they kindled on earth, they often believed it came from the celestial bodies. Some early people believed lightning came from the sun, others believed it fell from the stars to the clouds, and still others believed it came from the planets Jupiter, Saturn, and Mars, the most distant planets the ancients recognized.

The fire in the sky had power. Lightning flickered and flared like magic and conjured up images of gigantic sky creatures flashing supernatural fire from bright, flaming eyes. In many lands, this creature was the Thunderbird. In Finland and in Mexico, it was a snake. Some North American tribes too likened lightning to a serpent, because, like a serpent, the bolt zigzagged quickly and forcefully and struck both upward and downward. The Aztec had their lightning god Itzcoatl, the obsidian serpent, and the great sky snake who accompanied Tlaloc, the rain god, and confined the fertilizing force of the universe in his belly along with all the waters of the world. People in dry regions associated lightning with fertility and particularly with masculine virility. By extension, they associated it with snakes. The lightning came with the nourishing rain and fertilized the soil after long periods of drought.

People throughout history tried to control lightning and thunder, even though they perceived the electrical flashes as evidence of heavenly power. Up to the Middle Ages, people tried to control lightning by ringing church bells to try to disperse it. They thought the sound waves created by the ringing bells deflected the lightning but later realized it did nothing of the sort. By the Middle Ages people no longer believed Zeus hurled the lightning bolts, or Thor, or the Slavic Perun, but they still had many beliefs based on ancient myths. The oak tree, for instance was known as the Thunder Tree and held sacred to Thor because he was thought to manifest himself as his roaring thunder

rustled the branches. This led to the belief that oak trees ensured safety from lightning and the medieval practice of keeping oak branches from trees struck by lightning to ward off the dangerous force that seemed to fall mercilessly from the sky. (Cerveny 1994, Dennis 1992, Fiske 1996, McCartney 1932, Schonland 1964)

See also Fire and Fire Gods, Lightning Bird, Storms and Tempests, Thunder and Thunder Gods, Trees

LIGHTNING BIRD
The Zulu are among the many tribes in southern Africa who believe that lightning is a large bird who lays a large egg wherever lightning strikes. Some sources say the bird is a brown bird, others say it is a kind of heron or fish eagle, and still others say it is a shiny red bird with feathers like a peacock. Some claim they have found this bird, dead, in a spot where lightning struck, and others claim they have found the eggs. Although it is argued whether such finds bring good or bad fortune, it is generally agreed that the lightning bird and its eggs have great medicinal value. African medicine men use the eggs as a potent ingredient in their charms, as does the Zambian rain doctor, who digs up the eggs then uses them in remedies that cure burns and other injuries caused by lightning. (Knappert 1995a, Parrinder 1986)

See also Africa, Birds, Lightning, Rain and Rain Gods, Thunderbirds

LOTUS
Mythmakers associated the sea, like the earth, with life, and they used the lotus as a common symbol for the fertility of the waters. This plant was native to many areas of the world, so it occurred frequently in myths and was highly revered by people of many cultures. The Egyptians considered the lotus a solar symbol, and they dedicated the flower to Horus, the hawk-headed sun god. The ancient Persians likewise venerated the lotus as

The Hindu goddess of fortune and fertility, Lakshmi was believed to have risen from the ocean on a giant lotus flower with a lotus in her hand.

the symbol of sun and light. In the Hindu world, the lotus held Lakshmi, the fertility goddess who rose from the ocean of milk, and Brahma, the creator of the world. In Egyptian myth, the sun god Atum rose out of the primordial waters on a lotus. The behavior of the flower gave rise to its symbolism. The flower sank to the bottom of the water at night, then rose to the surface in the morning and spread its petals on the surface. Like the sun, who rose from the waters, the lotus was widely recognized as a symbol of life, fertility, and resurrection. (Campbell 1974, Lehner 1960)

See also Benten, Brahma, Churning the Ocean, India

LUGH

Lugh was a Celtic warrior, usually identified as a god of light and sometimes identified as a god of the sun. The name Lugh meant "shining one," and like sun gods of other lands, Lugh set out to conquer evil. In one of his most popular myths, he cast a slingshot into the evil eye of his grandfather Balor, a god of the Formorii, a group of deities associated with evil and darkness.

Some scholars have suggested that Lugh's sling represented the rainbow and his slaying of Balor represented the conquering of light over darkness. Like all Formorii, Balor lived in the dark recesses of the sea, and his powers of evil could only be conquered by the light force of Lugh. Balor tried to prevent his defeat long before Lugh's birth when it was prophesied that one of Balor's grandsons would kill the king of darkness. So Balor imprisoned his only daughter, Eithne, in a cave. But an enemy of Balor sneaked into the cave and seduced Eithne, and she gave birth to triplets. Balor threw them into the sea, but Lugh survived. He was raised by smiths and grew to be a warrior, a sorcerer, and a master craftsmen. (Rolleston 1990, Stewart 1990)

See also Celtic Lands, Darkness and Light

M

MAGELLANIC CLOUDS

The Magellanic Clouds are two small, irregular galaxies visible as hazy patches in the southern sky, near the Milky Way. The Polynesians used them as navigational aids and often as weather indicators, because their position and relationship to one another varied with the seasons and the wind changes. Myths of the Magellanic Clouds were told throughout the Polynesian lands, where the names of these two galaxies varied, though many had connections to mist and vapor. Because the Magellanic Clouds were always visible above the southern horizon at night, the Polynesians apparently considered them important enough to immortalize in their myths.

In a Tongan myth, two children of a great chief represented the Magellanic Clouds, and they resided in the sky along with a gigantic duck and a parrot-fish. The children were born to a lizard mother, and upon learning their true parentage, they went in search of the great chief Maafu, to live with him as his sons. As time went on, the boys caused more and more trouble for Maafu. When the chief had taken all of the trouble he could stand, Maafu sent them to fetch water, first from a pond and the home of a gigantic man-eating duck, and then from another pond and the home a gigantic man-eating parrot-fish. The boys managed to kill both these creatures and take them home to their father. Finally, the father gave up trying to trick them and sent them away. The boys, Maafu toka and Maafu lele, took the duck and the parrot-fish and as-

cended to the sky. There they remain, along with the duck and the parrot-fish, where the chief, their father, can see them each time he looks up into the night. (Alpers 1970, Makemson 1941)

See also Oceania

MAMA KILYA

Mama Kilya or Mama Quilla was the moon goddess of the Inca, the wife of Inti, the sun, and the mother of the stars. The Inca considered their sun god a divine ancestor and the father of their people, so they likewise considered Mama Kilya their divine mother. As a lunar goddess, Mama Kilya presided over women, especially in conception and childbirth, and she played a prominent role in timing the sequence of rituals and festivals that dominated tribal life. Just as the changing moon marked the passage of time, the goddess of the moon assumed the function of regulating the calendar.

Mama Kilya was revered along with Inti and other important nature gods in the Coricancha at Cuzco, or the Temple of the Sun. There in a silver shrine, her image shimmered and glowed on a silver disk with human features. The Inca believed that during a lunar eclipse, a mountain lion was attempting to devour Mama Kilya, or her celestial image. As was customary of early people, eclipse chasers gathered together during this frightening time and made a lot of noise in hopes of scaring the lion away and protecting their moon goddess. (Spence 1977)

See also Clocks and Calendars, Eclipses, Inti, Moon and Moon Gods, South America

MANANNAN

In Celtic mythology, Manannan was lord of the sea, a popular ocean deity similar in function to the Greek Poseidon. Mythologists often identified his father, Lir, as the primary Celtic sea god, but Manannan played a more active role; Lir remained an impersonal presence and represented the material sea, as did the Greek Oceanus. Manannan reputedly had a throne on the Isle of Man, which jutted above the waves of the Irish Sea between Ireland and Britain. Either beyond or underneath Manannan's island lay the Land of Youth or the Islands of the Dead.

Manannan was a craftsman as well as a noted magician. He had a helmet that made him invisible and a magic boat or sea chariot called Wave-Sweeper that sailed across the ocean simply by the sea god's command. In the myths, Manannan was surrounded by ocean imagery. He had a steed named Aonbarr who could travel on sea or land, and like Poseidon, he often rode in a chariot drawn by horses who personified the white crested waves. Manannan also owned a gigantic magic coat, which served as an allegory for the sea itself. This coat could change colors, as the sea appeared to do when viewed from different angles, appearing golden in the sunlight, silver in the moonlight, blue or black in the ocean depths, and frothy white when crashing in waves on the shore.

As a Celtic deity, Manannan was the object of a cult that lasted into the nineteenth century. In Wales, he was known as Manawydan, though in Welsh myth, the deity was much less developed as a sea god. (MacCana 1985, Rolleston 1990, Stewart 1990)

See also Celtic Lands, Horses, Poseidon, Sea and Sea Gods, Water and Water Spirits, Waves

MARDUK

Marduk was the creator god of Babylon. He ordered the world from chaos, created the sky and earth from the primordial sea monster, and fashioned numerous forms of natural phenomena out of the monster's body. The worship of Marduk assumed such importance in Babylon that it approached monotheism. Marduk was most likely at first a god of water and of the sun, but as his powers expanded,

he controlled many other natural phenomena as well, including the rain, the wind, the moon, the stars, and the seasons.

Marduk rose in stature as a deity when he slew the primordial dragon. Other gods in other cultures accomplished similar tasks when they battled their monsters and when they conquered their chaotic forces. Marduk was an ancient dragon-slayer, and he had tremendous power. He used his control of the wind to open up the dragon's body with a hurricane and his control of the storm to release the waters imprisoned in the dragon's body. As the eldest son of Ea or Enki, the water god, he was identified with water, and, like water, he could fertilize the land and make the vegetation grow.

The victory of Marduk over the dragon led to the establishment of an ordered cosmos. According to myth, this creator god split the monster's body in two and raised half of it to form the sky and left the other half to form the earth. From Tiamat's spittle he made the clouds, the rain, and the seven winds, including whirlwinds and sandstorms. From Tiamat's poison he made the fog, and from her eyes the two great rivers, the Tigris and Euphrates. He made the moon and the stars, and he assigned the moon control over the night and the ability to measure time. With the universe divided and in proper order, Marduk assigned the gods their rightful realms. In return for his success, Marduk himself inherited Babylon. He became the patron deity of that city, and his rise to power grew as Babylon itself grew as a great political power in Mesopotamia. (Mackenzie 1996, McCall 1990)

See also Cosmic Order, Dragon Slaying, Enki, Mesopotamia, Primordial Sea, Tiamat

MARSHES AND SWAMPS

In some parts of the world, in Africa, Australia, and parts of North America for instance, marshes and swamps once covered large areas of land. Over time, the land changed, and the areas either dried up or filled with more water, depending on the amount of rain that fell. In myth and legend, water spirits inhabited these swamplands just as they did the larger bodies of waters in the world. Limniads inhabited the marshes and swamps in Greece, njuzu inhabited them in Zimbabwe, and in Australia in the primeval period called Dreamtime, tribes of animal ancestors inhabited them and they played a large role in changing the structure of the land.

Some of the myths of marshes and swamps explained why these areas changed. The waters dried up, for instance, because the spirits that inhabited them moved away. The njuzu of Zimbabwe, it was said, hated noise, and so they left their watery abodes when the Europeans arrived, and when they left, the marshes and swamps that they guarded disappeared. The Australian Aborigines of Kimberly explained the disappearance of their marshes in another way. Long ago, according to Australian lore, a large part the land was covered with marshes and lagoons, and in the lagoons, many types of bird families lived, side by side with animals of other species who inhabited other areas of the marshland. The animal tribes lived in harmony and friendship until one day the birds suggested that they remain separate, that families of one kind should not associate with families of another kind. The animal families were quite upset with this, as it meant that no longer would they have access to the bird families' waters. So the animals searched for a plan to make the sea flow into the land. They found their solution when they discovered a magic bone. When they used the bone to dig in the ground, the sea came up. The lagoons and marshes disappeared, and the seawater cut into the continent, forming what today is Spencer Gulf. (Smith 1996)

See also Oceania, Water and Water Spirits

MARUTS

The Maruts were Hindu storm gods, handsome young men and companions of Indra, who rode on whirlwinds in a chariot that sparkled with lightning. They stirred up tempests, caused thunder with their booming voices, and shattered cloud-cattle and split cloud-rocks with their bows and arrows, axes, and gleaming spears. The Maruts were atmospheric deities with names like "wind-speed" and "wind-force." Always at Indra's side, they accompanied him on battles and gained recognition for helping him battle Vritra, the drought demon.

Some sources say the Maruts were born from the laughter of lightning, but other sources give a different account. Their mother Diti was the wife of Kasyapa, the sage, and the mother of the Daityas and Danavas, giant demons who Indra banished to the dark depths of the ocean. The loss of her children caused Diti great pain, and she vowed to take revenge on Indra by bearing a son who could overpower him and kill him. To have this son, however, she had to stay pregnant for one hundred years. In the last year, Indra intervened. As recounted in the *Puranas*, he shattered her womb with his thunderbolt and split the embryo into forty-nine pieces. Rudra then created boys from these broken pieces of embryo, and these Maruts became Rudra's sons. Some myths referred to the Maruts as Rudras and presented them as personifications of various aspects of their father's character. Diti's plan backfired in any case, and her offspring became not Indra's enemies but his constant companions.

The Maruts were described as luminous, with bright skins draping their shoulders, golden helmets, golden breastplates, and golden bracelets around their arms and ankles. (Ions 1984, Mackenzie 1971, Moor 1984)

See also India, Indra, Rudra, Storms and Tempests

MASON-WASP

The Mason-Wasp was the African Prometheus. He traveled to the celestial sphere and stole fire from the sun. Many myths of fire explain not only how fire came to earth but also the colors of many insects, animals, and birds. In many lands, animals owned fire before people did, and in Africa, it was the Mason-Wasp who possessed it. This insect, the most common insect of Africa, is yellow with blue wings and striped legs and builds mud nests, often in fireplaces. The Ila of Nigeria believe that they have fire in their fireplaces because of the Mason-Wasp's quest and that the sparks appear in various colors because they are the Mason-Wasp's children, colored as brightly as he is.

According to the Ila, a long time ago, the earth was without fire and the insects and animals came up with a plan to obtain it. The Mason-Wasp volunteered to fly to the sun and beg the sun for fire. He embarked on his long journey, accompanied by a vulture, a fish-eagle, and a crow. The vulture, the fish-eagle, and the crow withered away to bones and dropped from the sky, one by one, but the Mason-Wasp persisted higher and higher until finally he stopped to rest on a billowing cloud. God went down to meet him and inquire as to his mission, and the Mason-Wasp explained his needs. God made him chief over all the birds and reptiles on earth and told him to build nests in fireplaces. This myth explained how domestic fire came to the people of Nigeria. (Frazer 1996, Parrinder 1986)

See also Africa, Fire and Fire Gods, Prometheus

MAWU-LEZA

Mawu was the sky god and the highest deity of the Ewe people of present-day Ghana and Togo. Like the Greek Ouranos, the Polynesian Rangi, and the Hindu Dyaus, he personified the firmament, yet he also represented the great sky father married to the goddess of the earth. In one tradition, Mawu and Leza together formed this primordial couple, yet the two were perceived as one androgynous being rather than as separate partners. Sometimes Mawu was male and Leza was female, and sometimes it was the other way around. But whether perceived as separate gods or as a duality, this force moved the world.

Mawu and Leza, then, were creator deities. They represented the moon and the sun, day and night, and they created all the gods and assigned them domains in the earth, sea, or sky. Some of the peoples who considered Mawu alone the Supreme Being believed he used to live on earth but retreated to the heavens when smoke from people's fires burned his eyes. Mawu remained in the heavens as an omnipotent, benevolent sky force. He stored water in the firmament and let the rain fall in regular patterns to prevent drought or flood. Mawu's benevolence was typical of many other sky gods in world myths. He guaranteed survival so the people did not fear him. They therefore spent their time worshipping and sacrificing to the more personal deities he created, or he and Leza created together—the storm gods who often destroyed the land with fire and wind.

As the great sky father, Mawu was often visualized as a man who resided in the firmament while the other gods remained below to run the world. As the personified sky, the clouds were his robes; the blue color of the sky, his veil; and the light that illuminated the world, the oil with which he anointed his body. Some tribes connected Leza with meteorological phenomena and Mawu with the sky in general and with rain. Those who considered Leza alone the Supreme Being attributed to him all the powers attributed to other celestial sky gods. They considered him provider, protector, and guardian of the natural order of the universe. (Forde 1954, Frazer 1926, Herskovits 1938)

See also Africa, Sky and Sky Gods

MEDICINE WHEELS

Long ago, peoples of the North American Plains assembled rocks in circular arrangements to create what early settlers called medicine wheels. Most likely, they were used for tribal rituals, something the pioneers who named them believed a shaman or medicine man might have overseen. Archeologists today know of fifty or sixty medicine wheels, all of them along the eastern front of the Rocky Mountains, from Wyoming through Alberta and Saskatchewan. Ancient builders constructed each one differently, some as simple piles of rocks, and others in wheel configurations with a central pile of rocks, a ring of smaller piles, and rocks radiating from the center, like spokes.

The Bighorn wheel in Wyoming is perhaps the most famous of the medicine wheels and is believed to be a place where Crow Indians fasted during their vision quests. Some scholars connect it directly with the Sun Dance. A Crow legend attributes the Bighorn wheel to a young boy named Burnt Face, who assembled the rocks while he himself fasted in the mountains. The boy had fallen into a fire and become badly burned, and he retreated to the Bighorn Mountains to live his life as a recluse. There he fasted, and he spent his days assembling stones in a circular arrangement. Then one day a tornado came whirling toward Burnt Face in the form of an eagle, and because Burnt Face helped the eagle by making bows and arrows and getting rid of the otters who preyed on baby eagles, the big eagle miraculously healed his face. Ever since then, Crow Indians use Burnt Face's wheel in their vision quests, a process they undergo to commune with the nature powers. Some scholars theorize that the Bighorn wheel symbolized the center of the world, a place where shamans drew the sky powers down to earth. Some of the Crow said the Bighorn wheel was assembled by the sun himself, who made it his camping place. Scientists who analyzed the formation of the Bighorn wheel, and other medicine wheels as well, did discover alignments to solar events, among them the sunrise and sunset at the summer solstice, a time of year when the sun appeared to stop in its yearly path before it turned around and headed the other way. (Frey 1987, Krupp 1983, 1997b, Williamson 1984)

See also Astronomy, Clocks and Calendars, North America, Sun Dance

MERMAIDS

Legends of mermaids have permeated the sea lore of maritime nations since antiquity. Ancient people likely theorized that because men and women populated the earth, they also populated the sea. The mermaids of antiquity were beautiful maidens and enchantresses, both seductive and destructive, like the sea and like water itself. They personified both the beauty and the treachery of the ocean, and they represented the dangers of the rocks along the coastline.

The image of the mermaid probably stemmed from fish-tailed gods of early civilizations who had power over water. Mermaids date back to Babylonian myths and to the sea god Oannes and his female counterpart, Atargatis, both ancient sea deities and the earliest recorded ancestors of mermaids. Both Oannes and Atargatis were at first depicted as mortals in fish cloaks, but over time, their cloaks were modified to tails. Oannes was perhaps an earlier form of the Sumerian fish-god Ea or Enki, and he represented the positive side of the ocean, rising from the waves each morning and sinking below the waves each night, like a sun god. Atargatis, conversely, was worshipped as a moon goddess and represented the ocean's dark, destructive side.

The mermaids patterned after Atargatis's prototype had numerous attributes that identified them with the sea. They had long flowing hair, often green like seaweed or like rays of sunlight falling on the water, and they

The mermaids of antiquity were beautiful maidens, enchantresses—both seductive and destructive, like the sea.

often held mirrors to reflect the light of the moon and to identify them with the moon's control over the tides. Mermaids lived in undersea homes made of pearl and coral but were often seen basking on the sun-drenched rocks, gazing into their mirrors and combing their long, wavy locks. Sailors in many lands claimed to have seen these beautiful sea maidens, but rarely did they catch more than a glimpse. Mermaids seemed to fear mortals, and as soon as they saw one, they dove into the water and disappeared from sight.

This image of appearing and disappearing mermaids was a common image. These beauties were seductive and alluring yet just beyond reach. But mermaids, and their male

counterparts, mermen, longed to acquire human souls, and they could, it was said, if they captured the heart of a mortal. For this reason many mermaid tales involved trysts between these sea maidens and human men. In some tales, the men entered into the trysts willingly, seduced by the mermaid's beauty and charm. But in others, they were abducted, lured under the sea where the mermaids kept their human souls prisoners. The mermaid's love was deadly. If sailors saw mermaids, it usually foreshadowed such dangers as storms, shipwrecks, and possible drowning. Not all tales of mermaids told of death and destruction, but many told how vengeful mermaids became when angered. Fishermen off the coast of Ireland used to believe that angry mermaids caused uproarious winds and deadly tides. (Baring-Gould 1897, Benwell 1965, Phillpotts 1980, Rappoport 1995)

See also Nereids, Sea and Sea Gods, Sirens, Water and Water Spirits

MERU

Somewhere within the glorious snow-covered Himalayas lay the mythical Mount Meru, the cosmic mountain that rose up through the layers of Heaven to the home of the gods. The Himalayas stretch over India and Tibet and other parts of Central Asia, so the mythical mountain was worshipped by numerous groups of people in these lands. In the mythology of Mount Meru, this magnificent landform rose more than 80,000 miles from the deepest part of the Underworld to the highest point in Heaven. It connected earth, sky, and Underworld, and it ran right up through the center of the world.

Mount Meru, it was believed, lay just to the north of India, right below the North Star, which was connected to the other celestial bodies with ropes of wind. Sometimes it was said to rest on the backs of four elephants who themselves rested on top of a tortoise swimming in the ocean of life. The elephants represented the cardinal directions, and

Mount Meru, the north celestial pole and the pivot of the sky. The sun, the moon, the stars, and the planets therefore revolved around Meru, and the Supreme Deity had his throne on the summit. Indra or Brahma lived on the summit, and so did Buddha, just as Zeus and the high gods in the Greek pantheon lived on Mount Olympus. Half way up Mount Meru rested the chariots of the sun, moon, and stars.

An Indian myth explained why Meru supported the sun's chariot as well and why the mythical mountain was golden in color. Meru had strong connections to the sun as well as to the heavenly Lake Anavatapta and its waters of immortality. It was said that a magic shaft rose each morning from Anavatapta's magic waters to lift up the thrones of the sun and the moon. In myth, Surya, the sun, wanted a rest from his continuous revolutions around Meru, and he asked the mountain for permission to place the axle of his chariot on the sacred slopes. Because Meru agreed, Surya blessed the mountain, and from then on, Meru was golden, like the sun. (Bernbaum 1990, Mabbett 1983)

See also Fujiyama, India, Mountains, Olympus, World Axis, Ziggurats

MESOAMERICA

The myths of Mesoamerica emphasized the movement of natural forces and the interplay between them. Sky myths and agricultural myths defined the Mesoamerican calendars, rituals, and the people's perception of everyday life. The Mesoamerican tribes inhabited Central America, primarily Mexico, before the Spanish conquest in the early sixteenth century and included the Aztecs, the Maya, and their predecessors. Although scholars know much less about the mythology of these cultures than they do about that of the Indo-Europeans, archeologists have unearthed a world dominated by nature deities who kept order in the cosmos by virtue of the reverence and rituals of their worshippers.

The cultures of Mesoamerica immersed themselves in their deified world, and their mythology reflected a profound fear of catastrophic natural events. These people lived in a land of contrasts, and disasters plagued their world. They had rainforests and deserts, floods and droughts. They had hurricanes, volcanic eruptions, and earthquakes. Naturally, such instability influenced the myths the people created and instilled a profound fear of the natural forces and the gods who controlled them. The people knew that Tlaloc, their rain god, could provide adequate rainfall or could just as easily withhold the rain or send it down from his sky world in a torrential downpour. They believed that evil star gods could devour the moon, and they saw them do so. They knew that even though the sun rose reliably every morning, it just might sink below the horizon one day and never return. Concern with the sun's movement and the fear of such catastrophes as flood and eclipse permeated Mesoamerican culture. These people gave the sky gods primary roles in their myths, and they often viewed the interplay between them as cosmic battles.

The Aztec myth of the five suns involved the cosmic battles of Quetzalcoatl and Tezcatlipoca, two principal deities whose interaction brought about cyclic creations and destructions. The notion of multiple creations, or worlds, was common throughout Mesoamerica and among some other New World societies as well. The myth of the five suns outlined four previous world ages, or "suns," each characterized by a phenomenon of nature that defined the world and then destroyed it. The element earth devoured the world's inhabitants. The element wind blew the world to bits in a horrendous hurricane. The element fire exploded the world in a volcanic eruption. Then the element water annihilated the world in a deluge. In each of these eras, Quetzalcoatl and Tezcatlipoca battled and destroyed the world, and then they joined forces to reconstruct it.

The interaction between Quetzalcoatl and Tezcatlipoca conveyed the notion of complementary opposition. Dualism, it was believed, existed from the beginning of time. The Aztecs perceived a multilayered universe, with thirteen levels of Heaven and nine layers of Underworld. Ometeotl, the god of duality, resided at the topmost level of Heaven. He possessed both male and female principles and embodied creative energy. Ometeotl created both Tezcatlipoca and Quetzalcoatl and ensured cosmic order by doing so. In the Mesoamerican myths, opposition brought about world order. Night and day represented the most basic opposition, and Quetzalcoatl embodied the light of the Morning and Evening Star, and Tezcatlipoca the darkness of the night sky. Dawn, like light itself, represented stability and order, whereas night marked a time of chaos. The Mesoamericans feared the night sky, and they feared Tezcatlipoca for his association with it. But they knew that both light and darkness were essential to world order.

The Mesoamericans were so preoccupied with the sky forces that they symbolized the battles between them in myth and reenacted them in ritual. Most famously, they played a macabre ballgame in which players assumed the guises of gods and played out the scenes they witnessed in the heavens. Quetzalcoatl slaughtered Tezcatlipoca just as Venus, as Morning Star, slaughtered the darkness of night. The sun slaughtered the moon and the stars as it did every morning when it rose above the horizon. Playing a ballgame that involved ritual sacrifice today seems brutal and heartless, but to these ancient people it expressed reverence for the sky gods. That reverence was grounded in fear. When the player representing the sun killed those players representing the moon and stars, it ensured that the sun rise and renew the light. The players believed that by living out the order they witnessed in the sky, they had a hand in guaranteeing order in their world.

The fear the Mesoamericans had of disorder in the heavens led to the development of amazingly precise astronomical methods. The Maya in particular had a highly developed calendar, and it included elaborate eclipse tables and detailed observations of Venus, personified as Kukulcan, the feathered serpent. The Maya seemed to particularly fear the disappearance of Venus on the western horizon and the first yearly appearance of the planet on the eastern horizon, considered to be a bad omen. So they tracked the planet diligently and recorded these first appearances in their hieroglyphic codices. Pictures of Kukulcan wove through the pages alongside mathematical symbols, and the calendar represented an intricate weaving of science and myth. The Maya developed mathematical techniques unrivaled by any of the ancients except the Babylonians. They gained the practical knowledge to build their calendar because they wanted to predict events they greatly feared.

The myths of the Mesoamericans centered on natural phenomena, both in the sky and on the earth. Because these people knew firsthand of natural catastrophe, they wove myth with calendrics to predict times when the forces of nature might potentially destroy the world. These people ensured that the world stay in motion by continued worship, continued sacrifice, and the kindling of new fire at the end of every fifty-two-year cycle. At this time, the priests of the Aztec capital city, Tenochtitlan, performed the New Fire Ceremony. They knew that the world ended four times before and that it was just a matter of time before the current world ended as well. The sky would stop spinning, the sun would lose the strength necessary to rise, and the star demons of darkness, the tzitzimime, would plummet down to earth and annihilate human life. All this would occur, they believed, at the end of a fifty-two-year cycle. But the priests prevented this intrusion of chaos. They gathered on a barren hilltop at midnight on November fourteenth, and they watched the heavens closely. They watched for the descent of Kukulcan, the feathered serpent, who they then recognized in the Pleiades star group. When the serpent began its descent, the priests chose a victim for sacrifice, tore out his heart and lit a fire on his chest, and then threw the throbbing heart into the fire. A blazing light obliterated the darkness. In the New Fire Ceremony, sacrifice, the kindling of new fire, and the mysterious force of Kukulcan combined to ensure survival of the world. The ceremony marked simply one event in the lives of people propelled by worship and ritual and powered by the natural forces that moved the world and instilled order in the cosmos. (Aveni 1980, Bierhorst 1990, Brundage 1979, 1982, 1985, Markman and Markman 1992, Taube 1993)

MESOPOTAMIA

The ancient region called Mesopotamia generally referred to the fertile valley between the Tigris and Euphrates rivers and the land that extended northwest into Syria and Turkey and northeast into Iran. This area today is called the Middle East, but in the ancient world the northern part of the same area was termed Assyria and the southern part Babylonia. Some of the earliest nature myths originated in this part of the world. Because the land in this large area was subject to five long months of drought, the people relied on rain to swell the rivers. They depended on their fertility gods to battle the drought demons, restore the earth to fruitfulness, and maintain order in the world.

Due to the harsh climactic conditions, ancient nature worshippers saw forces of evil and chaos continually emerge to threaten their earth. The model for chaos in Mesopotamia, as well as in other places, was the sea, and the Babylonian creation myth began with nothing but the chaotic sea, personified as the she-dragon Tiamat. Marduk, the creator god, exploded Tiamat and formed the universe from her body. By doing this he organized the cosmos into three parts: He assigned Anu to rule the sky, Enlil to rule the earth, and Enki to rule the waters.

Division of the universe into three parts occurred in Greek thought as well, and just as Zeus, Poseidon, and Hades assumed primary importance in the Greek myths, so did the Babylonian triad. The supremacy of Enki attested to the importance of water in this semidesert landscape. The supremacy of Anu attested to the order the ancients witnessed when they watched the sky. Enlil, as earth god, embodied the wind that had the capability of blowing water all over the land. The Mesopotamians were agriculturists, yet no significant rain fell on their earth from April through October. Sterility consumed their world during these long, hot months. By the time the drought-stricken land had withstood all it could withstand, the earth had turned hard and the vegetation had died. The farming communities looked for supernatural help, and they prayed to the storm gods to bring relief.

When the rains finally did come, they poured hard. The Tigris rose quickly and flooded over a wide area. The Euphrates rose a little slower, but eventually it flooded as well. These rivers were fertilizing agents, but their propensity for violent inundations attested to their destructive power, as well as that of the gods who brought the heavy rains. Predictably, one of the most popular myths of this area was the myth of the Deluge. The Sumerian account came first and formed the basis for later versions, all of which conveyed the belief that water could obliterate life as easily as it could create it. Although the nature gods used rain to restore the land to fruitfulness, they also used flood as an expression of anger and a means of punishment.

Flood may have been a primary concern of the Mesopotamians, but drought, not water, posed the biggest threat. Because of the critical importance of rain, the storm god assumed primary importance, and the Babylonian storm god, Adad, belonged to the second triad of supreme gods, along with Sin, the moon god, and Shamash, the sun god. Adad had equivalents in other parts of Mesopotamia, among them Teshup, the Hittite storm god, and Baal, the storm god of Canaan. The mythmakers likened these deities to virile bulls who roared with power. Baal played a primary role in the myths of Canaan, and he took responsibility for fighting the forces of chaos. In the first of his battles, he swooped down from the sky like a vulture to fight Yam, the embodiment of the raging sea. Yam was a dragon, equivalent to Tiamat. He was tumultuous and dangerous and could rush over the land quickly and flood it in a short time. The people of this area clearly knew the strength of water, but perhaps they recognized that water's true power existed in the form of rain. Baal defeated Yam, then took on his other adversary, Mot. This second battle provided him with an even greater challenge, for Mot lived in the Underworld, so Baal had to die in order to conquer him.

The myth of Baal's war against Mot perhaps best described the climactic battles that went on in the Middle East. It was most likely a metaphor for the change in seasons, particularly the tension that accompanied the crucial turn from the period of drought to the period of rain. As a storm god, Baal embodied fertility, and Mot embodied the destructive power of drought. By descending to the Underworld and returning, Baal became a dying and rising god. In most myths of dying and rising gods, the earth god or goddess traveled through death and back. Such was the case with Ishtar, the Babylonian fertility goddess. But the storm god, too, embodied fertility. Metaphorically, he died in autumn when the drought demons took over the land, then he returned in winter or early spring to resurrect the earth.

The fact that the Mesopotamians lived off the land appeared to motivate their mythmaking as much as their activities. Worship of natural phenomena defined the nature of early Mesopotamian religion. The first deities existed in animal forms, and then eventually in human forms who represented the same nature powers. When Alexander the Great conquered the region in the fourth century B.C., these early gods became political powers. But this representation echoed nature worship. The order established by kings and the order established by nature appeared to be interconnected, as if the active forces in the universe defined the nature of true power in the world. (Black and Green 1992, Gray 1982, McCall 1990, Mackenzie 1996)

METEORS AND METEORITES

Meteors perplexed astronomers into the nineteenth century when they discovered them to be rock fragments of planets or asteroids, and sometimes, fragments of the moon that were hurled into space millions of years ago when other meteors blasted into the lunar surface. When these interplanetary fragments hit the earth's atmosphere, the friction fried them up, and at that point, they disappeared. But for a brief moment, the people witnessed a bright flame shooting down to earth. To the ancients that meant that someone from above sent these fiery messengers for a reason, and the frightened people believed that quite likely, these messengers meant harm.

Many myths about meteors emphasized their association with evil. Most commonly, ancient people believed these flaming rock fragments were demons, flying to earth for some malevolent reason. Given the significance ancient people assigned to fire and the fear they felt when some strange occurrence in the sky appeared to upset the cosmic order, it's easy to imagine how the appearance of a meteor caused trepidation and a sense of doom. But not all myths painted such a dark picture. In many ancient tales

A meteor shower over Niagara Falls.

meteors were simply weather portents, and in others, souvenirs of the thunder gods. In the latter case, the people actually found the rock fragments on the ground, because some of them survived their fiery falls and landed on earth as meteorites.

To early people, it appeared that some celestial being hurled these rock fragments from Heaven, just as Thor, the Norse thunder god, hurled his mighty hammer. The connection of meteorites with thunder gods was widespread. The ancients called their valuable finds "thunderstones," and often endowed them with the same fertilizing powers that they endowed the gods, their lightning bolts, and their mighty storms. The Mongols of China kept thunderstones and used them as tools, and the people in Scandinavia thought them to be actual pieces of Thor's hammer. People of many cultures told myths of meteors and meteorites, and many of those people believed them to be of celestial origin. The Hindus linked them to the severed body of Rahu, the eclipse demon. California Indians linked meteors with the moon; they called them the moon's children. Some New Guinea tribes thought the flaming light was the woman in the moon descending to earth to capture someone to take her place. Other groups connected them with stars, and, for thousands of years, people believed meteors were actual stars falling from Heaven. Some people in Oceania considered them children of the stars, a form souls of the dead assumed at night.

Mythmakers across the globe connected meteors with dead souls. People in Queensland believed they represented the ropes their dead relatives used to climb to Heaven and then dropped when they arrived safely. People in Islamic lands thought meteors were falling demons, hurled earthward by angels when the demons tried to reach Heaven and got too close to the angels' celestial abode. In parts of Europe, Africa, and Asia, every person had a star of their own in the sky, one that shone while the person lived and fell when he died. People in other lands had many different stories. The Australian Aborigines called meteors fire sticks of their dead enemies. Others called them fire sticks of sorcerers. Some tribes in central Asia called meteors fire serpents, and in Siberia, fire worms. The Siberian fire worms came to earth at night to prey on mortals and drink their blood.

Like comets, eclipses, and the occasional supernova, ancient people saw meteors as intruders in familiar skies, so they held supernatural forces responsible for their appearance. Incan priests used the fallen meteorites for divination, often to predict deaths and illnesses, and to determine the location of stolen items. The peoples of New Zealand believed their ancestor Tumatakokiri used them to predict the weather. These celestial fireballs could do amazing things because they came from amazing sky powers, storm gods like Thor and the Pawnee Tirawahat. In Siberia, the people believed they saw meteorites when the gods opened their sky roof made of hides and peeked down on earth. Others believed they saw them when the gods got bored and threw little pieces of coal from the fires in their palaces behind the dome of the sky. (Dennis 1992, Krupp 1991a)

See also Astronomy, Chaos, Comets, Demons, Rahu, Thor, Thunder and Thunder Gods

METZTLI

In the Aztec myth of the five suns, the god Tecciztecatl volunteered to throw himself into the sacrificial fire and rise as the fifth and current sun. He became Metztli, the moon, instead. The Aztecs believed in a succession of world ages, and a fifth sun had to rise in order for life to continue after the previous four suns died when cataclysmic natural forces destroyed their worlds. Tecciztecatl gathered with the other gods at Teotihuacan to bring about the new age and the continuance of life. Then he volunteered for the sacrifice. He threw himself into the sacrificial fire, but he did it too late. The diseased god, Nanahuatzin, proved more humble and more willing. Nanahuatzin became the sun, Tonatiuh, and Tecciztecatl became the moon, Metztli.

Tecciztecatl, at first, appeared more willing to sacrifice himself than did Nanahuatzin. But, feeling the heat of the flames, he hesitated. Nanahuatzin did not. Nanahuatzin jumped first into the fire, and then Tecciztecatl followed him, not to be bested. The gods waited. Soon, Nanahuatzin rose in the east as the bright new sun, Tonatiuh. Tecciztecatl rose after him, just as bright. The gods knew that two suns lighting the heavens would make the world too bright, so one of the gods threw a rabbit in the face of Tecciztecatl, which wounded him and darkened his face. From that day forward, Metztli, the moon, was forever dimmer than the sun, his face permanently marked with the imprint of the rabbit, visible in pattern of light and dark patches on the full moon.

Metztli was sometimes portrayed as a goddess rather than a god, and though she controlled fertility, she also represented night, dampness, and cold. The two hills prepared for the sacrificial fires of both Metztli and Tonatiuh were converted to temples, known today as the Pyramid of the Sun and the Pyramid of the Moon. (Brundage 1979)

See also Aztec Calendar Stone, Mesoamerica, Moon and Moon Gods, Moon Spots, Sacrifice, Tonatiuh

MICHABO

Michabo was the Great Spirit of the Algonquins of what is now the northeastern United States. He was sometimes referred to as their sun god, but he represented not only the power of the sun but also the breath of the winds and the force that rebuilt the earth after the great flood. Michabo created the sun, in fact, and was responsible for a great number of other creative acts, which included building beaver dams that became the Great Lakes, shooting arrows into tree trucks that became branches, floating pipe smoke over the hills to create the autumn haze, and sending a muskrat to the bottom of the sea to bring up the grain of sand that made the habitable land. The Algonquins worshiped him as the Great White Hare, which was perhaps a reference to his connection with the sun and his role as the spirit of light who dispelled the demons of darkness.

Michabo played a similar role to weather gods of other cultures and was worshiped by other neighboring tribes under such names as Manabohzo and Nanabush. In some myths, Michabo lived in the sky with his brother, Snow, and in others, on an island in Lake Superior or on an iceberg in the Arctic Ocean. Most commonly, however, he lived somewhere in the east, and from his home there, on the shore of the ocean thought to encircle the earth, he sent the moon and the sun on their sky journeys. Michabo ruled the weather, and he battled the serpent prince of the waters who lived in the lake and flooded the earth. Like serpent killers of other cultures, Michabo killed his adversary with a dart, symbolic of the mighty thunderbolt. His battle with the serpent prince, then, was likely an allegorical myth that explained the role of the sun god in advancing the seasons. (Brinton 1976, Fiske 1996, Spence 1989)

See also Dragon Slaying, Great Spirit, North America, Sun and Sun Gods

MILKY WAY

Throughout the world, the Milky Way fired the imaginations of skywatchers who imagined a great celestial path or river stretching across the heavens. In the dark skies of the ancient world, it stood out, white and sparkling, like a divine stream of milk from a celestial goddess. Though the Milky Way is really a system of stars, gas, and dust, to the ancients it looked like a trail, a path of spilled milk that graced the skies like a shining road to Heaven. That road they saw illuminated not by stars but by heavenly fires that guided travelers across the sky from one end to the other.

Most commonly, ancient peoples perceived the Milky Way as a river, usually a celestial counterpart to a river on earth. In Egypt, it was the Nile, and in India, it was the Ganges. In China, the Milky Way was the Tien Ho, or the Silver River, a heavenly counterpart to the Ho, or the Yellow River, that flowed through northern China into the Yellow Sea. Little fishes were said to swim in the Tien Ho, forever fearful of the crescent moon, which glistened above the celestial waters like a metal hook. Disembodied souls swam along this Milky Way river to reach the Otherworld, or the Land of Peaches.

In the Peruvian highlands, the Quechua viewed the Milky Way not simply as a celestial river but as a crucial player in the water cycle. These people regarded their Vilacanota River as an earthly reflection of the Milky Way, and they believed both rivers worked together to bring about the recycling of water from earth to sky. These Quechua recognized an exchange of fluid between the two realms, an exchange that connected the river on earth with the river in the heavens. They likely theorized then, that water could flow back and forth between these two rivers, circulating skyward to the Milky Way and falling back to the Vilacanota and to the earth as rain.

In some civilizations, the Milky Way represented not the connection of earth with sky but the connection of the two halves of Heaven. Perhaps this notion stemmed from a similar astronomical theory of the Milky Way espoused in the first century A.D. Some Siberian tribes may have ascribed to this notion, because they viewed the Milky Way as a seam where the two parts of Heaven were stitched together. They perceived the stars along the Milky Way as lights that shone through the stitch holes, lights that came from somewhere within the vault of Heaven and from palaces of the sky gods.

People in many lands saw the Milky Way as a path. It led to the sky gods' palaces, or to the Land of Peaches, or to whatever they envisioned as the Otherworld. They considered it a passage or a road traveled by souls of the dead in their transition from life to death. The Vikings knew the Milky Way as the path to Valhalla, the palace of the warrior Valkyries slain in battle. The Inuit of North America and the San of Africa called it the Ashen Path, lit not by glowing stars but by hot ashes from celestial fires. Some people saw the brighter stars along the Milky Way road as campfires built by dead souls as they traveled to their destination. Others considered the stars the souls themselves, shining brightly in the skies as, metaphorically, they had shone brightly on earth.

As a path from one world to the next, the Milky Way was likened to the rainbow, that elusive and ethereal bridge of color that appeared to span two realms. Both the Milky Way and the rainbow represented gates to the Otherworld, and in the Middle Ages, the Milky Way was perceived as a bridge that angels used to get to and from Heaven. Whether a bridge or a path, a celestial river or a stream of milk, the Milky Way linked the world of the living with the gods in the sky. It led to places that existed only in the imagination, and it vanished like a bird as it flew upward and disappeared into the heavens. The Estonians believed the Milky Way was a path for birds, and they told a tale to explain the Milky Way's function. They told of Lindu the Guardian of Birds, who fell in love with the northern lights and who pined away because her lover went north and never returned. Dressed in her wedding gown, Lindu waited and waited until finally, the South Wind swept her up to the sky. There she remains as Guardian of Birds, her wedding veil flowing like the Milky Way and leading the birds through the sky as they migrate south for the winter. (Allen 1963, Krupp 1991a, Staal 1988)

See also Bridges, Cosmic Sea, Rainbows and Rainbow Gods, Stars and Star Gods

MIRAGE

A mirage is an illusion, an optical phenomenon caused by the reflection and refraction of light in unique atmospheric conditions. Most modern travelers in the deserts and navigators on the seas know the phenomenon of mirage, as did people in antiquity. Desert travelers commonly see illusions of glittering lands and glistening water, and sailors commonly see images of sunken cities and mountains and phantom ships sailing in the distance.

When the ancients saw these images, they spun myths to explain them. Today's observers have access to facts. Mirages commonly occur in deserts and on seas because the phenomenon affects calm regions subjected to intense heat or cold. A mirage can also occur on flat plains, on ice fields, and in the sky, when the atmosphere acts like a lens and projects an image that is actually there, but many miles away. When there is a sharp temperature contrast, the layers of air have different densities. When the two layers lie next to each other, they create two images, one real and one imagined. The image is based on an inverted reflection. A layer of warm air over the colder seawater, for in-

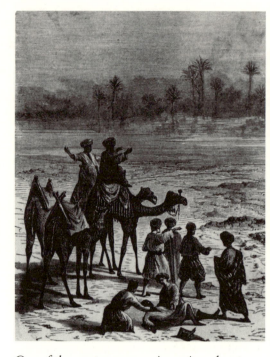

One of the most common mirages in a desert, an oasis in the distance.

stance, can give an inverted reflection of ships, sailing below the horizon. A layer of dense cold air over the desert reflects light from the clouds at sunset, and projects an image on the sand that looks like water. The sky acts like a mirror in this case, and the currents of air moving in the sunlight add to the mirage by creating the illusion of shimmering waves. Not surprisingly, this phenomenon gave rise to many myths and legends. People who knew nothing about the nature of reflection and refraction focused only on the images they saw, and they told tales of lakes and pools in the desert and of sunken cities and phantom ships on the seas. (Bassett 1971)

See also Deserts, Fog and Mist, Islands, Mermaids, Sea and Sea Gods

MIRRORS

Mirrors symbolize reflection and light, and in nature myths, specifically the light of the sun and the moon. This symbolism is linked to the ancient belief that mirrors trapped a person's soul. In a sense, they trapped the soul of many a moon goddess and many a sun goddess when these deities showed themselves to the world by gazing at their reflection in the glass.

The concept of the soul being trapped in the mirror led to the concept of the sun or the moon being trapped and to the belief that by using mirrors, it was possible to bring the sun or the moon mystically to earth. People couldn't look at the sun directly, but by looking in a mirror or in water, they could see the reflection of their light deity and watch her dance and whirl around. In some cultures, it was the shaman's job to capture these celestial light goddesses, as in Japanese myth, Uzume, the enchantress, captured Amaterasu by dancing in a mirror outside her cave. Mirrors and metal discs representing the sun and moon were common elements of shamanic costumes, and the shamans gazed into them to find their way to the Otherworld. The Mongul shaman believed he would see a white horse in the mirror, who would transport him to the sun or moon in a trance. The Yakur shaman wore a metal disc with a hole in it, called the Orifice of the Sun. This shaman believed he could descend through the hole to the Underworld, just as the sun itself descended to the Underworld each night. (Davis 1992, McCrickard 1990, Ono 1962)

See also Amaterasu, Mermaids, Shamanism, Sun and Sun Gods, T'ien Mu, Tsuki-yumi

MIST
See Fog and Mist

MITHRA
Mithra was the Persian god of light and heat, identified with the Vedic Indian deity Mitra and sometimes labeled a sun god. Mithra was born from beneath a rock on a riverbank on the day of the winter solstice, some say due to fertilization of the rock by the sun god's lightning. His emergence was a metaphorical expression of the light that arose from below the horizon. Mithra's light preceded the sun into the morning sky and dispelled the darkness of night, and his birth on the day the sun shone its weakest dispelled the darkness of winter.

Mithra was clearly a sky god who controlled the cosmic order. His emergence from the rock on the winter solstice made possible the rotation of day and night and guaranteed the immortality of the sun. Mithra slew the primordial bull in a cave beneath the earth and thus performed the act that identified him as creator. The primordial bull contained the seeds of creation, so when Mithra killed him, he created life. Mithra's birth and the bull-slaying incident symbolized the birth of time. When Mithra killed the bull, he set the world in motion. Plants and animals sprang from the bull's body, the stars revolved around the sky, the moon moved through its phases, and the sun continued on its westward path through the zodiac, guaranteeing the continuous cycle of life.

Mithra was widely worshipped in the ancient world but gained particular prominence in Persia in the eighth to sixth centuries B.C., then again in the Roman Empire in the second to third centuries A.D. Mithra knew all and could see all, as could other gods with solar attributes, and he acted as judge of the living and the dead. He was not the sun but rather the creative spirit of light and solar power. Representations of Mithra throughout the Roman world depicted the great god slaying the bull. (Curtis 1993, Frazer 1926, Krupp 1991a)

See also Balder, Darkness and Light, Persia, Shamash, Solstices, Sun and Sun Gods

MIXCOATL
Mixcoatl was the Aztec cloud serpent, alternately known as a storm god, a god of the Milky Way, and a representation of the tropical whirlwind. He was a shape changer,

sometimes taking the shape of scudding clouds and sometimes of a giant with a striped body, long black hair, and the face of a deer or a rabbit. As a cloud serpent, Mixcoatl was clearly associated with the Milky Way, that band of white that snaked across the heavens, as well as the storm, which the Mesoamericans identified with celestial serpents. As god of the Milky Way, Mixcoatl personified the souls of dead warriors who ascended to the sky and became stars, and as god of the sky, he personified the heavens, just as his wife, Coatlicue, personified the earth.

Mixcoatl had many functions, and, in one of his most popular myths, he introduced flint to mankind and brought fire into the world. In this myth, Mixcoatl appeared as the red aspect of the sun god, Tezcatlipoca, and with the flint, he successfully drilled fire and brought light and heat into Aztec life. The transformation into Tezcatlipoca clearly gave Mixcoatl solar attributes, and the Aztecs often worshipped their cloud serpent in solar rituals. He was said to have fathered the Centzon Huitznahua, or the four hundred warrior sons of Coatlicue, who represented the stars of the Milky Way. These stars were created to feed the sun, who devoured them each morning as he rose in the sky.

Mixcoatl was frequently depicted wearing a black mask that veiled his eyes like storm clouds veiled the sky and with red and white stripes like the stripes painted on sacrifice victims. In some representations, he carried a sheaf of arrows, his thunderbolts, which he used both as storm god and as god of the chase. Mixcoatl was worshipped in some areas of Mexico under the name Camaxtli. (Brundage 1979, 1982, Miller and Taube 1993)

See also Coatlicue, Mesoamerica, Milky Way, Star and Star Gods, Storms and Tempests, Sun and Sun Gods, Tezcatlipoca

MOIST MOTHER EARTH

The earth goddess of Slavic myth was associated with moisture and referred to as Moist Mother Earth. In Russia long ago, earth worship formed the basis of religion, particularly among the peasants and farmers who depended on the land to provide food even though it froze solid during the winter. Moist Mother Earth was possibly revered as Mati-Syra-Zemlya or as Mokosh. Her connection to moisture suggested her connection to the waters of both the earth and the sky. She was associated with streams and wells and was frequently evoked to end droughts with her life-giving rains.

Like earth goddesses of other lands, Moist Mother Earth was a fertility goddess. Some say she was the wife of Perun, the storm god, and that he clothed her in his sky waters, making oceans, rivers, and seas. The Slavic earth mother was a spinner, and she spun the waters that renewed life after the icy winds blew in and the winter gods cast their death spell on the land. Worshippers of Moist Mother Earth not only prayed to her to bring the rain but also to calm the winds and the whirlwinds, to subdue the snowstorms, and to lessen the severity of the winter cold. (Hubbs 1988, Larousse 1968, Simonov 1997)

See also Baltic and Slavic Lands, Earth and Earth Gods, Spinning and Weaving, Springs and Wells, Water and Water Spirits

MONSOONS

Monsoons, prevalent in southern Asia, change direction according to the seasons. They blow from the southwest all summer and bring heavy rains, then blow from the northeast all winter and sweep across the ocean with powerful force. This seasonal pattern gave rise to myths of supernatural beings materializing as monsoon winds and wreaking havoc on land and sea. Because the most destructive behavior of these beings occurred in winter when they blew in from the north, the north was feared as the home of the monsoon or the ocean wind.

The Chinese personified the monsoon as Yu Ch'iang, a bird deity classified as both a sea god and a wind god. In a myth that explained the monsoon pattern, Yu Ch'iang began his yearly flight in the north, then flew southward for six months to rest in the sea of the south. As a sea god, this deity had the body of a large northern whale with hands and feet, and he rode through the water on two dragons. But when Yu Ch'iang got angry, he changed into an enormous bird called a pheng, with a human face and the dragons, or sea serpents, clinging to his ears and feet. When the pheng flew south, it rose out of the ocean, flapped its gigantic wings on the water, then mounted a whirlwind to the sky and spread its monstrous wings over the ocean like dark storm clouds. Its furious flapping caused the gigantic waves, and the force of its movement as it flew south typified the powerful wind system that characterized the China Sea. (Christie 1985)

See also Rain and Rain Gods, Sea and Sea Gods, Storms and Tempests, Winds and Wind Gods

MOON AND MOON GODS

In sky myths all over the world, the moon stood for mystery, change, transformation, and immortality. The moon moved the tides and controlled the rain; it changed from one form to another, disappeared, and then emerged again. Because the moon appeared to grow, in ancient myth it made life itself grow. Moon goddesses all over the world represented the life cycle and controlled the growth and fertility inherent in nature.

Because the moon changed forms, as a sky force, it set a pattern. By tracking the behavior of the moon, early people established their own patterns and learned to rely on the silver sky goddess to set the cycles of their lives. The changing moon taught people when to plant, when to reap, and when to expect the annual migrations of game animals. It helped them build a calendar. But by deifying the silver orb, the people looked beyond the practical. They gave their goddess human qualities. When early people saw the moon wax, they thought their goddess was actually growing bigger, and when they saw it wane, they thought she was diminishing or being broken into pieces.

Many lunar myths explained why the moon waxed and waned and many conjured up events leading to the moon's destruction. In the Baltic lands, Saule, the sun goddess, sliced up her moon god husband, Meness, because he had committed adultery with the Morning Star, Auszrine, the sun goddess's rival. In Aztec Mexico, the sun god Huitzilopochtli also sliced up the moon, in this myth represented by his sister, Coyolxauhqui. In North America, the sun and moon were husband and wife, and when they quarreled, the sun god beat his moon goddess. He beat her when she passed through the hole at the edge of the sky before her husband, which was why the moon disappeared for a time. She pined away and lost her light. Gradually, she returned and regained her light. But each time her husband looked at her disapprovingly or beat her, she pined away again. Because the moon continued to renew itself, the people knew their silver sky goddess was immortal.

World myths are full of gods and goddesses who represented the moon in its various phases. People deified the rising moon, the setting moon, the waxing moon, and the waning moon. In Rome, Hecate represented the moon before rising and setting, Astarte when it was a crescent, and Diana or Cynthia when it was high in the sky. In India, Anumati represented the day before the full moon, and in a California tribe, Damhauja represented the moon just before renewal. In Sumeria, Nanna was considered the moon god, but Ensum was the same deity as a half moon and Suen the same deity still as a crescent. The Maori had a goddess for the dark phase of the moon called Hina-Uri, an aspect of their moon goddess Hina. The Romans deified the waxing moon as the goddess Postvorta. The crescent or the waxing moon was a symbol of increasing power. This moon appeared to have horns, like a cow, and it served as a symbol of fertility.

The fact that moon goddesses controlled fertility had more to do with their ability to wax and wane than it did with the appearance of horns. When it waxed, it appeared to be filling up with some sort of liquid, a magic liquid, the Water of Life, the Soma of Indian myth that made the gods immortal. Because the ancients believed the moon was full of water, they also believed their moon goddesses controlled rain, dew, snow, and ice, elements that fell from the heavens and fertilized the earth. The moon's watery nature connected it with life and, metaphorically, with the waters of the womb. But it also connected it with death. The mythical flood, it was said, caused the moon's death. As the lunar waters poured from the heavens, the moon's life blood was depleted. Then when the rain stopped, the moon began to fill up again.

Because the moon waxes and wanes, dies and is resurrected, myths of the moon often centered on time and rhythms. Moon deities governed the recurring cycles in nature, those of the tides and the rains, of the plant life and of the earth itself. So traditionally, moon deities ruled the seasons. The Peruvian moon goddess, Mama Kilya, regulated the calendar. The Egyptian Thoth was called Measurer of Time. These lunar deities set the cycles as they moved from barrenness to fertility, from death to rebirth. The moon encompassed these cycles and these dualities all by itself. It alone embodied the eternal battle between light and dark. The Japanese envisioned the moon as a white crystal palace inhabited by thirty princes, fifteen black and fifteen white. Each of the princes ruled the

moon for one day, and the crystal palace turned light and dark accordingly.

Moonlight is bright and powerful. It can penetrate the darkness and turn the night sky aglow, but it can never be as bright as the sun. Ancient myths attempted to explain why. In Bantu myth, the moon got splashed with mud in a fight with the sun. In India, Ganesha, the elephant-headed god, threw his tusk at the moon in anger because the moon laughed at him for eating sweetcakes. Often in myth, the moon as well as the sun was thought to retreat to the sea when it descended from the sky. In Maori legend, Tangaroa, the sea god, kept the moon out of the sky too long and it began to decompose. In a myth from Papua New Guinea, the moon stayed underground rather than in the sea, but it did not stay there long enough. A man plucked the moon out of the ground prematurely. Had he left it to grow there longer, it would have achieved maximum brightness. But as it was, it grew bigger and bigger in his hand, then it flew into the sky. (Harley 1969, McCrickard 1990, Proctor 1926)

See also Clocks and Calendars, Cosmic Order, Death, Dew, Moon Spots, Seasons

MOON SPOTS

The silver orb that dominated the night sky held people transfixed long before they began to unravel its mysteries. Early people knew nothing of the topography of the moon; they saw the moon as a god or a goddess, or an abode of the gods and goddesses, and they fancied all sorts of Immortals living there, their dark images silhouetted against the bright lunar surface. The lunar features have since been identified as seas and craters, but they were known to the ancients only as dark spots. Early moonwatchers saw patterns in those spots, and they struggled to find explanations for why and how those patterns appeared.

Many early mythmakers identified moon spots as animal forms and, commonly, as a hare or a rabbit. In one Native American legend, the gods struck the moon in the face with a rabbit, and it stayed there lighting the world on clear nights. In an Aztec legend, the moon was once as bright as the sun, but a god threw the rabbit into the moon's face and darkened it. The story of the rabbit in the moon took many forms and appeared in legends around the world. In ancient China, Sri Lanka, and Africa, the markings on the moon's surface were called the "Mark of the Hare." Chinese legends told of a hare who sacrificed its life to satisfy Buddha's hunger and was sent to the Moon as a reward. Many of these ancient tales glorified the rabbit as a symbol of enlightenment and good fortune—qualities the ancients often attributed to the moon.

The rabbit was not the only animal people saw etched on the moon's surface. There were many others—and human faces as well—with all sorts of legends attached to them. In Sweden, people saw two faces, a boy's and a girl's, and they believed them to be those of Bil and Hjuki, two children the moon took a fancy to and captured. In that story, the children appeared in the moon with their pail. In New Zealand, the moon goddess, Rona, appeared with hers. She had insulted the moon because it hid behind a cloud when she was getting water and caused her to trip in the darkness. For the insult, the moon captured her. Other people explained the spots in other ways. In New Guinea, an old woman hid the moon in a pitcher, but some boys opened the pitcher and the moon escaped. The dark spots were the marks left by the boys' hands as they struggled to hold the moon back. In myths of the Americas, the moon was the sun's brother, and the two had an incestuous relationship. But because they met at night and the sun could not see the moon in the darkness, she painted dark patches on his cheeks so she could recognize him later. A similar myth appeared in South America. In this story, the rain that fell was explained as a

continuing attempt to wash away the spots from the moon's face.

People struggled to decipher moon spots because the pattern of light and dark was so distinct. To some people, the light spots looked like toads. In Tahiti, the dark spots looked like the groves of trees. Later, when people formed more scientific explanations, Aristotle taught that the moon was smooth and that the dark spots were reflections of the earth's mountains. Even though it was not accurate, this explanation had come a long way from those based on the premise that the moon was living and feeling and capable of capturing or gobbling up people. To people of the Samoan Islands, the moon looked like a ripe and delicious breadfruit, and a woman who was hammering cloth on earth begged it to come down and let her child eat some of it. Insulted at the suggestion, the moon ate the woman, her mallet, and her child. They remained in the moon ever since. (Harley 1969, Krupp 1991a)

See also Heng O, Hina, Hjuki and Bil, Moon and Moon Gods

MOONBEAMS
See Sunbeams and Moonbeams

MORNING STAR/EVENING STAR
Astute skywatchers of the ancient world noticed that certain bright objects frequently dominated the eastern sky in the morning, disappeared for a time, then reappeared and dominated the western sky in the evening. Those who recognized the phenomenon deified the object, and they incorporated its sky travels into their myths and legends. The planets exhibited curious behavior in their sky world. Unlike stars, they wandered, and they flitted back and forth between east and west. All five planets visible to the naked eye behaved in this manner, but Venus moved the most obviously, and it always stayed close to the sun. Except for the sun and the moon, Venus is the brightest object in the sky.

Venus, the brightest object in the sky aside from the moon and sun, caught the eye of the ancients, who gave the planet the role of an enchanting goddess. Botticelli's Birth of Venus *is one of the best-known representations of this deity.*

Because of its brightness and its beauty, Venus often played the mythological role of an enchanting goddess. Astronomers named the planet after the Roman goddess of love, Venus or Aphrodite, who rose from the ocean, like the planet appeared to do when it appeared above the horizon. The Babylonians called this goddess Ishtar or Inanna, and the Slavs called her Auszrine. Both Ishtar and Auszrine were also exceptionally beautiful and radiant. In Russian mythology, in fact, Auszrine was considered more radiant than the sun. The moon could not rise for two nights because he was so transfixed by her, and when she rose from the sea in the evening, the sun set because Auszrine's beauty outshone her.

Myths of Ishtar and Auszrine and other deities who represented the Morning and Evening Star emphasized not only their beauty but also their behavior. Ancient sky-watchers observing the planets against the background of stars noticed the curious but regular cycles in the planets' movements, particularly in the movements of the illustrious Venus. This deity had a dual nature, so myth-makers sometimes identified it with twins. Some scholars identified the Aswins of Hindu myth as the Morning and Evening Star. As solar horsemen, they emanated light, and when they rose before the sun, they conquered the darkness. Chasca, the page of Inti, did the same thing in the myths of the Inca.

Venus rose before the sun, traveled next to it across the sky, disappeared for a time behind it, then descended after it below the horizon. For this reason, Venus seemed to die and to return to life. The Aztec called this dying and rising god Quetzalcoatl.

Unlike the promiscuous goddess identified in other lands, in Mesoamerica Venus was aggressive and masculine. In the myths of the Aztecs, Quetzalcoatl acted like the planet Venus. In the myths of the Maya, the adventures of the Hero Twins, Hunahpu and Xbalanque, have been shown to correspond to the movements of Venus as it alternated between Morning Star and Evening Star. The Maya assigned high significance to Venus, and they tracked the planet diligently and recorded its cycles. Hunahpu and Xbalanque moved like Venus through the constellations of the zodiac. The Popul Vuh, the sacred book of the ancient Maya, recounted the adventures and trials of these brothers as they fought and slew the monstrous bird Seven Macaw, or Vucub Caquix, then descended to the Underworld to battle the Lords of the Night. The battle Hunahpu and Xbalanque fought took the form of a ballgame. When the twins defeated the death gods, they arose from the Underworld, first Hunahpu as Venus, the Morning Star, and Xbalanque right after him, as the sun. The ballgame was a metaphorical enactment of the conflict the Mesoamericans imaged bright celestials engaged in when they fell into the Underworld and encountered the forces of darkness. The Underworld was represented as the ballcourt. Venus and the sun had to win the ballgame in order to rise, and they did. People chosen to represent the Mesoamerican gods often engaged in ballgames to re-enact celestial events the myth-makers witnessed in the night sky. (Krupp 1991a, Tedlock 1993)

See also Astronomy, Auszrine, Ballgame, Death, Ishtar, Planets, Quetzalcoatl

MOROZ

Moroz was the Jack Frost of the Slavic lands, and the pagans greatly feared him for his tendency to freeze people to death. Frost chilled the earth much of the year in this part of the country, so Moroz was a formidable presence. He was white as snow and had icy breath. He lived in the forest in a cottage covered with snow and dripping with icicles. Sometimes he was described as a blacksmith who forged chains of ice to shackle the earth and to bind the sea. He immobilized the world in a freeze-frame of death.

Moroz figured in many pagan legends in which an evil stepmother gave him her stepdaughter to be his bride. These stories appeared to illustrate that though frost had deadly tendencies, it also blanketed the earth and kept it from freezing too deeply. In one version of this legend, the stepmother planned to use the frost to kill her stepdaughter, and she left the young girl in Moroz's forest to die. But because the girl welcomed Frost instead of rebuffing him, he took mercy on her and covered her with his trees. This frost deity was believed to be wealthy because he owned the forest and everything he covered. He gave the maiden all his finery, and she survived. When the stepmother saw what Moroz had done for the girl, she sent her most beloved daughter to him as well. But this time Frost turned deadly. This second daughter was cruel to him, unlike the first, so Frost descended on her with his icy grip and froze her to death. (Ralston 1873)

See also Baltic and Slavic Lands, Frost and Ice, Snow

MOUNTAINS

Mountains are places of power. They evoke a feeling of mystery and magic, and they serve as sources of life, places of enlightenment, and pathways to sky powers. Mountains have been revered throughout history as sacred places, as elusive and enigmatic as they are vast. They hide in the fog and they glisten in the snow. They pour water from dark recesses that washes over the earth and fills up the rivers. Sometimes, they erupt in fiery explosions.

This air of mystery led many people to perceive mountains as the abode of high gods. They housed weather spirits and earth gods within them and powerful celestial deities on top. The ancient Greeks revered Mount Olympus as this sacred dwelling place, the home of Zeus and many of the most powerful gods in their pantheon. The Hindus revered Mount Kailas as the home of Shiva and Parvati. These magical peaks jutted up beyond the rain, behind the clouds, and reached far into the realm of Heaven. They made ideal highways for the gods to descend to earth and for people to ascend to the sky.

People who revered mountains often made no distinction between the power of the mountain and the power of the mountain gods. Though the Hindus considered Mount Kailas the abode of Shiva and Parvati, they also personified the entire mountain range as the god Himalaya. In Japan, people believed mountain deities called yama no kami to be both inhabitants of the peaks and a part of the natural world they inhabited. Some North American Indians continue to consider mountains their ancestors. Such beliefs often led to the practice of praying to mountains and offering sacrifices to them, because the people accepted the landform as an active deity capable of responding to this special treatment. The sacred mountains concealed power within their caves. They hid the weapons of thunder gods, held the brewing pots of rain gods, and kept the winds locked deep inside their rocks. When lightning flashed above the mountain summits, the Greeks believed Zeus had unleashed his thunderbolts. When rain poured over the earth, the Aztecs believed the children of Chac, the rain god, were brewing their magic waters. When gusts of wind whistled around the jagged peaks and swept over the land,

people of many cultures believed some mysterious power had released these winds from their mountain prison.

Some of the most sacred mountains of the world extended high enough to offer both a panoramic view of the earth and a spectacular vision of the heavens. People climbed mountains to gain both perspectives. The Japanese climbed mountains to achieve spiritual enlightenment. Native American shamans climbed them to acquire vision and revelation from nature's forces. The power of the peaks to reveal the spirit world led many people to simulate mountains by building high towers that linked the realms of the universe. The Mesoamericans and the Egyptians built temples and pyramids to the sky powers, and the Mesopotamians built ziggurats with long stairways leading to Heaven.

Mountains not only reached up into the heavens, however, they also extended down into the earth. This led to the common view of the mountain as a cosmic axis, similar to the world tree. Certain mountains were perceived as the center of the universe and a conduit linking Heaven, earth, and the Underworld. In India, the mythical Mount Meru was the pivot around which the sun and the stars revolved. Meru and other cosmic axis mountains served both as a cosmic center and a place of creation. Mountains anchored the world and steadied the directions and were therefore central to the order of the cosmos and the stability of the world. (Bernbaum 1990, Campbell 1974, Hori 1966)

See also Cosmic Order, Fujiyama, Meru, Olympus, Pyramids, Volcanoes, World Axis, Ziggurats

MUJAJI

Rainmaking is common practice in the hot, dry parts of Africa, and Mujaji, the rain queen of the Lovedu tribe, is a powerful rainmaker still worshipped today. Mujaji's story began around A.D. 1600 with one of her ancestors, Mambo, who ruled the area now called Zimbabwe. Mambo's daughter stole a rain charm and some sacred beads and fled with her son to the mist-covered Drakensberg Mountains where they formed the Lovedu tribe. The rain charm was passed down through generations and eventually fell to Mujaji, who at the time was the daughter of the king. Mujaji learned the secrets of the rain charm, and then succeeded her father as monarch. She became the first of a succession of rain queens, all named after her, who knew how to perform magic to either supply rain to their people or deny rain to their enemies.

The Lovedu rain queen is simply one of the many high officials or chiefs of African tribes entrusted with the crucial duty of rain-making. Each Lovedu rain queen inherits the previous queen's medicines and charms at the time of her death, so the rain magic always remains secret. Burning the medicines produces black smoke that is believed to induce black clouds to cover the sky and rain to pour down, and the most important ingredient in the rain-pots is believed to be skins from the queen's dead ancestors, who have to give their approval before the queen's magic will work at all. The Lovedu rain queen is believed to guarantee the cycle of seasons by bringing rain in times of drought. She does have help, however. A rain doctor, her assistant, uses divination to discover the cause of the drought and medicines to remove any forces that avert the queen's powers. (Forde 1954, Parrinder 1986)

See also Africa, Rain and Rain Gods

MUSIC

Mythological characters played musical instruments of many kinds, particularly the harp and the lyre. In Scandinavia, Odin chanted Runes; in India, the Gandharvas sang in Heaven; and in ancient Greece, Orpheus played his lyre. When the gods played or sang, nature danced. The winds blew, the rivers flowed, and the trees and the flowers wavered from side to side. Music in myths

was clearly a metaphorical expression of wind—its singing power, its moving power, and its power to stir the natural world.

The connection between music and wind was overt. Usually, when the gods played, nature moved; then when the gods ceased to play, nature stilled. When in Finnish mythology the sea gods played Wainamoinen's harp, the ocean winds sounded on the beach. When in Greek myths Orpheus played his lyre, or when in Celtic myths Dagda played his harp, music, like the spring breeze, awoke nature after its winter sleep. But in Slavic tales, music put nature to sleep. It was not the spring breeze in this case but rather the autumn wind that chilled the earth.

The sound produced by playing musical instruments had much to do with cosmic order and, perhaps, with the concept of Music of the Spheres. By producing music, the gods imposed harmony, and the myth-makers appeared to connect that harmony with movement in the natural world. The ancient Greeks coined the phrase "Music of the Spheres" to explain the belief that the planets revolved around the earth and that as they did, they made sound. The connection of movement and sound implied a sense of order. Perhaps Orpheus produced a similar kind of order when he played his lyre. It was said that the seven strings of the lyre corresponded to the seven known planets and that the lyre was a symbol of the harmony of cosmic forces. Lyre music rose up to the sky like smoke, and so did the ascending musical scale. The lyre appeared to symbolize a link between earth and sky, and music to represent an ordered pattern of the cosmos. (Baring-Gould 1897, Cox 1887, Graham 1979, Watson 1984)

See also Cosmic Order, Planets, Winds and Wind Gods

MYESYATS

Myesyats was the moon deity of the Slavic lands and the marriage partner of the sun.

The union of these two celestials was a popular theme in Slavic myths, and in most cases this moon deity was the male and his wife a beautiful and radiant goddess. The two of them lived together in the sun palace and conceived all the stars of the night sky. But the marriage was fraught with turmoil. The brightest of these star children grew more radiant and beautiful than his wife. Myesyats married his sun goddess in the summer when she shone the brightest, but he left her in the winter when her light began to fade and the light of the Morning Star outshone her.

Myesyats and his sun goddess fought bitterly over this, and by doing so, they upset the balance of nature. People felt the results of their battles when earthquakes shook the land. Myesyats was a philanderer, and he played a subordinate role to the sun goddess, who was much more worthy of praise and admiration. But people prayed to the moon god to heal their diseases. They invested him with this power because they saw him die every month and renew himself. They assumed he suffered from some affliction yet could cure it and bring himself back from death. (Larousse 1968, McCrickard 1990)

See also Auszrine, Baltic and Slavic Lands, Death, Moon and Moon Gods, Saule

NAGAS

In the myths of India and southeast Asia, Nagas were serpents who inhabited rivers and pools and the waters believed to exist beneath the earth. The Nagas of Indian myth appeared either as cobras or as half cobra and half man, and they had the ability to change forms at will. Some of the Nagas, like Shesha, the king, drank a few sips of Soma, gained immortality, and were worshipped as gods. But most of them were demons, powerful and dangerous and known to cause droughts and disturbances of wind and tide.

In a sense, the Nagas compared with the dragon-kings of Chinese and Japanese myths who lived in palaces under the sea made of coral, crystal, and glimmering gemstones. The Nagas also had palaces and gemstones they wore on their hoods that glittered so brightly they lit up the dark regions of the Underworld. Like the other demons of Indian myth, the Nagas inhabited a region called Patala, a luxurious land beneath the earth. But no matter how luxurious their abode, like many mythological snakes, these serpent gods personified evil. When their anger flared up, they tapped into nature's destructiveness, and they used their control over nature's most powerful forces to cause harm and death. (Howey 1955, Ions 1984, Werner 1995)

See also Demons, Dragon-Kings, Dragons, India, Serpents and Snakes, Water and Water Spirits

NEREIDS

The Greek sea nymphs, the Nereids, were mermaids said to personify the ocean waves. They were part of a large group of sea deities who attended the sea king, Poseidon, as he rode across the water with his wife Amphitrite, who was once a sea nymph herself. Like all mermaids, the Nereids had the top half of a woman and the bottom half of a fish and were exceptionally beautiful. Although the sea nymphs played peripheral roles in the myths, they appeared often, swimming in the water, frolicking in the waves, or sunbathing on the shore, where they were often seen drying their shiny, flowing tresses.

The Nereids were generally believed to be the daughters of Nereus and Doris, sea deities who personified the watery element itself. The Nereids personified not only the waves specifically but also the qualities and properties of the sea in general. These lovely nymphs lived in caverns at the bottom of the sea, some say seated on thrones in the sea palace of their father. They emerged to the surface when the waves rose and could be seen flashing through the sea like a play of sunlight on the water or dancing on the sand like the flowing tide that etched frothy patterns on the shore. (Bassett 1971, Graves 1988)

See also Amphitrite, Greece and Rome, Mermaids, Nereus and Proteus, Nymphs, Waves

NEREUS AND PROTEUS

Proteus and Nereus were ancient Greek sea gods, and both were commonly referred to as the Old Man of the Sea. Both Proteus and Nereus exhibited two characteristics common to sea gods around the world—the gift of prophesy and the ability to change shapes. These characteristics reflected the ancient perception of water. Early seafarers represented the multifaceted ocean with the changing forms of a deity, and they embodied

The Triton and the Nereid, *a late-fifteenth-century engraving by Jacopo de Barbari.*

the notion that the depth of the waters was somehow connected to wisdom as a wise and prophetic old man.

Nereus appeared in many early myths, but in later times Poseidon usurped his role. But whereas Poseidon had a violent temper, Nereus was kind and helpful and, like the Norse sea god Njord, represented the calm aspect of the sea. Nereus was depicted as an old man with long flowing hair and a white beard, and he lived in a magnificent palace in the Aegean. Proteus also lived under the sea, but he rose from the waters at noon every day and took a nap on the shore of the island of Pharos near Egypt—that was where, outside his element, people attempted to catch him and gain his prophetic powers. Proteus was perhaps most famous for his shape-changing ability, and Nereus for fathering the Nereids, the lovely nymphs who, like their father, represented the changing properties of the sea and the waves. (Murray 1935, Rose 1959)

See also Greece and Rome, Njord, Poseidon, Sea and Sea Gods

NIGHT

Creation myths usually began with darkness, a deep primordial darkness that the sun dispelled when creator gods introduced light into the world. Light was clearly a precious commodity, but mythmakers also recognized the essentiality of darkness. Although light enabled the formation of the world, with day and no night, time stood still.

According to some myths, in the beginning stages of the universe, night belonged to the sky or the sea but had not yet come to earth. In a legend from Brazil, it belonged to the sea. The sea serpent's daughter left the sea to live with her mortal lover on the sun-drenched earth. But she missed the darkness dearly, so her father sealed night into a bag and sent it back to his daughter with servants. Intrigued by the night noises coming from the bag, the servants opened it and spilled the night into the sky. In a similar myth of the Dayak of Borneo, a sky goddess also fell in love with a mortal, and she brought to earth with her another bag full of night. This goddess wanted the darkness to conceal her trysts with her mortal lover. But once again, someone opened the bag and the darkness of night escaped. For a while the mortals tried to capture the darkness and conceal it again, but it didn't work. It lifted for a time, but it returned every night.

Concealing night in a bag conveyed the value of darkness. Early people often feared it, but the mythmakers clearly realized its significance. In a myth from Sierra Leone, Africa, the Supreme Being gave Bat a basket to take to the moon, and darkness escaped when some animals opened it. Like the sky goddess in the Dayak myth, Bat tried to return the darkness to the basket. In Desana myth, the sun gave one of the earth people a sealed purse, and when the curious people opened it, black ants emerged and created the blackness of night. Again, nighttime was both necessary and evil. But a myth from India outlined the consequences of a world without night. In the beginning, only a pair of twins lived on earth, a boy named Yama and a girl named Yami. They loved each other dearly and they lived together in a world where it was always day and the sun never set. One day, Yama died, and Yami grieved inconsolably. Her tears flooded the land, her wracking sobs shook the earth, and her grieving heart set the world on fire. The gods knew she would destroy the world with her grief, and they knew the only way to ease her grief was to bring night to the world. So the gods created the first sunset, and soon darkness blanketed the earth. From then on, time moved on. Day turned to night and night to day. Over time, Yami's grief dissipated, and the earth moved through the seasons. (Ferguson 1996, Parrinder 1986)

See also Darkness and Light, Duality

NILE RIVER

The Nile River is the lifeblood of Egypt. The ancient Egyptians believed it had its source in the sky, just as the Chinese believed of the Yellow River and the Hindus believed of the Ganges. In the ancient world, before the construction of the High Dam, the flooding of the Nile was an annual event and the sole reason for the fecundity of the Egyptian river valley. Because of the crucial importance of this river and its floodwaters, a large body of Egyptian myths dealt with the sanctity of the waters and the gods of fertility who controlled them.

The primary Egyptian deities responsible for the Nile's function were Khnum, god of the Nile's cataract region; Hapi, the spirit of inundation; and, most importantly, Osiris, god of the flood and the personification of the Nile itself. Up to the sixth century, Nun was considered god of the Nile, Nun being, like the Mesopotamian Absu, an endless expanse of inert water envisioned as a primeval being. Later, the people believed the Nile flowed from Nun. It watered the world by drawing from the great ocean of water that surrounded the sky and the Underworld.

In Egyptian thought, Nun surrounded the floating earth and manifested himself in any source of underground water as well as in the flood water of the Nile. Hapi was in this sense identified with Nun and was said to emerge from the subterranean ocean through two whirlpools in the twin caverns of Elephantine. Hapi lived at the first cataract of the Nile, and Khnum guarded the entrance to his caverns. When Khnum unbolted the cavern doors, Hapi flowed out through the heavens, through the Underworld, and then divided up and flowed north through Egypt and south through Nubia.

The people of Egypt worshipped the gods of the Nile, sacrificed to them, and highly revered them for their life-sustaining powers. They considered Khnum a benefactor to the people because, by unbolting the doors and releasing Hapi, he created the flood. He also guided Hapi in both directions. Hapi himself unleashed the waters, and because of this, some people revered him even more than Ra, the sun god. They credited Hapi with making the land fertile and the harvests bountiful. Both Hapi and Khnum were fertility gods, identified with Osiris, who personified the Nile's fertilizing force.

Worship of Osiris as the god of the Nile was an important part of Egyptian belief. The death of Osiris was symbolically associated with the annual rising and flooding of the river and the subsequent vitalization of the land. In this tradition, it was thought that the rotting body of Osiris acted as a fertilizer that spread over the valley of Egypt and perhaps into the arms of two goddesses who personified the riverbanks and begged to be made fertile. The Nile waters were considered the sweat of Osiris's hands and the annual flood the tears of Isis, his consort, who grieved after the evil Seth locked her husband in a casket and sent him floating down the river to his death. Isis, too, played an important role in the flood. She appeared in the sky as the star Sirius, who rose each year in the predawn horizon to herald the overflow of the waters. To the Egyptians, the annual return of Isis as the star Sirius was evidence of the cosmic order that ancient people throughout the world witnessed in their skies. (Ions 1983, Lockyer 1964, Spence 1990)

See also Egypt, Ganges River, Isis, Osiris, Rivers and Lakes, Sirius

NINHURSAG

Ninhursag was the Sumerian earth goddess, and, like Gaia of Greek myth, she embodied the physical land in the area specific to her worship. In Mesopotamia, marsh waters covered the lower land, but the edge of the Arabian desert was dry and rocky. The name Ninhursag meant "Lady of the Stony Ground," and she embodied this rocky earth, yet still she served as fertility goddess. By

worshipping Ninhursag as the Great Mother, the Mesopotamian people affirmed their belief in the creative principle and in the ability of the earth to provide, even under harsh physical conditions.

Ninhursag figured prominently in Mesopotamian myths, but the story of her romance with Enki, the water god, perhaps best reflected the geographical conditions of the area. In the myth, Enki mated with the earth goddess, but then raped their daughter and went on to rape their daughter's daughter, producing offspring with each union. The series of rapes caused tension between Enki and Ninhursag and symbolized the opposition between water and earth. But most importantly, the union of these two elements led to the growth of vegetation. For this reason, the worship of Ninhursag as the Great Mother goddess was closely connected with agricultural rites. (Gray 1982, Jacobsen 1976)

See also Earth and Earth Gods, Elements, Enki, Gaia, Mesopotamia

NIOBE

The Greek myth of Niobe has been interpreted as a metaphor for numerous forms of natural phenomena, including the clouds, the mists, the ice, and the hard, cold winter. Niobe had beautiful children—so beautiful in fact, that she bragged that as a mother, she was better than Leto, the mother of Apollo and Artemis. But Apollo and Artemis got their revenge. They slew Niobe's children one by one with their arrows, just as the rays of sunlight and moonlight slew the mists. Niobe, like the clouds, dissolved to tears, which hardened to stone on the mountain summits, and her children, like the mists, died as the bright darts of Apollo and Diana penetrated them. Some scholars believe Niobe personified the clouds and others believe she personified the winter. Niobe's tears, in this winter theory, represented not the rain but the thaw that occurred when sunbeams penetrated the ice. (Graves 1988, Guerber 1992)

See also Apollo, Arrows, Artemis, Clouds, Fog and Mist, Greece and Rome, Rocks and Stones, Sunbeams and Moonbeams

NJORD

One of the three principal Vanir gods of Norse mythology, Njord was a fertility god associated with summer and the sea. The Vikings recognized several other sea gods, among them Aegir, who ruled the dark depths, and Mimir, who ruled the primordial ocean. But like the Greek Nereus, Njord represented the mild sea by the coast and was gentle and kind. When Aegir stirred up raging tempests, Njord stilled them, and he sent gentle winds to blow out wild fires. Because Njord personified summer and the summer sea, he was invoked often by fishermen and sailors, people who used the sea during the warm summer months, as well as by winter navigators who wished him to quiet the winter storms.

The most popular myth of Njord told of the summer god's marriage to Skadi, the winter goddess, and explained the changing seasons. In an earlier myth, Njord married his sister-wife, Nerthus, and begat the twins Frey and Freya, who, like their father, were powerful at sea. Njord left Vanaheim sometime later and, according to some myths, entered Asgard as a hostage of the Aesir. In Asgard Njord met Skadi, the beautiful goddess of the storm giant Thiazi. She chose him for her husband, and the two entered into a tumultuous marriage. Because they personified opposite principles they could never agree. Skadi personified the ice and cold and preferred to live in the snowy mountains at Thrymheim, the home of her father, whereas Njord personified the summer warmth and preferred to live in Noatum, his sparkling shipyard by the sea.

The marriage of Njord and Skadi explained the alternation of winter and summer. Because Njord could not bear the harsh mountain winters at Thrymheim and Skadi hated the sound of the waves and the gulls at Noatum, the two struck a compromise. They would spend nine months of the year in the frozen mountains and the remaining three in the warmth by the sea. But the myth of Njord and Skadi has a deeper meaning. Skadi's father was a storm giant, and after the Aesir gods killed him, the winter goddess went to Asgard to avenge her father's death. Skadi's anger was believed to symbolize the stubbornness of the ice-covered earth. The gods offered Skadi a husband to appease her, and she chose Njord, her opposite, the personification of summer warmth. For a short time, Skadi yielded to summer's embrace and winter relaxed its icy hold on the earth. But before too long, the earth froze again. This is when, in myth, Skadi returned to the mountains, taking Njord, and summer, along with her.

Skadi appeared as a beautiful giantess, the snowshoe goddess, wearing a white hunting dress, fur leggings, and snowshoes or skis and carrying a hunting spear that glittered with the frost of winter. Njord appeared as a handsome god wearing a short green tunic and a crown of seaweed and shells. Njord was considered wealthy and prosperous, to signify the fruitfulness and prosperity of summer and the riches of the sea. Some sources say that Njord's first wife, Nerthus, was a Norse Mother Earth and a symbol of fertility, like Njord. Some sources say that Skadi eventually married the winter god Uller, who, like her, was a symbol of cold and death. (Crossley-Holland 1980, Guerber 1980, MacCullough 1964)

See also Frey, Scandinavia, Seasons

NORTH AMERICA

Nature religion is still alive in North America. Large groups of Native Americans maintain their spirituality through a bond with the natural world. The essence of North American mythology is the notion of sacred geography. In the present, as they did in the past, these people recognize the sacred when they behold the power and beauty of their land.

Over two hundred ethnic groups settled in the vast North American continent, and the cultural differences among them led to a diverse body of myths and legends. Still, similar themes run through their stories, and their mythology as a whole reflects the concept of sacred space. People from the eastern woodlands to the northwest coast recognize sacred space in the mountains and waterfalls, the rivers and lakes, the rocks and caves. There they commune with nature and feel its spirit. Native American myths abound in spirits. These people know it pays to get in touch with the supernatural. Before the Europeans arrived, the people depended on the land for survival. They recognized a reciprocity between people and nature. Hunters and gatherers and agriculturists alike understood that if they took care of their earth, the earth took care of them. They depended on the benevolence of the earth spirit to survive.

Today's Native Americans continue to affirm the people-nature relationship that their ancestors so completely embraced. They strengthen their bond with the land by reenacting natural events in ceremonies that combine myth with ritual. The participants in these ceremonies wear masks or costumes, and in some cases, they absorb the power of the spirits of natural forces. The Navajo base their religion on such ceremonies, and they believe that each ritual gains its significance through an associated myth. These spiritual people account for everything in the universe by relating it to a supernatural equivalent in some previous, mythological world. They perform their rituals and recite mythical chants to achieve a harmonious relationship with the spirits of that world. Their intent is to acquire knowledge, a knowledge gained only through supernatural aid.

The necessity of communing with the spirit world reflects the belief that the nature spirits know the secret of world order. That order reveals itself in the structure of the earth and the sky. The Navajo occupy an area bounded by four sacred mountains, one for each direction. In myth, First Man and First Woman emerged from a hole in the ground and made these mountains with sacred soil. They fastened them to the earth with a sunbeam, lightning, a flint knife, and a rainbow, and they spread above the mountains the sky, the dawn, and the darkness. Each of these mountains have a deity in human form who gives the mountain its power and sacredness. The Navajo view their mountains as people and the watercourses as their veins and arteries. The Indians of the Central Plains hold similar beliefs about mountains. The Lakota consider the Black Hills in western South Dakota sacred. In one of their legends, these hills were the breasts of a divine female being, flowing with milk.

The notion that sacred milk flowed from the Black Hills was affirmed when the Lakota saw the water move down the mountains and nourish their land. They considered this movement a manifestation of the earth spirit. In hunting societies, the earth spirit was mother of the animals. In agricultural societies this spirit was the mother of corn. Because rain stimulates the growth of corn, rain myths permeate the lore of farming societies. Personifications of rainbows, clouds, thunderstorms, and winds dance through the myths, and they, too, uphold the world order. The Native Americans recognize that each phenomenon plays a crucial role in moving the earth through the cycle of seasons. The motion of the physical forces reveals the presence of the supernatural in nature, and those forces work together to bring about order in the world.

To people who believe movement in nature reveals its supernatural character, the rushing wind constitutes the most obvious manifestation of earth spirit. In some cases, the winds are perceived as four brothers who founded the race, because they brought the rains and thus guaranteed life. The Native Americans have numerous wind myths, and they divide the year based on the notion of four giants who rule the winds of the north, the east, the south, and the west. To the Pawnee of the Central Plains, winds act as intermediaries between humanity and the Great Spirit. They are defenders of order and spirits of the cardinal points. The Algonquin call the winds four brothers named Wabun, Kabun, Kabibonokka, and Shawano. Their behavior influences the weather. Kabibonokka, for instance, is the god of the north, and, like the North Wind, he acts fierce and wild. Because the four winds rule the four sacred directions, they play a significant mythological role. Their directional links connect them to the sacred order of the universe, an order established by the illusion of the spinning sky.

Native Americans model their behavior on the order established by their gods, and the gods of the sky set the best examples. By observing the movement of the celestial bodies, the people learned to understand the earthly cycles on which their lives depended. Hunters and agriculturists alike needed to understand the turning seasons. Long ago, these people relied on a complex knowledge of calendar and thus of astronomy. So numerous groups in the vast continent had well-developed cosmologies. They made skywatching a priority. Hunters of the northern forests used the movements of the celestial bodies to time the migration of animals. Farmers in the Midwest used them to determine times for planting, harvesting, and seasonal rituals. People continue to recite numerous legends of the sun and the stars. The proliferation of sky myths arose from an acknowledgment of the power of the sky gods and a respect for the sacred arrangement they set in the heavens.

Sun and moon watching occurred in cultures throughout the world, but perhaps nowhere did the observation of stars have a greater influence on mythology than among the North American tribes. This was particularly true of those groups who inhabited the Central Plains and who, long ago, had a clear, unobstructed view of the sky. The ancient Pawnee, for instance, had an extensive star lore, and their most sacred ceremonies were tied to the stars, who they believed to be ancestors of their people. They revered the North Star as a creator god, and they feared the South Star as a force of the Underworld. They made the Morning Star and the Evening Star their primary deities. The Navajo continue to regard the stars as primary deities. They call them Diyin dine'e or "Holy People," beings who take the form of single stars and about thirty-six prominent constellations.

Peoples throughout North America recognize the omnipotence in the sun, the moon, the stars, and the thunder. They know the power of fire and water and of earth and air. These forces are mysterious, but they can be persuaded, the people believe, through prayer and offerings, to use their powers to help mankind. In the Native American worldview, the forces that power the cosmos are simply manifestations of something much grander, the elusive Great Spirit. The Pawnee call this Great Spirit Tirawahat. The Lakota call him Wakan Tanka. This Great Spirit delegates his powers to all the nature gods. Most Native American groups strive to make direct contact with these gods and make indirect contact with the Great Spirit through them. This type of ritual and mythological existence enables the people to retain their spirituality and their respect for the world around them and to maintain their concept of sacred space. (Bierhorst 1985, Brinton 1976, Burland 1985, Hultkrantz 1981, Williamson and Farrer 1992)

NORTH STAR

The North Star is the point where the earth's axis meets the sky. Polaris serves as the North Star today, as it has since the Renaissance. But due to precession, or the slow wobbling of the earth's axis, over centuries the North Star changes. It takes such a long time to change, however, that the current North Star appears motionless, marking the point directly north. For this reason, the North Star has been used as a compass, revered as a powerful source of world order, and perceived as the most important star in the heavens.

Early North American tribes called the North Star "the star that never moves" or "the star that does not walk." Actually, though, it does. It moves over centuries, and it travels around the pole in a tiny circle, because presently, it is not right on the pole. Even so, ancient people noticed that it differed from the other stars. Because it appeared to remain in place, the ancients saw it as the model of stability, and they believed it played an important role in supporting the sky.

Legends of many lands attest to the celebrity of this star. To the Scandinavians, it was the glittering head of the world spike, hammered into the center of the universe to hold the sky together. To the Pawnee, it was a creator god. One Chinese legend called the North Star the throne of their sky god, Shang di, who ordered the world and maintained the balance between yin and yang. In India, it was Dhruva, the son of a king, who ascended to the sky in a meditative trance.

The story of Dhruva illustrates the ancient perception of the North Star as a model of stability and permanence. Dhruva was the son of a king and a woman named Suniti. But the king had a younger wife who had tremendous power over her husband. She exiled Suniti and Dhruva to the forest and forbade her husband from ever seeing them. When Dhruva visited his father anyway, the queen quickly sent him away. Greatly disturbed, Dhruva went in search of Narayana, another name for Vishnu as Supreme Being and preserver of order. He hoped that the powerful Narayana could be of some help. After traveling a long way, Dhruva met a sage who told him that Narayana was where he stood, and

the boy should sit down and meditate. That he did, and Narayana elevated Dhruva to the sky, where he remains fixed as the North Star, in union with Narayana. (Krupp 1991a)

See also Astronomy, Circumpolar Stars, Mountains, Shang di, Stars and Star Gods, World Axis

NORTHERN LIGHTS
See Aurora

NUT
Nut was the Egyptian sky goddess, the partner of the earth god Geb, and the mother of Ra, the sun, whom she swallowed each evening and gave birth to each morning. Although a goddess of the sky, Nut was essentially an earth mother. She personified the firmament, yet she assumed the role of creator and destroyer, womb and tomb, like earth goddesses from Indo-European myths. Nut gave birth to the moon and stars in the evening, and she swallowed them at dawn. Then she swallowed the setting sun when she descended on Geb and created darkness.

The mating of Geb and Nut was an essential element of the Egyptian creation myth. Earth and sky embraced, and for a time, the light between them dissipated. Ra, the sun god, did not want Nut to mate with Geb, but she did so anyway, against his wishes. So Ra decreed that Nut could never bear children on any day of the year. Thoth, the moon god, helped her out, however, by creating five new days in the year. The earliest Egyptian calendars had 360 days, but later ones had 365. The myth of Thoth and Nut explained the addition. On each of those five days, Nut gave birth, to Isis, Osiris, Horus, Seth, and Nephthys.

The term Nut meant the "great, brilliant one." Nut was the sky, sometimes pictured as a celestial cow, like Hathor, and other times as a sow with suckling piglets as the stars. Nut was usually shown as a blue goddess, however, with stars covering her belly and

Nymphs were beautiful female spirits imbued with personality traits that identified them with the types of landforms they inhabited and with the dangers these landforms presented. In this illustration, a Limniad (lake nymph) unsuccessfully tempts a youth.

her fingers and toes touching the earth at the four corners so her arms and legs held up the heavens. Nut was supported by Shu, the deified air, who separated her from Geb during the day and let sunlight fill the atmosphere. (Ions 1983, Krupp 1983, Spence 1990)

See also Egypt, Geb, Hathor, Shu, Sky and Sky Gods, Thoth

NYMPHS

The classical mythmakers populated many kinds of natural phenomena with nymphs, beautiful female spirits who possessed personality traits that identified them with the type of landform they inhabited. The ancients believed that every mountain, lake, river, grove, and sea had spirits living within it. The ancient Greeks called these spirits nymphs, and the Greek gods assigned each of these nymphs to a specific natural area. Nymphs were not immortal, but they had exceptionally long life spans. They personified the qualities and properties of their landforms and appeared in many myths, but usually in peripheral roles. The most common classes of nymphs were the Oreads, or the mountain nymphs; the Limniads, or the nymphs of lakes, marshes, and swamps; the Potomeids, or the river nymphs; the Oceanids, or the ocean nymphs; the Nereids, or the sea nymphs; and the Hyads or Hyades, who had been changed to stars. (Murray 1935)

See also Hyades, Mermaids, Nereids, Oceanus, Waves

OCEANIA

The nature myths of Oceania include those told by the inhabitants of Australia, New Guinea, and the numerous islands that dot the Pacific Ocean. A large part of this area was sea and the other part land masses surrounded by sea on all sides, places where tribal people depended on the ocean for survival. Oceania had its gods of the earth and the sky and of the sun, the stars, the clouds, the winds, the fog, the rain, and the mist. It had its gods of volcanoes and its gods of fire. But the sea gods were perhaps the most numerous. The nature myths relied heavily on water symbolism, and the sea gods personified the natural forces that affected the ocean realm.

Because of the crucial importance of the sea, many Oceanic myths attempted to account for the sea's existence. In Polynesia, the sea god Tangaroa was the primary deity and one of the offspring of sky and earth. In the beginning, Rangi, the sky, and Papa, the earth, remained locked in an embrace with their children trapped in Papa's womb, Tangaroa among them. Tangaroa emerged and created life. He formed all landforms and all living things from his body. Although sky and earth had to exist and separate before Tangaroa could emerge, the god of the sea created the world.

The myth of the separation of Rangi and Papa is well known, and it compares to the Greek myth of Ouranos and Gaia, the Indian myth of Prithvi and Dyaus, and the Egyptian myth of Geb and Nut. Variations of the myth

occurred within the Oceanic world as well. This type of creation myth revealed the belief that all forms of natural phenomena grew either from the union of sky and earth or from their separation. The gods of trees, wind, and water were the offspring of Rangi and Papa, and the atmospheric phenomena were the forms of grief this pair expressed at their separation. Rangi's tears fell to the earth as dew, Papa's sighs during the summer rose to the sky as mist, and her sighs during the winter froze and turned into ice.

The popularity of the Rangi and Papa myth accounted for another common theme in the nature myths of Oceania—sky raising, or why the sky stayed up above the earth. In some tales, Maui raised it. Maui was a culture hero and trickster responsible for all kinds of creative deeds, including fishing up the Pacific Islands, snaring the sun to slow it down, and creating from his blood the colors of the rainbow. Maui raised the sky by pushing it up with a poker. He fished up land from the sea using the jaw of his grandmother as a hook. When he raised the sky, Maui made way for the sun and the moon to move freely between the sky and the earth.

The raising of the sky paved the way for myths that explained the creation of the celestial bodies and myths that characterized the sun and the moon as beings who traveled between the earth and the sky, their earthly appearances heralded by thunder, lightning, mists, and clouds. The sun, the moon, and particularly the stars played a large role in Oceanic mythology, but all within the scope of the maritime culture. The early people of this area were navigators, so the celestial bodies served as reliable and convenient navigational aids. Aluluei was the Micronesian god of navigation, killed by his brothers, then restored to life by his father who gave him a thousand eyes so he could protect himself. These eyes became the stars of the heavens, the points of light in the night sky that guided sailors and kept them on course.

Polynesian navigators knew the sky well. They knew the sea well. They watched the stars and learned their patterns of rising and setting. They watched the waves and learned to understand their movements. They also watched the clouds move over the sky and materialize in all shapes, sizes, and colors. The stars, the waves, and the clouds had their deities, as did other forms of natural phenomena in all three realms. There were gods for every star and every star group the ancients recognized. There were gods of long waves and short waves and waves that broke into crests of white foam. Because the clouds of the Pacific often appeared light and airy rather than dark and foreboding, Ao served as both the god of light and the god of clouds, as well as the first ancestor of the Maori. Clouds, stars, and other celestial phenomena were often worshipped as ancestors and connected with the mythological ancestral clans that traveled across land and sea and created the world.

In Australia particularly, nature myths involved the adventures of wandering ancestral culture heroes. Physical features of the earth formed during the wanderings of these ancestors, characters who lived during a remote time in history the Aborigines called Dreamtime. During Dreamtime, these ancestors created the world by various acts they performed along their paths. They trekked across the land and carved out valleys; they urinated on the earth and made the lakes. The Rainbow Snake existed in Dreamtime, and with the other ancestors, he helped shape the landscape. Being a creature of rain and flood, his job, primarily, was to make the waterways.

The Rainbow Snake was but one manifestation of the animal gods that populated Oceanic myths, a gigantic python who heaved up from under water and caused storm and flood. Many gods of Oceania manifested themselves as sea creatures—sharks, sea snakes, crocodiles, eels, octopi, and gigantic hermit crabs. They personified the towering waves and the treacherous whirlpools. They controlled the ebb and flow of the tides. The sky gods too had intricate connections with the sea. The Milky Way, for instance, was perceived as a long blue cloud-eating shark.

The Pacific Ocean is the largest ocean in the world, and the land of Oceania is composed solely of islands, varying in size. Although the nature myths of this part of the world differed from island to island, they had common characteristics. Primarily, they relied on symbolism of the sea because the people relied on the water as a source of life. Living on island worlds, cultural groups from the gigantic Australian continent to the smallest coral atolls knew the same forces: the trade winds, the hurricanes, the tides, and the waves. These people had the largest body of water at the heart of their world and the top of their minds; they had common bonds because they shared the same sea and they shared the same sky. (Andersen 1995, Dixon 1964, Makemson 1941, Reed 1965)

OCEANUS

Oceanus was an ancient Greek sea god, both a god of the primordial ocean and a personification of the ocean itself. The Greeks believed that Oceanus encircled the earth, and they referred to him more commonly as a river than as an ocean. After the ascendancy of the Olympian gods, this body of water became known as the Outer Sea or the Atlantic Ocean, and Oceanus remained the god that embodied it. The other sea gods, such as Poseidon and Triton, presided over the Inner Sea, or the Mediterranean.

Oceanus was the oldest of the twelve original Titans, a race of giants and the offspring of Gaia and Ouranos in their roles as Mother Earth and Father Sky. Tethys was Oceanus's consort and one of these first twelve Titans as well. Oceanus and Tethys conceived all the rivers, all the sea gods except Poseidon, and 3,000 ocean nymphs called the Oceanids, who populated the Atlantic just as the Nereids populated the Mediterranean. But because all the world's rivers were thought to flow from Oceanus, the Oceanids were sometimes identified as nymphs of lesser bodies of water as well.

As a god, Oceanus was sometimes represented as a serpent encircling the earth and other times as an old man with a long beard and the horns of a bull. As the primordial sea itself, he held high rank. The Greeks believed the earth floated on Oceanus like a boat and that all the rivers and seas of the world flowed from his waters. They also believed the moon, the sun, and the stars ascended from his depths when they rose into the sky and sank back into them when they set below the horizon. (Graves 1988, Guerber 1992)

See also Cosmic Sea, Greece and Rome, Sea and Sea Gods

ODIN

Odin was one of the first of the Aesir gods in Norse mythology, a sky god, a storm god, and at one time, the highest god in the pantheon. Odin appeared to have combined the functions of two earlier deities, Donar, a god of the storm, and Tyr, an earlier god of the sky. Dressed in a blue-hooded garment spotted with gray, Odin clearly represented the sky with storm clouds and all the power that came with it.

Odin knew all and saw all; his right eye was the sun, and his left eye, the moon. Odin kept his solar eye but traded his lunar eye to Mimir in exchange for a drink of water from his well, the well of knowledge and life that Mimir guarded beneath the roots of the world tree, Yggdrasil. After drinking the water, Odin gained eternal wisdom. Sometimes, he was referred to as Ygg, which connected him to this world tree and the wisdom of the waters as well as the sky. Odin's powerful presence appeared to permeate the entire universe. In his role as sky god, he maintained cosmic order and guaranteed the rotation of day and night and the seasons. (Davidson 1964)

See also Eye, Scandinavia, Sky and Sky Gods, Springs and Wells, Storms and Tempests, Yggdrasil

OLYMPUS

The ancient Greeks conveyed the majesty of mountains when they created Mount Olympus, the abode of their high gods. Mountains have traditionally been associated with immortality because their summits reached the sky, the place where celestial deities dwelled and ruled. The conception of Mount Olympus may have originated as an ideal or it may have represented an actual mountain, possibly Mount Olympus in Thessaly, the highest mountain in Greece. But in the myths it was the ideal—it rose into Heaven, it sheltered the Immortals from the weather, and it served as their impenetrable fortress with gates of billowy clouds.

Mount Olympus was home to the twelve Olympians, the highest gods in the Greek pantheon, and among them the three gods who divided the world between them. Zeus controlled the sky, Hades controlled the Underworld, and Poseidon controlled the earth, yet all of them shared Olympus as their home. Clouds hid its summit. Snow blanketed its peaks. Mount Olympus, and the mountain in general, existed in the minds of early mythmakers as a place so beautiful, so lofty, and so mysterious, it could be only for gods. (Bernbaum 1990, Graves 1960)

See also Fujiyama, Greece and Rome, Meru, Mountains

OSIRIS

Osiris was one of the most widely worshipped deities in Egypt, a dying and rising god who symbolized life through death and the process of cyclic renewal. He was most commonly known as the god of the dead,

Osiris, god of the flood and personification of the Nile itself.

forms of natural phenomena. They called him a sky god because he maintained cosmic order, an earth god because he guaranteed fecundity of the soil, and a god of the waters because his physical resurrection coincided with the annual resurrection of the Nile.

The fact that Osiris was king of Egypt so infuriated his brother Seth, that Seth killed Osiris—that was how he died in the first place. Seth floated him down the Nile in a casket and then cut his body into pieces and scattered them over the land. Isis, his sister-wife and queen, resurrected him. Isis could perform this feat because she possessed magical powers, and, with the aid of Thoth, the moon god, she reassembled Osiris's broken body. Because his penis had been thrown into the Nile and eaten by fishes, his fertility went to the waters. But Isis fashioned a new penis for him that restored his own fertility. Osiris became immortal. This dismemberment and reassembly paralleled the behavior of the moon. The moon got smaller and smaller, died, got bigger and bigger, and then was resurrected. The moon too was immortal. So was the Nile. Osiris, as the Nile, rose every year to renew the earth and to guarantee that life continue.

The battle between Seth and Osiris appeared to symbolize the battle between desert and river valley, barrenness and fecundity, darkness and light. Osiris ultimately won the battle. The cult of Osiris was so popular it rivaled the cult of Ra, the sun god, and Osiris and Isis continued on as popular deities and became the central figures in one of the mystery religions that developed in the Greco-Roman world before the advent of Christianity. Osiris was usually depicted as a tall, bearded man, either black for death or green to symbolize his agricultural connection. He was wrapped as a mummy, he wore the crown of Egypt on his head, and he carried a crook and a flail, agricultural tools that revealed his connection with cyclic rebirth. (Budge 1969, Griffiths 1960, Spence 1986)

but he was first a nature god connected to corn and vegetation and the fertility of the Nile. In time, Osiris became the river itself. As Osiris rose from the dead, so did the Nile, and as Osiris embodied the fertility of the waters, so the Nile waters rose over the riverbanks and inundated the land.

The role of Osiris as god of the dead defined his persona. He embodied the concept of life as well as resurrection and cyclic transformation. For these reasons Osiris was a vegetation god, a god of the corn and the trees and a god of the seasons, of day and of light, and of the waters. He had lunar connections because the moon, too, died and was resurrected. He had solar connections because the sun went through the same process. Osiris was the king of Egypt, and scholars connected him with numerous

See also Death, Egypt, Isis, Moon and Moon Gods, Nile River

OURANOS

Ouranos was the primeval Greek sky god, both the offspring and the mate of Gaia, the earth. The name Ouranos had the same root as that of the Indian sky god, Varuna, *var,* which means "to cover, veil, or conceal." Like the ancient Varuna, Ouranos personified the veil of the heavens. He spread above Mother Earth like a giant canopy and fertilized her with life-giving rain. In this way Ouranos represented the primordial creative force. His rain made the land fruitful and plant and animal life grow and thrive. Together with Gaia, the earth, this Father Sky created the first races of mankind.

The mating of Ouranos and Gaia was related in Hesiod's *Theogony* and represents the most widely accepted Greek creation myth.

When Ouranos embraced Gaia, the two conceived the Titans, the Cyclopes, and the Hesperides, three races of giants that Ouranos feared would destroy him and take over the world. In one version of the myth, Ouranos threw the Cyclopes from his sky into Tartarus, the lowest region of the Underworld. In another version, he refused to withdraw from Gaia and kept all his monstrous children imprisoned within Gaia's womb. In either case, Kronus, the oldest of the Titans, took revenge and destroyed Ouranos, just as his father feared. At Gaia's request, he obtained a sickle and cut off his father's penis. When he castrated Ouranos, Kronus separated sky and earth and took over the world. (Graves 1988, Rose 1959)

See also Creation Myths, Cyclopes, Gaia, Greece and Rome, Sea Foam, Sky and Sky Gods

say he materialized from inanimate matter, the dual principle of yin and yang. But in either case, P'an Ku became the universe. His body became the cardinal points, and his head, the mountains. His voice became the thunder, his breath the wind and clouds, his tears the rivers and seas, his flesh the soil, his left eye the sun and his right eye the moon, his hair the stars, his eyebrows the planets, his sweat the rain, his flesh the soil, his teeth and bones the metals, rocks, and stones, and the fleas on his body became the people.

The account of P'an Ku is of Taoist origin, and several versions exist. Some legends say P'an Ku had the head of a dragon and the body of a serpent; others call him a dwarf who grew bigger and bigger over thousands of years until he finally filled up the world. In some representations of P'an Ku, he holds the sun in one hand and the moon in the other. In others, he holds a hammer and chisel, which in one version of his story, he used to shape the earth and chisel out the sky. P'an Ku sometimes appears with four fantastical creatures who possibly symbolized the primal forces of nature: The tortoise symbolized earth, the phoenix symbolized fire, the unicorn symbolized air, and the dragon symbolized water. (Mackenzie 1994, Werner 1995)

See also China, Creation Myths, Stoorworm, Tiamat, Tlaltecuhtli, Ymir

PACHACAMAC

Although the ancient Peruvians revered the earth as female, they considered Pachacamac the god who animated the earth. He was the spirit of plants and animals and all things that emerged from the earth, even human beings. In some traditions, Pachacamac married Pachamama, the spirit of mountains, plains, and rocks. Pachacamac created the earth and the earthquakes, and Pachamama manifested herself in lightning that flashed upward, earthquakes, landslides, and volcanic fire.

The coastal people of Peru venerated Pachacamac and Pachamama just as the people of the highlands venerated the sky gods. The coastal people considered Pachacamac the Supreme Deity, the creator god before the Inca conquest. After the conquest, Pachacamac joined the Inca pantheon but as a rival to Viracocha, the Supreme Being and god of the sky. Both Viracocha and Pachacamac were creators. In a popular myth of Pachacamac, he created the first man and woman, and by killing the woman's son, he was responsible for the growth of cultivated plants and maize that rose from the boy's body. (Cobo 1990, Parrinder 1971, Spence 1977)

See also Earth and Earth Gods, South America, Viracocha

P'AN KU

In Chinese mythology, P'an Ku was the first human being, a dwarf who turned giant and who created the world from the pieces of his body. Some myths say P'an Ku emerged from a cosmic egg and pushed up the sky. Others

PELE

Pele is a Hawaiian fire goddess who lives in the Kilauea volcano and embodies both its form and its power. She is both highly respected and greatly feared on the volcanic island, even today. Pele is fiery and impetuous, with a unpredictable temperament like that of the volcano she inhabits. Like the flames, she is both alluring and dangerous and can change shapes, charming men as a beautiful young woman, then destroying them when she turns into a fiery goddess. Pele often assumes her mortal form, sometimes as a

In Chinese mythology, P'an Ku was the first human being, who created the world from pieces of his body. P'an Ku often appears with the creatures that symbolized the primal forces of nature: the tortoise symbolized earth; the phoenix, fire; the unicorn, air; and the dragon, water.

young enchantress and other times as an old hag. But if provoked, she abruptly erupts and assumes the form of magma, steam, lava, vapor, and flames.

Myths of Pele vary from source to source, but most of them involve her traveling from island to island and spreading volcanic fire. This she did long ago, and in each place along her route, she dug a hole and created the volcanic calderas that characterize the Hawaiian islands. The route Pele took coincided with the geological order in which these landforms came into existence. She created Koko Head and Koko Crater on her last visit to Oahu, then finally settled in the active craters of Kilauea, where she lives today. People often say they have seen her appear in her mortal form just before the volcano erupts.

Pele moved from one place to another each time the crater she inhabited cooled down and stopped producing fire. The ancients spun myths to explain the deactivation, just as they did the eruptions. Some said Pele was a water goddess as well as a fire goddess, and she caused the ocean to encircle the Hawaiian islands. Again this involved Pele's travels, as she went from island to island with water just as she did with fire. The Polynesians have an equivalent goddess named Pere, and they say her mother gave her the ocean in a jar. As Pere traveled, she poured the ocean out around her until it surrounded the islands. (Beckwith 1970, Ching 1990, Frierson 1991, Vitaliano 1973, Westervelt 1963)

See also Earthquakes, Fire and Fire Gods, Kamapua'a, Oceania, Snow, Volcanoes

PERSIA

The myths of ancient Persia were revealed through the teachings of the sixth- and seventh-century prophet Zoroaster, or Zarathustra, who envisioned the world in a continuing battle of good and evil. Zoroaster embraced the view that cosmic order and cyclic renewal depended on the complementary opposition of natural forces. The Zoroastrians worshipped natural phenomena, and they allied each force to one of the two sides. Their Supreme Deity, Ahura Mazdah or Ormazd, personified the light and goodness associated with the sky, and his opponent, Angra Mainyu or Ahriman, personified the darkness and death associated with the Underworld.

Myths from all over the world characterized nature as an interdependence of opposites, but nowhere was the doctrine of dualism more evident than in ancient Persia. Ahura Mazda created a good world, but Angra Mainyu introduced evil by creating demons—the whirlwinds and sandstorms and the destructive natural forces that opposed the ordered world. The cosmic struggle between good and evil reflected both the opposition of the elements and their interdependence. Forces of the earth, of the air, of the water, and of fire assumed positions as warriors in the battle, and by continually dueling it out, they kept the universe in balance. (Curtis 1993, Hinnells 1973)

See also Darkness and Light, Duality, Elements

PERUN/PERKUNAS

The Slavic storm god Perun controlled rain, thunder, and lightning, and, like the Greek god Zeus and the Norse god Thor, he held high rank in the sky pantheon, perhaps even achieved the status of Supreme Deity. Perun and his Baltic counterpart Perkunas used the power of the storm to fertilize the earth. He was envisioned as a bull, with his bellowing as the thunder, and he was believed to inseminate the earth violently, with rain and lightning.

The Baltic Perkunas possibly ruled on earth before he ruled in the sky realm. Some say he lived as a king in a castle on the top of a mountain, then was sent to the sky after his death to a new castle floating above the clouds. Perhaps Perkunas's greatest feat was freeing the sun from its winter prison. When the storm god, as a bull, bellowed in the spring, he released the warm weather and renewed life.

Perun was usually depicted as a tall, dark-haired man with a long golden beard. He used a hammer, as did Thor, to hurl thunderbolts, and he rode in a flaming car or flew in the air on a giant millstone, supported by mountain spirits who caused storms. According to one tradition, Perun rode in his fiery car every spring, and using the rainbow for a bow, he shot demons with his arrows of fire. This myth metaphorically expressed the power of the spring lightning. When Perun's arrows pierced the demons, they poured blood, just as the clouds poured rain. According to another tradition, Perun's lightning arrow was a golden key with which he unlocked the earth. He released the water frozen in the streams and freed the rains imprisoned in the castles of clouds. (Gimbutas 1971, Hubbs 1988, Ralston 1872)

> **See also** Arrows, Baltic and Slavic Lands, Cows and Bulls, Hammers, Lightning, Storms and Tempests, Svarog, Thor, Thunder and Thunder Gods, Zeus

PHAETHON

Phaethon was the son of the sun god Apollo (some say of Helios) and Clymene, a sea nymph, making him in essence the son of fire and water. By his very nature, Phaethon was restless and full of tension, and he proved just how much so when he asked his father for permission to drive the Chariot of the Sun. The Greeks told the myth of Phaethon's ride to explain the formation of many phenomena, both terrestrial and celestial. When Phaethon steered the fiery chariot too close to earth, he parched the land and created the deserts. When he steered too close to the poles, he melted the snows and formed polar icecaps. He set the mountains aflame and turned them into explosive volcanoes, he left a scorched path through the sky that became the Milky Way, and then, set afire by Zeus, he

came tumbling down to earth in flames and became a shooting star.

Phaethon's story began when he was a young boy living with his mother, Clymene, and longing for proof of his divine parentage. Apollo did sire Phaethon, but Clymene alone reared their mortal son. Having been challenged by schoolmates to prove that he was really the son of a god, Phaethon set out to visit Apollo in his palace. The palace of the sun sparkled brilliantly, with silver doors opening to walls adorned with images of forests and trees, sea nymphs riding waves, and the twelve signs of the zodiac gloriously adorning the firmament over which the great sun god presided. Everything within glittered and radiated light. Phaethon was overcome. He then met with the sun god himself, his father, who was seated on a throne and attended by the four seasons, Spring with a crown of flowers, Summer with a garland of ripened grain, Autumn with feet stained from stomping grapes, and Winter, with hair glistening with frost. It was there that Apollo reluctantly consented to let Phaethon drive his chariot.

Phaethon failed at the task. As Night passed through the western gates of Heaven, Dawn threw open the doors of the east. Phaethon approached the golden chariot and mounted the jewel-studded seat. He took the reigns of the sun's horses. But almost immediately, he lost control. The horses swerved into uncharted parts of the sky, too close to the earth and then too close to the moon. Clouds began to smoke. Mountains, trees, cities, nations, and eventually the entire earth burst into flames. Zeus had no choice but to hurl his fiery spear at Phaethon, setting him on fire and plunging him into the waters. The infamous ride left the world a different place and the restless Phaethon dead. His sisters, the Heliades, wept so piteously when their brother died that they turned into trees that distilled amber. (*Bullfinch's Mythology* 1979, Snodgrass 1994, Staal 1988)

The phoenix rising from the fire, an illustration from Magister Joseph Beruerius's Bestuarius *of 1524. Although frequently associated with Greek myths, the phoenix appeared in other cultures as well.*

See also Apollo, Chariots, Cosmic Order, Greece and Rome, Helios, Sun and Sun Gods

PHOENIX

The phoenix was a mythical bird that served as a symbol of fire and the sun. The phoenix was Greek, although the concept of such a bird appeared in other cultures as well, in Chinese myths, in Arabic myths, and, some said, as the Bennu in Egyptian myths. The phoenix was a legendary creature, red and gold like the sun and resembling an eagle. Some claimed the bird lived in Arabia, and others claimed it lived in India. According to Herodotus, it flew to Heliopolis, Egypt, every five hundred years, built a funeral pyre, fanned its wings, then cremated itself and rose renewed from the ashes.

The myth of the phoenix fire stressed the regenerative aspect of fire and the sun. The phoenix was originally a sun symbol and the phoenix fire a mythological interpretation of the sunrise. The phoenix, like the sun, died in its own fires, then rose anew each morning. The Egyptian Bennu underwent a similar process, but he never burned. At the beginning of the world, the Bennu landed on a mound of earth that rose from the primeval waters, then took off in flight. As the bird flew, the sun rose for the first time. The Bennu was connected with the cult of Ra and was considered by some a secondary form of the all-powerful sun god. (Mercatante 1974, South 1987)

See also Birds, Elements, Fire and Fire Gods

PHOSPHORESCENCE

Phosphorescence of the sea baffled sailors for centuries. When the sea turned ablaze in shimmering ripples of light, it appeared something strange and supernatural was making an appearance. The oddity of this phenomena led ancient navigators to concoct many tales to explain the shining sea. To people who believed great sea gods ruled the realm from underwater palaces, it seemed logical that the glow came from the golden possessions of these sea gods or of other water spirits, or perhaps from jewels of the sea nymphs or Sirens, shining beneath the water.

Mariners in many areas of the world witnessed phosphorescent seas, and myths have been found to explain the phenomena from the Arctic to the Tropics. Scientists believe the illumination occurs when phosphorescent marine organisms, under certain conditions, glow like fire and sparkle like jewels. Breton sailors attributed the glow to shining gemstones, gemstones they believed came from a water demon's garden at the bottom of the sea. Phosphorescence has been attributed to other types of demons, evil spirits who sailed in ships full of burning lamps, and even to the devil himself, who navigated the water on a burning cask of tar. Sometimes the glow was so intense that something did appear to be on fire.

Myths from Java and the Gilbert Islands revealed that navigators in those lands believed fire had its origin in the sea. Similar myths appeared in the Pacific Northwest and Canada. The Haida said that Raven, their culture hero, brought fire from the sea depths, and the Nootka said that fire came from the house of the cuttlefish.

Because the "fire" appeared to move, the association with moving fishes seemed likely. Sailors on the Channel Coast believed that as starlight filtered through the water, it turned the fishes blue, and as the fishes swam beneath the waves, a shimmering blue glow rippled across the surface. Breton sailors believed the glow appeared when one enormous fish who lived at the bottom of the sea shot flames out of his nostrils and waged war against the smaller fishes. (Bassett 1971, Rappoport 1995)

See also Fire and Fire Gods, St. Elmo's Fire

PILLAN

Pillan was a powerful god of the Araucanians of Chile who controlled thunder and embodied the spirit of fire. He was a nature power, some say the primary nature power, and he had a violent temper that often flared uncontrollably. It was then that he caused all sorts of violent natural phenomena, not only thunder but also lightning, volcanic eruptions, floods, and tidal waves.

Pillan resided in the clouds and in the volcanic mountains, in any place where the sound of thunder was heard resonating through the earth or the sky. It was said that Pillan was the Supreme Deity and might have ruled a pantheon of the deities in the invisible world, much like the high chief of the Araucanians ruled the lesser chiefs in the visible world. The forces who worked under Pillan were demonic, and their evil ways caused destructiveness. The Araucanians considered most of their deities evil, and some said Pillan was inherently evil as well. Others say he might have been benevolent. Although he and the forces beneath him caused destruction, Pillan also served as the spirit of fire—and thus the life force—and the spirit of thunder that charged the earth. (Alexander 1964a, Osbourne 1986, Tierney 1990)

See also Fire and Fire Gods, South America, Thunder and Thunder Gods

PISCES, THE FISHES

Pisces is a faint constellation situated in the part of the sky called the celestial sea along with several other water signs. Like the other zodiacal constellations, the significance of Pisces lies in its function. Today it serves the purpose that Aries did long ago and Taurus did before then—it marks the vernal equinox. In ancient times, it presaged the rains. The Babylonians, the Persians, and the Turks all saw fishes in this star pattern, and the ancient Egyptians regarded it as the harbinger of spring and of the fishing season.

The most notable myth of Pisces was a Greek story of Venus and Cupid, who, like Capricorn, were among a group of gods feasting on the riverbanks and who jumped into the water to escape the monster Typhon. Gaia, the earth goddess, sent Typhon to attack the gods, and, out of fear, Venus and Cupid dove deep into the waters and turned themselves into fishes. On star maps, the two fishes are some distance apart and appear to be swimming in opposite directions, their tails tied with a cord. According to myth, Venus and Cupid tied themselves together in this way so they would not become separated in the deep waters. (Ridpath 1988, Staal 1988)

See also Constellations, Zodiac

PLANETS

Planets most likely confused ancient sky-watchers. These celestial objects looked like bright stars, yet they wandered, moving forward or eastward, then sometimes moving backward or westward, while all the other "stars" remained "fixed" in the background. The ancients recognized five planets: Mercury, Venus, Mars, Jupiter, and Saturn. Because they wandered, they put them in the same category as the sun and the moon, and they named them for some of their most powerful gods.

The names of the planets in use today came from Roman myths, and the characters who represented them had personalities and functions skywatchers identified with the celestial objects. Jupiter, or the Greek Zeus, was high king. He moved the most steadily through the stars and thus established order in the cosmos. Mercury, or the Greek Hermes, moved most swiftly. The ancients made him messenger because he appeared to be

delivering messages to the other gods when he sped back and forth from one side of the sun to the other. Mars, or the Greek Ares, fought battles. The ancients made him their war god because he shone blood red in the sky. Saturn, as Kronos, ruled the pantheon before Jupiter, and Venus, or the Greek Aphrodite, glowed most brightly of all as the goddess of love and beauty.

Mercury and Jupiter and the high gods of the classical myths stand out as some of the most colorful characters who graced the skies. But the Greeks and Romans were not the first to personify the planets, and the other groups who did gave their planetary gods similar characteristics. The Babylonians identified Jupiter with Marduk, their high god who bested the chaos monster Tiamat and established cosmic order. They identified Mars with Nergal, a violent god associated with war and with forest fires. The Egyptians too had their planetary deities, as did the ancient Chinese, who identified them with the five elements they considered the active forces in the universe. Many of the early people who personified the planets recognized the five visible to the naked eye, but most planetary myths centered on Venus. As the brightest of the celestials outside the sun and the moon, Venus appeared both as the Morning Star and as the Evening Star and often was featured in sky myths as a lovely and promiscuous goddess. (Krupp 1983, 1991a)

See also Ishtar, Morning Star/Evening Star, Quetzalcoatl

PLEIADES

The Pleiades is one of the most widely recognized star clusters in the night sky, and people all over the world assigned myths to it because its appearance signaled the change in seasons. Although the appearance of stars and star clusters is reversed from one side of the world to the next, people in both hemispheres noticed the Pleiades. In the northern hemisphere, it rose in the fall and signaled

In Greco-Roman mythology the Pleiades were sisters personifying the well-known constellation.

Atlas, with Merope the only one among them who married a mortal. Zeus placed all seven of the sisters in the sky to sparkle as stars. But Merope, ashamed of her mortal husband, hid her head in shame, which was why, the Greeks said, only six sisters sparkled visibly.

The Greeks offered other explanations of the missing Pleiad and so did many other groups of people. In Greece, if it wasn't Merope, it was Electra who faded away with grief over the fall of Troy. In Siberian myth, the lost Pleiad was stolen by seven old thieves identified with the stars of the Big Dipper, and in Iroquois myth, the star was a hungry child who floated to the sky and faded away. Connecting the Pleiades with hunger was commonplace in myths, particularly in North America. When the star cluster first rose above the horizon, it signaled the time to gather food for the winter. Then, as the cluster rose higher and higher, food became scarce.

The hunger myths worked because of the seasonal significance of the Pleiades. Myths of the southern hemisphere connected the cluster with seasonal rain and flood. But sky myths also dealt with origins, and many stories attempted to explain how the Pleiades got up in the sky in the first place. An Oceanic myth identified the Karakarook, or Krat-goruk, as a group of women who dug up ant eggs with yam sticks with coals of fire on the end. A whirlwind swept them up into the sky where they remain as the Pleiades—with fire at the end of their yam sticks. A Mataco myth of South America told of people who climbed a tree to the sky to get honey and fish. When they climbed back to earth one day, a woman stood at the bottom of the tree and asked for a share of their food. The climbers refused. Angry, the woman set fire to the tree. The people who had not yet descended remained in the sky and turned into the stars of the Pleiades. (Allen 1963, Krupp 1991b, Levi-Strauss 1964)

See also Hyades, Seasons, Stars and Star Gods, Tears

the onset of winter, and in the southern hemisphere, it rose in the spring and signaled the coming rains.

Myths of the Pleiades generally involved personification of the stars in the cluster, commonly as a group of children or a group of sisters. Six stars in the Pleiades are visible to the naked eye, but many early skywatchers counted seven, and astronomers offered suggestions to explain this discrepancy. Perhaps one of the stars was a variable star and flared up at times in the distant past, they said, or perhaps the ancients connected these stars to the seven stars of the Big Dipper; they formed a similar ladle pattern and were also used to signal the seasons. In any case, the Maori called the stars seven brothers; the Romanians, a hen and six chicks; the Japanese, seven maidens; and the Greeks, the seven daughters of

POLARIS
See North Star

POSEIDON
Poseidon was the Greek god of the seas, the son of Kronos and Rhea and the brother of Zeus, the sky god, and Hades, the god of the Underworld. In the earliest myths, Poseidon may have been a sky and thunder god, as well as a god of watered plains, valleys, springs, and lakes. But at the time of the *Iliad,* Poseidon and his brothers seized power of the world from their father and divided the universe among them. Poseidon inherited the oceans.

From that point on, Poseidon ruled his watery realm with unfettered violence. He had great powers and could calm the waters and grant safe passage to sailors, but he had an explosive temper and was more commonly known to cause storms and tempests, gigantic tidal waves, and landslides on the coast. Poseidon was associated with many destructive forces of nature, including earthquakes, which he caused by splitting open the earth and the mountains with a blow of his trident. The ancient Greeks logically connected earthquakes with their sea god because many of the tremors originated from under the ocean and caused tidal waves.

As lord of the seas, Poseidon appeared in many myths and had numerous affairs, which produced children like Polyphemus and the whirlpool Charybdis, who were as tempestuous and violent as their father. He ruled the Aegean, and he lived with his one legitimate wife, Amphitrite, and their one legitimate son, Triton, in a palace cave deep within its waters. In this underwater palace, Poseidon kept white horses who rose with him to the surface and carried him across the waves in a chariot. Some mythologists described these animals as half horse and half serpent and said that they represent the white-capped waves. Like foaming waves, the horses sprang swiftly from the water, their strength and might symbolic of both the force of the sea and the power of its king.

In art, Poseidon usually appeared as a bearded man, carrying a three-pronged trident and riding in his chariot surrounded by fishes, dolphins, and beautiful sea nymphs. Sometimes, he was accompanied in his sea voyages by his wife, Amphitrite, riding beside him in her chariot, and with their son Triton and the lesser sea deities trailing behind them. (Bassett 1971, Grimal 1986, Rose 1959)

See also Amphitrite, Greece and Rome, Horses, Sea and Sea Gods, Triton, Water Horses, Waves

PRIMORDIAL SEA
In many cultures, the first conception of the world was that of an ocean, boundless and endless, and full of enough raw energy to create a universe. This was the primordial sea, a vast expanse of undifferentiated matter embodied by androgynous serpent gods whose bodies exploded and gave birth to form and substance. The concept of such a sea reflected the fact that ancient people recognized creation as the emergence of form from formlessness. Water, it seemed, was formless. So from the water, earth and life emerged.

The concept of the primordial sea arose among people who knew the water around them. It arose among people who felt awed by its depth and captivated by its mystery. The Egyptians called the primordial waters Nu, and, like primordial waters of other people, Nu existed in the sky and contained the germs of life. This water, Nu, was the prototype of the world ocean, the circumambient ocean, which later people believed surrounded the world. Oceanus was this circumambient ocean to the Greeks, with a god of that same name who embodied it. In other lands, serpents embodied it; the Midgard serpent of Norse myth and Tiamat and Absu in Mesopotamian myth. The serpent symbolized formless chaos, the dark depths of the Underworld, and the fluency of the waters. Early people felt overwhelmed when they beheld the seemingly infinite waters. The sea, it appeared, extended into the earth and into the sky, so at one time, the ancients thought, it encompassed both. The sea defined the cosmos before its division into realms. (Campbell 1974, Freund 1965)

   See also Absu, Churning the Ocean, Cosmic Sea, Creation Myths, Sea and Sea Gods, Serpents and Snakes, Tiamat

PROMETHEUS

Prometheus was a Greek Titan and a trickster of sorts, who outwitted the gods and gave fire to mankind. Some myths say he stole the fire from the forge of Hephaestus, and others say he stole it from the sun. One myth explained how Athene granted him access to Mount Olympus, where he lit his torch from the sun's fiery chariot, broke off a piece of charcoal from the burning torch, and carried it back to earth in the hollow of a fennel stalk. He gave humanity a most precious gift, worthy only of gods, and because of this, Zeus punished him. Zeus chained Prometheus to a mountaintop where an eagle pecked continually at his liver. Some stories connect Prometheus's struggles against the chains and the eagle with the tremors of earthquakes.

   Prometheus's name may have derived from the Sanskrit term for fire drill, and he may have been an ancient fire god who became eclipsed in later years by Hephaestus. Like Hephaestus and fire gods from other cultures, Prometheus was a master craftsman. But Prometheus was considered a creator deity as well. Some say he made the first people from clay. Zeus didn't like them and denied them fire. So Prometheus had to steal it from the gods' abode to provide for his people. Prometheus, like fire, was a generous life force. (Frazer 1996, Graves 1988, Snodgrass 1994)

   See also Earthquakes, Fire and Fire Gods, Greece and Rome, Hephaestus

PROTEUS

See Nereus and Proteus

PYRAMIDS

Ancient architectural monuments often replicated sacred landforms. The builders constructed the pyramids, for instance, to tap into the sacredness of the earth and, because they extended toward Heaven, to tap into the sacredness of the sky. The Mesopotamian, the Mesoamerican, and most famously, the Egyptian pyramids shared a common symbolism. They mirrored the structure of a multilayered universe, and they reflected the cosmic order upheld by the deities within it.

   Among the landforms the pyramid builders intended to replicate, the mountain was perhaps the most obvious. But because the pyramids tended to mark the center of the world, they replicated not just any mountain, but the cosmic mountain, the mountain that itself marked the center of the world and that emanated power. The builders of the Egyptian pyramids oriented them to the cardinal directions, and in most cases constructed corridors aligned to the circumpolar, or the "undying," stars in the heavens. The Egyptian pyramids may have served as temples and tombs of the pharaohs, but they also led to the sky world. They provided an access route for the dead rulers to join the immortal sky gods in the undying realm of the heavens.

   Most pyramids built by the Mesoamericans were artificial mountains, perhaps volcanic mountains, and they too likely symbolized a multilayered world. They had bases that extended into the earth and a series of platforms or stairways that led to the immortal sky gods—the sun, the moon, the stars, and the planets. In the ancient city of Teotihuacan, the Pyramid of the Sun and the Pyramid of the Moon provided access to the gods who controlled the order of the cosmos. These monuments had clear connections to sky power. The Aztec sun and the

PROMETHÉE DÉCHIRÉ PAR UN VAUTOUR.

Prometheus tortured by a Vulture.

Prometheus durch einen Geyer zerrissen.

Prometheus door een Gier verscheurt.

A Greek Titan, Prometheus outwitted the gods and gave fire to mankind. In revenge, Zeus chained Prometheus to a mountaintop where an eagle pecked continually at his liver, as portrayed in this eighteenth-century engraving by B. Picart.

Aztec moon held high rank in the pantheon because they moved the world. It appeared likely that early people who worshipped the sun and moon wanted to reach them. So they built stairways they could climb to get close enough to tap into their powers.

Pyramidal temples were connected to solar power and lunar power and power that emanated from such celestial deities as Venus, who the Mesoamericans assigned great mythological significance. These structures were analyzed for astronomical alignments and interpreted in relation to the myths and rituals of the people who built them. Although the scientists studying these alignments found clear connections to the celestials, the pyramids represented more than paths to their abodes. They represented the place of creation and, it has been said, the primordial mound of earth. The Aztec believed that the sun and the moon were created at Teotihuacan, so they built their two greatest pyramids on the spots designated as the places the gods threw themselves into the sacrificial fires. There the gods burned, then rose as the new great sky powers. (Campbell 1974, Krupp 1997a, Lurker 1980)

See also Circumpolar Stars, Egypt, Metztli, Mountains, Ziggurats

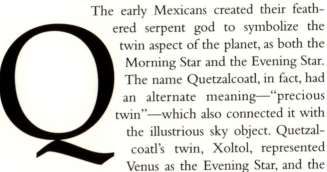

watchers of ancient Mexico tracked Venus. The early Mexicans created their feathered serpent god to symbolize the twin aspect of the planet, as both the Morning Star and the Evening Star. The name Quetzalcoatl, in fact, had an alternate meaning—"precious twin"—which also connected it with the illustrious sky object. Quetzalcoatl's twin, Xoltol, represented Venus as the Evening Star, and the Feathered Serpent himself represented Venus as the precious Morning Star who was resurrected in the east and lit the morning sky with a beautiful light.

Because Quetzalcoatl rose in the east, he was a kind of sun god or, at least, a dawn hero like Viracocha to the Inca or Michabo to the Algonquin. Like them, he had white skin, a long robe, and a long, flowing beard. Quetzalcoatl, Viracocha, and Michabo all maintained cosmic order by representing the stable forces that moved the world. They ordered the sky; they renewed the earth. Quetzalcoatl, as well as his Mayan counterpart, Kukulcan, represented life and fertility. As a bird he was resurrected like the stars and the sun. As a serpent he not only renewed the earth but he drew power from the waters. The Aztecs also saw Quetzalcoatl as Ehecatl, the wind god who swept the roads for Tlaloc to bring the rains. So as wind god and water god, as earth god and sky god, Quetzalcoatl was fertilizer and demiurge. He battled the sun to light the morning skies, and he blew life into the universe.

Quetzalcoatl was generally depicted in the codices with a conical hat, half dark and half light to represent his sky-earth duality. He was adorned with jewels, and he wore a feather headdress or, as Ehecatl, a red bird-beaked mask. In Mayan culture, the cult of Kukulcan reached its peak in the tenth century A.D., when the legendary leader Quetzalcoatl

QUETZALCOATL

The feathered serpent of Mesoamerican lore, Quetzalcoatl, was a god of Heaven and earth, light and darkness, and life, death, and rebirth. He was a culture hero, some say a deified king, but he gained primary significance as a mythical figure who died and was resurrected as Venus, the Morning Star. The Maya identified this feathered serpent as Kukulcan; Quetzalcoatl was an Aztec deity. He had many aspects, and the Aztecs connected him not only with Venus, but with earth, sky, and water and with rain, wind, and rebirth.

The contradictory nature of the feathered serpent symbolized the dual nature of Quetzalcoatl as both earth and sky god. *Quetzal* meant "bird" and *coatl* meant "snake," so this snake-bird deity represented the link between sky and earth, between humanity and the stars. It appeared the Mesoamericans recognized this link when they observed a particular "star," the planet Venus. In the Aztec myth of the feathered serpent, Quetzalcoatl died just as Venus appeared as the Evening Star, and he cremated himself in the funeral pyre just as the Evening Star disappeared below the western horizon in the "fire" of the setting sun. Then Quetzalcoatl, as Venus, returned to life. Eight days later, as his heart rose out of the flames and ascended to the sky, he appeared as the Morning Star rising in the east.

Scholars have long recognized that sky-

conquered the Yucatan then went on to become the most widely revered god in the Aztec pantheon. (Brundage 1979, 1982, Nicholson 1967)

See also Birds, Ehecatl, Mesoamerica, Michabo, Morning Star/Evening Star, Serpents and Snakes, Tezcatlipoca, Viracocha

R

RA

The religion of ancient Egypt was dominated by sun worship, and Ra, or Re, was the primary sun god. Ra was the primeval sun called Atum, and he existed in the waters of Nu, the primordial ocean, then emerged to create the other eight principal gods. Ra and these other gods formed a group of deities called the Ennead, who were worshipped at Heliopolis, the City of the Sun. But the worship of Ra entered into the rituals of every cult. The sun god was a cosmic hero. He battled the forces of evil each night in the Underworld, and then renewed the world each morning as he emerged reborn from the womb of Nut, the sky goddess.

Preoccupied with the sun's movement and the sun god's hand in cyclic renewal, the ancient Egyptians spun myths of Ra that involved his passage through the heavens. They told detailed accounts of his famous sky journey, beginning at the eastern horizon where he emerged from Nut, to the western horizon where he sunk into the waters of the Underworld, then back to the eastern horizon again where he returned to life. During Ra's daytime passage, he aged, from a young child at dawn, to a mature man at midday, to an old man at sunset. During his nighttime passage, he entered into battle with the serpent Apep. Ra had to fight Apep and conquer him in order to renew the world. He had to overcome the darkness demons to guarantee continued light and continued life. The sun god always won the battle.

Ra was identified with the Greek sun god,

Helios, who also traveled across the sky. Helios traveled in a horse-drawn chariot, but Ra traveled in a boat. The image of the sun god in a boat combined several concepts: first, that a great cosmic sea flowed through the heavens and, second, that the Nile River culture permeated Egyptian thought. The boat was the vehicle needed to cross these waters, and the sun god was a fitting driver. But the mythical imagery of Ra's sky travels involved much more than the portrayal of a man sailing a boat. Ra assumed many forms during his cycle. At dawn, he was a scarab beetle named Khepri, pushing the sun along its path in the same way the scarab beetle rolled a ball of dung in the dirt. At midday he was a falcon who had soared to the highest point in the heavens. Then at night, when he sank into the Underworld, he was a human with a ram's head and a crown. In art, Ra was typically depicted in his human form but with the head of a hawk or a falcon with a sun disk on top. (Krupp 1981, Rosalie 1980, Spence 1990, Wainwright 1938)

See also Amon, Apep, Aten, Cosmic Sea, Egypt, Helios, Nile River, Scarab Beetle, Sun and Sun Gods

RAHU

Rahu was a Hindu demon who continuously pursued the sun and the moon around the heavens and caused eclipses. In the beginning of the world when the gods and demons churned the ocean to get Soma, the elixir of immortality, Rahu disguised himself as a god and drank some. But the sun and the moon saw him do this, and they told Vishnu, the Hindu Supreme God, who intended the Soma only for the gods. Vishnu sliced off Rahu's head before the elixir reached his throat. As a result, Rahu's body died, but his head was made immortal, and his head continued to circle the sky in search of the sun and moon, who told Vishnu of his deception.

The myth of Rahu explained total eclipses, partial eclipses, and the phenomenon of the waxing and waning moon. When Rahu caught the sun or the moon, he swallowed them and an eclipse occurred. The eclipse ended when the moon or the sun dropped out of Rahu's mouth. Rahu dropped his prize often because the Hindu people attempted to prevent the disappearance of their celestial bodies by banging pots and pans and making a lot of noise. Sometimes, the noise scared Rahu before he swallowed his prize completely, and in those cases, a partial eclipse occurred. The constant feud between Rahu and the moon explained waxing and waning, as the moon got larger and larger as it filled up with the magical Soma and smaller and smaller as the Soma disappeared down the demon's throat.

Rahu was depicted as a monster with a dragon's head and a tail like a comet. He had a chariot drawn by eight black horses that represented the clouds of the night sky. Some scholars call Rahu a dual deity, a planet or a meteor god and the personification of the two nodes of the moon's orbit. In this view, both parts of Rahu survived after Vishnu cut him in half. Rahu was the ascending node, or the demon's head, and Ketu was the descending node, or the demon's tail. (Knappert 1995b, Krupp 1991a)

See also Chaos, Demons, Eclipses, India, Soma

RAIDEN

Raiden was the Japanese thunder god, a malicious deity with claws, red skin, and the head of a demon. Although most of the myths about Raiden tell of his malevolence, he was credited with preventing the Mongols from invading Japan in 1274 by creating a great storm and destroying all but three men. Raiden was usually depicted sitting on a cloud and shooting arrows of lightning down on the Mongol ships coming in for attack.

Raiden kept the company of other super-natural storm beings, particularly his son Raitaro, a ptarmigan named Raicho, and Fugin, the god of winds. Raitaro, unlike his father, was associated not with malice but prosperity. A poor farmer named Bimbo found the boy one day, and he took the baby home and raised him as his own. The farmer and his wife called the baby "Child of Thunder," and the child helped his foster parents by calling to the clouds and asking it to rain on Bimbo's fields whenever they needed it. The clouds obliged, and the farmer's fields were always watered. Then when Raitaro, the Thunder Child, turned eighteen, he turned into a small white dragon and flew up to the clouds. (Davis 1992, Knappert 1995c)

See also Japan, Thunder and Thunder Gods, Thunderbirds

RAIN AND RAIN GODS

To the ancients, rain seemed to fall from the sky like magic. It replenished the waters, it fertilized the earth, and it guaranteed the growth of food and the continuation of life. When the gods of winter surfaced and clutched the earth with their grips of death, the gods of rain emerged soon afterward to repair the destruction. The notion of the Water of Life may have originated from these seemingly magic spring rains. Like semen from the celestial sky god, they planted seeds deep into Mother Earth, and soon she delivered the gift of life.

The gods who released the rains made possible this gift of life and thus had considerable power. Sometimes they were great sky gods who controlled the storm as well as other mighty forces that emanated from the celestial sphere, and sometimes they were lesser gods, still powerful, but who showed themselves only at certain times of year. The rain gods often lived in the clouds, and they poured their precious sky water from pots or containers of some sort that they could open at will. In Africa, some tribes say the rain falls when their ancestors in the sky throw calabashes full of water. Other tribes say it falls when their god's son, a water carrier, spills the water. The Peruvians say that their rain goddess sits in the clouds with a pitcher of water, poised and ready to pour it out at the right time. If she waits too long, her brother intervenes. He controls the lightning and thunder, and he uses them to smash the pitcher to pieces and cause violent storms.

The rain deities lived in the clouds because ancient weather watchers recognized the connection between clouds and rain. The Chinese believed that dragons rose to the sky each spring and fought with each other, pressing their enormous feet on the clouds and pushing out the water. People in other lands perceived the clouds as cattle herded by the storm god. In Indian myth, Vritra, the drought demon, imprisoned the cloud-cattle in caves, and Indra, the storm god, released them. Some African tribes called their rainmakers sky herds, and they gained their power to herd the clouds only after eating meat from the lightning bird, a bird reputed to have value as a rain charm.

Rainmaking was one of the most practiced rituals of times past, and among some people, remains so today. The process of rainmaking combines religion and magic, and persons trained to perform these rituals are reputed to have special abilities to tap into nature's water supply. Rainmakers do things like sprinkle water to simulate rain, as did Ix Chel, the rain goddess of the Maya, or they dip tree branches into springs, as did the Chinese rain god, Chhih Sung-tzu. All over the world, rainmakers imitate the techniques of rain gods and spirits. The Chinese attempt to make it rain by making paper dragons, the rain spirits of China. The Pueblo wear masks and assume the mythological roles of their rain spirits, the Kachinas. In some parts of Russia, the people attempt to make rain by pouring water over a young girl selected to represent the earth. They dress her in green leaves and flowers, and by showering her with water, the people believe they can encourage the clouds to shower her and the earth as well.

Rain rituals, however, involve the practice of both producing rain when it is needed and halting the flow of it when the land is threatened by flood. In dry lands, such as Africa, rainmaking is big business, but on tropical islands and other places where rain falls abundantly, rituals for preventing rain commonly occur. These rituals often involve avoiding water at all costs. Some of the rain doctors refrain from bathing, and others drink no water at all, only red wine. Still others kindle fires to avert the rain. Too much rain, people know, can be as devastating as too little. Floods can occur anywhere, and they did, as evidenced in flood myths of many cultures. In Zambia, a sitando is both a rainmaker who sings to the clouds to persuade them to drop water and a rain doctor who pleads with the clouds to disperse.

It is important to remember, however, that although rainmakers reputedly have magic powers, they get those powers from the Great Spirit or the sky god. They know the weather well, they make appropriate sacrifices, and they use rain charms, but their object is to communicate with and receive the blessings of the deities with the real power to release the water. Sometimes the spirit of the god possesses the rainmaker. Sometimes, the god appears to the rainmaker in a dream. During their rituals, rainmakers usually keep their eyes peeled on the sky, not only to observe the celestial objects but to make contact with the rain spirits.

The practice of rainmaking generally assumes that the rain spirits have the water in their possession already and that they need to be persuaded to make their sky waters fall. To the Ganda of Africa, rainmaking is a joint effort of several gods. They say that Mayanja, a river god, blows his waters into the sky, and then Musoke, the air god, beats it, distributes it through the clouds, and lets it fall back to earth again. People in some cultures equated the falling of the rain with the falling of tears. Tlaloc, the Aztec rain god, required the sacrifice of thousands of children to encourage the flow of their mothers' tears. The Zulus threw a bird into the water to encourage the heavens to cry for the dead bird. In Liberia (West Africa), the Supreme Deity, Meleka, lived high in the sky above the clouds with his daughter, Sia, who cried all the time. Sia looked down on earth and saw the unfeeling ways of human beings and she cried and cried. Then when her father punished the sinful mortals by hurling his thunderbolts, she cried even harder. Sia's tears, of course, were the rains that fell abundantly on the earth. But because Meleka and Sia lived in only one part of the sky, Sia's tears fell on only one part of the land. Meleka remedied the situation by calling on the winds for help. He asked them to blow his family all over the sky so Sia's tears would distribute the rains evenly instead of flooding the land in one place while allowing drought to persist in other places. Even today, shamans and rainmakers summon the winds when they want to make it rain. They ask the winds to locate Sia and invite her to the drought-stricken areas of land. (Donnan 1977, Ferguson 1996, Frazer 1950, Krupp 1997b)

See also Chhih Sung-tzu, Clouds, Drought, Floods and Flood Gods, Indra, Kachinas, Lightning Bird, Mujaji, Storms and Tempests, Tlaloc

RAINBOW SNAKE

Gigantic water snakes that coiled around the earth and manifested themselves as the rainbow appeared in many mythologies, particularly in those of Africa and Australia. Generally, they existed in the primeval waters, then continued to exist after the world's creation, submerged in whirlpools or waterholes or in any body of running water. Usually the rainbow snake remained submerged, writhing in darkness and moving the waters. When the snake surfaced, his massive movements drew up the waters and caused rain and flood.

The concept of the rainbow snake combined the belief in snakes as symbols of flowing movement and the notion of serpents or dragons as water gods. These snakes were so monstrous and their magic so powerful that by writhing underneath the earth, they set the world in motion. Aido Hwedo, the rainbow snake of Dahomey in Africa, kept the celestial bodies moving around the heavens, and he supported the earth with his coils. Rainbow snakes who inhabited waters visited by other tribes of people performed similar functions and were greatly feared for their ability to flood the land. When Aido Hwedo remained coiled in the waters, he kept the universe stable and prevented the earth from sinking into the sea. When he surfaced and unleashed the waters, he upset the balance of nature.

The actions of the rainbow snake served a dual function, however. This snake was powerful as both creator and destroyer. He produced the fructifying rain but also the monsoons and the devastating floods. He ensured fertility and regeneration but also caused death and destruction. Tribes that worshipped the rainbow snake both feared and revered him for the strength of his powers. Rainmakers and medicine men in some tribes of Australia tried to tap into those powers by manipulating quartz crystals and pearl shells, from which they believed the snake's powers emanated.

Belief in the rainbow snake still exists among some tribal people, including the Gagudju of Australia, who consider her the most important of all spirits. The rainbow snake of their myths is female, and she created hills and stones and pools back in the primeval period of creation called Dreamtime and continues to bring rain and renewal to the earth. Perhaps the best-known Australian myth of the rainbow snake is the myth of the Wawilak sisters, two women who traveled across the land, one pregnant and one with child in arms. The pregnant sister gave

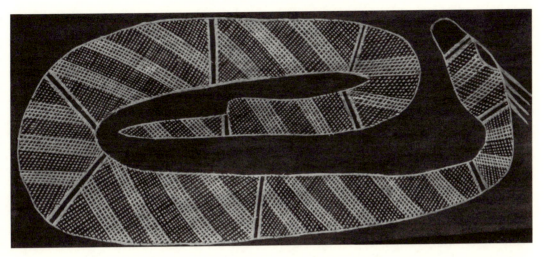

A bark painting of a Rainbow Snake from Arnhem Land, Australia, where the snake is considered an extremely important spirit.

birth, and then, while fetching water from a well, she allowed some of her postpartum blood to flow into the well where the rainbow snake resided. The snake got mad at her for polluting his waters. He rose up and flooded the land, then swallowed both women and their children. The snake emerged from the waters when the flood subsided and regurgitated the people he had just devoured. This myth conveyed the dual nature of the rainbow snake and of the power of water in general. It drew connections to death when the snake, like the flood waters, swallowed up the women, and it drew connections to life and fertility when the snake regurgitated them in an act of creation. (Parrinder 1986, Poignant 1967)

See also Dragons, Dreamtime, Floods and Flood Gods, Oceania, Rain and Rain Gods, Serpents and Snakes

RAINBOWS AND RAINBOW GODS

Long before scientists unraveled the mystery of rainbows, people from every culture pondered their existence. The ancients saw them as magical because they seemingly appeared out of nowhere and disappeared just as mysteriously. Astute observers of nature understood that rainbows appeared in connection with rainshowers, so in the myths of many lands, rainbows appeared as weather portents and rainbow gods and goddesses appeared as powerful deities with control over earthly waters. In some myths, those deities took human forms. But in others, the rainbow was itself a living spirit, capable of causing either good fortune or devastating harm.

The rainbow's use as a weather forecaster stretches back to the earliest myths, when skywatchers used these colored arcs to predict either good rains or life-threatening storms. Many notions of these early skywatchers held true. In the northern hemisphere, the belief that a bad rainbow appears in the morning and a good one at night, for instance, is based on fact. Rainbows usually appear during passing rain, and weather usually moves from west to east. Therefore with the morning sun in the east and the rainbow in the west, the arc serves as a predictor of oncoming storms. In the evening, the sun has moved to the west, and the rainbow in the east indicates that the storm has passed.

The Chinese were among the groups who attributed the prominence of certain colors in the rainbow to particular weather conditions.

Red meant wind, for instance, and green meant continued rain. But the rainbow's connection to weather made it more than a handy predictor. The arc became a useful weapon of storm gods. Ancient storm gods of Siberia and Russia, Finland, Lapland, India, and Africa used the arc as a bow to fire thunderbolts at their enemies.

Although many myths draw parallels between rainbows and rain, the bow's formation requires sunlight as well. When the sun rises or sets behind a sheet of falling water, a band of color is projected on the opposite horizon. This works with moonlight too, causing a more subtle phenomena called a moonbow. It took centuries to understand the physics of rainbows, but even in prehistory many people recognized rainbows' association with light. In South America the rainbow was the husband of the moon; in other cultures, the companion or servant of the sun.

Rainbow myths prevailed in Oceanic and Polynesian lands and in South America where agricultural communities depended on long rainy seasons for survival. Because rainbow deities in these areas controlled rainfall, the benevolent gods and goddesses rejuvenated the land and often served as fertility gods. But other rainbow deities exercised their powers of destruction. With the ability to cause drought, flood, and storms at sea, the evil powers of the rainbow god caused people in many lands to live in fear.

The fear of rainbows crossed many cultures. Some Australian tribes viewed the rainbow as the rain's son, who caused droughts in an effort to prevent his father from falling down. These tribes performed elaborate rituals to drive the rainbow away by imprisoning the arc. But drought was not the worst of their fears. Some groups thought the rainbow would devour them, like a thirsty crocodile or snake touching the earth to drink the waters and with them, any person or animal who crossed its path.

The crocodile as a rainbow symbol prob-ably stemmed from the reptile's dual nature as land dweller and water dweller. Some cultures likened the rainbow to a chameleon or lizard. But the snake is the most prevalent symbol of the rainbow. In myths of Europe, Africa, South America, and most commonly of Australia, rainbow serpents and snakes emerged in the literature as powerful gods.

Perhaps the best known of the rainbow deities is the Greek goddess Iris, daughter of Thaumas, the god of wonder. This parentage seems to reveal the ancient Greeks' fascination with the rainbow—as if it were the creation of wonder itself. Iris was probably a wind and rain goddess before she inherited the rainbow, and in some early myths she was the fiancée of the rain. But through time, her role as messenger prevailed. In some myths, Iris personified the rainbow, but in other myths the rainbow simply indicated the route Iris took as she flashed across the sky.

The rainbow as a route or path is a common theme in myths around the world. Because the bow appears to touch the earth at one end and the sky at the other, the rainbow served as a bridge between worlds; it was the path that connected Heaven and earth. In Norse mythology, a rainbow bridge called Bifrost connected the world of people with the world of the gods. In myths of Japan, China, Iran, Central Africa, and North America, similar rainbow bridges and paths led from one realm to the next, revealing a common belief that the rainbow led to paradise.

Rainbow myths cross all cultures because people in all areas of the world have been awestruck by their mysteries. From prehistory to the modern day, people have chased these arcs and fruitlessly searched for the rainbow's end. But by nature the bow can never be reached; when approached, it appears to retreat or disappear completely. This inaccessibility combined with its beauty led the ancients to deify the bow. What scientists now understand as a "natural" phenomenon once achieved divine status in the histories and myths of people across the globe. (Boyer 1987, Graham 1979, Krupp 1991a)

See also Bifrost, Bridges, Iris, Milky Way, Serpents and Snakes

RIVERS AND LAKES

Water worship was prevalent in antiquity, and by deifying rivers and lakes, the ancients showed reverence for water's strength. This strength the ancients witnessed in river water particularly, as it coursed through the earth, fell through rapids and waterfalls, and often, whether for good or for bad, overflowed and flooded the land. River water moved, it appeared alive, and the ancients believed some supernatural force caused the movement. River gods, they said, caused the coursing and flooding. River spirits set the whirlpools and waterfalls in motion.

To control the movement of sacred waters, these river gods had to possess great powers. The Ashanti considered the spirits of rivers the most powerful of all the nature spirits, the children of the Supreme Being sent to earth and distributed throughout the land. The people of Benin, Nigeria, considered the Olukun River the source of all waters on earth and its god, Olukun, the Lord of All Waters. The rivers these gods ruled and the realms they inhabited were sacred, for within them pulsed the Water of Life. Sometimes, the world's river deities created those life waters by pouring it out of bowls or urns. In Babylon, when the swollen river waters turned red from the soil, the people attributed it to the river god's blood.

River worship was prevalent the world over, but perhaps the most noted water cults and shrines appeared in the Celtic world. The Celts named the rivers and lakes after their presiding deities, deities who in ancient times received offerings and sacrifices. Ritual offerings to the spirits of lakes and rivers were believed to discourage the gods from using the water's destructive power and encourage them to activate the healing and fer-

A distressed mother with her baby being pulled into a lake by Nicor, a Celtic water demon.

tilizing powers; they were deemed necessary for the well-being of the land. The Celts built shrines over the sources of rivers, as well as over holy wells. The temple over the source of the Seine, for instance, was once an ancient water shrine to the goddess Sequana. Early people deemed river sources sacred because they appeared to harbor the Water of Life and immortality. They deemed other features of rivers sacred as well, such as certain waterfalls or rock hollows that were thought to have healing powers.

The search for the Water of Life occurred in many lands. By drinking or immersing in this water, people became immortal. Ho Po, the Chinese Count of the River, gained immortality when he threw himself into the Yellow River, and so did Achelous, the Greek river god, when he threw himself into his river, the largest watercourse in Greece. Achelous, like all the Greek river deities, was male, and there were three thousand of his kind, according to the Greek poet Hesiod, all the sons of Oceanus and Tethys. But most areas of the world had female river deities. The ancients associated the fertilizing power of water with the life-giving power of women.

The fertility goddesses that inhabited rivers and lakes took many forms. They were the Rusalka in the Slavic lands and mermaids of many sorts, lovely maidens who graced the world's freshwaters just as they did the seas. Although many of these spirits were benevolent, many others caused harm. The Cailleach of Scotland caused storms. The Nokke of Norway demanded annual sacrifice to prevent them from taking human victims. But Yemoja, the goddess of water and the mother of all rivers to the Yoruba of Nigeria, made barren women fertile. In return for offerings of yams, maize, animals, and fishes, she gave them water in a jar from the country's primary river, the River Ogun.

River and lake deities demanded regular sacrifices because, benevolent or not, they did have the power to pull people into the depths of their waters. They also had the power to send their waters surging over the land. Many myths of lakes and rivers involved drowning and flooding. So Ho Po in China received human sacrifices and gifts of jade. The Kawa-no-Kami in Japan received offerings, as did Ganga in India, Osiris in Egypt, and deities in other bodies of freshwater throughout the world. In a sense, the power of these river gods extended to all three realms. The deepest parts of their waters led to the Underworld, and often major rivers on earth had a celestial counterpart as the Milky Way in the sky. (Bord and Bord 1985, Michell 1975, Pennick 1996, Vitaliano 1973)

See also Achelous, Canyons, Ganges River, Nile River, Springs and Wells, Water and Water Spirits, Well of Life

ROCKS AND STONES

In many lands people connected the worship of rocks and stones with reverence for the earth mother. Solid and immutable, the rocks were the great goddess's bones, the foundation from which she gave birth, and the framework that protected the hollows of her womb. In mythology, high gods and human beings alike emerged from rocks, an indication that early people regarded them as a source of life. These solid structures symbolized the permanence of the great mother's presence, and they contrasted the stability of her body structure to the fragility of the bodies of human beings.

Mother Earth manifested herself in rocks and stones that appeared in various shapes, sizes, and colors. The Celtic named stones after the part of the body they resembled. Some looked like heels, for instance, and others looked like elbows. All over the world, people found stones that resembled human beings or animals. In myths and legends, some of these stones actually were people at one time. In a Papago Indian myth, the boulders on the mountain tops were once people who asked the Great Spirit to save them from the flood. In a myth from Greece, the queen Niobe turned to stone while grieving the murder of her children, and in a legend from North America, so did another woman grieving when her husband married someone else. The Native Americans believed this woman turned into the Standing Rock on the Upper Missouri River. Then, in a reverse instance of such metamorphoses, certain North American tribes claimed that they descended from stones. It appeared that in their way of thinking, if human beings could become stones, then stones, in turn, could become human beings.

The humanization of stones was an ancient belief, as was the notion that stones grew and reproduced. The Hawaiians believed that rocks had sex, that solid rocks were male and porous ones female, and that together they created children, the small pebbles that they found dotting their land. In Maori myth, Rakahore was the Father of Rocks. With one of his two wives he produced land stones and rocks, and with the other wife, the rocks and reefs of the ocean. In Greek myth, the Titan goddess Themis told Deucalon and Pyrrah, the survivors of the great flood, to throw the bones of their mother behind them in order to save mankind. These bones were the rocks and stones. Those thrown by Deucalon became men and those thrown by Pyrrah became women.

The prominence of rocks and stones in creation myths of this sort meant that early people infused these objects with spirit. In China and some other countries, people believed the color of a stone revealed the character and attributes of the spirit within it. Stones that had five colors, for instance, contained the spirit of the gods of the four quarters and the god of the sun. The Chinese called colored stones dragon's eggs, so their dragon gods, it appeared, emerged from the stones just as such gods as Mithra did when they came to power in the world. The Japanese Buddhists venerated certain stones because they believed the Buddha's spirit and knowledge had seeped into the rock. Some African tribes continue to believe that rocks harbor spirits of the dead and that particularly large rocks harbor many of these spirits.

Rock spirits assumed evil guises in myths as often as they assumed benevolent ones. The spirits that inhabited rocks in the water and along the sea coasts were especially considered evil. Rock demons in the waters of Africa and Australia sometimes carried off women or stole fishes from nets, and other times they raised storms over the waters, storms with strong enough winds to wreck boats and drown their passengers. The Greeks symbolized the dangers of the waters by creating Scylla, the monster who embodied the treacherous rocks in the Strait of Messina, and the Sirens, who turned into rocks but who first lured men to their deaths with beautiful songs. In Finnish myth, Luonnotar, the mother of the waves, created the rocks and reefs to kill mariners. In Greek myth, Poseidon put rock islands and reefs in the Aegean to help him battle the giants. The Titans of Greek lore and the Stone Giants of North America may have embodied the treachery of the rocks, and the gods had to battle them to maintain supremacy in the world.

Whether individual rocks or stones harbored good or bad spirits, they did have power and they did represent the divine, so people in many cultures venerated them. Because rocks and stones had divine powers, they made valuable magic charms. Sometimes the rock spirits made barren women fertile. Sometimes they helped procure the rains. The magical use of stones for these purposes likely stemmed from the belief that, as an avatar of Mother Earth, the spirit within the rock held the powers of creation. In the world of the Lakota Sioux, Inyan was the Spirit of the Rocks. He was a primordial omnipotent power, the first of the high gods and the oldest deity known. Inyan created the earth from his body. He created the waters from his blood. Because Inyan was the source of all things, stone in itself was seen as sacred and immutable. (Eliade 1958, Krupp 1997b, Mackenzie 1994, Rappoport 1995, Vitaliano 1973)

See also Ayers Rock, Earth and Earth Gods, Huacas, Inyan, Scylla and Charybdis, Sea and Sea Gods

ROME
See Greece and Rome

RUDRA
Rudra was a Vedic Indian deity, a forerunner of the widely worshipped Shiva and usually identified as a god of hurricanes, storms, and winds. Unlike Shiva, Rudra was most often

demonic and terrifying and known for shooting arrows of death and disease at human beings and animals. The name Rudra meant "howler," and like the hurricane winds, this deity was wild and tempestuous and often described as a bull. He stirred up storms and agitated the waters as he rode on a whirlwind and terrorized the land.

Rudra fathered the Maruts, storms deities who were thought by some to represent various aspects of his character. The Maruts were sometimes called Rudras, and they had both good and bad qualities, as did the storms and the winds themselves. Although Rudra acted both as creator and destroyer, he was most commonly known for his destructive side. (Ions 1984, Thomas 1980, Zimmer 1962)

See also Demons, Hurricanes and Tornadoes, India, Maruts, Shiva, Storms and Tempests

RUSALKA

The Rusalka of Russian lore was primarily a water maiden, connected to the fertility of the water she inhabited and to the concept of life and death embodied by the figure of Mother Earth. The Slavic people commonly believed that when a maiden drowned, she became a Rusalka, and that Rusalki were thus spirits of the dead. The belief in these water spirits occurred throughout the Slavic lands, where the maidens appeared to embody the dualistic quality of nature. The Rusalka was both a spinner who rejuvenated the earth and controlled the cycle of seasons and a dweller of the dark recesses of the waters who represented nature's destructive, uncontrolled side.

Water spirits permeated Russian lore, and Rusalki were perhaps the most common. Like the Sirens of Greek lore, they enchanted men with their lovely voices, then turned deadly and lured them to watery deaths. These beautiful women lived in the water during the winter months when the earth was dead and the waters were cold and fitting abodes for these dead souls. Then in the spring when the sun's rays warmed the waters, they rose up to the trees in groves or in dark forests and perched on the branches. The Russians believed the green trees to be the abode of the dead, so the Rusalki, as death maidens, remained there a while. Then they slid down the trees' trunks, danced on the earth, and showed their life-maiden side. The fertility of the waters they embodied brought life to the grass and renewed the earth during the upcoming summer season.

Because the Rusalka embodied both life and death, she was a fitting symbol of Mother Earth. She was the maternal womb, the Water of Life, and the tomb that embodied the dead. When the Rusalka perched in the tree branches, she watered them, as did the Norns of Norse myth who watered the cosmic tree, Yggdrasil, and who were also spinners who decided when people should live and die. The rising of the Rusalka from the waters to the treetops suggested the rising of the life-giving waters to the sky, where they fell to the earth as rain. In some traditions, the Rusalka as spinner and fertility goddess also regulated the moon and the weather, directed clouds, and caused the rain to fall, sometimes when she combed her hair. (Hubbs 1988, Ralston 1872)

See also Baltic and Slavic Lands, Mermaids, Sirens, Spinning and Weaving, Water and Water Spirits

RYUJIN

Ryujin was a benevolent water god and the Sea King of Japanese myth. He was a dragon-king, like those of China, and he lived in a magnificent palace under the waves, a palace believed to exist in the deepest part of the sea near the Ryukyu Islands. Ryujin had a human body, yet he was in essence a dragon. This gave him power over the storm. Ryujin controlled the rain, the wind, and the thunder. He was attended in his underwater palace by fishes and sea creatures of every sort, and he had untold riches, among them magic jewels he used to control the tides. His daughter Benten gained much more significance than he, and she played a starring role in many Japanese sea myths. (Anesaki 1964, Davis 1992)

See also Benten, Dragon-Kings, Dragons, Japan, Sea and Sea Gods, Tides

SACRIFICE

The horror with which most people today view the practice of sacrifice is perhaps surpassed only by the sacredness with which it was viewed by many people of the past. Blood sacrifice was one of the most universal acts of piety; it was, and continues to be by some, the height of reverence for the gods. In polytheistic cultures, the gods controlled natural phenomena, so sacrifices ensured that these nature powers looked kindly upon the earth. What justified the practice of sacrifice to those who worshipped in this manner was their belief in appeasing the nature gods to gain their favor.

The idea of propitiating the nature powers with blood and flesh recurred throughout history. Human sacrifice perhaps reached its zenith with the Aztecs, but the Maya before them and indeed cultures all over the world practiced sacrifice, both human and animal. These rituals did not mean the practitioners loved the gods, but only that they feared them. They represented the forces that could destroy life on earth. When water flooded the plains, when earthquakes split the earth, or when hail or lightning or any other destructive force made its appearance, people witnessed the gods' angry outbursts. It was then that they found it necessary to sacrifice, so the gods would know of their piety and, they hoped, repair the destruction.

The ritual of sacrifice, like many other ancient rituals, was an attempt to control nature. When the nature powers wreaked havoc, they upset the cosmic balance and people felt the need to do something to restore it. When drought plagued the land, sacrifice offered the promise of rain. When ice froze the crops, sacrifice offered the promise of sunshine. The Inca sacrificed to the mountain gods to ensure the flow of water down the peaks. The Aztec sacrificed to the sun to keep him moving on his path. Many people sacrificed at planting time to ensure that the crops grew and the earth renewed itself and continued moving through the seasons.

Through the act of ritual sacrifice then, people took responsibility for maintaining order. They took this responsibility seriously, and they chose their sacrifice victims carefully, as part of the plan. People sacrificed rams to the sky gods because rams symbolized celestial power. They sacrificed horses to the sea gods because horses symbolized the power of the mighty waves. People sacrificed bulls to waterfalls because they likened the roar of the bull to the sound of the falling water, and they sacrificed black sheep to the rain gods because they likened their dark fleecy bodies to the dark fluffy clouds. When the Greeks sacrificed horses to the sun, they believed the sun god needed new horses to drive his chariot because the old ones got tired. When the Aztecs sacrificed children to Tlaloc, the rain god, they believed the flow of tears from both the children and their mothers made the flow of water fall from the heavens.

Sacrifice occurred universally and throughout history, perhaps because in many creation stories, life on earth—and indeed the earth itself—emerged from the broken parts of a sacrificed god. Death, in creation myths, generated life, and in many other kinds of myths, life and death depended on each other and comprised one of the inherent dualisms of the ordered world. Death and life alternate in all realms of nature, in the earth as the seasons change, in the sea as the tides ebb and flow, and in the sky as the celestial objects rise and set. That people of all ages incorporated death into their rituals was perhaps as natural to them as a subtle prayer for the Great Spirit's mercy. (Brundage 1985, Tierney 1990)

See also Cosmic Order, Death, Mesoamerica, Tonatiuh

SAGITTARIUS, THE ARCHER

Sagittarius is the ninth constellation of the zodiac, half horse, half man, and is considered to be either a centaur or a satyr. An ancient constellation, Sagittarius appeared in the early zodiacs of Egypt and India as well as on monuments from Babylonian times. Sagittarius was an archer, perhaps represented as such because in ancient times, the sun entered Sagittarius when hunting season began. Today, the sun reaches Sagittarius on the first day of winter, so the constellation marks the winter solstice.

In star maps, Sagittarius wears a cloak and carries a bow and arrow that points to Antares, the star that marks the heart of Scorpio. According to Greek myth, Sagittarius avenged Orion by slaying the scorpion that stung him and caused his death. Some mythologists have confused Sagittarius with another celestial archer, Centaurus, who was perhaps a representation of Chiron, the centaur who was placed among the stars after Herakles shot him with a poisoned arrow. But other mythologists say Sagittarius represented Crotus, the son of Pan and Eupheme who lived with the Muses on Mount Helicon and invented archery. The Muses asked Zeus to put Sagittarius in the sky, and Zeus obliged.

Most of Sagittarius lies in a dense part of the Milky Way. Because many early people considered the Milky Way a path of the dead, some scholars have suggested that Sagittarius guarded the door to the Underworld. In these times, the sun moved through Sagittarius just before it reached the point of the winter solstice, the lowest part of the sun's journey across the sky. (Ridpath 1988, Staal 1988)

See also Constellations, Zodiac

ST. ELMO'S FIRE

Aside from the aurora borealis, St. Elmo's Fire is probably the most familiar phenomenon of the glowing sky. It appears between the masts of a ship as a flash of lightning, usually resembling a blue candle flame, and generally accompanies thunderstorms. St. Elmo's Fire is caused by an electrical discharge from a sharp object, and it is visible only in the dark, so sailors navigating the seas on stormy nights commonly saw it, sometimes as one flame and other times as two. The eerie appearance of this dancing light stimulated the imagination of many superstitious mariners of times past. They viewed the odd fire not as a benign electrical phenomenon, but as an indication of the presence of water spirits or some other strange and supernatural force.

The fire of St. Elmo was alternately seen as evil and fortuitous. Ancient mariners observed that the phenomenon normally occurred about six hours after the center of a storm passed, so they considered the glow an indication of good fortune, of fair sailing weather ahead. Others connected the eerie appearance to the presence of dead souls, particularly the souls of drowned sailors who returned either to warn others of danger or to try to climb back aboard ship. The Greeks and Romans saw the flame as an indication of the presence of Castor and Pollux, two warrior brothers who served as protectors of ships and sailors, even after Zeus placed them in the sky as stars. On star maps, Castor and Pollux always appear directly above the constellations that form Argo Navis, and in the myth of the Argonautic trip, the two flames danced around the heads of Castor and Pollux just before the tempest ceased. The Greeks thought Castor and Pollux produced the double flame as an indication that the two brothers were escorting the ship through dangerous waters. They thought Helen of Troy produced the single flame. Although the double flame in the rigging meant good fortune, a single one spelled disaster, just as Helen spelled disaster for Troy.

In the Middle Ages, when patron saints took over the function of the pagan gods, St. Elmo was considered the patron saint of sailors. The mysterious light indicated his presence, and sailors around the world told tales of when and why he would appear. Some considered his presence fortuitous, and others, a warning of disaster. (Rappoport 1995, Ridpath 1988)

See also Gemini, Lightning, Phosphorescence

SAND AND SANDSTORMS
See Deserts, Whirlwinds

SARASVATI
In the Hindu world today, Sarasvati is worshipped as Brahma's wife, the goddess of wisdom, but in Vedic times, she was most likely goddess of the river Sarasvati, which at the time flowed from the Himalayan mountains into the sea. The ancients worshiped rivers because they believed in the fertilizing and purifying powers of water. As goddess of the river, Sarasvati embodied these powers, and she was thus revered as one of the three great river goddesses of India.

Vedic India refers to a time when the Aryans settled in India, 1500 B.C. to approximately 600 B.C., and during these early years, the river Sarasvati flowed right through these first settlements. It spilled out into the Indian Ocean, a body of water ruled by the powerful water god Varuna. But today the river stops in the desert and never reaches into the great god's waters. According to legend, an ancient curse halted the flow. Varuna stole the wife of a sage named Utathya, and to force Varuna to give her up, Utathya decided to deprive Varuna of seawater. The name Sarasvati means "flowing," and it relates both to her ancient role as river goddess and to her current role as goddess of wisdom and eloquence. (Ions 1984, Moor 1984, Thomas 1980)

See also Benten, Ganges River, India, Rivers and Lakes

SAULE
In the Baltic lands, Saule was the sun goddess and, like Amaterasu of Japan, an exception to the traditional Indo-European conception of a male sun. Saule was beloved and highly revered among the ancient Latvians, Lithuanians, and Old Prussians. All-seeing and all-knowing, she warmed the earth, nourished the crops, subdued the thunderstorms, and guarded and protected all the people in the land.

Saule shared many characteristics with other sun deities; she rode across the sky in a golden chariot, she reached a magnificent palace in the west each night, and she returned to the east through the Underworld waters each day. But elements in her myths gave her persona a unique flavor. Because the Balts witnessed the sun's appearance during rainstorms, they said that Saule created the rainbow's colors. She also gilded the treetops for her daughter's dowry, and cried red tears at sunset that colored the clouds. According to one tradition, Saule drowned each night in the western sea, which explained why her children, the "orphan" stars, appeared in the sky without her. Saule's daughter, Auszrine, the sun maiden or Morning Star, had to plead every night with the ruler of the dead for a key to the Underworld. Each night, the ruler of the dead surrendered the key, and Auszrine rescued her mother. Saule then rose to the sky again the next morning, with Auszrine.

Saule had many children in addition to Auszrine. Wakarine, the Evening Star, was her daughter, and so was the fire goddess and the many stars of the night sky. Saule also had three husbands, sometimes identified as the three phases of the moon and other times as the sky father Dievs, the moon god Meness, and the storm and rain god Perkons. But her relationships with these men were tumultuous. Perkons and Saule fought constantly, as the storm does the sun, and Meness and Saule did not get along much better. Meness was an adulterer and seduced Saule's daughter

Auszrine, the Morning Star. So Saule sliced up the moon, which is why the moon appeared in phases, or pieces.

The cult of Saule was widespread in the Baltic lands, and the beloved sun goddess was the subject of many myths, legends, and dainos, or Lithuanian songs. Perhaps her popularity stemmed from the belief that she descended to earth and interacted with the people. She appeared to them as an elegant woman, dressed in traditional Baltic costumes spun from threads of red, gold, silver, and white, the colors she used to light the sky. (Greimas 1992, McCrickard 1990)

See also Amaterasu, Auszrine, Baltic and Slavic Lands, Morning Star/Evening Star, Myesyats, Sun and Sun Gods

SCANDINAVIA

The nature myths of Scandinavia reflected a harsh winter landscape: stormy seas, snow-capped mountains, and an ice-covered earth that thawed for just a few months each year then froze again. In this area of the world, winter dominated, and the people faced long, dark days and bitter cold nights. Frosts were prevalent in the Nordic lands, even in the summer. When the first settlers came to this area, they found the frozen landscape foreboding and hostile, and they personified nature's forces in myths of monstrous giants made of frost and ice.

Much of Norse mythology came from Icelandic sources, particularly the *Poetic Edda*, a collection of poems that likely date to the early years of the Viking age, and the *Prose Edda*, written in the thirteenth century by an Icelandic scholar named Snorri Sturluson. Iceland is a volcanic island, often referred to as the Land of Ice and Fire. A layer of ice covers the land most of the year, but underneath the ice lies a fiery subterranean world. The myths in the Eddas combined the forces of ice and fire and told of entire races of fearsome giants, frost giants who waged constant battles with the gods and fire giants who

eventually led the world to destruction. The influence of these two forces was so strong that the Norse creation myths involved the existence of two primeval worlds in opposition: Nifflheim, the home of mist and ice, and Muspelheim, the land of flame and fire. In between the two worlds lay the great void called Ginunngagap, formed by water flowing into the dark abyss and freezing over. In Ginunngagap the first person, a monstrous ice giant named Ymir, was born, created when ice from Nifflheim and sparks from Muspelheim mingled together.

Such harsh, driving forces permeated every aspect of Norse mythology. The natural world was a constant force to be reckoned with, so these mythological giants were constant forces to be reckoned with as well. In the Norse myths, the gods had to destroy the first race of giants before they could create Aesir, the home of the gods. Many of the giants were drowned in the blood of Ymir, whose icy body parts formed various features of the frozen landscape. But enough of the giants survived to continue the race. These were the frost giants who mingled with the gods, most of whom opposed them, but some of whom became their friends and lovers. Like the sparkling ice and the glistening snow, these creatures were lovely and alluring but at the same time terrifying. Some the gods battled and tamed, but, ultimately, the race of frost giants took over the earth.

In the Norse myths, mythological beings inhabited each of the three realms. The frost giants, called Jotuns, lived underneath the earth in Jotunheim, and the two races of gods—the Aesir, or sky gods, and the Vanir, or earth gods—lived in realms above them. In myths all over the world, gods and spirits inhabited nature, and in animistic cultures, they inhabited every element, form of life, or type of vegetation. In Norse myths, these spirits were the giants, elves, and dwarves. The giants embodied large-scale natural phenomena, such as hurricanes, volcanoes, snowstorms, and hail. Elves and dwarves embodied the smaller elements of nature and resided in woods, mountains, lakes, and streams.

The earth and sky forces entered into all of the Norse myths, but because many of the northern European people were navigators, the stormy North Sea cropped up in many myths as well. Northern sea giants terrorized sailors and threatened to pull their ships into the icy waters. Gigantic wave maidens pulled sailors to their deaths. These horrific beings personified different aspects of the raging sea. The bubbling cauldron of the sea god Aegir represented the ferocious whirlpools that hissed and swirled as Aegir brewed ale for the gods in his underwater hall. Storms constantly waged battle over the sea, like some monstrous storm giant battling with an angry water serpent. Such was the myth of Thor fishing for the Midgard serpent, Jormungandr, who twisted and thrashed as the thunder god struggled to reel him in. Hymir, the giant who accompanied Thor on his fishing trip, got frightened, however, and cut the fishing line. So most mythologists say Jormungandr is still in the sea, where he continues to battle storms, lashing at cliffs and icebergs and causing untold hazards to northern navigators.

The Scandinavian land embodied harshness, but in the summer there was some relief. In the summer the unending darkness abated and the vegetation that cropped up appeared miraculous in a land where most of the year nothing grew at all. For this reason, Norse myths were full of seasonal metaphors, and in two popular stories, gods of summer and light married frost giantesses. The gods, Njord and Frey, were Vanir gods who ruled over rain and soft winds and represented the fertile summer earth, whereas their lovely goddesses embodied winter and cold and frozen seed.

Most of the good gods in Norse mythology were fertility gods and represented in one form or another the land in the summertime, when light overcame darkness and life began anew. The summer god, Uller, was credited with the near ever-present light of the aurora borealis, and Balder, the primary light god, was the most loved and most beautiful god of all. Balder's death at the summer solstice was mourned piteously as an allegory for the onset of a long, dark winter. But the longest winter, the winter to end all winters, characterized the end of the world. The myth of Ragnarok, or the Twilight of the Gods, began with Fimbulvetr, the long winter, characterized by continuous frost, snow, and cold for three years with no summers in between. Ragnarok represented the end of the Nordic race and the return of the world to its original state of chaos and darkness. It seemed fitting that the end of the world begin with darkness and cold. The stars fell from the sky and the moon stopped shining. The frost giants and fire giants destroyed the world. At Ragnarok, the same elements responsible for creating life led to life's end. (Crossley-Holland 1980, Davidson 1986, Guerber 1980)

SCARAB BEETLE
In ancient Egypt, the scarab beetle symbolized solar rebirth. Perhaps more than in any other land, the people of the Nile River valley were preoccupied with the sun, and particularly, with the sun's movement as it traveled across the sky. Solar symbols permeated Egyptian myths, and they represented the sun in its every aspect and function. The scarab beetle represented the rising sun. By instinct, the beetle gathered his dung into a ball, then rolled the ball in front of him. He buried the ball in the ground, then new beetles arose, just as the sun arose each day after its "burial" beneath the horizon.

The sun cult of the Egyptians was one of the most widespread sun cults in all of antiquity. As the scarab beetle, the Egyptian sun god Ra took the name of Khepri, which meant "self-created." The beetle, the Egyptians believed, recreated himself from his own dung. In reality, he laid eggs in a ball of dung before he buried it. Then a new beetle emerged. Khepri, as an aspect of Ra, was portrayed as either the insect itself, or a man with the face of the beetle. He was often depicted rolling in a ball of dung to represent the sun's movement across the sky. (Krupp 1991a, Mercatante 1978)

See also Cancer, Egypt, Ra, Sun and Sun Gods

SCORPIO, THE SCORPION

The stars of Scorpio, the eighth sign of the zodiac, clearly outline a creature with extended claws and a curved tail. With its distinct shape, this constellation is the easiest of the twelve zodiacal groups to find. Legends from many lands center on this constellation, particularly in countries of the southern hemisphere where the star group appears almost directly overhead. In the skies of the South Pacific, the curved portion glistens like a metal hook, and New Zealanders wove it into legends of their hero Maui, who used the hook to fish islands out of the sea. In northern lands, the hook becomes a tail that lies in a dark portion of the Milky Way. There, the constellation remains low on the horizon, the tail buried in darkness, like the tail of the scorpion who dwells in deep crevices of rock.

According to Greek myths, Scorpio represents the scorpion who stung the hunter Orion and killed him. In one version of this myth, Artemis sent the scorpion after Orion when he tried to rape her. In another version, Gaia, the earth, sent the scorpion after Orion bragged that he could kill any beast that walked the earth. The myth of Orion and Scorpio appears to symbolize the battle between light and dark. The scorpion, a symbol of darkness, and Orion, a symbol of light, appear opposite to each other in the sky and pursue each other continually. The death of Orion is reenacted on the celestial stage when Orion sets as Scorpio rises. (Ridpath 1988, Staal 1988)

See also Constellations, Libra, Zodiac

SCYLLA AND CHARYBDIS

In Greek mythology, the sea monster Scylla and the whirlpool Charybdis represented dangers met by navigators of the open seas. These two monsters inhabited a narrow strait off the coast of Sicily, where sailors were forced to encounter Scylla on one side and Charybdis on the other. If the sailors steered their ships too close to Scylla, she reached out and devoured them. If they steered too close to Charybdis, she sucked their entire ships into the watery depths.

Scylla and Charybdis did not always terrorize the seas. Scylla was once a beautiful sea nymph whom the enchantress Circe saw bathing in a tidal pool one day. Because Circe and Scylla loved the same man, Circe took revenge on her rival and threw poison into the pool. The poison disfigured Scylla, leaving her a woman from the waist up but turning her into six barking dogs from the waist down. Scylla threw herself into the sea, where she came to embody the treacherous rocks of the Straits of Messina. When a ship passed too close to Scylla, the dogs around her waist seized and devoured the sailors.

Charybdis battling soldiers of the sea.

Charybdis was never a beautiful sea nymph, but a greedy, monstrous woman, the daughter of Zeus and Gaia. Charybdis was so greedy that Zeus threw her into the sea, where she continuously gulps water then spits it out. Charybdis embodied the whirlpool opposite Scylla in the Straits of Messina. When a ship passed too close to her side of the strait, the whirlpool greedily devoured it. In Homer's *Odyssey*, Odysseus navigated his ship between these two sea monsters and found it impossible to escape their clutches completely. He chose to sacrifice some of his sailors to Scylla rather than loose his entire ship to Charybdis. (Bassett 1971, Graves 1988)

See also Greece and Rome, Rocks and Stones, Sea and Sea Gods, Whirlpools

SEA AND SEA GODS

The sea has always represented magic and mystery. It symbolized life (many called it the source of all life), and it existed in the beginning of time long before the earth was formed. The notion of the primordial sea arose in cultures around the globe and was founded on the notion that water, as an element, held a myriad of possibilities. The ancients perceived the sea as both creator and destroyer, and they saw it as an animate being, singing or moaning with each rush of the waves and sighing and breathing with the ebb and flow of the tides.

The ancients formulated many beliefs about the sea, the waves, and the tides and about the winds and storms that swept across the water's surface. Because the sea had so many aspects, early people created different sea gods, one for every aspect they witnessed. Many of these sea gods had the ability to change shape, to transform from one face to another just as the ocean itself changed. Sea gods could change from an angry demon lashing its gigantic body over sinking ships to a lovely maiden frolicking gently on calm, sunlit waters. Early people populated the sea

with all sorts of gods and sea creatures, many of them composite creatures, portrayed as half man and half animal to represent the diverse nature of the waters.

The world's climate also accounted for the diversity of sea gods. The Norse sea gods like Aegir and Ran were fierce and terrible, and they were responsible for the drownings and shipwrecks common in the stormy waters of the North Sea. Greek gods like Pontus and Nereus were kind and calm and characteristic of the gentle waters of the Mediterranean. Hine-moana, the Ocean Woman of the Maori, constantly assailed Papa, the earth, who was protected by Sand Woman and Rakahore, the Father of the Rocks. She did this in myth because in reality, when the waters of the South Sea lashed up against the shore, the sandy beaches stopped the rising waters from inundating the land.

As the ancients got acquainted with the waters around them, they began to distinguish between the ocean that they believed surrounded the earth and the sea that they fished and navigated. The outer ocean they feared. They imagined it more like a river than a sea, and they also thought it unnavigable. The Greeks called this ocean Oceanus, but in reality it was the Atlantic, a sea that held dangers unknown to those familiar only with the calm waters of the Mediterranean. The outer ocean, they surmised, was larger, deeper, perhaps even infinite, so natural phenomena on such waters, they assumed, presented themselves on a larger scale. The Egyptians knew of this outer ocean. They too feared it, and they considered sea travel sacrilegious. The Nile River was their sea, the sea they traveled and the sea that brought them life and fertile ground.

Given the shortcomings of the vessels of early navigators, people who sailed the open seas faced battles with all kinds of dangerous phenomena. Rocks, whirlpools, waterspouts, tempests, monsoons, and gigantic tidal waves threatened the lives of these seafarers at every turn. Classical writers often dealt with the theme of perilous sea journeys, and in the *Odyssey*, the first great sea epic, Homer filled the ocean with unknown terrors. Sea demons, rock demons, multiheaded serpents, and ravenous whirlpools emerged from the waters and exercised their power over the winds and the waves. Sea demons stirred up horrendous storms in a matter of seconds or pulled the heaviest of vessels beneath the waves in just seconds more. But the myth-makers combined the treachery of the sea with its allure. Mermaids and Sirens perched seductively on rocks and mesmerized sailors with the lull of their voices, hypnotic voices representative of the melodic, repetitious sound of the sea. These sounds mesmerized sailors, then steered them off course, and in an instant their ships crashed upon the very rocks where seconds before the sailors swore they saw mermaids. Like a mirage, the mermaids had disappeared.

The sea held mysteries, and the depth of the waters held secrets. The Nereids frolicked on the waves and mermaids sunned on the rocks, but some of the most powerful sea gods lived at the bottom of the sea in palaces full of glittering treasures. These palaces added to the imagery of a sea full of riches. Early people relied on the sea for food, so they associated sea gods with abundance. Aegir had a magnificent hall shimmering with booty from drowned ships and a cauldron in which he brewed ale for all the Norse gods. The Japanese dragon-kings hoarded pearls and jewels. Sailors and fishermen on these waters got glimpses of these riches from their boats up on top. What they witnessed was a scientific phenomenon known as phosphorescence, but to the early navigator, it was the sparkle of sea gods' jewels, shimmering so brightly they shone from the depth of the sea to the surface of the water.

These jewels, these sea treasures, metaphorically linked the sea to fertility. The births of the Greek Aphrodite and the Hindu

Lakshmi occurred when these goddesses arose from the sea foam and legitimized the notion of life from the waters. In a Finnish account of creation, Luonnotar, the daughter of Nature, fell from the sky to the sea, floated on the white-crested waves, and became fertile. The water deities in American mythology were primarily female—Sedna of the Arctic lands, for instance, and Chalchihuitlicue of Mexico—and they had the ability to guarantee survival. Kianda, a Poseidon-like sea god of Angola, served the same function. These deities, like the sea, were providers. People who recognized their power and worshipped the life-giving properties of the ocean gave their sea gods offerings and sacrifices, and in exchange, the sea gods let them partake in the abundance of their waters. (Baker 1979, Bassett 1971, Beck 1979, Rappoport 1995)

See also Cosmic Sea, Primordial Sea, Sea Foam, Sea Monsters, Serpents and Snakes, Water and Water Spirits

SEA FOAM

In several ancient myths, sea foam was likened to semen and made responsible for the birth of such goddesses as the Greek Aphrodite and the Hindu Lakshmi. In the Greek creation myth, when Kronus castrated his father, Ouranos, and threw his penis into the sea, water foamed up around the sky god's severed genitals. From the white froth, Aphrodite was born. This myth clearly identified the concept of sea foam with genital sperm. Water, like semen and the life-giving seed within it, represented fertility and the vital fluid of life.

Aphrodite was the goddess of love and fertility, and so was Lakshmi of Hindu myth. Lakshmi rose, like Aphrodite, from the froth of the ocean—the ocean of milk that the gods and demons churned in the beginning of the world to get Soma, the elixir of immortality. Lakshmi rose out of the frothy sea-waters seated on a lotus, a beautiful Hindu

Mother Goddess who became the wife of Vishnu. Lakshmi, the lotus, and the seawaters from which she sprang represent procreation, fertility, and immortality. Sea foam produced a goddess connected with love and fertility, the essential elements needed to assure the future of mankind. (Mercatante 1974)

> *See also* Churning the Ocean, Lotus, Ouranos, Sea and Sea Gods, Soma

SEA MONSTERS

The human mind has a tendency to exaggerate when it beholds something vast and mysterious, like the ocean. To the ancients, the great expanse of water seemed boundless, and whatever moved within the water often appeared larger than life. Some myths of sea monsters were attributed to ocean plants moving in the water like the coils of some fabulous sea serpent. In the sea, everything became magnified. Big fish became gigantic fish, big snakes became gigantic serpents, and enormous whales, often covered with shells or seaweed, became even more enormous scaled giants. From witnessing these creatures, people created myths of sea monsters.

People in most areas of the world believed in sea monsters at some time, beginning in far ancient history in Akkadia, where scholars found depictions of them on clay tablets. Sea monsters reputedly frequented oceans and other large bodies of water, from the fjords off the coast of Norway to the sea surrounding the Pacific islands. The sea serpent was the most common type of sea monster and was thought to be gigantic. The Hebrew Leviathian was perhaps the best known, but there were many more ancient ones, including the Midgard serpent of Norse myth, Jormungandr, who encircled the world and raised storms when he moved his monstrous coils.

Nature myths across the globe contained tales of sea monsters. The Kraken terrorized the North Sea and the Hydra and other similar creatures terrorized the Mediterranean. Many scholars who have studied myths of sea

Stories of horrifying sea monsters abound in every seafaring culture.

monsters believe that most of these myths were cloud myths. The heroes who battled these monsters were often sun gods, and the sea monsters, the scholars say, personified the vaporous clouds rising over the sea to dissipate the sun's power. Such was the case in Greek myth when Perseus battled Cetus, the sea monster poised to attack Andromeda, and such was the case when Hercules battled the Hydra. Krishna fought the serpent Kaliya and the serpent-eagle Garuda, and Thor fought Jormungandr. The heroes in these stories all had solar characteristics, and their monsters ate maidens like clouds ate sunbeams. (Bassett 1971, Ellis 1994, Gould 1989)

> *See also* Clouds, Dragon Slaying, Sea and Sea Gods, Serpents and Snakes, Sun and Sun Gods

SEASONS

People have always looked for rhythm and order in nature, and they found it in the earth realm when they witnessed the changing seasons. Three goddesses called the Horae ordered the seasons in Greek myth, because the early Greeks, like other people of ancient times, saw cyclic time and cosmic recycling as evidence of the supernatural. Understanding time and the rhythm of nature provided a sense of stability in the world. Understanding when and why the seasons changed gave people hope that although some forces of nature emerged to destroy the earth, in time, others emerged to renew it.

Early people did not know that the seasons changed because the earth revolved around the sun; they merely assigned each season significance by connecting it with agricultural rites or rites associated with the migration of animals. Because each season played a crucial role in the life cycle, mythmakers gave each one human characteristics and assigned the deity a starring role in myths that reaffirmed renewal of the earth. These deities usually battled deities of other seasons, those with opposing characteristics and motives. The Greek Niobe, for instance, suffered at the hands of Apollo, the sun god. Niobe appeared to represent the winter. She was hard and cold and her children were said to represent the winter months. When Apollo killed them one by one, they succumbed to the force of his solar rays. Some scholars believe the tears Niobe shed at the death of her children represented the thaw that accompanied the spring. Winter slipped away, the snows melted, and the sun rose victorious and dominated the spring sky.

The discordance between the gods of one season and the gods of another metaphorically expressed the discrepancy in climactic conditions. When Norse mythmakers married the frost giantess Skadi to the fertility god Njord, they gave them a marriage fraught with dissension and turmoil. When in Algonquin myth the Summer Elf thawed the earth and returned warmth to the land, she accomplished her task by melting the Winter Giant. Summer and winter battled in Pueblo myth when Shakok, the spirit of winter, and Miochin, the spirit of summer, fought over the goddess of corn. Shakok wore a shirt of icicles and had a violent temper, like the violent winds that froze the earth, and when he married Yellow Woman, the corn maiden, the corn stopped growing. One day Yellow Woman traveled far from

home and met Miochin, dressed in corn silk and moss, and Miochin offered Yellow Woman corn to eat. Yellow Woman in turn offered some to her people. At their request, Yellow Woman returned to Miochin and brought him home with her. Shakok and Miochin fought over Yellow Woman, Miochin with summer lightning and Shakok with icy winds. Miochin won and made a deal with his adversary. He got Yellow Woman for half the year, in summer and spring, and Shakok got her the other half of the year, in the winter and fall. Shakok froze the earth, and Miochin renewed it.

The arrangement between Miochin and Shakok guaranteed the change in seasons. Each year when winter turned to spring, the fertility god confirmed his commitment to order. He reaffirmed his ability to resurrect the dead. Scholars labeled the character the Pueblo called Yellow Woman the dying and rising god. They called this story an Adonis myth. Adonis was simply one deity who remained in the Underworld during the winter and returned to the earth each spring. Yellow Woman did the same. When Miochin and Shakok agreed to share the corn goddess, they struck the same deal Demeter and Hades did in Greece long before. Hades kept the earth goddess in the Underworld each winter and returned her to the earth each spring. Fertility goddesses in other lands made similar travels to the Underworld and back. The powers of death claimed them for a time, then restored them to life.

These gods and goddesses survived their deaths because, like the earth, they were immortal. They stilled for a time, but then they stirred, like the leaves on the trees and the flowers that burst into bloom at the sound of some deity's magic harp. In Norse myth, the earth goddess, Idun, represented the seasons. Idun was young and beautiful and she supplied the gods with magic apples that gave them their immortality. In this capacity, Idun personified spring and its connection to immortal youth. She symbolized the change from summer to fall when she fell from the branches of Yggdrasil like the autumn leaves. Idun landed in Nifflheim, the world of frost, ice, and cold, and her husband, Bragi, found her there and covered her with a wolfskin blanket, white as the winter snow. Bragi stayed with Idun throughout the winter, but his magic harp remained silent. Bragi's harp stirred the world to life. When he played, the trees and flowers bloomed. Dagda of Celtic myth had a similar harp, and Orpheus of Greek myth had his lyre. When these gods played, they released the seasons and awakened the earth like the singing of birds. (Frazer 1950, Krupp 1991a, 1997b)

See also Cosmic Order, Death, Frey, Glooskap, Music, Njord

SEDNA

The story of Sedna, the Sea Spirit, is an Inuit origin myth with the goddess of the sea a type of earth mother and creator deity. Because the Inuit believed in the divinity of the sea and the game animals within it, Sedna's myth held an important place in Arctic culture. Sedna was the daughter of two giants who lived long ago at the beginning of the world. Her father, Anguta, created the earth, the sea, and the heavens, and Sedna herself populated the sea with animals and became the essence of the most powerful force in Inuit life.

Sedna's story appears in many sources and in varying detail. In one legend, she was a beautiful maiden, carried off by a raven one day who took her to be his bride. Her father then rescued her and fled from the raven in a kayak while the raven stirred up tremendous storms. In another legend, she was a hideous giantess with an explosive temper and an insatiable hunger for human flesh. In this tale, Sedna began gnawing on her parents' limbs one night while they slept, and her father was forced to take her out to sea. But in every story, Sedna ended up in a kayak

with her father, who, for one reason or another, had to sacrifice her. He threw her over the boat, but she clung on to the side. Grief-stricken but determined, her father then chopped off her fingers at the joints, and Sedna sank to the bottom of the sea.

The struggle with her father at the side of the boat must have been agonizing, because her father kept hacking away at his daughter's fingers, one joint at a time, while she tried desperately to hold on. The severed joints then became the sea animals, her fingertips the smaller fishes and seals, her middle joints the larger ones, and her last joints the walruses and whales. Sedna became the Spirit of the Sea. She governed storms, set the times for the migration of sea animals, and, in her modified earth goddess role, had the power to either provide or destroy. When food was scarce in the Arctic lands, shamans turned to Sedna for help. In a trance, the shamans traveled across the sea to a whirlpool that sucked them down to Adlivun, her underwater home, where they pleaded with the goddess for food. Sedna either denied their requests and told them to move on, or she promised to provide game to see the people through the harsh winter. (Burland 1985, Gill and Sullivan 1992, Wood 1982)

See also Arctic Regions, Sea and Sea Gods, Shamanism

SELENE

The Greek Selene, or the Roman Luna, was a moon goddess and the sister of Helios, the sun god. She and her brother shared the duties of lighting the sky, Helios during the day and Selene during the night. Both Selene and Helios drove chariots across the heavens; Selene's was drawn by white horses. While Helios drove his chariot, Selene bathed in the ocean. Then just as he descended to the ocean, she emerged from the waters, donned her shining robes, and rose up to the heavens to take her turn at brightening the sky.

The most popular myth of Selene told of

her love for Endymion, a handsome young prince she found so beautiful that she put him to sleep forever so she could keep him youthful and gaze upon him each night and make love to him while he slept. Endymion was not Helios, but he represented the setting sun. He lay sleeping in a cave and lit up Selene's face as she passed over him, just as the sun lit up the moon. Every night at sundown the love-struck moon goddess rose above Endymion and watched him sleep. While he slept, she bore him many children. The myth of Selene and Endymion, then, was simply another sky myth, an expression of the partnership of the sun and moon. Selene's path to her lover marked the moon's journey across the night sky to the sleeping sun. (Fox 1964, Graves 1988)

See also Greece and Rome, Helios, Moon and Moon Gods

SERPENTS AND SNAKES

When serpents or snakes slithered their way through myths, they represented the forces of darkness associated with the earth and the sea. These creatures existed in primeval times and embodied not only the physical earth and the water but also the power within them, the force that existed in the primordial abyss before the birth of the world. Snakes symbolized power. They also symbolized evil. Because snakes and serpents embodied the primeval waters, they had tremendous creative energy. When they emerged from the primordial darkness they demonstrated their destructive power. They threatened the world order established by the sky gods and continually tried to return the world to its original state of chaos.

By its nature, the serpent or snake symbolized many natural forces. Its venom symbolized destruction, and its ability to strike, the quick and deadly bolt of lightning. Its undulating movement represented the flowing water and waves, and its skin-shedding ability represented cosmic renewal. The

snake emerged from beneath its dead skin and was metaphorically resurrected. The snake curled itself into a circle and symbolized the cyclic character of the universe. (Cirlot 1971, Gubernatis 1872, Howey 1955)

See also Apep, Chaos, Dragon Slaying, Dragons, Rainbow Snake, Sea Monsters

SHAMANISM

Shamans are intermediaries between nature and people. They descend into mountain caves, go into trances, and then travel to the height of the sky and the bottom of the sea to communicate with the spirit world. Shamans are found in the Americas, the Far East, Australia, the Pacific Islands, northern Europe, the Middle East, and the Mediterranean. They act as guardians, as calendar keepers, and as skywatchers. They protect people from natural disasters, and by maintaining communication with the gods, they ensure that the gods use their power over natural phenomena to provide rain, food, and fertility to the land.

Those cultures who practice shamanism rely on the belief in magic. They rely on the belief that their shamans, often the most powerful persons in the tribe, have the ability to control natural phenomena. Finnish shamans are thought to brew rain and mist, and Inuit shamans, it is said, persuade Sedna, the sea goddess, to provide food. These people gain their power by going into trances then allowing their spirits to leave earth and travel to different worlds. Then they use their power to bring the helpful spirits to earth and to drive the harmful spirits away.

To travel to the spiritual world, shamans have to know the structure of the universe. They must adhere to the belief that the universe has three levels, connected with a central axis, and they must know how to use that axis to reach the different levels and to move freely between them. The central axis is often believed to be a mountain or a tree that extends from the Underworld, through the earth, then passes through a hole in the sky.

The shamans' souls traverse these landforms—or sometimes the Milky Way or the rainbow. They move through the stages of Heaven, often to Polaris, at the top of the sky. There they make offerings to the gods and then return home. But only their souls do the traveling. When Inuit shamans travel to the bottom of the sea to visit Sedna, for instance, they tie themselves with ropes so their bodies will remain on earth.

When the shamans return to earth, they remove themselves from their trances. That the shamans often achieve their trances in a cave stems from the ancient idea that power originates in darkness. However, that the shamans gain such significant powers at all stems from the belief in animism—the notion that every force of nature has spirit. The shaman's spirit and that of the natural forces must connect. Only then can these powerful magicians achieve a harmonious relationship with the nature powers and use them to benefit their people. (Campbell 1977, Eliade 1964, Hultkrantz 1967, Krupp 1997b)

See also Animism, Totemism, World Axis

SHAMASH

Shamash was the Babylonian sun god, kind and just, and representative of the benevolent aspect of the solar force. He was considered the son of the moon, because in ancient Babylon sun worship took a back seat to moon worship, and Shamash held an inferior rank to the moon god, Sin. Under the later kings of Assyria, however, Shamash gained prominence. At that time, the people revered him as the chief of gods, as supreme lawgiver, judge, and dispenser of morality. Shamash was linked with the Vedic Indian god Mitra. Both gods were all-seeing, all-knowing, and widely worshipped for their power to guard against evil and to illuminate the world.

Shamash made his journey across the heavens as did sun gods in other parts of the world. He traveled on foot when the Babylonian people traveled on foot; later when they acquired chariots, Shamash too used a chariot on his solar journeys. At daybreak, he emerged from behind the blue vault of the sky through the eastern gate to Heaven and arrived on the Mountain of the Sunrise. At nightfall, he arrived at the Mountain of the Sunset. He then passed through the western gate of Heaven and disappeared into the abode of the gods, where he spent the nighttime hours feasting with his wife.

The sky journeys of Shamash likened him to the Greek Helios and to other personifications of the physical sun. But Shamash was perhaps most noted for his role as moral guardian, a role shared by solar deities in other parts of the world. He judged mortals during the day, and he judged the dead in the Underworld at night. He upheld the laws of the universe, dispensed justice, and fought for the good of the world. Shamash's oracular duties connected him with death and the Underworld, similarly a province of sun gods because they spent half their time in the abode of the dead. In addition to the traditional solar links, Shamash may have controlled rain as well. In the Gilgamesh epic, he decided when the floods flowed from the heavens.

Shamash was symbolized as simply a disc with water streaming from it like solar rays. Sometimes he was represented as an old man with a long beard, often with sunbeams streaming from his shoulders. In this human form, he was usually depicted riding on a horse or sitting on his throne, where he doled out justice and defended the world against evil and wrongdoing. Shamash was widely worshipped and received many offerings and sacrifices. His temple at Babylon was called "the House of the Judge of the World." (Frazer 1926, Mackenzie 1996)

See also Mesopotamia, Mithra, Sin, Sun and Sun Gods

SHANG DI

The sky god of ancient China had two names, Shang di and Tien. Tien meant

"Heaven," or rather, the celestial place where spirits dwelt, the place where the Supreme Being ruled and where he doled out rewards and punishments. Shang di and Tien may have at one time been worshipped as separate deities, then later they fused, or Tien may have supplanted Shang di at a later date. But Shang di was at first the Supreme Being and moral guardian. He was omnipotent and invisible, and he guaranteed that the rain and the sun and all the other forms of natural phenomena work properly to ensure a balance of nature.

As supreme sky god, Shang di upheld the order of the universe. The Chinese considered order a balance of yin and yang, and, every year, the emperor made a sacrifice to Shang di to ensure he maintained that balance. Shang di was considered Emperor on High, and, as was true of sky gods in some other cultures, he was believed to be the ancestor of the earthly emperor and his family. Shang di was not only an ancient ancestor but also the celestial counterpart of the emperor, and his celestial abode was the counterpart of the imperial palace. Shang di's palace sat at the height of the heavens, in the area of the circumpolar stars, those that circled around the north celestial pole and never set. Shang di himself represented the north celestial pole, and the undying stars surrounding him were his imperial court. He anchored the world and maintained order. Because of his connection with the emperor, only the emperor could worship Shang di directly. The Taoists worshipped him as the August Jade Emperor, who lived in the highest level of Heaven and controlled all the nature powers, the spirits of the earth and the air below him. (Frazer 1926, Krupp 1997b, Werner 1995)

See also China, Circumpolar Stars, Sky and Sky Gods

SHANGO

The most prevalent nature deities of Africa were storm gods, and Shango, a god of the Yoruba of Nigeria, was a particularly powerful one. Shango was once an earthly king noted for his tyrannical rule and for causing death and destruction by spouting fire from his mouth. Shango reputedly hanged himself in a forest after fleeing from an angry minister who opposed his violent rule. But fire continued to sweep the plateaus during lightning storms, and many people held Shango responsible. In fact, Shango's followers and enemies alike believed the tyrannical king had not hanged at all but ascended to the sky, where he continued to rule by thunder.

Shango was classified an earth god of the Yoruba; he was born on earth, lived as a king, and was then deified after death. Thunder and lightning shook the earth on the day Shango was born, and because the violent ruler could sustain his powers in the afterlife, his storm powers continued to shake the earth forever. This tempestuous god appeared in myths of Haiti, where he was connected with the anger of St. John the Baptist, possibly because storms and hurricanes in Haiti generally occurred on St. John's Day. In Nigeria, he sometimes kept the company of Oya, the goddess of the River Niger and of winds and squalls. She spread her destructive winds as Shango spread his storms.

Some mythologists liken Shango to Zeus of Greece or Amon-Ra of Egypt. Like Zeus, Shango had sole control over the thunder, and like Amon-Ra, he had connections to the ram. Shango was often depicted with a ram's head and horns, and the sound of his thunder was likened to the ram's bellowing. The tyrannical Shango was a terrible king, but he had many followers. They sacrificed to him at many temples and shrines, and some, yearning to avenge his death, consulted a magician who told them how to destroy with fire, as Shango had done during his rule. Some people today believe that these worshippers of Shango use magic powers to make lightning strike. (Courlander 1973, Parrinder 1986)

See also Africa, Rain and Rain Gods, Storms and Tempests, Thunder and Thunder Gods

SHEEP AND CATTLE

Sheep and cattle commonly appeared in nature myths as representations of clouds and waves. In Greek sea myths, these animals were the herds of Poseidon, and in sky myths, they were the cattle of Helios. In India, the cloud-cattle were imprisoned by Vritra, the drought demon, inside a mountain cave. The mention of Poseidon's herds clearly conjured up images of waves rising from the water's surface, and the myth of Vritra imprisoning the cattle clearly meant that the drought demon had imprisoned the puffy, full rainclouds. When the storm god Indra released the cattle from their mountain cave, the clouds metaphorically burst, and rain poured from the heavens.

Some scholars interpreted the myth of Indra and the cloud-cattle as a solar myth as well as a storm myth. Indra, they said, was a light god, and his herd of cattle the bright colored clouds, tinged purple and golden by the sun's rays. Some scholars said that the herds of Helios were tinged golden because Helios, as the sun, lit up the clouds as he rose and set. They also connected mythological sheep in other lands to solar phenomena. Some likened the solar rays to the horns of the male sheep or the ram butting against the clouds, and people in some parts of Africa likened the sheep to the rainbow. (Bassett 1971, Frazer 1926, Gubernatis 1872)

See also Clouds, Drought, Indra, Rain and Rain Gods, Waves

SHIPS

Ships symbolize voyages, and in nature myths, they symbolize the voyages of the sun and the moon as they cross the heavens and the voyages of the clouds as they waft through the atmosphere. Mythological ships, such as the Argo in Greek myth or Skidblad-

nir in Norse myth, tended to move by themselves, like the sun or the clouds. They carried solar heroes on metaphorical missions to capture the light of the sun; to reach their desired destinations, they sailed across earth, sea, and sky.

This type of travel was equated with the notion of a cosmic sea. The Egyptian Ra sailed this cosmic sea, across the heavens in the daytime and beneath the earth, in the waters, at night. What lay beyond the cosmic sea one could only guess, but people from many areas of the world guessed it was some mythical paradise, a paradise the Greeks and the Celts calls the Islands of the Blessed. Ships transported gods through the heavens to the Otherworld, and sun gods from many lands traveled this way—Frey, Ra, Jason, Icarus, and Daedulus. They traveled to paradise or to the land of the dead. Either way, they traversed the sky realm on a ship, and thus they sailed through the waters of Heaven.

The belief in waters of Heaven stemmed from the perception of water as infinite. It seemed to disappear at the horizon, but because the ancients envisioned water in Heaven, they thought the horizon extended into the sky. Mythologists likened the sun, the moon, and the clouds to ships. They all disappeared on the horizon. The moon sailed through the clouds and so did these mythological ships. The clouds wafted through the aerial sea by the wind. Ships were commonly likened to the moon in myths—the crescent moon, with horns up, like the bow and stern of a silver boat. In the story of *Jason and the Argonauts*, Jason sailed the ship Argo in search of the golden fleece, which some believe was a metaphor for the sun's rays. Icarus and Daedulus traveled on a metaphorical cloud ship, and Icarus got too close to the sun. The wax on Icarus's wings melted, like the dissolution of a cloud by the sun's rays. (Baring-Gould 1897, Bassett 1971, Cirlot 1971)

See also Clouds, Cosmic Sea, Skidbladnir

SHIVA

Along with Brahma and Vishnu, Shiva is one of the three principal deities in Hindu India and worshipped as the god of cosmic destruction. The name Shiva did not appear in Vedic times, the ancient period before 600 B.C., but the god perhaps existed then as Rudra, a storm god known for the devastation he brought to the land. The term "destruction" when it applies to Shiva, however, carries the promise of new life. He destroys in order to create new forms and thus serves as a protector of the world and a restorer of cosmic order.

Shiva is sometimes referred to as the moon god of the mountains. When he appeared on earth, he was a wanderer but was known to meditate under the full moon on Mount Kailas, a mountain in the Himalayan range. Shiva had several distinct characteristics, among them hair that lay in a mass of mats and a third eye that could obliterate anything with one gaze. Shiva used his third eye to restore order. His other eyes were said to be the sun and moon, and in a myth when Uma, his consort, held her hand over his eyes, Shiva opened his third eye to restore light to the world. He used his matted hair to protect the world. When the river goddess Ganga threatened to rush down from the Himalayas and flood the land, Shiva siphoned her through his hair and allowed her to flow into many small streams and rivulets. (Ions 1984, Thomas 1980, Zimmer 1962)

> *See also* Brahma, Cosmic Order, Eye, Ganges River, India, Moon and Moon Gods, Rudra, Vishnu

SHOOTING STARS

See Meteors and Meteorites

SHU

Shu was primarily the Egyptian god of the air, although sometimes he was also considered a god of the sunlight, particularly to account for the fact that the air he personified was permeated by the rays of the sun. He was one of the original nine gods of Heliopolis created by Ra, as was his sister-wife, Tefnut, the goddess of moisture. As a personification of the air, Shu separated the earth and sky by pushing Nut, the sky goddess, upward. Then, with the help of Tefnut, his mate, he supported the sky with his arms.

The name Shu derived from the hieroglyph that meant "to raise." Shu raised the sky, and then, like the air, he kept the sky and the earth separated forever. Because he held up the sky with his arms, he compared with the Greek Atlas, who served the same function, as well as with creator deities in other mythologies responsible for separating their parents. This monumental act enabled the creation of the world to take place.

Shu and Tefnut both comprised elements that the ancients recognized between earth and sky—air and moisture. They were companions, both as brother and sister and as husband and wife. It has even been said that they shared the same soul. The Egyptians may have created Shu and Tefnut to describe two opposite aspects of the atmosphere: Shu when the air was dry and Tefnut when it was filled with moisture.

Sometimes Shu and Tefnut were represented as lion and lioness, and other times Shu was depicted as simply a column of air. Shu was usually represented as a bearded man, however, standing or kneeling over Geb, the earth god, with his arms upraised to support Nut. Often he wore an ostrich feather on his head, which was a hieroglyph for his name. In an alternate view, Shu's name also meant "to be empty." In this sense, he was, like the air, emptiness deified. (Ions 1983, Spence 1990)

> *See also* Air and Air Gods, Egypt

SIN

Sin was the Babylonian moon god; in Sumeria he was a god by the name of Suen, Nanna, or Nannar. Moon worship was prevalent in ancient Babylon, so Sin played a prominent role in Babylonian myth. Sin held a chief place in the astral triad, along with Shamash, the sun god, and Ishtar, the planet Venus, both thought to be Sin's children. Whereas in other mythologies the moon was often the sun's spouse, in Babylonian myth he was the sun's father, as well as the father of Ishtar and, some say, of Nusku, the fire god. That Sin fathered these three deities revealed the belief that light arose from the night.

Sin sailed through the night in his crescent moon boat, lighting the sky and the earth and serving as a deterrent to demons and evildoers who worked in darkness. He was perceived as a kindly deity for serving this function and many others. Sin had the power to measure time, control the seasons, and fertilize the earth, because his cycles determined the times for planting and harvesting. He was beneficent but mysterious, forever changing form from a crescent alternately perceived as a boat and as a weapon to a full, round disk often perceived as his crown.

Sin was depicted as an old man with a long blue beard and a turban on his head. His chief seat was the ancient city of Ur, in Sumer. Sin married Ningal and, in addition to fathering the three children mentioned above, was sometimes said to have fathered the twins Mashu and Mashtu, similar to the Norse moon children Hjuki and Bil. (Jacobsen 1976, Mackenzie 1996)

See also Hjuki and Bil, Mesopotamia, Moon and Moon Gods

SIRENS

In Greek mythology, the Sirens were sea nymphs who perched on rocks that jutted out from the ocean and lured sailors with their beautiful songs. The original Sirens were generally thought to be the daughters of Achelous and Calliope, and their names were Ligeia, Leucosia, and Parthenope. During the Argonautic journey, the song of Orpheus overpowered the songs of these deadly maidens, and all three of them jumped off their islands into the sea and changed into rocks.

The songs of the Sirens were death songs, and their alluring voices were metaphors for the dangers of the sea. In later myths, the Sirens were sometimes confused with mermaids; originally, however, the Sirens had the faces of beautiful women but the bodies of birds, not fishes. The name Ligeia meant

Two of the Sirens with Triton, a Greek sea god who was the son of Poseidon and Amphitrite. Taken from a Roman relief, this engraving appeared in Dr. Paul Barutaut's La Légende des Sirènes.

"harmony," Leucosia meant "white," and Parthenope meant "virgin face." The three of them together represented the white surf whose harmonious hum and intense brightness both lured sailors and destroyed them. (Benwell 1965, Graves 1988)

See also Greece and Rome, Mermaids, Rocks and Stones, Sea and Sea Gods

SIRIUS

Sirius was given a starring role in sky myths because it was the brightest star in the night sky. People noticed it, and they used it to keep time because they could easily track its cycles. In the northern hemisphere, Sirius made its first yearly appearance around the summer solstice and in the southern hemisphere around the winter solstice. For this reason, ancient people from all parts of the world considered this stellar deity a harbinger of the seasons.

Skywatchers who tracked the movements of celestial objects regarded the patterns they recorded as evidence of cosmic order. The reliable rise and set of Sirius reassured these people that the sky gods were doing their jobs. The Persians identified Sirius as the god Tishtrya, who brought rain to the land and prosperity to the people. The Maori identified Sirius as Takurua, the goddess who shone brightly in the sky to warn people of upcoming frosts. But Sirius perhaps had the greatest significance to the Egyptians, who identified the star with their beloved fertility goddess Isis. In ancient Egypt, Sirius rose in the predawn sky about the time of the annual flood of the Nile, so in myth, Isis brought on the flooding. The annual inundation of the river water sustained life in this desert land. When skywatchers saw Isis make her first annual appearance on the predawn horizon, they knew their river would flood and their world would continue. (Krupp 1991a, Olcott 1911, Staal 1988)

See also Astronomy, Cosmic Order, Isis, Nile River, Stars and Star Gods, Tishtrya

SKIDBLADNIR

Skidbladnir was the magic ship of Frey, the Norse god of rain and sun. The ship could expand to hold all the gods and their artillery or contract to fit into a pocket, tucked away and out of sight. When the trickster god Loki cut off Sif's golden hair as a prank, he turned to the dwarf Dvalin to spin her some new hair. Dvalin did, at the same time making a spear called Gungnir for Odin and the ship Skidbladnir for Frey. Skidbladnir, like the Greek Argo, could sail through the sky as well as on land and sea and represented the bright summer clouds. Like the clouds, the ship got larger and smaller and always sailed overhead, conveyed by the winds.

Skidbladnir rightly belonged to Frey, because as the god of sun and rain, he was also considered a fertility god. Ships were identified with fertility and the life cycle in many ancient myths, and Skidbladnir, as the manifestation of the summer cloud, brought new life and summer to the northern lands. Ringhorn, another ship in Norse mythology, had a contrasting function and symbolized the opposite phase of the life cycle. As the light god Balder's burial ship, Ringhorn symbolized death and winter. (Bassett 1971, Guerber 1980)

See also Balder, Clouds, Cosmic Sea, Frey, Scandinavia, Ships

SKY AND SKY GODS

The sky covers the earth like a veil. It is infinite, immovable, and awe inspiring. In a time long ago, it was much more awe inspiring. People today will never see the sky as the ancients saw it. The night sky will never be so dark; the daytime sky will never be so unobstructed, so clear. Long ago, the sky was a sensation, and by its very essence it emanated power. So from this overwhelming sensation of sky, the ancients made the heavenly vault their model of order and their highest god.

Connecting the sky with the concept of God and power came from watching the sun rise and set, the moon wax and wane, the wind blow the clouds across a sea of blue, the clouds dissolve to water, and the rain pour down and fructify the earth. These marvels occurred with cyclic regularity and revealed continuity and immortality in the heavens. Skywatchers of the ancient world, then, looked to the sky as their model. Then from careful observation of the rhythms they witnessed, they internalized the movements of the heavens and made them the focus of their life and ritual.

The most ancient conceptions of sky power stemmed from the natural forces that emanated from the celestial realm and then penetrated the earth with strength and might incomprehensible to human minds. So the minds that beheld these lofty forces put them in terms they understood: They endowed them with the feelings and capacities they knew in themselves. The fact that the sky could act by pouring rain and booming thunder and lighting the world with the power of a thousand stars meant that the sky had volition. It had a mind of its own. The sky power itself was invisible; it came from somewhere above the clouds, beyond the rain, and far behind the blue vault that canopied the earth. But that power manifested itself nevertheless. It manifested itself in the physical phenomena of the rain, the hail, the snow, the wind, and the light. Such was the earliest conception of sky. Sky was both an embodiment of the heavens, a god with power and volition, and the place where he dwelled.

This dual conception of sky gave way to the notion of a sky land. It gave way to the notion of the sky god as creator. Then after many myths of how the sky got up there, separated from the earth, and after many myths of sky gods who married earth goddesses and begat the world, there came a time for specialization. The sky god had children. These children were mere manifestations of the sky god himself, physical phenomena

that served as his messengers and conveyed his wishes to the world. In contrast to the Supreme Deity, the sun gods and moon gods, the atmospheric gods, and the gods of rain, hail, thunder, clouds, halos, and rainbows were widely worshipped and greatly feared. The all-knowing father remained up there, aloof and untouchable, but these personal gods entered into the human sphere. They affected everyday life and drove the world with their power.

The power of these gods, however, came from the sky god himself, whom the Native Americans called the Great Spirit, the force that empowered the world and the gods from his celestial sky palace. This Great Spirit, the Sky Father, was omnipotent and immortal, so the gods he created were immortal too. The irony about the omnipotence of these supreme sky gods was that they were pushed aside in favor of the lesser powers who had more staying power, more brute strength. The Finno-Ugric Jumala, the Mongol Tengri, the Chinese Tien, the Aryan Dyaus were all passive deities, despite their great powers. But then the sky gods became storm gods and revealed themselves in the power of nature. They became upholders of order and renewers of time. Worshippers then saw the true power in their immortality. The emphasis switched to the fertilizing powers of these deities and on their ability to continually renew the earth.

Continuity and renewal is what sky power is all about. These gods stabilized the cosmos, they ordered the world, and they moved in regular patterns. By observing the movements of these deities, people knew how to pattern their lives. They knew when they did wrong, because the sky gods either sent streaks of lightning to warn them or they flooded the land. They knew when they behaved properly, because the sky gods rewarded them with fruitful harvests or an abundance of fish from the sea. The sky gods had eternal wisdom and acted as moral guardians, acting of course through messengers the people knew as light, rain, hail, and wind. They used thunder as their voice, lightning as their weapon, and the moon and the sun to control the passage of time and explain day and night and the seasons. The sky gods themselves remained passive, sitting on thrones or in palaces in the highest layer of Heaven, above the atmosphere, where all is still and unchanging. From there they made and enforced the rules of the cosmos.

So the sky was the archetype of cosmic order. The sky god guaranteed the continuation of life. Creation was up to the sky god, because his celestial realm established world direction, oriented the landscape, and set the rhythms of time and change on earth. The Native Americans patterned their homes to model the heavens, and early people in many societies established ritual behavior in accordance with the movements of the celestial bodies. They did this because the forces of nature revealed the presence of an infinite, unending power. People understood the sacred when they looked to the heavens and beheld the sky. (Frazer 1926, Krupp 1991a, 1997b)

See also Astronomy, Cosmic Order, Sun and Sun Gods, World Axis

SNAKES
See Serpents and Snakes

SNOW

In the ancient world, snow was lovely and alluring but at the same time a deadly threat to survival. As ancient people battled the harsh forces of winter, they feared the snow as much as they admired its beauty. In myth, these people created embodiments of snow that reflected the dual nature of this winter spirit. Snow's cold breath could still the earth in a freeze frame of death yet cover the world in lovely layers of glistening white, then simply melt away

The Finns personified snow as a three-hundred-year-old king named Snaer, the son of Iceberg or Frost and the father of three daughters, Thick Snow, Snowstorm, and Fine Snow. But more commonly, a young maiden embodied the snow, a pale and beautiful maiden who was the possessor of deadly power. The Japanese called this snow woman Yuki Onna, and travelers in snowstorms often fell prey to her charms. Yuki Onna was young with an alluring body, but she was ghastly white, like a ghost. When she encountered travelers weary and weak from battling winter blizzards, she lulled them to sleep, then blew her icy breath over their bodies and froze them to death.

In one tale of Yuki Onna, she married a mortal, then left him when she melted away. The melting of snow appeared in other myths as well. In Algonquin legend, a snow bridegroom named Mowis took a bride one cold night then disappeared the next morning as the sun warmed the earth. In Russian legend, a Snow Child, created by a childless Russian couple out of snow in their garden, went to the forest one day with friends, who lit a bonfire and spent the night frolicking in the light and jumping playfully over the flames. When the Snow Child took her turn, she disappeared. A Navajo myth explained why the snow melted. Coyote melted it in the first year of the world because he was thirsty and wanted to drink it. From then on, heat melted snow. In these early days, snow was considered good nourishment. It melted and flowed down the mountains in spring and stimulated new vegetation.

Snow is powerful, creative moisture, like rain. Not only does it nourish the earth when it melts in the spring, but it extinguishes fires from summer heat and explosive volcanoes. A Hawaiian legend tells of Poliahu, the snow goddess of Mauna Kea, who came down from her mountain to enter a sled race with the fire goddess Pele. Pele lost. She pursued the snow goddess with fingers of lava that grabbed at Poliahu's white robe, which started to melt. But Poliahu pulled her

This Celtic depiction of the Snow Queen represents the classic image of a young, pale, beautiful woman who also possesses deadly powers.

robe free and spread it out over the mountain. The mantle of snow melted some more and froze Pele's lava to stone. It sealed off the passageways from her volcano. The power of snow defeated the power of fire. Pele could no longer rule Mauna Kea and had to move on. (Davis 1992, Westervelt 1963)

See also Frost and Ice, Pele

SOLSTICES

The ancients tied their solstice ceremonies to their belief in the sun as a supernatural being with a mind of his own. The word *solstice* is derived from Latin and means "sun stand still," and on two days of the year, the sun did appear to stand still. On the winter solstice, the sun stopped its southerly journey to turn around and head north again, and on the summer solstice, the sun stopped before beginning its journey south. Those who participated in solstice ceremonies feared these two critical days. What if the sun decided not to turn? The people knew they had to do something to ensure that it did.

Solstice myths and ceremonies exemplified how early people tried to control natural phenomena—in this case, the sun's path across the sky. As the year approached the summer or winter solstice, the sun gradually slowed its movement, then stopped at the farthest point it could go on the horizon without disappearing below it and darkening the world. Each solstice is just an instant in time, but naked-eye observers could not detect any north-south movement of the sun for five or six days, so it seemed as if the sun paused, as if to deliberate its future course. The sun never did continue its southward movement; it always turned around and headed the other way. But many groups of people thought it needed help and encouragement to do so. Participating in solstice ceremonies meant that people had control over the sun's behavior and therefore played a crucial role in maintaining balance in the world.

Because the sun's northward turn at the winter solstice was crucial to the restoration of warmth and light, winter solstice ceremonies often involved more elaborate rites and rituals than did the summer ceremonies. Native American shamans or sky priests watched the sun's movement for weeks in order to predict the critical day well in advance. The solstice ceremonies of the California Chumash were among the most elaborate and the most studied. The Chumash employed shaman-priests to use their supernatural powers to drive the sun back onto a northerly course. The people dug a pit for the ritual sunstick. Then the chief priest, called Image of the Sun, and twelve assistants, called Rays of the Sun, began the ceremony. The Rays of the Sun formed a circle around the ceremonial pit, each of them holding a feather. Then the chief put the sunstick into the pit, called to the sun to "go into the house," and tapped the stick twice to summon the supernatural powers. (The house, in Native American lore, referred to the points in the sky the sun reached at the solstices.) In times past, the Chumash placed great importance on this ceremony because they knew that only the sun's northward turn would renew their world. Most of the tribe stayed inside during the solstice period, fearing that the sun's strength would overpower and consume them.

Like many other groups, the Chumash conducted such rituals to manipulate the celestial sphere for the good of society. The Pueblos, too, had elaborate winter solstice ceremonies in order to ensure the return of vegetation in the spring. To agricultural people, the return of vegetation meant the rebirth of the earth, and in myths of this rebirth, metaphor ran thick. The winter solstice symbolized the beginning of a new sun and renewed light, or in the myths, the beginning of a new god of sun and light. Balder, the Norse light god, was born on the winter solstice, and so was Mithra, the Persian god of light. When the sun reached its most southerly point, the northern hemisphere experienced its shortest days and longest nights. The earth was at its darkest, which was clearly the time for sun gods to emerge.

Because the sun underwent a cycle of life, death, and rebirth, the deity was considered an immortal. The deified sun, like Mithra, had the capability to renew life when, like the physical sun, he arose from the darkness and brought light to the world. Throughout history, people attempted to bond with nature, to manipulate the natural world, and to simulate desired events in myth and ritual. They felt the need to control nature's most powerful forces. At the solstices, skywatchers observed the earth and sky spirits at work, so they conducted ceremonies to help them. Many archeological sites throughout the world exhibit alignments to the rising or setting sun at the solstices, a reminder that people for centuries assigned mythical and ritual significance to the solstices as crucial events in the fate of their world. (Krupp 1994, Williamson and Farrer 1992)

See also Astronomy, Balder, Cosmic Order, Mithra, Sun and Sun Gods

SOMA

Soma was both the magic elixir of immortality and the Hindu moon god who embodied the elixir. The ancient Indians drank Soma themselves, making an intoxicating drink from a plant yet to be identified, and a mixture of buffalo milk, honey, barley, and water. The Hindus used this drink in rituals, and they incorporated it into their myths and legends. As a powerful liquid, Soma not only fortified the gods but also represented the Water of Life and the vital fluid in all beings. This connection with water led to the perception of Soma as a moon god and the absorption of Chandra, an earlier moon god, into Soma's persona. Because the ancients regarded the moon as the storehouse of life's waters, they created Soma to personify the power of those waters. Soma, like the moon, was the vital fluid of nature and the source of fertility and growth.

As a liquid, Soma was often called amrita, a substance that arose in the process of creation when the gods churned the ocean of milk. Both gods and demons coveted Soma because they knew it had the power not only to strengthen them but also to make them immortal. The use of Soma became an integral part of Vedic sacrifices, and the ritual pressing of Soma juice through a sieve became a metaphorical reenactment of water's powers. Some scholars suggested that the sieve symbolized the sky; the juice passing through the sieve, the rain; the yellow color of the juice, the lightning; and the noise the juice made as it passed through the sieve, the thunder. Soma itself symbolized the fertilizing power of the waters as represented by the watery nature of the immortal moon.

Soma was linked as much with the moon's immortality as with its role in regulating the waters. The moon contained the Soma, and as the gods consumed its immortal properties, the moon got smaller and smaller. Of course, the gods' drinking of Soma did not steal the moon's immortality completely; it replenished itself every time, consuming water from the cosmic sea. The Hindus wove a myth around Soma, the god, to further explain this phenomenon. Soma had twenty-eight wives, said to represent the twenty-eight stations of the lunar zodiac, called Nakashtras, each of whom the moon visited each month as he passed through his cycle. (Myths from other lands also speak of the moon having twenty-eight wives or lovers. The number twenty-eight refers to the number of days it takes for the moon to pass through the zodiac and revolve around the earth.) In the Hindu myth, these wives were the daughters of the sage Daksha, who grew angry when twenty-seven of his daughters complained that Soma preferred one of his wives, Rohini, over them. So Daksha cursed

Soma with a disease. From thenceforth, Soma gradually weakened each month until he finally disappeared. He then gradually recovered, only to weaken again. This cycle the ancients witnessed each month as the moon waxed and waned.

In primeval times, Soma was omnipotent. In a sense, he was the Supreme Deity because he alone gave the other gods their power. Over time, the use of Soma as an intoxicant died out, but the perception of Soma as a moon deity remained. Although Soma didn't become fused with Chandra until much later, he appeared as a deity in the early Vedic period. The entire ninth book of the ancient text, the Rig Veda, dealt with Soma's properties as an elixir of the gods. (Ions 1984, Knappert 1995b, Mackenzie 1971)

See also Churning the Ocean, India, Moon and Moon Gods, Sea Foam

SOUTH AMERICA

The cultural groups who inhabited South America long ago had a unique perspective on the natural world. They lived close to the equator in a land of contrasts, with sandy beaches, tropical rainforests, and the magnificent Andes mountain range, with its snow-capped peaks, grasslands, volcanoes, and rushing rivers. The people of Pre-Columbian South America settled primarily in the Andes region, and despite the differences among them, they shared a belief in an animate earth. Although they focused their worship on their environment, they looked to the sky with awe, and the sky looked different in the tropics than it did anywhere else on earth.

Small clans of aboriginal people lived throughout continental South America, but the people of the Andes were the most culturally advanced. Scholars refer to these civilizations as highland or high culture and the civilizations of the tropical rainforests and coastal areas as lowland or low culture. Distinct differences in nature myths existed among them. Each group of people in the

low culture had their own mythology that focused on nature deities, which attested to their worship of the earth and the sea. The people of the high culture had a highly developed pantheon with its primary emphasis on deities of the sky.

Living in a tropical rainforest quite naturally influenced the types of nature myths people created. The forest closed them off from the rest of the world and protected them from atmospheric elements that affected those people living on the open plains. There were thunder gods in these societies, but not many. There were rain gods, but little need to placate them because rain fell in abundance. Most of the spirits who inhabited these forests embodied the rocks, the stones, the waterfalls, and other natural phenomena in the jungle. The people of the rainforest worshipped the earth and needed supernatural help in protecting it. The Tupi of Brazil knew Corupira as the guardian spirit of the forests. He was not malevolent, but he did disorient people who tried to destroy the forests or harm the trees or animals. The knowledge that animals existed in the forests long before people led to a proliferation of animal spirits, many of whom served as guardian spirits of the clans.

The early peoples of South America practiced totemism, a form of religion that generally involved the association of a clan with an animal spirit. But forces of nature served as totems too—powerful forces such as thunder, water, lakes, mountains, and stones. In Peru, totemism existed in pre-Incan times, and the totemic system these people established remains one of the distinguishing archeological features of Andean culture. These people called their totemic spirits "huaca," and they worshipped them at sacred shrines and revered them as protective deities. These early people particularly revered the spirits of mountains and stones, and they worshipped them in connection with the earth goddess Pachamama. When the Inca established their civilization, they maintained the shrines but revered Inti, the sun god, above all other deities. The sun held little significance to the pre-Incan cultures, who made their primary totems the phenomena of the earth and, along the coastlines, the sea itself.

The coastal people and the inland people viewed the sea differently. The inland people considered the sea harsh and foreboding, so they gave the goddess of the sea malevolent characteristics. The people along the coasts, however, made their living as fishermen, and they knew the sea as a provider and a source of life. They worshipped their sea goddess Mamacocha as a benevolent deity and considered her the mother of all waters. They called the springs and lakes her daughters. Lake worship was preeminent in South America, because many Andean tribes believed their ancestors came from lakes or springs. The Indians of Cuzco believed their great god, Viracocha, rose from Lake Titicaca. Lakesides were desirable habitats, and perhaps this led to their prominence in myths and legends. Concern with water was central to Andean ideology. The ocean was the source of all waters, and the snow-capped mountains and mountain lakes the sources of major rivers. Shamans performed sacrifices on mountaintops and poured blood down the mountains to imitate the flow of water to the thirsty rivers. Viracocha, the Inca creator, rose from the water and became a powerful deity, worshipped as both a water god and a sun god.

The Inca appeared to be more interested in their own creation that in the creation of the world. They said they descended from the sun—not Viracocha, but Inti. Viracocha, however, made the sun at the beginning of time. The sun and the moon took precedence in the Andean high culture, and Inti gained prominence over Viracocha. Chosen women called Acllas served the royal family and the cult of Inti. Sun worship became the official state religion. The Inca sacrificed to Inti on a regular basis, and they held festivals to honor him. His wife, Mama Kilya, the moon, received sacrifices as well. Moon goddesses in South America were generally believed to control the sea and the tides, the crops, the thunder, and the lightning. Numerous myths centered on relationships between the sun and moon, and people created these myths to explain eclipses, moon spots, and the phenomenon of waxing and waning. Some Andean societies considered the moon more powerful than the sun because he showed himself both day and night. He also had the ability to eclipse the sun. In a partial lunar eclipse, the moon was sick, they said, and in a total eclipse, it was dead, and it might fall and kill everyone. People of the Peruvian lowlands considered Pachacamac, the earth, the Supreme Deity and the sustainer of the universe. It was he, they believed, who cured the moon when it was resurrected from death.

With the exception of the high culture and some cultures in Brazil, the sun and moon often took subordinate roles to the gods of the stars. Some said people rose from the stars, and they held in particular esteem the Milky Way, the Pleiades, and Orion. The sky looked different in the tropics than in other parts of the world. Perhaps most noticeably, Polaris, the North Star, appeared directly on the northern horizon while the other stars moved up and down in straight lines. Skywatchers in the tropics tended to think they lived at the center of the world. They considered the vertical paths of the sun and stars important links that connected the earth with the sky. The Inca recognized sacred power in the celestial phenomena they saw moving in their heavens, and they tried to imitate the sacred arrangement on earth. They erected poles called gnomons, or shadow sticks, to represent the vertical paths of the sky gods. In Brazil, important tribal chiefs climbed up the poles to talk with the star gods they believed to be ancestors. These people believed that after their death, they too would follow one of the vertical paths and go straight up to the sky world to become stars. (Brinton 1976, Cobo 1990, Hultkrantz 1967, Osbourne 1986)

SPINNING AND WEAVING

Spinning and weaving were ancient arts practiced by females and, in myth, by females connected with the fertility of the earth and the moon. Goddesses with lunar attributes spun thread as an expression of their creative powers. With the spindle or distaff a symbol of life, these goddesses controlled the life cycle and ensured cosmic order and the continuity of the world.

The act of spinning was a cyclic process. It was an act of creation, as was the moon's movement through its phases and the earth's movement through the cycle of seasons. Thus, the birth and death of the moon and the earth related to the concept of fertility, so it was the fertility goddess who often sat at her spinning wheel and spun the sky, the sea, or children into existence. In Norse myth, Frigg sat at her spinning wheel and spun the clouds, in Greek myth the Fates sat at their spinning wheels and measured lives by the lengths of their threads, and in Dogon myth the Nommo Spirits wove together the four elements of nature to create the world. These deities, and lunar goddesses in other cultures, spun together their endless nets of invisible threads and wove together earth, sea, sky, and human destinies.

The Fates, as well as the Norns of Scandinavia, not only drew thread from their spindles to create life but also cut thread to bring about death. Thus, the ancients connected the act of spinning to controlling time, which was the essence of the lunar connection. There were three Fates in Greek myth, clothed in white like the moon and representative of the moon's three phases. Isis, in Egyptian myth, was goddess of the earth and the moon, and she taught the weaving arts to

women. These spinning deities, like the moon, symbolized the cyclic nature of life and the necessity of cosmic order. In Japanese myth, Amaterasu was weaving in her sky palace when her brother Susanowo disturbed her by creating menacing storms. He interrupted her weaving and thus upset the order of the cosmos. (Eliade 1958)

> **See also** Cosmic Order, Frigg, Isis, Moist Mother Earth, Moon and Moon Gods

SPRINGS AND WELLS

Springs and wells have long been perceived as healing powers. The water moved, so to the ancients it had spirit, and through the powers of that spirit, spring and well water held magic. Since antiquity, springs and wells were revered for their curative powers, particularly in Celtic Europe. In each spring lived a water deity, usually a goddess, and people led pilgrimages to thermal springs to propitiate the goddess and to reap the benefits of her healing graces.

Some springs, particularly hot springs, actually did have the power to heal; their water harbored minerals used in making medicines. But more than that, spring water was sacred. Fresh and clear, it flowed miraculously from below the earth, like a gift from the earth goddess. The spirits of wells were usually perceived as female because the creamy consistency of some well water connected it with the milk of the earth mother. Wells were also viewed as shafts to the Underworld. Both wells and springs appeared to link two worlds, and they provided a way of tapping into the secret powers that lay in the dark recesses of the sacred earth.

People who led pilgrimages to curative springs and wells were part of healing cults, and they participated in many kinds of rituals. These people prayed to the presiding deity and then made offerings of coins, trinkets, cauldrons, and other objects made of glittering metal. Often times, the person wishing to be healed bathed in the water, then left a model of a diseased body part for an offering, hoping that in return the presiding deity would substitute a body part that was healthy. These water spirits had amazing powers. They could cure eye diseases, repair diseased limbs, and, often times, make barren women fertile. Sometimes, the pilgrims went into a kind of healing sleep in special dormitories, hoping that the deity would appear to them in their dreams and heal them with their water magic.

Many myths involving springs and wells conveyed the ancient belief that water healed not only the body but also the mind and spirit. The ancients thought flowing water held the key to wisdom and universal truth. In Norse mythology, the Spring of Mimir flowed from underneath the roots of Yggdrasil, the world tree, and the great god Odin sacrificed one of his eyes in return for permission to drink from this spring and thus gain wisdom. In Irish legend, the hero Finn acquired wisdom from a well, particularly from the Salmon of Knowledge who lived at the bottom. Finn met Finnegas the Bard, who had spent the last seven years fishing for this Salmon of Knowledge. When he caught it, he gave it to Finn, and upon eating it, Finn became eternally wise.

Curative springs and wells appeared in the mythologies of many people, but they assumed particular prominence among the Celts. The Celtic Mother Goddess, Brigit, presided over many wells, and the Celtic Apollo, Apollo Grannos, presided over many curative springs with his consort Sirona. Sulis was the greatest British curative deity, and she presided over the gushing hot springs under the great temple at Bath. People throughout Celtic Europe built shrines over springs and wells, some of them sacred stones and megaliths. These edifices appear to have been designed as homes for the gods and receptacles for the spirits of the waters. (Bord and Bord 1985, Freeman 1995, Green 1993, Michell 1975, Pennick 1996)

See also Celtic Lands, Grannos, Mirrors, Sulis, Water and Water Spirits, Well of Life

STARS AND STAR GODS

The stars of the night sky have captured the attention of skywatchers for eons. In times when no artificial light polluted the heavens, stars illuminated the night and gazed down upon the earth like thousands of sparkling eyes. People all over the world felt awed by the beauty these mysterious strangers brought to their world. They emerged out of the darkness like magic and turned the night into a glittering wonderland.

On a dark night with no clouds obscuring the heavens, a skywatcher might see about six or seven thousand stars. Mythmakers have offered numerous explanations for their existence. According to one theory, the giants in the early days of the earth threw stones at the sun and pierced holes in the sky. The stars were the sun's light shining through the holes. In a similar theory, fires from the gods' palaces shone through the holes and created stars. Commonly, people identified stars as jewels or crystals. They were also called sparkling eyes. Because skywatchers on earth looked up, it likely made sense to them that whoever resided in the sky world looked down. In Greek myth, the stars were the eyes of the monster Argus, and in Norse myth, they were the eyes of the storm giant Thiazi. In Polynesian myth, they were the many of eyes of Aluluei, the god of navigation, whose sparkling brightness guided seafarers on their journeys.

The notion of stars sparkling or twinkling was as common in the ancient world as it is today. Some stars, in fact, do twinkle. They are called eclipsing binary stars, and each one is actually two stars held together by gravity. The stars continuously orbit around each other and, from time to time, the dimmer of the two stars moves in front of the other one and blocks its light, thus creating the twinkling effect. Although the ancients arguably

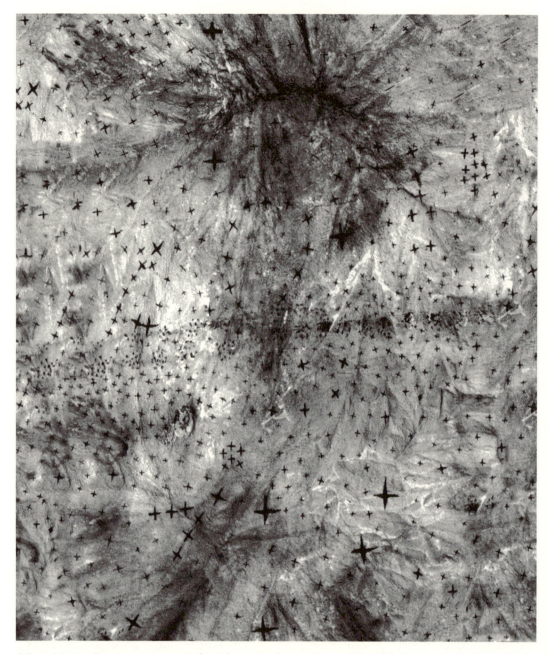

Many Native American astronomical myths centered around stars. The Pleiades are clearly represented on this Pawnee buckskin map of the heavens.

had no knowledge of this phenomenon, they had an explanation for it—and again they connected it to eyes. The Greeks, for instance, considered the eclipsing binary star Algol a dangerous star. To them, it was the blinking eye of Medusa, the Gorgon slain by Perseus, who opened and shut her evil eye in Heaven as she did on earth.

Medusa and Argus once lived their lives on earth and then became immortalized as constellations in the heavens. In death, their eyes became stars. Other people also deified the stars, sometimes as souls of the dead. In Chinese thought, certain stars were souls before birth that entered human embryos as shooting stars and became emperors; these star souls could be either human or animal. The ancient Peruvians thought that every animal on earth had its likeness in the sky. The San of Africa also believed the stars once lived on earth, and some tribes of North America said the animals became stars after they climbed to the sky on a rainbow. In the myths of New Zealand, the stars were the souls of dead warriors, and the more victims they had claimed in battle, the brighter they shone in the sky.

Particularly bright stars fired the imagination of the ancients. Starwatching in times of old led to many widely known legends that featured the brightest stars in the night sky. But often, the stars collectively appeared in the myths, commonly as children of the sun and the moon. The Peruvians thought them these children and so did the Slavs. In West Africa, it was said that the stars that shone at that time belonged to the moon, but at one time, the sun too had had children. The sun and moon decided to kill their children, but only the sun went through with the act. The moon changed her mind and hid hers in a jar. So today, while the sun remains in the sky alone, the moon has company. She releases her children from the jar every night and they sparkle beside her and help her light the dark sky.

The fascination with stars led to a reverence for these bright celestials, and, in fact, star worship, or sabianism, was one of the earliest forms of religion. To some the importance of the stars rivaled the importance of the sun. The California Chumash regarded the stars, rather than the sun, as guardians of world order. The Pawnee of the Central Plains believed certain "patron stars" ruled the sky and guided the lives of the people on earth, and the Navajo believed the stars helped people live their lives and follow divine law. The Navajo also believed the stars

supported the heavens. It has been suggested that the star ceilings on rock caves in Navajo territory were created to hold up the caves just as the stars held up the sky.

Myths and legends of the stars occurred frequently in early myths, and stories of mortals falling in love with stars and marrying them illustrate the stars' allure. An Oceanic myth told of two women who slept out under the stars and fell in love with two of them. The women were gazing up into the dark night, captivated by the sparkling lights, when one of the sisters picked out two exceptionally beautiful stars and wished aloud that she and her sister could become their wives. Soon after, the two found themselves in the sky world with their new husbands. (Allen 1963, Krupp 1991a, Olcott 1911)

See also Astronomy, Circumpolar Stars, Constellations, Hyades, Moon and Moon Gods, North Star, Pleiades, Sirius, Zodiac

STONES
See Rocks and Stones

STOORWORM
Stoorworm was the great primeval water monster of British legend, comparable to the Midgard serpent of Norse mythology. Rising from the sea, it caused gigantic waves that swallowed entire islands. Because too many maidens were being sacrificed to appease this horrendous monster, a young British boy named Assipattle attempted to kill him. He succeeded by cutting a hole in his liver and filling it up with burning peat. This act of destruction led to the formation of landforms. Stoorworm vomited out his insides. His teeth formed the islands of Orkney, Shetland, and Faroe, and his tail formed the strait between Norway and Sweden then fell into the sea and formed Iceland. According to myth, the burning peat that Assipattle used to fill the water monster's liver still burns, which explains the volcanoes and thermal areas. (Matthews and Matthews 1995)

See also Celtic Lands, P'an Ku, Serpents and Snakes, Tiamat, Tlaltecuhtli, Ymir

STORMS AND TEMPESTS

Metaphorically, storms symbolize a union between sky and earth. When the thunder rumbles and the lightning strikes, they energize the earth spirit, and when the rain falls, it fertilizes the goddess of the land. Storm imagery often involves a sky god, virile with storm power, who inseminates the earth goddess by imbedding the planted seeds deep inside her womb. The storm god does this in spring, and shortly after, the earth goddess gives birth to the trees and herbs and food plants that enable the world to survive.

Understanding the storm as a creative force means that the gods who sent the storms did so out of benevolence. But, as with much of the work of deities, benevolence was not always the reason. In most nature myths, the storm god hurled his thunderbolts out of anger and as punishment. Often times evil giants or monsters caused storms. Typhon caused them in Greek myths; his counterpart, Seth, in Egyptian myths; and thunderbirds of many sorts—often times evil—caused them in myths from tribes throughout the Americas. The ancient Chaldeans believed air demons caused storms, and many other people attributed storms to demons of wind and wave. But the people who attributed storms to the sky gods thought of them as celestial forces rather than as atmospheric forces. Ancient people saw the storm forces emanate from the realm of the sun and the moon and the stars. It made sense to these people that storms originated there. After all, storms exhibited unbridled strength, and the sky gods, they knew, had the greatest strength of all.

Such sky gods as the Greek Zeus or the Pawnee god Tirawahat caused storms. These were the supreme beings, and the storms were the supreme unleashing of both their creative power and their destructiveness. In the ancient world when people lived on the open land, storms assumed gigantic proportions and caused untold destruction. The gods who caused them were as much feared as they were revered. They guaranteed life and fertility, but no one knew if they would keep their powers in check. They could just as easily cause flood and famine and death.

Because storms had tremendous impact on the open seas, sailors particularly feared the storm gods. Navigators from the earliest times tried to determine ways to predict their appearance, and they developed a myriad of ways to use changes in the natural environment as portents. Sailors watched the sky and attached significance to the appearance of clouds, of rainbows, and of halos around the sun and the moon. Some sailors knew the forces so well they actually could predict the weather. Sailors personified the storm winds as demons or giants. In Greenland, it was said that a giant kayaker caused tempests. In Greece, Poseidon, the sea god, had that power. Some scholars suggested that Poseidon's trident may have been a thunderbolt, and that Poseidon shared storm-raising powers with his brother, Zeus.

Whether or not Poseidon used his trident as a thunderbolt, the sky gods clearly did possess weapons and that made them mighty warriors. In Norse myth, Thor had his hammer, Mjollnir. In the Slavic lands and in Asia, the thunder gods often used arrows for weapons, and they used the rainbow as the bow that enabled them to shoot their lightning bolts to earth. Possession of these weapons symbolized not only the strength of the storm but also its virility. Thor knew the power of his hammer, for it never broke and it always returned to his hand. Yet in one popular Norse myth, the frost giant Thrym stole Thor's hammer and demanded the goddess Freya for its return. Freya was a fertility goddess, and only she could replace the virility lost by surrendering the hammer. But Thor tricked Thrym, cracked his skull, and got both Freya and the hammer back—and with them all the power and fertility associated with the storm. (Rappoport 1995)

> *See also* Churning the Ocean, Hail, Hammers, Hurricanes and Tornadoes, Lightning, Monsoons, Rain and Rain Gods, Snow, Thunder and Thunder Gods, Waterspouts, Whirlwinds, Winds and Wind Gods

SULIS

Sulis was a healing spring deity who presided over the hot springs at Bath, the ancient springs called Aquae Sulis. She was one of the most important British water deities, and she had solar attributes, perhaps because of the heat in the spring water. The hot springs of Bath gushed water from the ground at the rate of one quarter million gallons a day. The ancients thought that surely indicated the presence of a deity. Because they believed Sulis to imbue the waters with curative powers, pilgrims traveled to her springs to worship the goddess and bathe in the hot water.

The name Sulis came from the root *suil,* which meant "eye," and perhaps the name referred to the sun as the eye of the heavens. Sun gods and goddesses throughout the world derived power from the solar properties of heat and light, and in myth, they descended into underground waters at sunset only to return to the sky the next morning. The worshippers of Sulis likely believed she too descended into the springs and heated the water with her solar power. Miniature sun wheels were cast into the springs as offerings, as well as many coins bearing the image of a phoenix, a symbol of sun and fire and an indication of the magic power of underground heat. (Green 1992, McCrickard 1990)

> *See also* Celtic Lands, Grannos, Phoenix, Springs and Wells, Water and Water Spirits, Well of Life

SUN AND SUN GODS

People long ago relied on the rhythms of the sky, and the sun exhibited the most obvious and dramatic rhythm of any celestial object. This force disappeared every night in what appeared to be the waters of the Underworld, then it reappeared the next morning to provide the world with light and heat. People across the globe from the most ancient of times recognized the power of the sun as provider, creator, and sustainer of life. Their myths reflected their reverence. They deified the golden orb as an all-powerful god and the ruler of the sky forces, because the sun, like a god, died and returned to life. The sun made survival possible.

Some of the earliest sun myths attempted to explain the phenomena of the sunrise and the sunset. When the sun disappeared each night, the sun god sank into the abode of the dead, and ancient people feared for the fate of their world. In Greek myth, the sun god Helios bathed his horses every night in the western sea, and in New Zealand, the sun descended to an underground cave where he bathed in the Water of Life, which renewed his immortality and enabled him to rise again. Those myths painted a pleasant picture. Others attributed the red sky at sunset to the sun god's death blood. In Egypt, the sun god Ra descended into a realm of serpents and demons who tried to destroy him during the night. Ra always arose victorious but only after a perilous battle. In cultures lacking the scientific knowledge to explain the sunset, the "death" of their sun god terrified them. When people watched their creator sink below the horizon, they also witnessed the extinction of their life-sustaining light. They knew the importance of a resurrection.

Scholars know that far back in antiquity people not only monitored the sunrise and the sunset but also tracked the sun's movement across the heavens. The ancients told myths to explain how the sun moved, through the day, through the night, and through the year. Because early people personified natural phenomena, they endowed them with human capabilities. It seemed natural to them then that the sun moved like they did. In European myths, the sun generally traveled across the sky by chariot. In North America and Australia, the sun traveled on foot. In Egypt, the sun steered a boat across the firmament, just as the people on earth steered their boats along the Nile. Fortunately, these sun gods knew their paths well and could keep their sky vehicles on course. The Greek myth of Phaethon outlined dire consequences should they fail. Yet still, some myths of solar movement involved the intervention of a culture hero who played an important role in keeping the sun on course. The Polynesian Maui was one such character. He caught the sun in a noose and beat it to slow it down.

The myths of solar movement, throughout the day and throughout the year, reaffirmed the sun god's role as creator. By maintaining a steady, reliable course, he upheld the order of the universe and guaranteed not only his own resurrection but also the resurrection of the earth. Life began anew each day the sun rose and each year when at the winter solstice the sun god turned northward. For this reason the sun god was crowned king of the sky, ruler of all the other celestial deities, and sometimes, the progenitor of the highest powers in the land. In Japan, the sun goddess Amaterasu was the ancestress of the imperial line. In Peru, the sun god Inti was the ancestor of the entire Inca race. In ancient Egypt, Ra was this great father, and all the pharaohs of the land were said to be his sons. The Egyptian Ra, as well as the solar aspect of Osiris, assumed primary importance in Egyptian religion, and the people worshipped different aspects of their solar deity as different aspects of the sun—the light, the power, the heat, the rays, and so on.

Egyptian religion centered on the sun for centuries, but in the fourteenth century B.C. a young pharaoh named Akhenaten replaced Ra and his rival god, Amon, with a new deity—Aton, a simple representation of the solar disk. The worship of Aton, or Atonism

as the religion was called, represented one of the most extreme forms of sun worship. In contrast to the earlier Egyptian gods, with their golden accouterments and their barques to sail the heavens, Aton was simply a disk, with rays that bestowed blessings on its worshippers. Atonism died when Akhenaten died and his successor, Tutankhamen, restored the old order. But sun worship continued around the world. In ancient Greece people sacrificed horses to the sun, most likely to provide new force for the sun's chariot. In Mexico people sacrificed to the sun to give it strength to continue its routine and to return to life every morning.

Because the sun did rise to life each morning, the sun god was a cosmic hero. He battled the demons of death and darkness and he won. Sun gods all over the world fought similar battles, battles not only against darkness demons but also against the storm-clouds that blocked the light and the numerous forces of evil that stood in opposition to sun and light and goodness. War gods often had solar characteristics, particularly in the Aryan cultures. Although in India Indra was most noted as a storm god, he assumed the role of a solar warrior as well. Other storm gods like Indra fought to save the world as they traveled across the sky and shattered the demons that challenged them from their abodes in the earth and the sea.

Emphasis on solar power permeated the myths, so much so in fact, that the renowned scholar Max Muller called almost everyone in the myths a sun god, or at least a solar hero. He gave almost everyone a solar mission: Jason searched for the golden fleece, perhaps a symbol of the golden sun, and Hercules accomplished his twelve labors by traveling, like the sun, through the twelve signs of the zodiac. Whether or not all these characters were solar heroes, the sun did figure in all kinds of myths. Often times, the sun was male and if not a warrior, at least a symbol of power and might. When the powerful sun god married the moon goddess, they often engaged in marital disputes. In another myth of celestial movement, for instance, the sun and moon ran a race. At the beginning of the race, the moon nearly reached the sun, but later, she slipped behind. The sun overtook the moon at the end of his course in an act described as a rape. Similar myths appeared all over the world.

The force of the sun reached far beyond the sky realm where he overpowered the moon goddess. It reached into the realm of the earth and the waters that ran beneath it. Sun worship had close connections to water worship, perhaps best illustrated by healing cults associated with thermal springs. But the sun god was a celestial, nevertheless, and as a celestial, he wrote the laws of the universe. He acted as judge and as moral guardian. The sun god healed, instructed, and gave the people their power. When the sun god spoke, the people listened. As light giver and life giver, he knew all and saw all, and he served as the omnipotent eye of the heavens. (Frazer 1926, Green 1991, Krupp 1991a, McCrickard 1990, Olcott 1967)

See also Clocks and Calendars, Cosmic Order, Death, Phaethon, Sky and Sky Gods

SUN DANCE

The Sun Dance is primarily a prayer to the sun god. Many tribes in North America perform it still; it is a sacred ritual conducted for the purpose of worshipping the Great Spirit in his manifestation as the sun and for requesting blessings from the greatest of all the nature powers. Dancers who participate in the ritual ask the sun to grant their wishes. They believe that all the nature powers, even the mighty sun, can be appeased through prayer and offerings and be persuaded to use their supernatural powers to benefit the tribe.

Sun Dance ceremonies were a prominent form of sun worship among many tribes, but the Plains Indians in general and the Dakota

Sioux in particular had elaborate Sun Dance ceremonies, and some continue to conduct them today. According to one Sioux legend, the ritual began when a young brave got a blessing from the sun god to marry a beautiful maiden, and in honor of the marriage blessed by the sun, people danced and worshipped the sun all day. The ritual has since become an annual event. The Plains Indians believe in an all-pervading supernatural power that manifests itself in all forms of nature, and the sun, they believe, is the greatest manifestation of that power. During the Sun Dance, the dancers seek visions from the spirit world. They deprive themselves of food and water, dance in the hot sun, and sometimes perform self-mutilations. Because of the severity of the routine, the dancers often do have visions. They hold their ceremony at the summer solstice during a full moon, illuminated by the supernatural light of the Great Spirit. They believe that the ritual—and the sun—gives them strength, so they perform their Sun Dance to pay homage to the mysterious life-giving force. (Gill and Sullivan 1992, Hultkrantz 1967, 1981)

See also Medicine Wheels, North America, Sun and Sun Gods

SUNBEAMS AND MOONBEAMS

The rays that extend from the sun and the moon penetrate the sky like darts. So in sky myths, that's often how they were symbolized—as darts or as arrows released from the bows of solar and lunar archers as they moved through the sky on their hunting trips. These sun and moon deities needed accouterments to embellish their stories and to add glitter and glitz to their personas. So mythmakers made sunbeams and moonbeams their shimmery weapons. The Aztec sun god Huitzilopochtli used his fire serpent, and the Greek deities Artemis and Apollo used bows and arrows. These gods and many others slew the darkness when their weapons pierced the sky.

Early depictions of sun gods and sun symbols often included solar rays to enrich the deity's appearance. If the sunbeams weren't weapons, they were simply part of the god's physical self, such as the golden locks of his hair or the tawny-colored beard on his chin. The Greek Helios had golden hair and so did the Hindu sun god Surya. Apollo had a flowing beard. In many places, the lion symbolized the sun, and the lion's golden mane, the solar rays. In the Norse myths, the sun god Frey rode a boar whose golden bristles symbolized sunbeams.

Myths that explained the sun and solar power were among the most common nature myths, and they often had connections to fire. In some stories, culture heroes who procured fire from the sun used sunbeams to bring the fire down from the sky to the earth. In a myth from the Gilbert Islands, the sea lord's child, Te-Ika, caught a sunbeam in his mouth and brought the fire to earth. The Thompson Indians of British Columbia said they learned to catch sunbeams too. A long time ago, when people had no fire, they sent messengers to the sun to retrieve it and to carry it home in seashells. This method proved troublesome, however, because each time the fire died out, another messenger had to travel back up to the sky world to retrieve some more. Some men in the tribe solved this problem when they learned to catch sunbeams. They drew the sunbeams down from the sky without ever having to leave the earth. Sunbeams brought fire to the world. (Frazer 1996)

See also Apollo, Arrows, Artemis, Helios, Huitzilopochtli, Sun and Sun Gods

SURYA

Surya was a sun god, one of the primary deities in Vedic India and both a representation of the physical sun and a personification of the sun as a deity. Surya was the son of Dyaus, the sky god, along with his brothers Indra and Agni, and the three of them comprised a triad of the most widely revered gods of the Vedic period. Surya often appeared in three forms, like the Egyptian Ra, and incorporated in his persona the force of the rising sun and the force of the setting sun. At first, the three appeared as separate deities, but eventually they fused into one solar force. Surya, Savitri, and Vivistat represented the all-powerful sun that stimulated life in the world.

Surya played a different mythological role in later years than he did in the Vedic period. The later Hindus considered Surya either the son of Aditi and the sage Kasyapa or of Brahma, the first of the Hindu triad and the greatest of all sages. Surya fathered the Aswins in Hindu myth, his twin horsemen, and they preceded his chariot on its sky journeys just as the solar rays preceded the sun into the sky.

In the Vedic period Surya also drove a chariot, a golden chariot driven by seven mares, one for each day of the week. This early Surya had golden hair, golden arms, and golden tongues, while the Hindu Surya appeared as a dark red man with three eyes and four arms. Surya was sometimes objectified as a gemstone glittering in the heavens or as a weapon the sky gods Mitra and Varuna concealed with rainclouds. (Frazer 1926, Ions 1984)

See also Aswins, India, Sun and Sun Gods

SUSANOWO

In Japanese Shinto mythology, Susanowo was the god of turbulent storms and typhoons. He was the brother of the sun goddess Amaterasu and of the moon god Tsuki-yumi and was born from the body of Izanagi, the creator deity. Whereas his sister and brother emerged from the eyes of Izanagi, Susanowo emerged from his nose. That connected him to breath or wind. He rode through the autumn skies on dark cloud horses and chased away his sister, the sun, in autumn, and then was exiled in the spring when the sun goddess returned.

In the myth of Amaterasu and the cave, Susanowo overshadowed his sister, just as the storm clouds obscured the sun. But the sib-

Swan maidens appear in many cultures and in various guises, associated with both sea and sky.

lings were not always at odds. In one myth, Amaterasu gave Susanowo shining jewels that he used as hail and lightning. Susanowo was described as impetuous rather than evil. He controlled the life-giving rains as well as the turbulent winds and thunder, but when his anger flared up, he caused massive destruction, ravaging the land and sea like the typhoons that swept the Pacific. Susanowo's tears, which caused the rain, were tears of destruction. Like the tears of the Egyptian Seth and of angry gods in other lands, they dried up the oceans and withered the forests. Typhoons that raged across the Pacific were accompanied by dark skies and lots of rain. These were the work of Susanowo, riding the dark clouds across the ocean and weeping his destructive tears. (Davis 1992, Piggott 1983, Mackenzie 1994)

See also Amaterasu, Japan, Storms and Tempests, Tears, Typhoons

SVAROG

Ancient people in Russia and the Slavic lands deified the sky as the Supreme Being then later personified him as Svarog. Svarog created life and light by having two sons, the sun god Dazhbog and the fire god Svarovich. Long ago when the people in the Slavic lands continually battled cold and darkness, they considered fire and the sun their greatest allies. Svarog presented them to the earth as gifts. He got tired of ruling the universe, so he transferred his creative powers to his two sons, who then assumed their roles as sustainers of life.

Svarog, as the original Supreme Deity of Russia, may have been displaced at a later time by Perun, the god of thunder and lightning. Svarog himself was connected to lightning, as it was he who created Svarovich, the personification of celestial fire. Svarog created fire by kindling it in the clouds. Then he sent the lightning to earth and gave fire to human beings. He created the sun by slitting open the clouds with his lightning and letting Dazhbog into the sky. (Ralston 1872, Simonov 1997)

See also Baltic and Slavic Lands, Chariots, Fire and Fire Gods, Perun/ Perkunas, Sky and Sky Gods, Sun and Sun Gods

SWAN MAIDENS

The ancient Aryans envisioned the heavens as a great sea and the clouds either as ships or as swans sailing over the cosmic waters. The swans in Aryan lore were commonly lovely young maidens, some covered with white feather plumage resembling the fleecy white cirrus clouds, and others were mermaids who frolicked in the great blue sky-sea. The ancients didn't know the composition of the heavens, but they knew the sea met the sky at the horizon and the two appeared to mesh. They didn't know that clouds were vaporous, but they knew that they floated through the sky like graceful white birds.

Swan maidens appeared in Greek myths as the Muses, in Norse myths as the Valkyries, and in Hindu myths as the Apsaras. They all had connections to earthly waters, then appeared to transfer their watery nature to the watery nature of clouds in the celestial realm. The Muses originally inhabited springs and fountains. The Valkyries sometimes inhabited lakes and pools, although most commonly they wore white-plumed garments and flew through the air like swans. Some say the Apsaras rose up from the ocean like vapors when the gods and demons churned it to obtain the elixir of immortality. The Apsaras bathed in the cosmic sea and could change shape, like clouds. The name Apsara meant "moving in the waters," which they appeared to do in the blue expanse of the heavens. Sometimes they descended to the earth and married mortals, but then they flew away, back to the sky. (Baring-Gould 1897, Fiske 1996)

See also Clouds, Cosmic Sea, Mermaids

T

TANE

In Polynesian lore, Tane was one of the sons of Rangi, the sky god, and Papa, the earth goddess. He was the son who succeeded in separating his parents and thus in raising the sky to allow light into the world. In some traditions, Tane was considered the god of light, but more commonly he was known as the god of trees and forests. Tane, along with his brothers, featured in many Polynesian myths as one of the most active deities in the pantheon.

Before the birth of the universe, Tane was trapped inside Papa's womb along with his siblings, and by pushing up the sky with his feet, he divided the world into realms. After he separated sky and earth and emerged, he clothed the naked bodies of his parents by covering his mother with trees and plants and his father with the Milky Way, the mist, and the luminous stars believed to be their children. Tane created various forms of natural land features by mating with certain beings and producing children, phenomena such as stones, grass, and creeks. In the Maori version of Tane's myth, he then made the first woman from the sand of the Hawaiki island, and with her he produced a daughter whom he mated with as well, the Dawn Maiden. (Alpers 1970, Andersen 1995)

See also Oceania, Tangaroa, Tawhiri-
matea, Trees

TANGAROA

Tangaroa was a principal god of the South Sea Islands, worshipped primarily as the god of the sea. In some myths, he was the creator deity, existing at the beginning of time within the confines of a cosmic egg, floating in the primeval darkness. The relationship of the demiurge Tangaroa and his role as ocean god probably stemmed from the prominent role the sea played in Oceanic culture. In some traditions, the sea existed first, and from the sea, all forms of life emerged.

Tangaroa figured prominently in the Maori creation myth of the separation of Rangi, the sky, and Papa, the earth. Rangi and Papa were locked in an embrace, and their children, Tangaroa among them, were trapped within Papa's womb struggling to be born. Tangaroa's brother, Tane, the forest god, succeeded in pushing his parents apart. Then trouble began among the children. Tawhirimatea, the storm god, stirred up ravaging storms, and Tangaroa fled to the sea for safety. But the battles among the brothers continued. Tane killed many of Tangaroa's children, the fishes, by using his trees to supply fishermen with canoes, fish hooks, and spears. Tangaroa, in anger, sent surging waves to swallow the canoes and high tides and flood waters to ravage the forests. Forever more, it was Tangaroa who was held responsible for destruction by ocean and flood waters.

The worship of Tangaroa spread over many of the Polynesian islands. He was a demiurge, a sea god, and a god of fishes, and in some myths, a god of the wind, a god of the tides, and in some way and in some traditions, a kind of sun god as well. Myths from the Society Islands and Samoa indicate a close relationship between Tangaroa and the sun, and the people of New Zealand sometimes claimed to have seen him, shining in the misty spray of seawater visible when the sun shone. In some stories, Tangaroa married Hina, the moon goddess, and together they ruled the tides. When Tangaroa breathed, only twice in twenty-four hours, his breaths caused the ebb and flow. (Alpers 1970, Andersen 1995)

See also Creation Myths, Oceania, Sea
and Sea Gods, Tane, Tawhiri-matea, Tides

TANIWHA

The Maori believed that water spirits called
Taniwha inhabited the oceans and inland
waters of the South Pacific. Volcanic eruptions, earthquakes, and other forms of thermal activity played a large role in shaping the
landscapes of this area, but the Taniwha were
held responsible. Taniwha, it was said, caused
the landslides by lakes and rivers. They lived
in deep pools or in caves, and the people
were alerted to their presence whenever
river currents flowed strong or huge waves
broke on the ocean.

The Maori believed that every person had
a Taniwha of their own and that usually the
Taniwha served as its person's guardian.
These guardian spirits were sometimes spirits of the drowned, and they often protected
people from drowning themselves. Not all
Taniwha were good, however, and some of
them drowned people as punishment. So
people appeased them with offerings. Taniwha usually materialized as large reptiles,
some as big as whales, and at other times, as
rocks or floating logs. (Dixon 1964, Orbell
1985, 1996)

See also Oceania, Water and Water Spirits

TARANUS

Taranus was the Celtic god of thunder and
lightning. He was closely connected to
Jupiter, but he represented the thunder aspect
of the great sky god. In that sense, he constituted a separate deity. Taranus was represented in statues with a thunderbolt and a
celestial wheel, the celestial wheel a common
image in the Celtic world and generally connected to the power of the sky and the sun.
But the word *taran* meant "thunderbolt," and
the name Taranus meant "thunderer." So
Taranus was first and foremost an embodiment of the booming noise and the destructive force that accompanied the storm.

Taranus was a true Celtic deity, unlike
many other gods the Celts adopted from the
Romans. But Taranus may have existed long
before the Romans arrived in the Celtic
lands, and in these early years, he may have
had connections with the sun and, perhaps,
with the rain. Rain gods are more common
in parts of world where rain is scarce, and in
the Celtic lands, rain fell from the sky often.
Because little evidence suggests a true Celtic
rain god, it has been suggested that Taranus
probably controlled rain as well as thunder
and lightning. (Green 1992)

See also Celtic Lands, Thunder and
Thunder Gods

TATE

Tate is the wind god of the Lakota Sioux, created by Skan, the sky, to be his companion.
He is a benevolent spirit, and, like the other
benevolent spirits, he has no material body
but appears more like a shadow. Tate remains
outside of the realm of human affairs and lets
his four sons influence the lives of the people
on earth. The notion of four winds is a common one, in North America particularly, and
the four sons of Tate personify these winds.
Each one has a distinct personality, and each
has a connection to one of the four cardinal
points and one of the seasons.

Tate is a sky spirit, but long ago he fell in
love with Ite, the lovely daughter of First
Man and First Woman, and he wished that he
and his sons could remain with her on earth.
So Skan agreed they could, on the condition
that Tate's four sons travel around the world
and establish the four directions. Tate built his
lodge at the center of the earth and his sons
departed to set up their homes in the north,
east, south, and west. Skan created a season for
each of these directions and decreed that each
son take turns bringing his season to the
world and controlling the weather during
that time. Waziya, god of the north wind,
brings snow, ice, and frost. Yanpa, god of the
east wind, sleeps most of the time. Okaga, god

of the south wind, brings warm, good weather, and Eya, god of the west wind, brings rain and thunderstorms. (Walker 1980)

See also Cardinal Points or Directions, North America, Seasons, Thunderbirds, Winds and Wind Gods

TAURUS, THE BULL
Considered the second sign of the zodiac, Taurus is one of the earliest constellations and contains some of the most celebrated stars in the sky. It led the zodiac for a long time, marking the vernal equinox from 4000 B.C. to 1700 B.C., and in these early years, was regarded as a bull in many lands. The stars in Taurus outline the bull's head and the front part of his body. Aldebaran, the brightest of these stars, marks the bull's eye, the Pleiades star cluster marks his back, and the Hyades star cluster marks his face. Near the bull's right horn is the notable Crab Nebula, the result of a supernova explosion in the year 1054.

Taurus has been likened to the bull god aspect of Osiris in Egypt; to Marduk, the spring sun, in Mesopotamia; and to Mithra, the primordial bull of Persia who ascended to the sky after his battle with Angra Mainyu, the spirit of evil and darkness. Some mythologists say that in Greek myth, Zeus was the bull, and he raised the animal to the sky because the form of a bull served him well when he transformed himself to be with his lover Io, who he had turned into a heifer to escape his jealous wife. But the most popular myth of Taurus involves Zeus as another bull and Europa, the daughter of King Agenor, as the object of his affections. Zeus fell in love with Europa, and to attract her attention, he disguised himself as a handsome white bull with golden horns. Thinking the bull as attractive as Zeus intended him to be, Europa climbed upon the bull's back. The bull took off over the sand, through the waves, and across the sea to Crete. Only the front part of the bull appears in the stars, perhaps to depict him crouching so Europa

could mount his back, or perhaps to depict him carrying her across the water, when the back part of the bull remained immersed as he charged through the waves. (Ridpath 1988, Staal 1988)

See also Constellations, Hyades, Pleiades, Zodiac

TAWHIRI-MATEA
Tawhiri-matea was the Maori storm god, a god of winds and the elements, and a child of Rangi, the sky, and Papa, the earth. Tawhiri-matea had five brothers, and in the beginning, with their parents stuck together, these brothers agreed that Tane, the forest god, should push trees and plants between the two to separate them. All the brothers consented to this plan, but Tawhiri-matea protested. The storm god waged war on his brothers. First he sent his children, the winds, to the four corners of the earth, and then he sent gales, whirlwinds, squalls, hurricanes, rain, and storm clouds of all sorts to destroy the land and the sea.

Tawhiri-matea's defiant act structured the Polynesian islands. He destroyed the trees and forests of his brother, Tane, and sent fierce waves lashing at the waters of his other brother, Tangaroa, the sea god. The winds and rains worked in tandem with Tawhiri-matea to terrorize Tangaroa and Tane in a furious attempt to seek revenge on them for separating Rangi and Papa. Tawhiri-matea, the spirit of the hurricane, continues to terrorize the Polynesian islands. He wreaks havoc on the sea and then sweeps over the islands, which, as a result of his initial act of vengeance, represent only a small portion of Papa. The rest of her remains covered by water. (Andersen 1995, Poignant 1967)

See also Hurricanes and Tornadoes, Oceania, Storms and Tempests, Tane, Tangaroa, Winds and Wind Gods

TEARS
Mythmakers have traditionally used tears, both human and divine, as a form of creative,

fertilizing water. Most commonly, tears symbolized rain and dew, particularly those tears shed by the gods. When a Great God or Mother Goddess shed creative tears, those tears usually caused the trees to grow, or, sometimes, they fell to the earth and created stones or minerals.

Weeping deities appeared in myths of many lands and their tears most often vitalized the earth. In creation myths where the world was formed from the body and secretions of a giant, his tears usually filled up the earth's rivers and seas. In creation myths that involved the separation of earth and sky, tears were sometimes shed by one or the other of the partners in grief over their separation. In Polynesian myth, Rangi, the sky god, cried tears of grief when his son, Tane, pushed him upward and out of the earth's embrace, and in Egyptian myth, Geb, the earth god, cried tears of grief after Shu, the air, came between him and his sky goddess. Geb's tears, as creative bodily fluids of an immortal, filled the oceans and seas.

The notion of tears as droplets of celestial rain led to the belief that tears stimulated the growth of vegetation. In classical myths, the Hyades shed tears of grief over their brother's death each spring when the seasonal rains rejuvenated the earth. Tears of benevolent deities produced good vegetation, whereas tears of evil deities produced poisonous plants. For example, in Egyptian myths, the tears of Seth grew the poisonous plants and the tears of Isis and Osiris grew herbs. In Japan, Susanowo the storm god grew the noxious foliage with his tears of rage. The tears of destructive deities had the opposite effect from the tears of creative ones. They parched the forests and dried up the oceans. (Mackenzie 1996)

See also Creation Myths, Hyades, Water and Water Spirits

TEZCATLIPOCA

Tezcatlipoca was the Aztec sky god, a god of duality who personified both night and the summer sun. This sky god originated as a god of the air and wind, then over time achieved the rank of Supreme Deity, a Mesoamerican counterpart of Zeus. The name Tezcatlipoca meant "Smoking Mirror," a reference to the black obsidian mirror used by sorcerers and carried by Tezcatlipoca to foretell the future. Like a sorcerer, he knew all and saw all, and he could change shapes, most commonly to a jaguar, a formidable predator and a symbol of the dark night sky.

Tezcatlipoca was a complex deity who assumed many guises and served many functions. As the jaguar, he personified darkness, and some myths indicate that he controlled storm, drought, famine, barrenness, and plague. Tezcatlipoca had four primary aspects, each of whom stood at one of the four cardinal points, like the Mayan Bacabs. As Blue Tezcatlipoca he stood at the south, and as White Tezcatlipoca he stood at the west. But his primary personas were those of the east and north. As Red Tezcatlipoca, this enigmatic sky god ruled the east and the daytime sky, and as Black Tezcatlipoca he ruled the north and the night. Thus, he represented both light and dark, good and evil, sky and Underworld.

No matter how many guises Tezcatlipoca assumed, however, his black aspect prevailed. In the myth of the five suns, Tezcatlipoca was the first sun, the dark sun, a jaguar sun, ruler of night and a world populated by giants. In one version of the myth, he became a jaguar and destroyed the giants. Then Quetzalcoatl, his rival, knocked him out of the sky and into the waters that surrounded the earth. Some say Tezcatlipoca, as the jaguar, can still be seen in the heavens as the constellation of Ursa Major. They call his fall from Heaven and the accompanying loss of his left foot a metaphor for the setting of Ursa Major and its accompanying loss of stars. As Tezcatlipoca's constellation dipped below the horizon, the ancients saw it descend into what they believed to be the Underworld and the waters.

Tezcatlipoca is usually depicted black, with a mirror in his left hand and another one replacing his severed foot. The myths of Tezcatlipoca were commonly reenacted in ballgames in which the player impersonating the dark sky god battled the forces of daylight. (Brundage 1979, 1982, Taube 1993)

See also Aztec Calendar Stone, Duality, Jaguar, Mesoamerica, Quetzalcoatl, Sky and Sky Gods

THOR

Thor was the Norse thunder god, and like the element he personified, he was both powerful and destructive. The most popular god of the Viking period, Thor was a sky god like Zeus, violent and unpredictable yet looked upon with reverence and worshipped more as a protector than as a destroyer. Thor was perceived as a kind god and believed to hurl his thunderbolts only at giants, monsters, and other enemies of humanity. The ancient myths of Thor's battles with these monsters likely symbolized mountain thunderstorms and emphasized the necessity of exerting power over the natural world.

Thor was generally thought to be the son of Odin and Frigg, and even as a child he revealed his explosive temper. Because his mother could not control him or his violent outbursts, she sent him to be raised by foster parents, Vingnir and Hlore, who were said to personify sheet lightning. After Thor grew up, he joined the other gods in Asgard and was given the realm of Thrudvang, or Thrudheim, where he built a magnificent palace called Bilskirnir, a name that meant "lightning." From then on he hurled his mighty hammer and sent sparks flying to earth. He cracked the skulls of frost giants to break up icebergs and smashed the skulls of cliff giants to cause avalanches of snow that fertilized the land. Each time Thor threw his magic hammer, like a boomerang it always returned.

Thor was the strongest of all gods and had three mighty possessions to aid him in battle.

The Norse god of thunder, Thor, wields his mighty hammer.

Mjollnir was the hammer, red-hot and representative of the force of the lightning bolt. He also had a pair of iron gloves that enabled him to hold Mjollnir and a magic belt that, when worn around his waist, doubled the thunder god's strength. Over time, Thor's powers as high god and the properties of his magic hammer expanded. Although he originated as a thunder god, in later myths he assumed the role of fertility god as well. His worshippers turned to him for protection and believed it was Thor who tamed the wild forces, calmed the winds and seas, and prevented famine and disease. Perhaps his connection with fertility stemmed from the association of thunder with rain, but perhaps it also lay in the symbolism of the hammer. Likened to a phallus, Thor's hammer represented the electrifying strike that energized and fertilized the earth.

Thor was depicted in many Viking Age carvings and on wooden statues in temples throughout the Scandinavian world. He appeared as a young man, tall and muscular, with red hair and a beard that spewed sparks of fire when he was angry, just as sparks of fire danced on the bark of a tree when lightning struck. Sometimes, the thunder god wore a crown with a bright star or a burning flame on each point, thus encasing his head in a halo of fire. The other gods feared Thor and believed he would set their rainbow bridge, Bifrost, aflame if he crossed it. So he traveled from his home in Asgard by wading through rivers and streams. His eyes blazed like lightning, his voice boomed like thunder, and his red beard (and in Sweden his hat) puffed out around his face and was said by some to symbolize the stormy sky.

Thor was popular in all the Teutonic lands, particularly in Norway and Iceland. Donar was his equivalent in Germany. Numerous myths of Thor appear in the Eddas and in later sagas. In many of the stories, thunder roars as he rumbles across the heavens in his chariot, drawn by two goats named Tanngniostr and Tanngrisnr, who steer the great god across the firmament with sparks of fire flying from their teeth and hooves. Thor sometimes answered to the names Vingthor and Hlorridi, names he assumed out of respect for the stepparents who raised him. (Crossley-Holland 1980, Davidson 1986, Guerber 1980)

    See also Hammers, Lightning,
    Scandinavia, Sky and Sky Gods, Thunder
    and Thunder Gods

THOTH

Thoth played numerous roles in Egyptian myths, but primarily he ruled the moon. Some myths said he created the moon himself, and other myths said that Ra, the sun god, created it for him. Thoth was said to have retrieved the eye of Ra when it escaped and to have returned it to the great sky god. Ra gave Thoth the moon as a reward. From then on, Thoth served as Ra's representative in the night sky, and Thoth's eye symbolized the full moon, just as Ra's eye symbolized the noontime sun. Thoth guarded the moon as it moved through its phases and regulated the passage of time.

Because the ancients used the moon's phases to create the first calendars, moon gods from many lands controlled time and the seasons. Thoth was called the "Measurer of Time," and he played an important role in establishing the Egyptian calendrical system. One myth of Thoth recounts how he played draughts with the moon and, over the course of several games, won one seventy-second part of the moon's light. This portion of light amounted to five extra days, which Thoth added to the official calendar of 360 days, just before the New Year. On each of these five days, the sky goddess Nut gave birth—to Isis, Osiris, Seth, Nephthys, and Horus.

Thoth had many names in his role as moon god. He was the "White Disk," the "Governor of the Living Sky Gods," and the "Bull Among the Stars.'" Sometimes he appeared as a dog-headed baboon or as an ibis, but most commonly he appeared as a man with the head of an ibis. On his head he wore a crown resembling a moon disk cradled in a crescent. The beak of the ibis too represented the crescent moon, the silver sliver of light that in some myths Thoth used as a boat to sail the heavens and to transport souls of the dead across the night sky. (Ions 1983, Pinch 1994, Spence 1990)

    See also Clocks and Calendars, Egypt,
    Eye, Moon and Moon Gods, Nut, Ra

THUNDER AND THUNDER GODS

Thunder is evidence of sky power. To the ancients, it seemed celestial. It seemed to emanate from the realm of the sky gods and from the weapons they used to strike the earth. In many cases, the sky gods used their weapons in anger. They destroyed, yet at the same time they fertilized; with rumbling noise and sailing lightning bolts, they heralded the coming of spring and the rains.

Agricultural people revered their thunder

deities and relied on them to restore fertility to the earth. Thunder was a seasonal power, so after long, dead winters, the thunder god's appearance meant that life would continue, that the people could once again rely on the earth goddess to provide. For this reason, some groups of people considered their thunder gods benevolent beings. The Iroquois considered their thunder god, Hino, benevolent. With his companion, Oshadagea, the dew eagle, he brought moisture back to the earth. In India, Parjanya, a rain and thunder deity who preceded Indra, was also considered benevolent, and so were the dragons of Chinese and Japanese myths. The dragons made the thunder rumble when they engaged in battle. In the spring, they rose up to the sky from their underwater homes, and as they fought in the clouds, the rains poured down.

The ability of thunder spirits to bring the rain meant that they served a creative function. The Skidi Pawnee clearly recognized the creative power of thunder gods. They believed that the world was made during the earth's first thunderstorm. But thunder and the gods who controlled it had dual characteristics. The gods acted as both creators and destroyers. Zeus and Perun, the high gods of their pantheons, clearly had creative power, yet they often hurled their thunderbolts in anger. The sound of thunder was frightening and threatening, so people often perceived it as punishment.

World myths include many metaphors for the sound of thunder. It was the rumbling of the sky gods' chariots as they drove across the heavens. It was the voice of the Great Spirit, speaking through the clouds. It was the bellowing of a ram, the howling of a dog, or the hissing of worms or serpents in the beak of Raven, who was himself a symbol of the dark storm cloud. Ancient weathermakers often imitated the sound of thunder to bring about the rains. In Slavic lands, people used to imitate thunder by beating on a kettle with a hammer. King Salmoneus of Greece imitated

thunder by riding his chariot over a bridge. However, because in many lands only the greatest gods had such power, those who imitated the storm were severely punished. Zeus burned Salmoneus for committing an act he considered the height of sacrilege. Zeus alone had power to sound the thunder, to hurl the lightning bolts, and to send the rains.

The mighty rumblings of Zeus, of Thor, or of thunder gods from any land resonated through the trees and the forests. In ancient times, much of the world was covered with natural woods, so people heard the sound of thunder clearly in the rustling branches. For this reason, the worship of thunder gods like Zeus and Thor was closely connected to the worship of sacred oaks. The thunderbolts hurled from the great gods' hands split open the trees and transmitted their celestial fire to the earth. Perhaps mythmakers drew the connection between oaks and thunder gods for this reason, and because people too kindled fire in wood, just as the thunder gods did when they struck their trees. But these mythmakers also offered fanciful explanations for why thunder hit trees. According to the Thompson River Indians of North America, Thunder asked Mosquito why he was so fat, and Mosquito replied that he sucked on trees. He didn't want to admit that he really sucked on people, because he didn't want thunder to eat up all the people and deny him of his prey. Mosquito's plan worked, and his story explained why thunder now shoots trees instead of people. (Krupp 1991a, McCartney 1932)

See also Hammers, Lightning, Meteors and Meteorites, Perun/Perkunas, Rain and Rain Gods, Storms and Tempests, Thor, Thunderbirds, Zeus

THUNDERBIRDS

In the myths of the Americas, thunderbirds were gigantic winged creatures responsible for storms. It was a widespread belief in the ancient world that birds controlled the weather, perhaps because they made their appearance in spring, just as the rains came and the land began to get warmer. As rain bringers, the birds were beneficial, ending droughts and propagating fruitful harvests. But thunderbirds were generally connected to violent storms and tempests. They beat their gigantic wings to produce thunder, shook their bright plumage to release the rains, and flashed their monstrous eyes to streak the lightning. People throughout the Americas greatly feared thunderbirds as creatures of destruction.

The belief in thunderbirds was not unique to the Americas however; it occurred across the globe. The Chinese thunder god Lei Kung was originally believed to be a bird, the Japanese thunder god Raiden had a companion thunderbird named Raicho, and the Indian Garuda bird was a similar creature connected to wind and storm. In West Africa, So was the lightning bird who flapped his wings and caused thunder, and in Kenya, a crowing cock made the rumbles. Most commonly in the myths, the bird resembled an eagle, although it was rarely seen because it hid behind the dark clouds during flight. The African bird Umpundulo dived from the clouds and flashed through the sky, as the lightning appeared to do in dry countries when it emanated from the bottom of the clouds, then branched out and traveled through the air below.

Some people believed that the Thunderbird used his wings to shoot arrows of lightning, that the rebound of his wings made the booming noises, and that that was why thunder was heard in different parts of the sky. A story of the Lengua Indians in South America explained why the Thunderbird caused storms in the first place. This story was based on the belief of the Lengua Indians that fire was kindled from the Thunderbird's lightning. An Indian discovered the fire one day when, while fishing for snails, he noticed a large bird carrying the snails off to the forest, under a tree, where a column of smoke swirled up into the sky. The Indian followed the smoke and noticed that the bird had kindled fire and did not have to eat his snails raw, as he and his people did. So the Indian stole the Thunderbird's sticks and kindled his own fire, which made the bird angry. He soared up into the sky in a rage, stirring up black clouds and creating a terrible storm with crashing thunder and piercing flashes of lightning. From then on, whenever it stormed, the Lengua said the Thunderbird was showing anger for the theft of his fire. (Eels 1889, Ingersoll 1923)

See also Birds, Garuda Bird, Hino, Imdugud, Lei Kung, Lightning, Lightning Bird, Raiden, Thunder and Thunder Gods

TIAMAT

The story of Tiamat, the chaos dragon, appears in the Babylonian creation story, *Enuma Elish,* and may well represent the first of the dragon myths. Tiamat existed as a primeval force in the form of an enormous dragon, and she represented the chaotic waters of the salt sea that existed in the beginning of the world. This dragon was the mate of Absu, god of the freshwater ocean, and the two of them existed together until a trio of younger gods destroyed them and took over the world. These three gods were Anu, Enlil, and Enki, and Marduk, the storm god, was their champion. The story of Marduk's slaying of Tiamat represents not only the end of one world and the beginning of another but also the victory of order over chaos. As the embodiment of preexistent, chaotic matter, Tiamat had to be destroyed, broken into pieces, and restructured. From her broken body, Marduk created the world.

Tiamat had the body of a python, the jaws of a crocodile, the teeth of a lion, the wings of a bat, the legs of a lizard, the talons of an eagle, and the horns of a bull. She was fearsome and monstrous, and engaging her in combat was no small task. Nevertheless, Marduk rose to the challenge. Arming himself with a net, a bow, lightning bolts, and the winds, the storm god mounted his chariot. He caught Tiamat in his net, opened up her mouth and her body with his mighty winds, then sliced her in half. From one half of her body he created the sky and installed in it the moon and the stars. From the other half he organized the earth. He erected mountains from her head and breasts, channeled the Tigris and Euphrates from her eyes, and built reservoirs of water from her nostrils. Then he filled up her body with dust to create the earth's surface.

Although the slaying of Tiamat was a creation myth, the story was also in a sense a fertility myth. Dragons embodied—and often imprisoned—water, and the dragon-slayers were often storm gods. When Marduk slew Tiamat, he released her waters and restructured them to make a new, fertile world. (Huxley 1979, McCall 1990, MacKenzie 1996)

See also Absu, Chaos, Creation Myths, Dragon Slaying, Dragons, Mesopotamia, P'an Ku, Stoorworm, Tlaltecuhtli, Ymir

TIDES

Tides are the rhythmic motion of the sea; they're predictable and provide a sense of order, like the movement of the celestial bodies and the rotation of the earth's seasons. Philosophers attempted to explain the motion of the tides for a long time before they got it right. Pytheas thought they were caused by the moon, but Aristotle thought that they were caused by the sun moving the wind around. Others attributed them to the alternating decomposition of the sea by the air and the air by the sea, ice melting at the poles, or ferocious winds escaping from underwater caverns. Less scientific explanations attributed tides to sea serpents, evil water genii, or supernatural beings. Plato believed tides were the earth's breaths. When the earth inhaled, the tide ebbed, and when the earth exhaled, the tide flowed.

Tide myths were created in areas where waters were rough and the tides were forces to be reckoned with. Because the Mediterranean was a gentle sea, tides were unfamiliar to the ancient Greeks. But navigators of the North Sea and the Pacific Ocean knew tides well and created myths and legends to explain them. In Scandinavia, Thor caused the tides with his powerful breaths, and in Polynesia, Tangaroa caused them with his breaths—one inhalation and one exhalation every twenty-four hours. In Chinese myth, two warring nations cause tides as they waged their battles. These nations grew from the one hundred children of a princess, fifty of whom formed a nation in the mountains and the other fifty a nation on the beach. When the nation on the beach won a battle in the war, the tide flowed, rushing inland toward the mountains. When they lost a battle, the tide ebbed and the beach people retreated further out to sea.

Several stories from the Pacific Islands involved controlling the tides with jewels owned by the dragon-king who guarded them in his palace under the waves. The white jewel caused the ebb tide and the blue jewel caused the flood tide. A Japanese myth told of the High Tide Jewel and the Low Tide Jewel, precious gifts from the dragon-king used by the Japanese Empress Jingo centuries ago when she sent the Japanese fleet to invade Korea. When the Korean fleet sailed forth to face the Japanese, Jingo threw the Low Tide Jewel into the sea and the tide instantly receded, leaving the Koreans stranded on the beach. The Koreans jumped out of their ships, planning to attack. Then the empress threw in the High Tide Jewel, and the tide instantly rose. The Koreans drowned, and the Japanese successfully invaded Korea. (Bassett 1971, Davis 1992, Rappoport 1995)

See also Death, Dragon-Kings, Ryujin, Sea and Sea Gods

T'IEN MU

When the Taoists came to China, they established a mythological tradition in which a Ministry of Thunder, comprising several deities, controlled various aspects of the storm. T'ien Mu controlled the lightning. She made it flash by using two mirrors to deflect the light from the celestial sphere down to earth through a hole in the sky. The Chinese regarded lightning as female because they believed it came from the earth, part of the yin, or the female, principle. T'ien Mu sent her lightning to earth and set fires with it. As the source of terrestrial fire, T'ien Mu, also called the Mother of Lightning, dressed in colorful clothes—blue, green, red, and white, like flickering flames. In some traditions, she appeared as the thunder god's wife, and she worked together with him, the rain god, the wind god, and the little boy who piled up the clouds. (Hackin 1963, Werner 1995)

> *See also* Chhih Sung-tzu, China, Feng Po, Fire and Fire Gods, Lei Kung, Lightning, Mirrors

TILO

Many sky gods of the Indo-European lands controlled all forms of atmospheric phenomena, and Tilo of Africa did as well. The Tonga of South Africa and Mozambique called Tilo their sky god, and they greatly feared him as a force of evil. Sky gods in most parts of the world had dual characteristics: they destroyed and they fertilized. But Tilo brought death and disease. He controlled the same cosmic forces as other sky gods, but whereas they maintained order in the world, Tilo introduced chaos.

Storm gods of Africa were often frightful personages. Although the continent thirsted for rain, the rain quickly escalated into raging storms. Strong winds swept the storm all over the land and spread death and disease as it moved along. Those who feared and revered Tilo believed he sent the disease. They believed he decided who lived or died. Tilo was

the Great Spirit, the Supreme Being, a mysterious power because thunder and lightning were mysterious phenomena. He was omnipotent and invisible, but he made himself known when he sent every force that appeared to emanate from his sky world plummeting down to earth. (Mbiti 1970)

> *See also* Africa, Storms and Tempests

TIRAWAHAT

Native tribes throughout North American believed in a Great Spirit, or an invisible sky presence who created the world and served as the driving force of the universe. To the Skidi Pawnee of the Central Plains, that Great Spirit was Tirawahat. Tirawahat lived above the clouds, directly overhead in the unchanging blue vault of Heaven. He ordered the course of the sun, the moon, and the stars, and he gave all the gods their power. Tirawahat, as Great Spirit, was the omnipotent creative force and the Father of the Sky.

The Skidi Pawnee saw Tirawahat manifest himself in many forms. As a sky god, he was impersonal and invisible, yet his people recognized him in the lightning that flashed, in the wind that rustled the branches, and in the light that filtered through the wafting clouds. Like sky gods in cultures all over the world, Tirawahat controlled the storm, and he used the rain, the hail, the sun, the clouds, and other forms of atmospheric phenomena as his messengers. These forces acted as intermediaries between the people and the great sky presence, and they transmitted to the people Tirawahat's power and thus, the power of the sky. (Chamberlain 1982, Dorsey 1997)

> *See also* Creation Myths, Great Spirit, North America, Sky and Sky Gods, Storms and Tempests

TISHTRYA

Tishtrya was the Persian rain god, a stellar deity identified with the star Sirius because of the star's prominence in the sky during the rainy season. Some said Tishtrya was a god of the primeval waters; he produced the primeval rain, and then Vayu, the wind god, carried the rain to the edge of the earth where the cosmic sea formed. Tishtrya may have been present at the beginning of time and responsible for the formation of the lakes and seas, and he continued to produce rain after that. He provided the water necessary for the seasons to turn and the earth to rejuvenate after the long periods of drought that plagued the land.

The Persians associated Tishtrya and Sirius with fertility and prosperity. Sirius rose when the rains came and returned the earth to fruitfulness. The myth of Tishtrya's battle with the drought demon typified the Zoroastrian battle between good and evil. Tishtrya, fighting for good, opposed the evil drought demon Apaosha, as well as Duzhyairya, the witch who spoiled the harvests. In Tishtrya's battle with Apaosha, he assumed the form of a white horse and Apaosha the form of a black horse. At first, the black horse won and drought plagued the land. But then Tishtrya appealed to Ahura Mazda, the Great God, for help. To win the battle, Tishtrya attested, he needed the power and strength of sacrifice. So the people fed their rain god sacrifices, and he defeated the drought demon. Sirius rose in the sky, and life-giving rains renewed the earth. (Curtis 1993, Hinnels 1973)

See also Cosmic Sea, Drought, Duality, Indra, Persia, Rain and Rain Gods, Sacrifice, Sirius

TLALOC

Tlaloc was a powerful rain god worshipped by the Aztecs and their ancestors, the Toltecs. He lived in a southern paradise, on a mountaintop dwelling called Tlalocan, and he controlled not only the rain but the wind and the lightning bolts as well. In some myths, Tlaloc ruled the storms along with his companion sky serpent, who held all the water of Heaven in his belly. In other myths, Tlaloc poured his rains from four jugs that held both the beneficent rains that watered the crops and the destructive rains that ravaged the earth.

Tlaloc was both highly revered by the ancient Aztecs and highly feared. Rain in the Valley of Mexico was a precious commodity, but storms could cause massive destruction. The first of Tlaloc's four jugs held the good water. It fertilized the earth and made the vegetation grow. But the water in the other three jugs caused problems. The second jug held water that delivered blight to the grains; the third jug held water that turned to frost on the fields. The fourth jug too destroyed all the fruits and devastated the Aztec lands.

Tlaloc was one of the most powerful gods in the Aztec pantheon, but he didn't work alone. During storms, he worked in tandem with Ehecatl, the wind god aspect of Quetzalcoatl, who first blew the winds. He worked with his wife, Chalchihuitlicue, the water and flood goddess, and with the Tlaloque, the spirits of rain clouds, who lived on hilltops throughout the country and distributed rains to different areas. Tlaloc had perhaps one of the bloodiest cults in all of history. Both Tlaloc and the Tlaloques received sacrifices of babies and young children who were rounded up, then slain and their flesh eaten by priests and members of the nobility. If the mothers of these children or the children themselves cried during the ritual slayings, the Aztecs rejoiced, because they believed their tears meant the rain would fall.

Tlaloc was represented in art as a black man with teeth like tusks and large circular eyes. He sometimes carried an axe, the symbol of thunder, and appeared with the sky serpent, a symbol of lightning. The Tlaloques, his attendants, were represented as statues called Chac Mool figures, which had shallow dishes, believed to either catch the rain or hold the hearts of sacrifice victims. Because the Tlaloques were rain bringers, the

Chac Mool figures were bumpy and irregular, carved to resemble the shape of floating clouds. (Brundage 1985, Klein 1980, Markman and Markman 1992)

See also Chac(s), Chalchihuitlicue, Ix Chel, Mesoamerica, Rain and Rain Gods, Sacrifice

TLALTECUHTLI

Tlaltecuhtli was an Aztec earth monster pictured as a gigantic toad and believed to have existed in the primordial waters. The story of Tlaltecuhtli was a creation myth, similar to the Norse myth of Ymir, the Babylonian myth of Tiamat, and the Chinese myth of P'an Ku. The two primary Aztec creator deities, Quetzalcoatl and Tezcatlipoca, dismembered Tlaltecuhtli and fashioned the world out of its body. They transformed themselves into two giant serpents, coiled themselves around the monster's arms and legs, and ripped it apart. Then they used the top part of Tlaltecuhtli's body to make the earth, and they threw the bottom part into the sky to make the heavens. Trees, flowers, and herbs grew from the monster's hair, mountain ridges formed from its nose, grasses and small flowers sprouted from its skin, wells, springs, and small caves issued from the hollows of its eyes, and rivers and caverns issued from its mouth. Tlaltecuhtli was often called "Earth Lord," yet was most often considered female. As an embodiment of the earth, this Earth Lord, or Earth Lady, swallowed the sun every evening and vomited it back up each dawn. (Markman and Markman 1992, Muser 1978)

See also Creation Myths, P'an Ku, Stoorworm, Tiamat, Ymir

TONATIUH

Tonatiuh personified the Aztec Sun, the visible disk in the sky whose movement through the heavens guaranteed the continuation of the world. Four previous suns, or sun gods, had existed before Tonatiuh, each as ruler of his own cosmic era. But in succession, each of them died. Tonatiuh was the first moving sun, and he ruled the present world. The Aztec sacrificed blood and hearts to Tonatiuh to fortify him and to ensure that he had enough strength to continue his celestial movement.

The myth of Tonatiuh began after the extinction of the fourth sun when the gods gathered in Teotihuacan to create a new sun. They built a bonfire, and Nanahuatzin, the diseased god, volunteered to sacrifice himself by diving into the flames and being resurrected. Tecciztecatl, another god, volunteered as well, but threw himself into the fire after Nanahuatzin. Tecciztecatl was resurrected as the moon, but Nanahuatzin, having jumped first, was resurrected as the bright Tonatiuh.

After the burning of Nanahuatzin, the gods waited and waited, watching the horizon for Tonatiuh to rise. But none of the sun gods of previous eras moved, so Tonatiuh didn't either at first. At that point, the gods decided to sacrifice to him to give him strength. Quetzalcoatl cut out the hearts of sixteen hundred gods, wrapped them in bundles, and offered them to the sun. This myth justified the practice of human sacrifice that permeated the Aztec religion. Because Tonatiuh rose into the sky after the blood sacrifice, the Aztecs believed that human beings must continue to sacrifice to ensure that the sun keep moving and stay on its path.

Tonatiuh appears in numerous representations throughout Mexico and is reputed to be the face in the center of the Aztec Calendar Stone. Usually, he appears within a large rayed solar disk, wearing red paint and an eagle feather headdress. Tonatiuh is associated with the eagle because the sun, like the mighty bird, swoops down low and ascends high into the sky. This fifth sun is a warrior who shoots his darts, the solar rays, through the heavens and lights up the world. (Brundage 1979, 1982, Taube 1993)

See also Aztec Calendar Stone, Fire and

Fire Gods, Mesoamerica, Metztli, Phoenix, Sacrifice, Sun and Sun Gods

TORNADOES
See Hurricanes and Tornadoes

TORTOISE

Some early people envisioned the world as a tortoise swimming in the primeval ocean, with the belly of the tortoise as the earth and the shell of the tortoise as the sky. This animal, with its hardy shell and its consequent ability to support heavy loads, symbolized strength and permanence. It not only embodied the universe, but it also assumed the mythological role of supporting the earth on its back.

The tortoise played the role of earth supporter in many world myths. North American tribes perhaps most notably held this conception of the tortoise and believed that in the beginning, human beings lived within the animal's body. Some tribes even called the animal the mother of humanity. In Chinese myth, the goddess Nu Gua used the legs of a tortoise to hold up the heavens, and in Hindu myth, Vishnu took the form of a tortoise to support the earth while the gods churned the ocean to obtain the Water of Life. In North America, some believed that earthquakes occurred when the Great Turtle got tired and shifted or moved his feet. The Hindus believed that when the tortoise got too tired to support his load any longer, the animal would sink into the sea and the earth would be destroyed by flood. (Fiske 1996, Mercatante 1974)

See also Elements

TOTEMISM

Totemism was a common form of religion for many people of Oceania, of parts of Africa, India, and the Americas, particularly in tribes of the Arctic and along the northwest coast. Adherents of totemism believed in a supernatural relationship between a human being and a nonhuman force, in many cases an animal but quite often a phenomenon of nature, such as thunder, lightning, river, or rain. The natural phenomenon was seen as a living spirit and an ancestor of a particular person, clan, or group of people. That spirit protected its people and gave them power. Some people claimed lightning as their totem, others thunder, the wind, or the sun. Totemism pervaded the societies of the Peruvian Andes, and people there considered themselves descendants of fountains, rivers, lakes, mountains, stones, rocks, and the sea. (Brinton 1976, Durkheim 1995, Lang 1996, Levi-Strauss 1963)

See also Animism, Dreamtime, Shamanism, South America

TREES

In times long ago, the ancients worshipped trees because forests covered much of their land. In parts of Asia, trees lined the sea coasts, and in old Europe natural woods dominated much of the countryside. The Celts may have established their earliest shrines and temples in sacred groves, and the Lithuanians worshipped trees right up to the time they were converted to Christianity. People revered trees for the energy within them, for the spirit that inhabited the tree and infused it with life. Sacred trees seemed alive with this spirit. They moved and swayed, they spouted sap like precious milk, and when the wind rustled through their branches, they appeared to speak in whispers.

Tree spirits assumed a variety of forms. People who lived in heavily forested areas such as North America and Europe worshipped forests as a whole. People in ancient India worshipped groves and credited grove deities with bringing rain and fruitful crops. Different groups of people worshipped different kinds of trees, depending on what species grew in their countries. The Iroquois believed each species had a separate spirit. The Celts worshipped the oak and connected it to

This undated woodcut depicts a malevolent tree spirit in Fiji.

thunder gods and gods who had power to bring rain. In Oceania and in some parts of Africa, people particularly revered the spirit in the coconut tree, because, like a mother, it gave milk. People in West Africa revered the silk-cottonwood trees as the abode of a spirit named Huntin. Massive and overpowering, the silk cottonwoods seemed to attest to the permanence of nature and to validate the belief that trees had spirit that could never die.

Nature worshippers of times past venerated trees in part because they witnessed their immortality. Trees renewed themselves every year after dropping their leaves and fruits and dying a winter death. The mythmakers used trees as symbols of immortality by associating them with powerful gods and goddesses. The ancient Egyptians identified

Osiris with a tree that formed the vault of the heavens. The Indians identified their creator god, Brahma, with the eternal asvattha tree. These trees, and many others like them, symbolized the vitality of the universe. Tree worship constituted a form of earth worship. People of many cultures considered tree spirits creator deities, and they connected the tree with life and fertility. Some people believed that tree spirits bestowed blessings in the form of sun and rain and that they made the crops grow. Others considered them manifestations of the Mother Goddess. In ancient Persia, the cosmic tree grew out of the cosmic sea, Vourukasha, and that tree was the source of all life on earth.

The ancient perception of the tree as Mother Goddess led to the symbolic representation of a tree of life. It led to the concept of a world tree that bridged the chthonic and celestial spheres—from the Underworld to the sky—and that served as the axis around which the entire world revolved. This world tree structured and supported the universe. It validated the belief in a layered cosmos. Yggdrasil of Norse myth best exemplified this tree, an enormous evergreen ash that marked the center of the world. Water from underground springs and wells nourished it; celestial dew fell on its leaves and gave it life. This tree, like the cosmos, was immortal. It emanated spirit. When the ancients beheld life and energy in the trees of their world, they felt the need to immortalize that spirit in myth. So they symbolized the earth's vitality in one powerful image that they knew attested to the belief in cosmic renewal and the notion of stability and permanence in the world. (Eliade 1958, Frazer 1926, 1950, Leeming 1990)

See also Forests, World Axis, Yggdrasil

TRICKSTERS

The trickster played an important role in nature myths, sometimes as a creator deity and culture hero and other times as the introducer of chaos. He was mischievous and un-predictable, and he popped up often in myths and manipulated natural forces, such as thun-der, the sun, the moon, and the stars. These clever figures appeared most commonly in myths of the Americas, Australia, and Africa, although such characters as Loki of Norse myth and Hermes of Greek myth were also labeled tricksters. They were cunning and clever, and, quite often, they upset the order of nature.

Tricksters were part god, part animal, and part human. They existed before the world was formed, and generally, they played a large role in forming it. The North American trickster, Coyote, created waterfalls on the Columbia River as a gift for a maiden who wanted a secluded place to bathe. He cut through hills, made a slanting rock wall, and made water gush out of the earth and fall over the rock wall into a splash of mist at the bottom. Commonly, characters like Coyote entered into solar myths, particularly as thieves of the sun. In one myth of Raven, the trickster of the American Northwest, Raven decided to put light in the world, and he found that a powerful shaman had impris-oned a bright ball of light in a box. Raven set his sights on obtaining it. He turned himself into a tiny pine needle in a container of drinking water, and the shaman's daughter drank the water then gave birth to Raven. Raven, as a baby, cried for the box, and when his mother gave it to him, he changed back into his bird form and flew away, the ball of light in his beak.

Raven kept flying, higher and higher into the sky. But because the sun was a precious commodity, the shaman chased the bird. Soon, Raven got tired. When the ball got too heavy and Raven could hardly hold it any longer, he broke small pieces off of the ball with his beak and scattered them across the sky. They became the stars. When he felt the ball get heavier still, he broke a larger piece off, which became the moon. Then finally,

when he reached the top of the sky, he let the largest piece go, the piece that he still had in his beak. It became the sun. Raven gave light to the world.

In another version of this myth, Raven took light away. He hid the sun in a bag to punish the people for killing all the animals he made. It this version, it was Raven's brother who returned the sun to the sky. Sun stealing was a serious offense in myths all over the world, and usually the trickster committed the crime. But, as in the myth of Raven, the trickster sometimes stole the sun back or rescued it from someone else who abducted it. In a similar myth from Siberia, a hero named Main returned the sun to his people after an elk impaled it and ran off with it into the forest. Darkness persisted until Main returned with the sun. People often told such myths to explain the absence of the sun during the night. Main was said to perform his solar rescue every night and to return the bright ball of light to the sky every morning.

To steal the sun and perform similar feats, the trickster deity had to be clever. His cre-ative aspect had to prevail even when he did evil deeds. Many trickster deities created the world. Coyote of the American Southwest crafted the sun. Raven and the Ashanti trick-ster Anansi created the sun, moon, and stars. Maui, the trickster figure in Polynesia, fished up islands, raised the sky, snared the sun to slow it down, and, as did many other trick-sters, stole fire for humanity.

Despite their performance of crucial cre-ative acts, tricksters were mischievous, and that meant, in nature myths, that they also in-troduced chaos into the world. The African trickster, Legba, enticed the sun and the moon to change houses. The South Ameri-can Mataco trickster, Tokwah, flooded the earth by releasing the waters of the ocean, which were enclosed in a tree. Coyote, in North America, upset the order of the heav-ens. According to Navajo legend, Black God, the creator deity, planned to create constellations to represent every animal on earth. He gathered up a pouch full of crystals and began placing the crystal in the sky in an orderly fashion, starting in the east, and moving in a circular path in a clockwise direction. But Coyote wanted to have his say in ordering the heavens. While Black God rested, Coyote grabbed the pouch and flung the remaining crystals haphazardly into the sky. His careless action created the Milky Way but also upset the intended order of the stars. Because of the interference of this mischievous trickster, there were then many unnamed stars among the constellations. (Lopez 1977, Parabola 1979, Pelton 1980, Radin 1955)

See also Chaos, Cosmic Order

TRITON

The son of Poseidon and Amphitrite, Triton was a gigantic Greek sea god and a merman. Like all mermen, Triton was a man from the waist up and a dolphin from the waist down. He rode through the sea on a sea horse and commanded the waves by blowing into the twisted conch shell he used as a horn. When he blew hard into his shell, the waves assumed gigantic proportions. When he blew softly, the waves subsided and the sea became quiet and calm so Poseidon and Amphitrite could glide through the waves.

In early myths, Triton appeared to personify the sea, but in later myths, he primarily heralded the appearance of his father. More importantly perhaps, Triton served as one of the early prototypes for mermen, a race of sea beings that appeared in legends of many lands. Triton's descendants were likewise called Tritons, and they had bodies covered with scales, gills under their ears, and fingernails that looked like rough, spiny shells. The Tritons appeared in Greek myths as peripheral sea deities, trailing Poseidon's sea train and giving rides to many of the other creatures that peopled the sea. (Graves 1988, Guirand 1963, Rose 1959)

A massive Greek sea god, Triton commanded the waves by blowing into a twisted conch.

See also Amphitrite, Greece and Rome, Mermaids, Poseidon, Sea and Sea Gods, Waves

TSUI'GOAB

Tsui'goab was a great hero worshipped as a rain god by the Khoi Khoi of South Africa. He was a creator deity, some say the Supreme Being, and he was believed to have made the first human beings out of rocks. The Khoi Khoi worshipped Tsui'goab as a great warrior chief and a sorcerer, perhaps in the form of a peculiarly shaped stone. His name meant "Red Dawn," and his worshippers connected him with dawn and light and with stone worship. However, he was primarily associated with rain, and in that capacity, Tsui'goab provided nourishment for the land and the people.

The worship of Tsui'goab was a form of ancestor worship, a common practice in Africa and prevalent in this South African society. Tsui'goab may not have existed as a living being at all, however, but simply as an ideal, worshipped as a spirit or ghost and invoked at dawn to bring the rain and the stormclouds. According to legend, Tsui'goab was wounded in the knee in a battle with Gaunab, a warrior chief thought to be evil. Because of Tsui'goab's connection to dawn and Gaunab's to night, their battle perhaps represented the battle of light and dark, good and evil. (Lang 1996, Parrinder 1986)

See also Africa, Darkness and Light, Rain and Rain Gods

TSUKI-YUMI

The moon god of Japanese Shinto, Tsuki-yumi, was one of the three supreme deities, along with Amaterasu, the sun goddess, and Susanowo, the storm god. He was born from the right eye of Izanagi, the creator deity, just as Amaterasu was born from his left. Tsuki-yumi differed from many moon deities, because, unlike the silvery goddesses that appeared in most other lands, Tsuki-yumi was male and little worshipped, perhaps because he ruled the land of the dead. Just after his birth from Izanagi's eye, he inherited the kingdom of night and climbed the Ladder of Heaven to join Amaterasu in the sky. But he was soon banished from his high kingdom and sent down to earth. He never shared his sister's sky again.

The story of Tsuki-yumi's exile from Heaven involved his slaying of the food goddess, Uke-mochi. Amaterasu sent Tsuki-yumi down from Heaven to check up on Uke-mochi and make sure she was providing an adequate supply of food. The food goddess acted rudely, showing off, and vomited food onto the land and into the seas. Tsuki-yumi took offense at her actions and killed her. Although upon her death the body of Uke-mochi became the plants and trees and provided food for the Japanese people, Amaterasu got angry at her brother's reaction and vowed that she would never again look him in the face. This myth explained why the sun appeared only in the day and the moon only at night.

Tsuki-yumi was silver and radiant, befit-ting a moon god, and, like Amaterasu, he was thought to manifest himself in a mirror placed in his shrine at Ise. (Davis 1992, Piggott 1983)

See also Amaterasu, Japan, Mirrors, Moon and Moon Gods

TUPAN

Tupan was the thunder god of the Guarani, or Tupinamba, Indians of Brazil. He was an important deity among these people, but he was demonic and, unlike the thunder gods of other lands, associated only with thunder and lightning and not with rain. Thunder gods like Thor and Perun had dual natures; they hurled their storm hammers to punish evildoers, but they also acted as fertility gods and sent rain to water the land. But among the Tupinambas, the goddess Kasogana sent the rain. Tupan only caused destruction.

In some myths, Tupan was portrayed in human form as a hefty man with dark curly hair. He caused storms when he traveled across the sky in a boat, attended by two birds, beginning from his home in the west and arriving at his mother's home in the east. The hollow seat of his boat made the thunder sound as he traveled swiftly through the air. When he reached his mother's house, the thunder stopped. In other myths, Tupan was not a man attended by birds, but a gigantic bird himself, the Thunderbird, a common concept in tribes of the Americas. (Brinton 1976)

See also South America, Thunder and Thunder Gods, Thunderbirds

TYPHOONS

Hurricanes in Asia are known as cyclones or typhoons. They occur in the South China Sea and the western Pacific Ocean and cause mass destruction with heavy winds, torrential rain, and massive flooding. The Greek monster Typhon personified the hurricane or the typhoon, and it seems likely that Typhon had his origin in Asia. The Greeks sometimes referred to him as the Anatolian Typhoon, a demonic spirit who lived in the Corycian cave in Sicily. He was the largest monster ever born, with a hundred serpent heads for hands, eyes that flashed lightning, and wings that darkened the entire sky. He emerged from his cave and stormed through the land with such force that he gouged great furrows in the land, which became the beds of rivers.

Typhon was a dragon, the offspring of Gaia, the earth, and Tartarus, the depths of the Underworld. Gaia produced entire races of hideous monsters, but Typhon was the youngest and most hideous of all. He was taller than the tallest mountain. He spat fire and vomited rocks. In the myths, he terrorized Zeus and all the other Olympian gods, causing them to change shape to escape him and flee in fright.

In a popular myth of Typhon, the monster battled with Zeus and cut out his sinews, immobilizing the great sky god and forcing him into the Corycian cave. Hermes came to the rescue, stole the sinews back, and repaired Zeus's broken body. Zeus, of course, got his revenge. He assaulted his attacker with thunderbolts, then buried him alive under Mount Aetna. There, he continues to twist and writhe and cause earthquakes.

Like the typhoon itself, Typhon destroyed the land in many ways. His writhing movements under the earth caused earthquakes, and his emergence from the Corycian cave, volcanic eruptions. Ancient people commonly believed that strong winds emerged from caves where something trapped inside the cave struggled to escape. So the Greeks attributed the winds to Typhon—all except the gentle winds of the south and west. As the spirit of the typhoon, Typhon's noises caused the roaring winds, his gigantic strides through the sea caused tidal waves, and his continually violent movements caused whirlwinds, hurricanes, and volcanoes. (Graves 1988, Rose 1959)

> *See also* Aetna, Earthquakes, Hurricanes and Tornadoes, Monsoons, Storms and Tempests, Susanowo, Volcanoes, Winds and Wind Gods

TZITZIMIME

The night demons of Aztec lore were stars, evil supernatural beings called Tzitzimime who continually threatened to destroy the world. The Aztecs believed the night sky was an evil place, and they believed the star demons would eventually destroy the world when they dove down to earth and caused the firmament to collapse. The Tzitzimime symbolized the terror these ancient people felt when they looked into the dark night. The stars appeared to them as evil eyes gazing down from an evil realm and waiting for the opportunity to annihilate mankind.

Given the demonic nature the Aztecs assigned the stars, the outlook for humanity seemed grim. Some believed four Tzitzimime held up the firmament, which explained their power to collapse the sky. But according to others, the stars only transformed into tzitzimime at certain times and during certain celestial events. These malevolent night demons were female beings, some say souls of women who died in childbirth. They posed the biggest threat during solar eclipses when they waged battle against the sun. During a solar eclipse, the stars appeared close to the sun, so it looked like they could attack it, and the gradual disappearance of the sun appeared to confirm the people's greatest fears. (Brundage 1982, Taube 1993)

> *See also* Demons, Mesoamerica, Quetzalcoatl, Stars and Star Gods

U

UKKO

Ukko was a god of thunder, clouds, and rain, widely worshipped by the Finns and the most commonly evoked deity in the Finnish epic poem the *Kalevala*. Ukko replaced the earlier Finnish sky god Jumala as Supreme Deity and assumed a role similar to the Scandinavian Thor. Ukko, too, carried a hammer or, in some areas, a rainbow bow and a lightning arrow. With these weapons, he drove away evil spirits by sending thunder and lightning down to earth.

Ukko was a benevolent god and helped his people in times of need. His worshippers sacrificed sheep to him and placed them in birch bark chests along with liquor and beer on which, it was believed, Ukko feasted during the night. No one ever saw Ukko in human form, only in the form of rainclouds that covered the sky before thunderstorms. But Ukko made his presence known in other ways. He stirred up the ocean waves, he ensured fruitful harvests and fended against drought, and after the sun, moon, and stars were stolen by the wicked Louhi, he restored fire to the people by sending lightning down to earth. Ukko lived in the thunderclouds; his domain was the sky. But like Jumala and other sky gods who achieved the status of Supreme Deity, Ukko's power extended beyond the sky, to the earth and the sea. (Harva 1964, Muller 1897)

See also Baltic and Slavic Lands, Hammers, Sky and Sky Gods, Thor, Thunder and Thunder Gods

V

VARUNA

Varuna was a complex deity in the Hindu pantheon, at first the supreme sky god and later the god of the oceans. In his original position as sky god, he was thought to possess infinite knowledge and acted not only as creator but also as divine judge, controlling the destiny of humanity and upholding the laws of the universe. Varuna kept his high position for only a short time, however. By the end of the Vedic period, he had surrendered his powers to Indra and become lord of the seas and rivers. As sea god, he watched over demons in the darkness beneath the waves, and he ruled from the western ocean from whence the rains blew to India.

In the early years when Varuna ruled supreme, he was said to have created the universe by standing in the air and measuring out the three worlds: Heaven, earth, and the atmosphere. This act and others established Varuna as the emperor of order, and, like the Greek Ouranos, the personification of the sky. His breath was the wind, his eye the sun, and his house a golden sky palace with a thousand columns and a thousand doors. He caused the rain to fall and the rivers to flow, and he performed other acts to ensure cosmic order, such as guiding the moon on its course and keeping the stars in the sky.

Whereas Varuna compared with the Greek Ouranos as sky god, he compared with Poseidon in his role as sea god. Varuna ruled the ocean, and he lived with his wife, Varanani, in an undersea heaven on the mountain Pushpagiri and rode through his realm on Makara, the sea serpent. Where Varuna was once surrounded by celestial trees and glimmering jewels, he was there surrounded by serpents and ocean demons, along with spirits of the cardinal points and the mountains and many spirits of rivers, seas, lakes, and pools.

Varuna was depicted as an old man with a club and a noose called Nagapasa. As sky god, he used his noose to seize whoever opposed his cosmic laws, and as sea god, he used it to subdue the ocean demons. In a sense, Varuna had always controlled the waters, even as sky god when he guarded the mythical sea of heaven and caused the rains to fall and fill the rivers and oceans. In later years he inherited the terrestrial waters, descending into the dark ocean depths, destined to rule only the demons who resided there to escape the wrath of the gods. (Ions 1984, Knappert 1995b, Mackenzie 1971)

See also Cosmic Sea, India, Sea and Sea Gods

VAYU

Vayu was a wind god who appeared in the nature myths of India and Persia. In Persian myths, Vayu was the god of the air, and he inhabited the realm between the light sky world of Ahura Mazda and dark earth world of Angra Mainyu. In Hindu myths, Vayu traveled all over the earth, but he lived in the northwest, and from there he blew the winds down the mountains to India.

Vayu was an important deity in ancient times, because as wind god, he controlled life's breath, the force that animates all things. Some sects considered him gentle, a god of breath and of the soft breeze, but other sects considered him violent. Commonly in the myths, this mighty wind god had a nasty temperament and combined it with the ability to destroy at will. In his most noted act of violence, he battered the summit of Mount Meru, the world mountain, then finally broke it off and hurled it into the sea. Like mountaintops of other lands that were broken off by violent gods of natural phenomena, the summit of Mount Meru became an island, the island today known as Sri Lanka.

In Hindu mythology, Vayu was commonly depicted in the company of Indra, the storm god, and often as his charioteer. Sometimes, he rode in a chariot of his own, drawn by deer, or on the back of an antelope, an animal known to move swiftly, like the wind. Sometimes he was called Sadagata, which meant "ever-moving," or Gandhavaha, which meant "bearer of perfumes." In Persian myths, Vayu was considered a warrior who chased away evil. (Ions 1984, Knappert 1995b)

See also Aeolus, Air and Air Gods, Ehecatl, Indra, Meru, Winds and Wind Gods

VENUS
See Morning Star/Evening Star

VIKHOR

The Vikhor bird of Slavic myth was one manifestation of nature's fury. The winds blew hard in northern Europe, and the pagans watched them manifest themselves as frightening beasts. Vikhor was one such beast. He personified the whirlwind. Whirlwinds were commonly seen in the Slavic lands in the summer, so that was when Vikhor made an appearance. He flew in a gale and seized whatever he found in his path.

Whirlwinds are much like tornadoes, only smaller. They swirl and they twist and they do seize things; they suck things up and carry them away. Giant birds like Vikhor personified the winds and whirlwinds in myths of other lands as well. Vikhor behaved much like the Harpies of Greek myth who seized things forcibly. In one legend, the Vikhor bird seized the queen. Her three sons, distraught over her disappearance, finally located her in Vikhor's palace on a high hill. When one of the young princes confronted Vikhor, he grabbed hold

of the bird's little finger, just as his mother had instructed him to do. Vikhor flailed around violently, as winds often do, and he tried to shake the prince loose. Finally, the whirlwind dissipated. Vikhor fell to the ground and turned to sand. (Ralston 1873)

See also Baltic and Slavic Lands, Birds, Garuda Bird, Harpies, Imdugud, Whirlwinds

VIRACOCHA

To the Inca of Peru, Viracocha was an omnipotent presence in the universe. Although he was a sun and storm god, Viracocha was more distant and impersonal than the primary sun god, Inti, and the primary thunder god, Illapa. Viracocha delegated power to Inti and Illapa and to the four winds he created and sent to civilize the world. Viracocha was both culture hero and creator deity. The mythmakers said he emerged from Pacari, the cave of dawn. But more commonly, they said, he rose from Lake Titicaca, created the sun, moon, and stars and sent them on their sky journeys, then traveled westward himself, like the sun, and disappeared below the horizon into the ocean.

The circumstances of Viracocha's birth and the metaphorical interpretation of his name identified him as a sea god and a water god as well as a sun god. The name Viracocha meant "Fat Foam of the Sea," and he was white, like the sea foam but also like the light at dawn that emerged above the horizon, as did the great god, from what appeared to be below the waters. Viracocha could hurl thunderbolts, as could any storm god, and he did, to show his anger at people who opposed or attacked him as he continued on his westward travels. But he had much more power than that. Because he existed as a primordial being in Lake Titicaca, he represented not simply the rain, but the procreative power of the liquid element in general.

Viracocha was often depicted as a white man crowned with the sun and sometimes holding a thunderbolt and weeping tears of rain. He had a long flowing beard, a common characteristic of water gods, and a sister-wife named Mamacocha, a sea deity and a goddess of rain and water. (Brinton 1976, Mishkin 1940, Osbourne 1986)

See also Inti, Sea and Sea Gods, Sea Foam, Sky and Sky Gods, South America, Thunder and Thunder Gods

VIRGO, THE VIRGIN

The sixth constellation of the zodiac, Virgo, glistens in the night sky as a maiden and an earth goddess, with the bright star Spica marking the sheaf of grain she holds in her hand. The star Virgo symbolized earth goddesses of many lands, though in old star maps she held not grain but scales, suggesting a connection to justice. Mythologists have connected Virgo to both. In Babylonia she was Ishtar; in Egypt, she was Isis; and in Greece, she had many identities, among them the earth goddess Demeter, her daughter Persephone, Dike, who controlled the seasons, and Astraea, the goddess of justice who symbolized innocence and purity.

Mythologists may have connected Virgo with agricultural deities because fifteen thousand years ago, the constellation marked the vernal equinox. The sun moved into Virgo in those days just as spring arrived and people paid homage to the goddesses responsible for renewing the earth. The myth of Demeter explained one version of Virgo's story. Demeter left earth for a while to search for her virgin daughter, Persephone, whom Hades had abducted and carried to the Underworld to be his bride. The earth goddess traveled far and wide to reach Hades' realm, then remained there for a long time trying to per-

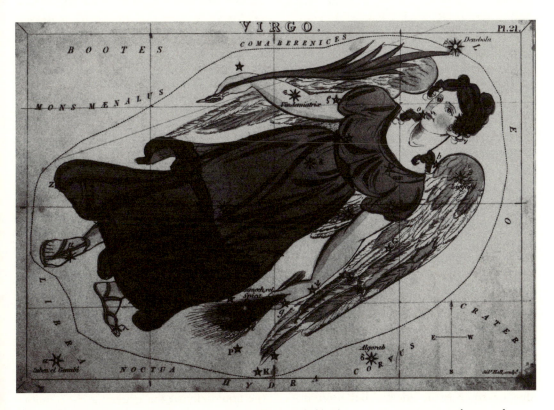

The constellation Virgo symbolized an earth goddess, probably due to its appearance at the vernal equinox in ancient times.

suade the god to release her daughter. With the help of Zeus, Hades relented. Persephone remained in the Underworld each winter but returned to the earth each spring.

Although the myth of Demeter and Persephone neglected to explain which of the story's goddesses brought the spring back to earth, it drew clear connections between the return of the earth goddess from the Underworld and the arrival of spring. Legends from other lands told similar stories. In Babylonia, the earth goddess, Ishtar, caused winter when she left to find her husband, Tammuz, and caused spring when she returned. The same happened in Egypt when Isis left to search for Osiris. It was believed that Isis formed the Milky Way when she scattered grain along her route. The sheaf of grain in Virgo's hand clearly identifies her as an earth goddess, whether Isis, Demeter, or any other fertility goddess responsible for the growth of the land in spring. (Ridpath 1988, Staal 1988)

See also Constellations, Demeter, Earth and Earth Gods, Libra, Zodiac

VISHNU

In Hindu mythology today, Vishnu is one of the three aspects of the Supreme Being. He's the Preserver and Restorer, and, together with Brahma the creator and Shiva the Destroyer, he symbolizes the divine essence of the universe. Though Vishnu is widely worshipped today, he appeared in the Vedic period as well, probably as a kind of sun god. Even today he is believed to alternate between sleeping in the cosmic waters and rising in one form or another to restore order and sustain the cosmos.

According to Hindu thought, Vishnu emerges from his sleep when the world is in danger. The forms he assumes are called avatars, or incarnations, and as each of these avatars he fights the forces of evil that threaten to upset the balance of the world. As Matsya, the Fish, for instance, he saved human beings from the flood. As Kurma, the Tortoise, he helped the gods churn the ocean to obtain the elixir of immortality, and as Varaha, the Boar, he raised the earth out of the ocean. As Vamana, the Dwarf, he took his famous three strides, and it was agreed that as much ground as he could cover would belong to him. Vishnu's strides measured out the entirety of the universe. Vamana's three giant steps have been interpreted as the sun at sunrise, at noon, and at sunset, so that by taking these strides, Vishnu's light penetrated the earth, the air, and the sky.

Vishnu assumes many forms in his role as Preserver, ten of which are well known. In his true form, he usually has five heads and twenty hands. He is often depicted either riding on the Garuda bird or reclining on the sea serpent Shesha with a lotus flower, with Brahma on top of it, rising from his navel. The serpent has been identified as a symbol of the earth, and Vishnu, by resting on top of it, serves as the earth's preserver. (Campbell 1974, Ions 1984, Thomas 1980, Zimmer 1962)

See also Brahma, Cosmic Order, India, Shiva, Sun and Sun Gods

VOLCANOES

Volcano myths attempted to explain many things. Some explained what caused volcanic eruptions in general, whereas others explained events that caused specific eruptions the ancients may have witnessed. Others, like the Japanese story of a giant who created Mount Fuji when he tried to fill up the Pacific Ocean with earth but got tired and dumped the last shovel full in a large heap on the land, explained why certain volcanic mountains existed in the first place. Volcano myths also explained what rendered certain volcanoes inactive and what might make them erupt again. The ancients attributed frightening displays of nature to frightening gods and demons, for instance, to horrendous giants struggling against binding chains or to tempestuous fire goddesses who exploded in anger by hurling liquid rocks and flaming spears.

The word *volcano* came from the Latin word *Vulcanus,* the island off the coast of Sicily where the Roman fire god, Vulcan, had his forge. Vulcan, or in Greece, Hephaestus, crafted armor for the gods in his forge, and the smoke that escaped from the top of the mountain indicated the fire god was hard at work. In classical myths, underground metal shops explained not only the smoke that rose from volcanic mountains but also the tremors, believed to occur when Vulcan or Hephaestus pounded the metal with his mighty hammer. Often demons trapped underneath the metal shops explained the tremors. Sometimes these demons were fire-breathing monsters, sometimes they were fierce roaring winds imprisoned in underground caves, trying to escape. Most commonly perhaps, they were hideous giants, like the first children of Gaia and Ouranos. These children personified the volcanoes as well as other violent natural forces, such as earthquakes, hurricanes, lightning, and thunder. Their father imprisoned them in the earth, and their struggles to escape resulted in earth tremors and fiery explosions.

The prominence of fire worship in antiquity led ancient people to postulate reasons for the existence of natural fire, like that of volcanoes. In Hawaii, the most popular fire goddess, Pele, set fires inside the mountains she reached as she traveled from place to place. In Madagascar, some people explained fire in volcanoes as the result of fighting between the Flames of the Sun and the Thunder. The Flames were the sun's soldiers, proud and cruel and willing to fight to prove their ultimate power. But Thunder challenged them with his power and scared them with his loud noises. The two sides got into a power struggle and met on the tableland in a horrendous lightning storm. Thunder shot out from behind dark clouds, and the Flames stood on each other's shoulders and climbed higher and higher into the sky. Then Thunder let loose a torrent of water from the clouds, and the Flames surrendered, fleeing to the mountains and hiding deep within them. There they have remained ever since, surfacing from time to time from crevices in the top and shooting out into the sky.

The myth of the Flames fighting the Thunder was only one myth of a battle causing eruptions. Volcanic action is violent, so the ancients commonly attributed it to violent battles, often between gods or tribal chiefs who inhabited mountains and basaltic hills. A Native American legend from the Northwest told of a fight between two chiefs, Llau on Mount Mazama in Oregon and Skell on Mount Shasta in California. The chiefs hurled rocks and spat lava at each other until Mount Mazama finally collapsed on Chief Llau, driving him underground with such force that it caused a large depression in the land, a caldera, now called Crater Lake. Calderas like Crater Lake, thermal springs, and geysers resulted from underground heat connected to volcanism. Other tales of volcanic battles explained the formation of these landforms, and still others explained the broken cones of volcanic mountains. Rivers were formed by the paths of angry gods retreating from their battlefields. A Maori legend told of the spirit of Taranaki (now Mount Egmont), who fought with the spirit of Ruapehu over the love of another volcano, named Tongariro. When Ruapehu swallowed the top of his mountain, melted it, and spat it out at Taranaki, Taranaki fled to the sea, digging a path that became the Wanganui River. Taranaki followed this path up the coast, where he remains brooding to this day, deciding how to take revenge on his rival. The Maori believe that when he decides, Mount Egmont will erupt once again.

Volcano myths were common in the Pacific Islands and especially in Polynesia, where they explained the origin of fire. A

Maori legend told of a medicine man named Ngatora who climbed Tongariro with his slave, and, deeply chilled by the high altitude cold, he prayed to his sorceress sisters to send fire and warmth. The sisters sent fire demons who swam under water to New Zealand, bringing fire and heat along with them. Wherever they surfaced, they created volcanoes and thermal springs. A myth from Samoa told of a man named Ti'it'i who stole fire from Mafuie, the earthquake god, and the two got into a horrendous fight. Mafuie blew up Ti'it'i's oven and scattered the burning stones. Then Ti'it'i tore off Mafuie's arm. To ensure that Ti'it'i would not tear off his other arm, Mafuie gave him fire to take to his people. But Mafuie himself continued to cause volcanic fire. Whenever the volcanoes in Samoa erupted after that, local people said that Mafuie caused them and that the eruptions would be much more violent if the earthquake god had both arms. (Bullard 1962, Frazer 1996, Vitaliano 1973, Westervelt 1963)

See also Aetna, Earthquakes, Fire and Fire Gods, Fujiyama, Pele

WATER AND WATER SPIRITS

In many cosmogonies, the world began with water alone. Water contained the seeds of life, so it had infinite possibilities and power—power to create the universe and to circulate through all three realms. The mythology and symbolism of water is pervasive and complex, and it encompasses the duality that defines the character of many natural forces. Water as creator and water as destroyer fostered the development of a wide range of spirits, some who ensured life and fertility and others who caused death.

The spirits who inhabited the world's waters stirred those waters to power. Whether they used that power for good or evil depended largely on what part of the world they inhabited and what type of people created them. People in rain-drenched areas feared flood, and ancient mariners and fishermen faced numerous perils in their waters every day. So the water spirits they created embodied their deepest fears. But people in lands threatened by drought populated their water myths with benevolent spirits, spirits who embodied water's creative power and so dispensed life and guaranteed the fertility of the soil.

The world's water spirits took a myriad of forms and dwelled in a myriad of places. They empowered rivers, lakes, streams, fountains, waterfalls, wells, springs, and rock pools. They rode over waves in the sea, and they hid in treasure palaces in bottomless lakes or within the confines of swirling whirlpools. People depended on all of these waters for life and sustenance, so they naturally assumed that the spirits who inhabited the liquid realm had fertilizing powers. They could wash over the land and replenish the soil after droughts, and they could provide food by sending fishes into the nets of fishermen. People who revered water as a creative force tended to make their water spirits female. They considered water the source of life and the mother of all things. Mamacocha in Peru was one such mother goddess and so was Chalchihuitlicue in Mexico. Anahita was the water goddess of ancient Persia, and the Zoroastrians regarded her as the source of all life and of the cosmic ocean. Those who perceived an ocean flowing through the heavens likely connected that ocean with the fertilizing waters that fell from the sky. So Anahita drove a chariot pulled by four horses: wind, rain, cloud, and sleet. Water appeared to have procreative powers, and Anahita embodied them. The Persians believed she could purify the female womb and the male seed that fostered life. Childless women bathed in her waters to make them fertile, and sick people bathed in them to cure their illnesses. Like the Hindu Sarasvati and the Aztec Chalchihuitlicue, Anahita not only had the power to create but also the power to heal.

Other water deities used their powers to cause harm. Many of these spirits had explosive tempers. The Vodyanoi, one of the many Slavic water gods, guaranteed mariners safe travel and provided fishermen with food, but if provoked, he dragged them under the waters and made them slaves in his crystal palace under the waves. The Rusalka, his female counterpart, seduced men into her waters, and in some legends, so did mermaids. Vumurt, the Finnish water spirit, lived primarily in the deep waters of rivers and seas and was especially evil in winter. It was then that he broke the ice under people and caused them to sink into the water and drown.

The range of characteristics assigned to water spirits and deities clearly reflects the duality of nature. This German illustration of a waterfall demon reflects the terrible fear of drowning.

Drowning was a common theme in water myths all over the world because people in antiquity abhorred drowning as a form of death. If a person drowned, he was denied the possibility of a ground burial and the return to Mother Earth; he remained lost in a realm where sea monsters ruled as well as all manner of devils and demons who lived in the depths of the waters. In South America, the Choroti of Gran Chaco believed a black water dwarf abducted children, and in Japan, a magic dwarf named Kappa pulled people under the waters. Crater Lake in Oregon harbored water devils who drowned trespassers, and serpents and similar creatures existed elsewhere. The Inuit believed that malevolent sea spirits called Atalit seized people, and the Estonians said the Nakk devoured them with his fishlike teeth. The

Nakk appeared in various forms and was always dangerous. If he or any other malevolent water spirit set its sights on a person, many people believed they had no business interfering. Often times people refrained from saving a drowning man for fear of defying the water spirit. Sailors often even sacrificed a member or two of their crew to propitiate the spirit and plead for safe passage across the waters.

The ability of the Nakk to change forms was a common characteristic of water spirits. Many of them appeared in human form but then transformed to fishes or serpents or some type of fantastical composite creature, like a mermaid. The shape-changing ability of water spirits was rooted in the knowledge that water itself changed form. As it glistened in the sun and moved with the wind, it exhibited different characteristics, sometimes moving gently and quietly and other times rushing down rocks, fast and furiously. The rushing water of rapids, the swirling water of whirlpools, and even the gently flowing water of rivers and streams impressed the ancients; this force moved spontaneously and therefore had supernatural power. The water spirits infused it with power. They not only activated it, but they kept the water in the pools. When the dragons left their underwater abodes in China, they took the water with them up to the sky. When the rainbow snake left his water hole in Australia, he overflowed the waters onto the earth. The Zuni of the American Southwest believed that a serpent lived in the water of their sacred springs, and they refused to kill him for fear of reducing the water supply. (Eliade 1958, Frazer 1950, Rappoport 1995)

> **See also** Marshes and Swamps, Mermaids, Moon and Moon Gods, Rivers and Lakes, Rusalka, Sea and Sea Gods, Springs and Wells

WATER HORSES

Water horses were common creatures in myths throughout the world. They went by different names in different countries but were usually classified as water sprites, often malicious ones. Perhaps the most commonly known water horse was the kelpie of Scottish lore who inhabited lochs and pools and drowned human victims. The kelpie appeared as a black horse, induced travelers to mount him, then rushed back under the water, carrying his victim along with him.

Kelpies and similar water horses rose from the depths swiftly and powerfully, as did the mighty waves. Horses symbolized waves in many legends. The Celts called the waves the horses of Manannan and the Greeks called them the horses of Poseidon. Poseidon's horses had white manes, like the white crested waves on the Mediterranean. But the kelpies were usually black, and their neighing and whinnying could be heard from beneath the depths during thunderstorms. This was when the waves turned dark and foreboding and seemed to pounce out of the water with violent force. Then, like the legendary water horses, they pulled people under. In the northern lands, the water horses were strong enough to break through the ice, and they did so when the ice cracked at winter's end. They rose from the water and pushed through the frozen surface. (Bassett 1971, Benwell 1965)

See also Horses, Manannan, Poseidon, Waves

WATERFALLS

Nature worshippers saw the manifestation of spirit in water, especially in water that moved forcefully when it plunged over cliffs and cascaded downward in a dramatic display of power and might. Wherever water moved rapidly, spirit seemed particularly to make its presence known. Spirit made the thundering noise of the falling water, and spirit made it pulse and rush and splash up from the ground in a spray of mist and foam.

People who perceived nature as a show of supernatural power considered the waters of the world sacred. Waterfalls, like springs and

wells, housed deities, and water worshippers believed both the deities and the waters themselves had healing powers. In Celtic myths spirits cured with the power of water, and in African myths, spirits in waterfalls made sick children healthy. Fudo, the Japanese waterfall god, had a shrine on a slope of Mount Shiratake in the province of Awa and had the ability to cure blindness.

Niagara Falls is one of the most impressive waterfalls in North America, and to the Iroquois, it was an extraordinary manifestation of spirit in nature. The term *Niagara,* to the Iroquois, meant "thundering water," and the Iroquois explained the rushing noise the water made as the voice of the water spirit. They sacrificed to the water spirits, usually by sending a young maiden down the rapids in a canoe. In one legend, a great chief and the father of the maiden chosen for sacrifice rushed into the rapids and attempted to rescue her, but they both fell to their deaths as they plunged over the falls. Their spirits live in the falls: he in the cataract, and she in the mist. The Iroquois also had a legend to explain the creation of the falls, and that too involved a maiden in her canoe. The canoe crashed to pieces against the rocks, but a great thunderbird living behind a waterfall on the river saw the canoe crash, and he swooped up the maiden before she too was torn to bits. The thunderbird told the maiden of a great snake monster who was coiled under her village and bringing illness to her people. The thunderbird attacked the snake with his lightning bolts. He killed the monster and wedged his body up against some rocks in the river. The Niagara River then, had to rise above the monster's body and then fall down over it. (Edmonds and Clark 1989)

See also Rivers and Lakes, Springs and Wells, Water and Water Spirits

WATERSPOUTS

Sailors have always feared waterspouts. The wind blew from all directions, the water swirled around with great speed, and the strength of the two forces moving together could often capsize small vessels. From antiquity through the Middle Ages, sailors considered waterspouts the work of dragons. The columns rising from the depths spiraled upward like twisted serpents ascending from their abodes underneath to cause some type of trouble.

For thousands of years, sailors tried to frighten away these sea dragons, at first by beating drums and gongs and later by firing canons at the moving columns. These actions accelerated the fall of the columns and made passage through the area less foreboding. But sailors still believed they were traveling through dragon territory, and they feared the dragons could cause them trouble, even though these sea creatures may have temporarily halted their movements. The Chinese thought waterspouts occurred either when the dragons ascended to the clouds or descended back to their undersea palaces. The Japanese thought these dragons had long tails, and the tails materialized as vertical columns of water. Arab mariners of the Middle Ages also connected waterspouts to dragons and believed they caused the spouts when they swooped down from the clouds and raised up the waters with their tongues. In Brittany, early people called these dragons or sea serpents tannin. Like water dragons from other lands, tannin entered the clouds in the winter when the clouds touched the water's surface and remained imprisoned within them until the clouds rose up to the sky in the spring and released the rains. (Bassett 1971, Rappoport 1995)

See also Dragon-Kings, Dragons, Hurricanes and Tornadoes, Whirlpools, Whirlwinds

WAVES

Most people of antiquity perceived the sea as an animate being, and they perceived the waves as the deliberate movements of the spirit of the sea. Gods presided over the waves: to the Greeks, the great sea god Poseidon; to the Inuit, Aulanerk; and to the Vikings, nine giantess daughters of the sea gods Aegir and Ran. Personifying the waves led to nature myths that used the sea spirits' strength to account for the waves' forceful pulses. The wrath of these spirits caused destruction, and the moaning of these spirits made the sounds of crashing waters on the shore.

Because the force of the waves was at times powerful enough to capsize ships, the mythology of waves often made use of other metaphorical symbols of power. Horses were likened to waves in many stories, for instance, the horses of Manannan to the Celts and the horses of Poseidon to the Greeks. As these sea gods rode their horses across the water, they metaphorically rode the waves that sprang up from the ocean depths. The white crests resembled the horses' billowing manes. Breakers, or particularly strong waves, were sometimes referred to as wild bulls, and the wildest bull of all, it was sometimes said, was the ninth wave. This wave, for some reason, could sink ships. This wave led to drownings.

Sailors across the globe knew the dangers of the waves. Navigators of the South Sea encountered the ocean demons Aremata-Rorua and Aremata-Popoa, or Long Wave and Short Wave, and navigators of the North Sea encountered the wicked sea goddess Ran, whose nine wave maidens assumed gigantic proportions and pulled ships and their crews underneath the water to remain as captive souls in Aegir's underwater hall. The personification of waves as evil spirits revealed the sea's dark side. Some myths identified waves as portents of death. The noise of the waves was attributed to the sea spirits wailing as a warning, or the spirits of drowned people moaning because their bodies were never recovered. The Celtic god of waves, Dylan, embodied the sea's darkness. He plunged into the water right after his birth and was considered the son of the waves. Dylan was eventually killed

The notion of the Well of Life or the Fountain of Youth was a common belief in the ancient world; its water was believed to bestow the gift of youth, vigor, and immortality. This sixteenth-century woodcut shows the elderly climbing into the Well of Life and emerging young and spry.

by his uncle, Govannan, and the waves continually mourn their son. When the waves crashed on the shore, the Celts said it was the waves expressing their anger at Govannan and their ardent wish to avenge Dylan's death. (Bassett 1971, Dixon 1964, Rappoport 1995)

See also Aegir, Horses, Manannan, Mermaids, Nereids, Poseidon, Sea and Sea Gods, Tides, Triton, Water Horses

WELL OF LIFE

The notion of a Well of Life or a Fountain of Youth was a common belief in the ancient world, founded on the notion that water had curative and restorative powers. People believed water from the Well of Life bestowed the gift of youth and vigor and immortality. Ancient explorers searched far and wide for this well, presumably located in some earthly paradise. They believed that by drinking a mere drop of water from the well a person miraculously recovered from near death and by immersing oneself one achieved immortal life.

The universal search for the Well of Life led to speculation of the well's location. Some people said it existed in the mineral springs of Siberia, others said it was somewhere in Africa or Asia. But many others said it lay on an island paradise or somewhere in the celestial realm, beyond the cosmic sea. In India it was thought to be the celestial Ganges, and in Egypt, the celestial source of the Nile, which lay under the Mountain of the Moon. The moon played a crucial role in Well of Life myths because the moon served as a model of immortality. The Water of Life, then, was perhaps moon dew, the magic elixir with which the Norse Hjuki and Bil filled their pail or the Soma or amrita of Indian myth, which was the liquid that fortified the moon and many other Hindu gods. A Maori legend also explained that the Water of Life, presumably from this magic well, renewed the moon each month after she died and made her full again.

The story of Alexander the Great told of his search for the Well of Life and the ultimate power of immortality. Some people in Africa believed that the Well of Life existed beneath the earth, perhaps as a submerged lake beneath the Sahara. So Alexander the Great, accompanied by his servant Khadir, went under the earth by entering a cave in the mountains. In some versions of the story, he went in search of the Tree of Life, believed to be located beside the well. In the darkness underneath the earth, however, Khadir fell into the well. Having immersed himself in the magic waters, he gained immortality and some believe became known as the Green Man, or the spirit of vegetation. But many ancient gods and goddesses owe their lives to the water's magic. The gods of India drank the immortal liquid to gain strength and power, and the Egyptian sun god Ra washed his face in the spring of the sun every morning in Heliopolis to renew his immortal powers. For these same reasons, Tung Fang So, a magician in the Chinese Han dynasty, bathed in the Purple Sea. He too became immortal but turned purple instead of green like Khadir. In the feng shui doctrine of the Asian world and in Well of Life myths around the world, water was perceived as the source of all life. (Eliade 1958, Knipe 1989, Mackenzie 1994)

See also Islands, Moon and Moon Gods, Soma, Springs and Wells, Sulis, Water and Water Spirits

WELLS
See Springs and Wells

WHIRLPOOLS
Ancient people thought whirlpools were both fearsome and awe inspiring; they seethed and they hissed and they swirled up in gigantic spirals, attesting to the vigor of water. Water was perceived as a source of energy, and swirling water, evidence of the life force. The ancients considered whirlpools magic, and they held all kinds of beliefs as to what kinds of magic lay beneath these dynamic spirals in the world's waters.

Spirals appeared as symbols in nature myths throughout the world. The spiral manifested itself in whirlwinds and seashells as well as in whirlpools, and it represented the creative life force of the waters. To ancient people, movement meant life, and the waters they observed in the world always moved. The rivers coursed, the tides ebbed and flowed, and the rain fell from the sky and streamed down the mountains to wash over the land and energize the crops. Swirling water was this creative motion at its extreme. Confined in a whirlpool, water appeared to have enough energy to create gods and goddesses or even the entire world. Such was the notion of the World Mill, which the Norse gods used to create the earth, sea, and sky from the body of Ymir, the frost giant. The Greek goddess Aphrodite was born from whirling water and so was the Hindu goddess Lakshmi. Ancient people in many lands revered water for its life force, and they respected the whirlpool as a manifestation of water's natural energy.

Whirlpools appeared to validate the magic of the waters, and ancient people held underwater creatures responsible for that magic. In Austria, whirlpools were evil spirits, and in Scandinavia, they were the work of Aegir, the sea god, boiling ale in his magic cauldron. In many lands, gigantic fishes were held responsible for the swirling waters: whales in some stories and sharks or sea demons in others. A kind of dragon was thought to produce whirlpools in the Nile River, and in Japan, a well-known whirlpool called Uwa no

Naruto was believed to lead to a dragon palace. Whirlpools off the coast of Russia led to the houses of water sprites, and the people thought it necessary to throw bread or salt into the waters to appease these spirits. Then another tale from Scandinavia used a mill to explain the water's movement. In this myth two giantesses grinding salt in a millstone explained the presence of a gigantic whirlpool or maelstrom off the coast of Norway and explained why the sea is salty. The giant women were turning the millstone in a boat, and the millstone got so heavy it sank to the ocean depths, spilling out enough salt to fill the seas. Where the millstone fell, it dug deep into the ocean bed, and the waters foamed and swirled and rushed up around the millstone in a monstrous spiral.

Of the celebrated whirlpools in antiquity, Charybdis off the coast of Sicily was perhaps the most famous. Charybdis made the waters swirl with unfettered force, and she sucked many a ship down into the watery depths. People in the American Northwest told the story of another dangerous whirlpool in their river called Keagyihl Depguesk, which also sucked people down into the waters. But a beneficent spirit named Hanging Hair got all the powers of the storm and water to work together to deflect the river water and turn the whirlpool into a gentle eddy. The powers succeeded. What was once a source of death became a source of life. The eddy now draws fishes to the area, and fishermen know it as a reliable place to find food. (Bassett 1971, Mackenzie 1970)

See also Dragons, Scylla and Charybdis, Water and Water Spirits, Waterspouts, Whirlwinds

twisting, twirling, and carrying within them the potential to vivify the world—and to destroy it. Because the ancients considered wind a powerful god, they considered energetic, whirling wind a particularly angry god, as well as the vehicle that carried him.

Supernatural beings of many kinds traveled in whirlwinds, across land, across sea, and sometimes upward to Heaven or downward into the Underworld. The ancients feared the power in the twisted air columns, so they commonly envisioned them as vehicles of devils, witches, ghosts, demons, or souls of the dead. Some tribes in North America threw sticks into the moving air to scare the spirits away. Other tribes thought whirlwinds were made from dead shamans' dust and believed that they killed people by capturing their souls or their shadows.

The gods and spirits connected with these twisting wind columns likely caused the whirlwinds with their rapid movement rather than simply rode within them. To the Aztecs of Mexico, Mixcoatl, the cloud serpent, caused them, and to the Greeks, the hideous Typhon, a monstrous serpent-dragon, was responsible. In China and Japan, dragons caused the ascending whirlwinds, as well as thunder and rain, as they wound their way from the sea to the sky during storm season. In Chile, the Araucanians represented the descending whirlwind as a lizard who disappeared under the ground when a typhoon broke. (Bassett 1971, Mackenzie 1970)

See also Dragon-Kings, Dragons, Hurricanes and Tornadoes, Vikhor, Waterspouts, Whirlpools, Winds and Wind Gods

WHIRLWINDS

Whirlwinds, like whirlpools, represented a source of natural energy. Characterized by a spiral, they symbolized motion, life, and the evolution of the universe. Whirlwinds confined the winds in powerful movements,

WINDS AND WIND GODS

Winds were prominent deities in world myths, in part because the ancients connected them with life and breath. Winds moved, and as they sailed through the atmosphere, they breathed life into the universe.

Wind gods from many lands displayed this creative side when they blew life into human beings originally made of clay or some inanimate substance. But like rain and sun and other natural forces, the winds had a destructive side. They cropped up at inconvenient times, changed directions at will, and reduced large areas of land to ruin.

Because the winds moved but could not be seen, the ancients saw a supernatural connection. Some people believed wizards brewed the winds or sorcerers or witches sent them from far away. Others thought ghosts and souls of the dead materialized as winds and hovered in the air, in the space between Heaven and earth. The gentle sea breeze, to the ancients, was a different being than the demonic storm wind or the angry gale or the whirlwind. Gods who controlled the winds resided in all three realms. In the sky realm, gods like Zeus and Odin controlled them, Odin as he rode on his horse Sleipnir, who some say personified the wind itself. In the sea realm, Poseidon and Nereus roused the winds from the ocean depths, winds that forcefully lashed giant waves angrily on the shore. On earth, the winds were often attributed to the struggles of giants or the breaths of monsters; in Siberia, they were attributed to a furious mountain spirit hiding in a cave. Wind gods materialized in all forms and in all areas of the world. In Greek myths, when the monstrous Typhon moved across the land, he caused storm winds, typhoons, and hurricanes.

Storm gods and wind gods were one and the same in many lands. Thunderbirds conjured up the winds when they flapped their gigantic wings. The Harpies conjured them up when they rushed through the atmosphere and spread filth and debris, as winds tended to do. The Garuda Bird caused winds in India; the storm bird Imdugud, in Mesopotamia; and Hraesvelgr, a giant disguised as an eagle, caused them in Scandinavia. Though the storm bird was the most

common wind deity, there were many others. The mischievous Greek messenger god Hermes, a winged god, raised the winds, especially the North Wind, when he flew over the land with great speed. In the tribes of the Iroquois and the Huron, Ga-oh controlled the winds and the seasons. In China, the tiger raised the winds, and in Japan, a tigerlike god named Abbuto raised them, and another wind god, Shintatsuhiko-no-kami, drove away morning mists. In Polynesia, Raku and his children blew the winds through holes at the edge of the horizon. In Greece, Orpheus stirred up winds when he played his lyre, but Aeolus controlled them and kept them concealed on his Island of Winds somewhere off the coast of Sicily.

Wind gods throughout the world kept their treasures locked up, as Aeolus did, confined in pots, calabashes, or leather sacks, or imprisoned in underground caves or tied into knots to render them inactive. Generally, some sorcerer or supernatural creature imprisoned the winds, someone who had the power to release them at will, usually for destructive purposes. When the winds escaped or were let loose, they blew out of their prisons with great force and caused volcanoes, tornadoes, and violent tempests.

The wind deities who caused this destruction were predominantly male, robust and fearsome and full of raw energy. Sailors perhaps feared these winds the most, sailors who faced long journeys and the perilous task of navigating through a realm where strong winds could sink their ships in a matter of seconds. Every maritime nation had their myths and legends of winds. Mariners worshipped the wind gods, and they knew that these deities could either help them or kill them. Early sailors often bought winds from the wind gods—or from the sea itself—in an attempt to control the natural forces that moved their ships. For similar reasons, sailors attempted to placate the wind gods with offerings and sacrifices in hopes that the powers that be would send favorable winds instead of menacing ones and would help them steer their vessels on the proper course.

Deities of wind, then, could be either good or evil. Their temperament depended on many things, primarily on the direction from which they blew. People generally personified four principal winds, those of the north, the east, the south, and the west. Each of these winds had distinct characteristics, and their deities, distinct personalities. In Algonquin myth, Wabun, Kabun, Kabibonokka, and Shawano represented the four winds and resided in the four corners of the world. The Lakota called the winds the four sons of the wind god Tate. Usually in North America the winds were birds, and gods and heroes often tried to control them. The trickster Coyote snared the wind, and Glooskap broke one of the wind bird's wings. Wind birds controlled their phenomena by flapping their wings. When Glooskap broke the bird's wing, he exercised control over the wind. The bird could only flap one of his wings from then on, and the winds lessened in severity. (Bassett 1971, Brinton 1976, Cox 1887, de la Rue 1955, Frazer 1950, Watson 1984)

> *See also* Air and Air Gods, Birds, Cardinal Points or Directions, Feng Shui, Garuda Bird, Hurricanes and Tornadoes, Imdugud, Raiden, Storms and Tempests, Tate, Thunderbirds, Waterspouts, Whirlwinds

WONDJINA

To the Kimberly of Australia, supernatural beings called Wondjina existed in Dreamtime, when wandering ancestral spirits roamed the earth and shaped the land. The Wondjina were mythological ancestors of the Aborigines, and some people believe in them today. These spirits personify rain, and, according to some, they originally existed in the sky. According to others, the Wondjina lived at the bottom of springs, rivers, lakes, and rock pools, and they surfaced sometime

in the Dreamtime and brought water with them wherever they roamed.

Whether the Wondjina came from the sky or the earth, they had an intricate connection to the waters of the universe. As sky beings, they dressed in rain and encircled their heads with lightning and thunder. In addition to bringing rain to the earth, the Wondjina completed other creative tasks, such as forming the hills and plains. Some people also credit them with the creation of rock paintings. It was said that the Wondjina emerged from their underwater homes at the places where the rock images appear today and that they made the impressions in the rock when they lay down on them in the early stages of land formation, before the stone fully solidified. (Campbell 1988a, Eliade 1973, Mudrooroo 1994)

> *See also* Dreamtime, Oceania, Rain and Rain Gods, Rainbow Snake, Taniwha

WORLD AXIS

To describe the positions and movements of astronomical objects, scientists consider the sky a hollow sphere, and the world axis, or the north celestial pole, the point on that sphere around which the sky appears to rotate. The north celestial pole points due north, toward the North Star, or Polaris, which mythmakers recognized as the unmoving sky god they relied on to uphold the cosmic order. Because the sky world seemed to revolve around this invisible pole, the world axis and the North Star above it implied stability and permanence. It marked the center of the world.

The ancients considered the center of the world sacred. They often symbolized the center with a tree or a mountain, and they worshipped that landform as sacred space. Perhaps the most vivid imagery of the world axis appeared in Norse mythology with the magnificent ash tree the Norsemen called Yggdrasil. This tree, it was said, was the reason the world existed. It miraculously renewed itself with dew from the heavens and with magic waters from the wells and springs that flowed beneath the roots. Yggdrasil was so large that its roots extended to the Underworld and its branches reached far into the heavens. It supported nine worlds and provided a path for communication between them. The goddesses of fate, the Norns, spun the threads of life beneath the tree and controlled the passage of time.

Yggdrasil was not the only world tree in nature mythology. The Yakuts had a similar tree and so did the Turks, complete with replenishing waters and a goddess who, like the Norns, controlled time. The people of Central Asia symbolized the world axis with a mountain, a golden mountain in the Himalayas called Mount Meru to those of the Shinto faith or Mount Sumeru to the Buddhists. In Greek mythology, the god Atlas represented the world axis. He supported the world on his shoulders. In aboriginal Australia, Numbakulla created the link between earth and sky. Numbakulla was one of the supernatural beings who wandered around and helped form the land in the primordial creation period. He created the world axis. He planted a pole in the ground and climbed it to Heaven and disappeared. The Dogon of West Africa used the pillar of their creator god, Amma, as the world axis, symbolized by the granary and, particularly, by the spindle that arose from the roof. The Dogon believed the sun, moon, stars, and planets revolved around Amma's Pillar, so the pillar itself stabilized the universe and established the patterns of life and the movement of time. (Eliade 1964, Krupp 1991a, 1996b, 1997a, 1997b)

See also Amma, Cardinal Points or Directions, Meru, Mountains, North Star, Shamanism, Trees, Yggdrasil, Ziggurats

XIUHTECUHTLI

Xiuhtecuhtli was the Aztec fire god, who some said presided over the birth of the sun, raised the four trees that held up the sky, and cast Tezcatlipoca, as the sun god, into the four cardinal directions. Also referred to as Huehueteotl, the Old God, the fire god was the oldest of gods. The Aztec understood fire as the sole reason for their advancement. So they placed Xiuhtecuhtli at the center of their world and considered him the driving force of the cosmos.

The worship of Xiuhtecuhtli as the fire god was, in some way, almost monotheistic. The Aztec called this Old God Lord of the Pole Star, and thus considered him the pivot or spindle of the universe. Xiuhtecuhtli turned time and controlled the calendar. He was central to all the cults and present at all the temples and ceremonies. His primary ceremony, the New Fire Ceremony, occurred at the end of every fifty-two years when all fires were extinguished and then rekindled over the heart of a sacrifice victim. Everyone partook of the new fire, passing it from temple to temple and home to home. Fire ensured the continuance of life, and Xiuhtecuhtli ensured that time kept moving.

The Aztec generally considered Huehueteotl and Xiuhtecuhtli two aspects of one deity, an example of the duality that lay at the heart of their religion. As Huehueteotl, the fire god appeared aged, and as Xiuhtecuhtli, as young and dynamic, accompanied by a fire serpent known as Xiuhtecoatl. (Brundage 1985, Burland 1967)

See also Fire and Fire Gods, Mesoamerica, North Star

YGGDRASIL

Yggdrasil of Norse mythology was an enormous evergreen ash and a classic illustration of the world tree, a concept common to many European and Asian cosmologies. Yggdrasil marked the center of the world and it overshadowed everything in existence. Its roots delved into the Underworld and its branches spread over the sky. Its leaves became the clouds, its fruits the stars, and its trunk the support of the nine worlds that made up the earth, the sky, and the Underworld.

The concept of the world tree encompassed the notion of world order and the threat posed to that order by violent forces of nature. Yggdrasil was the symbol of order, and it housed and nourished many animals, each symbolic of a phenomenon of nature. A squirrel ran up and down the tree, imitative of the vertical motion of rain, snow, and hail. Four stags named Dain, Dvalin, Duneyr, and Durathor lived in the branches and nibbled off new roots, imitative of the blowing winds. An eagle who perched on the highest branch suggested the air, and a hawk or a falcon who rested on the head of the eagle and illuminated the tree's limbs perhaps symbolized the high status of the sun. A serpent named Nidhogg slithered underneath the great tree and constantly gnawed at the tree's roots. The serpent, it seemed, symbolized the subterranean volcanic forces that threatened to return the world to chaos.

The ash tree was the Nordic symbol of life and strength. Yggdrasil was the strongest of trees, timeless and immortal, like a god. De-spite the forces that threatened the tree's stability, Yggdrasil lived on, nourished constantly by the life-giving power of water—the Spring of Mimir underneath the tree that held the waters of wisdom, the Spring of Hvergelmir that filled eleven rivers and the Well of Urd that nourished Yggdrasil and gave it everlasting life. Well water renewed the tree continuously, as did celestial dew that fell from the sky and dripped on the trees, leaves, and branches. (Crossley-Holland 1980, Lehner 1960)

See also Scandinavia, Springs and Wells, Trees, World Axis

YMIR

Ymir was the first Norse frost giant, born from the mingling of ice and fire. In the beginning of the world, nothing existed but a region of fire called Muspellheim, a region of fog and ice called Nifflheim, and in between, a great primordial abyss of frozen water called Ginunngagap. When ice blocks from the streams of Nifflheim and sparks of fire from the land of Muspellheim blended together in the icy abyss, Ymir emerged, along with an ice cow named Audhumla who nursed him with her streams of frozen milk. Ymir personified the frozen ocean and the numbing cold.

When the Vikings first arrived in Scandinavia, they encountered glaciers and volcanic mountains and thought they had settled in a land of ice and fire. They visualized these threatening landforms as giants, giants they had to destroy to make the area habitable. Ymir was the first of many frost giants. From under his armpit grew the first man and woman, and from them, an entire race called Jotuns. But the gods emerged early on too, among them Odin and his two brothers, Vili and Ve. The three of them slew Ymir and pushed his body back into Ginunngagap. From his frozen corpse, they created the world.

The story of Ymir's death exemplifies the life-out-of-death creation myth and compares to the African legend of Minia, the Babylonian story of Tiamat, and the Chinese myth of P'an Ku. The bodies of all these creatures became the universe too. Odin and his brothers ground Ymir's body in a mill. The giant's blood and sweat formed the sea, his flesh formed the earth, and his skull formed the dome of the sky. As the gods continued to grind, the world took shape. Ymir's bones became hills, his teeth became cliffs, and his hair became trees and vegetation. Sparks of fire flew up into the heavens during this grinding process and became stars, and the brightest sparks became the sun and the moon. The gods then scattered Ymir's brains across the sky to make billowing clouds. Although Ymir's blood drowned many of the Jotuns, enough survived to continue the race. So the gods used Ymir's eyebrows to create an enormous wall to protect the world from these fierce frost giants. (Crossley-Holland 1980, Guerber 1992, Page 1990)

See also Creation Myths, Frost and Ice, Giants, P'an Ku, Scandinavia, Stoorworm, Tiamat, Tlaltecuhtli

mer-wielding deities who sent their mighty bolts to earth as punishment for actions deemed infractions of moral law. Zeus ruled from Mount Olympus, the sacred peak that disappeared behind the clouds and reached into the realm of the Immortals. He descended to earth from time to time and interacted with human beings, but he lived on Olympus, where he had his throne, his wife Hera, and many of his offspring, the other high gods of the Greek pantheon. From there he enforced the laws and let people know of his pleasure and displeasure.

The union of Zeus and Hera was unique. Whereas sky gods of other cultures married earth goddesses, Hera represented the heavenly light and the varying atmosphere, and she shared her husband's realm and nursed his children, her divine milk splashing across the sky to form the Milky Way. Although Hera was generally regarded as Zeus's legitimate wife, he had many lovers, and with them he sired all of the Olympians and many other gods and heroes. Some of his unions have been interpreted as solar myths, others as metaphorical expressions of other forms of natural phenomena. His constant battles with Hera over his loves and his illegitimate children, some say, were mythological enactments of thunderstorms or of meteors and other atmospheric phenomena.

Zeus was depicted in human form, robust and bearded, although he had the ability to disguise himself and appear to his paramours in various forms. His symbol was an eagle, the king of birds; his most noted attribute was his thunderbolt; and his attire, an aegis or a goat skin coat that may have represented the thundercloud. (Eliade 1958, Graves 1988, Murray 1935, Rose 1959)

See also Cosmic Order, Greece and Rome, Sky and Sky Gods, Thunder and Thunder Gods

ZEUS

Zeus was the Supreme Deity of the Greeks, their sky god, their weather god, and their upholder of law and order. At first, Zeus was simply a sky god, having usurped the power of the previous sky god, Kronos, who had usurped the power of Ouranos, the sky god before that. But Zeus achieved a stature that far surpassed his predecessors. Not only did he control all forms of atmospheric phenomena, but he also became the all-powerful god of Heaven and earth. In the minds of the people, he advanced to high king, and as king, he used his functions as sky and weather god to deliver discipline in the form of thunder and lightning and blessing in the form of rain.

Zeus was so widely worshipped that he appeared to control every aspect of nature in some respect and all of human activity as well. He transformed himself into animals of all sorts, animals thought to represent electrical phenomena, such as clouds and storms. In his atmospheric role, Zeus frequently hurled thunderbolts, but he also gathered the clouds, blew the winds, and sent the rain, the hail, and the snow from Heaven to earth. Because he controlled the weather, he fertilized the land, and because he fertilized the land, his role extended into the earth realm, where his powerful presence permeated every part of the natural world.

Zeus has been compared to high gods in many other cultures, primarily to thunder gods like Thor or Perun and to other ham-

ZIGGURATS

The symbolism of the mountain in world mythology was of such crucial importance to the concept of cosmic order that the ancient Mesopotamians tried to replicate the mountain by building pyramidal mud brick towers called ziggurats. These towers were constructed in most major cities between 2200 and 550 B.C. and most likely served as the observatories from which the Babylonians calculated the movements of the celestial bodies and developed astronomical methods unrivaled even by scientists of the Victorian age. But the ziggurats of the ancient world served a loftier purpose than mortal skywatching. Like the world mountain itself, they provided paths for mortals to reach the sky realm and paths for gods to descend to earth.

As man-made imitations of world mountains, the Mesopotamian ziggurats attempted to connect the earth, the sea, and the sky. They attempted to link man with the gods. Sumerian skywatchers saw the universe as a mountain that rose from the sea and extended into the sky. So the ziggurats they built had their base in the Underworld and steep external stairways climbing toward Heaven and to the temples of the gods, built on the summits. The most famous ziggurat was the Tower of Babel, which accommodated on its summit a temple to Marduk to honor him for his role in creation. Other ziggurats had temples to other gods, such as the ziggurat at Nippur with the temple to Enlil, the god of air, and the ziggurat at Ur, the best preserved example, with the temple to Nanna, the moon god.

The vision of the earth and the sky to a large extent determined early perceptions of the universe. The Mesopotamians felt the need to build ziggurats high enough to afford them a panoramic view of the world, and the Mayans tried to achieve something similar with their pyramids and temple towers. These early people replicated the world mountain, and thus, they believed, simulated the power of the peaks. With their stable bases, their high tops, and their stairways toward Heaven, the ziggurats connected the earth to the sky and the Babylonian people to the divine order of the heavens. (Campbell 1974, Hadingham 1984)

See also Cosmic Order, Mesopotamia, Mountains, Pyramids, World Axis

ZODIAC

Twelve constellations form a ring around the sky and lie along a path called the ecliptic. These constellations compose the zodiac, and the ecliptic denotes the path the sun takes in its journey through the heavens. Many ancient people noticed that it takes one year for the sun to move through the zodiac, so they associated each constellation of the zodiac with a particular time of year. They didn't know until centuries later that the earth revolved around the sun and that the sun's movement was an illusion. To early people, as the sun moved through the zodiac, the months changed, the seasons turned, and time marched on.

Where the sun appeared in the sky seems

This illustration of the sun surrounded by a calendar showing the seasons and signs of the zodiac first appeared in an 1841 almanac.

to have had a lot to do with the form the ancients assigned to the stars behind it. When the sun moved through a certain star group at the summer solstice, for instance, people assigned to that star group an image they connected with the summer sun. The pictures these people created were symbols more than anything else. It took a great deal of imagination to see the animals or figures the ancients placed there, and because some of the constellations were faint and the stars inconspicuous, it took something more than imagination to even recognize patterns at all. The ancients noticed these star groups because they lay along the sun's path and could therefore be used to mark the seasons.

Although many signs in our zodiac originated long before ancient Greek civilization, the zodiac we know came from the classical world. The Greeks made a picture book out of the heavens, and they told captivating myths of gods and heroes to explain the placement of each constellation in the sky. Some of the Greek stories link the constellations together and explain the movement of these star groups as they appear and disappear over the horizon. But not all of their star stories draw connections. Most of them are separate myths, told as separate legends of the sky.

The constellations recognized as the zodiac today are Aries, the ram; Taurus, the bull; Gemini, the twins; Cancer, the crab; Leo, the lion; Virgo, the virgin; Libra, the scales; Scorpio, the scorpion; Sagittarius, the archer; Capricorn, the goat; Aquarius, the water carrier; and Pisces, the fishes. See individual signs for specific myths and legends. (Allen 1963, Olcott 1911, Ridpath 1988, Staal 1988)

See also Constellations, Stars and Star Gods

APPENDIX
Guide to Primary Sources

The following list identifies ancient sources of myths for most broad geographical areas covered in this book. English translations of many of these sources, as well as literary commentaries, are available in most large libraries.

Much of what scholars have learned of nature myths they deduced from studying the art and artifacts of early civilizations. Many myths and legends were never recorded in writing but simply transmitted orally, from generation to generation. This is particularly true of the myths and legends of Africa, Oceania, and the Americas. In these areas no truly "ancient" sources exist. The earliest works from these areas were compiled by Christian missionaries and chroniclers of individual societies and were written well into the nineteenth and twentieth centuries. For a thorough treatment of the best sources for study in these areas, as well as in the areas of the ancient world listed below, refer to the entries for each geographical area in Mircea Eliade's *Encyclopedia of Religion*.

BALTIC AND SLAVIC LANDS
Most early myths from this area of northern Europe survive in over a million songs, which in the Baltic lands are called dainas or dainos. They describe the deities of the pagan people and recount myths and legends that emphasize a reverence of nature and, particularly, of the sun.

The *Kalevala* is a Finnish epic poem consisting of fifty individual runes, or songs, recounting the adventures of Finnish gods and heroes. It was compiled by Elias Lonnrot from the oral songs of folk singers over a period of time.

CELTIC LANDS
The pagan Celts were nonliterate, so scholars derived much of their early mythology from archeological finds and from written documents of the medieval period. Classical writers of the first century A.D., such as Caesar and Lucan, contributed to the collection of early Celtic myths by writing about early ritual practices like Druidism, divination, human sacrifice, and water worship.

In Ireland three collections compiled in the twelfth century A.D. contain myths and legends of earlier times. Students interested in Celtic nature myths will find frequent reference to the myths of the "Fionn Cycle," the "Ulster Cycle," and the "Mythological Cycle," the latter of which contains the most renowned source of information, the *Book of Invasions*.

CHINA
Primary sources for Chinese mythology include the *Feng shen yen i*, or *Creation of the Gods*, in eight volumes, and the *Sou shen chi*, or *In Search of the Supernatural*, in ten volumes. Confucian works include the *Shih ching*, or the *Book of Odes*, which is the earliest anthology of Chinese poetry; the *Shang shu* or the *Shu ching*, or the *Book of Documents*, which is the earliest Chinese historical work;

the *I ching,* or the *Book of Changes,* which is an ancient manual of divination; and the *Li chi,* or the *Book of Rites,* which contains a series of texts on various topics, including magic, ritual, and the meaning of sacrifice.

EGYPT

A collection known as the *Pyramid Texts* is one of the oldest religious works in the world and contains prayers and spells that were carved in hieroglyphs on pyramid walls around 2400–2280 B.C. The collection contains hymns to individual nature gods and particularly emphasizes the supreme rule of the sun god.

The *Coffin Texts* came into being in the Middle Kingdom, about 2040–1786 B.C., and contain original material from the *Pyramid Texts* and new spells as well. In this collection, Osiris, rather than the sun god, rules supreme.

The *Book of the Dead* is a collection of funerary texts consisting of hymns, prayers, and incantations found on the walls of pyramids and tombs. From various times and places, they were collected by tomb robbers and compiled into one volume. Many of the spells in this book originated in the *Pyramid Texts* and the *Coffin Texts.*

GREECE AND ROME

The Greek classics the *Iliad* and the *Odyssey* contain accounts of all the major figures in Greek myth. The *Iliad,* the famous epic poem written by Homer about 900 B.C., contains twenty-four books or chapters dealing with the Trojan War and particularly with the hero Achilles. The *Odyssey* was written by Homer about 900 B.C. and recounts the adventures of Odysseus as he travels home after the fall of Troy.

The *Argonautica,* the epic poem written by Apollonius of Rhodes in the third century B.C., contains the most celebrated version of the journey of Jason and the Argonauts.

Theogony, written by the poet Hesiod in the eighth century B.C., includes the most widely accepted myth of creation and a genealogy of the Greek gods.

The *Aeneid* was written by the Latin poet Virgil about 90–70 B.C. and has been hailed as the most influential book of Roman myth and literature.

The *Metamorphoses,* a collection of poetic tales composed by Ovid from 43 B.C. to A.D. 17, contains about 250 myths and legends in fifteen books and includes many famous constellation myths. These are a Roman account of the Greek gods.

Other early sources of astronomical and constellation mythology include the *Catasterismi,* commonly attributed to Eratosthenes and likely written in the first century A.D., and *Fabulae* and *Poetica Astronomica,* both attributed to Hyginus, and written at the beginning of the second century A.D.

INDIA

The Vedas comprise the earliest record of Indian mythology, dated possibly between 1200 and 800 B.C. They consist of a collection of hymns and chants that contain the spiritual insights of ancient sages. There are four Vedas, among which the Rig Veda is the oldest and most well known. The central theme of the Rig Veda is the myth of creation; the primary hymns are devoted to Indra, the storm god, Agni, the fire god, and Surya, the sun god.

The *Ramayana* and the *Mahabharata* are the two great epics of Hindu India. The *Mahabharata* was attributed to the sage Vvasu and composed between the fourth century B.C. and the fourth century A.D. It tells the story of Vishnu in his avatar as Krishna. The *Ramayana,* attributed to the sage Valmiki, was composed in the third century A.D. and tells the story of Vishnu in his avatar as Rama.

JAPAN

The *Kojiki (Records of Ancient Matters),* written in A.D. 673–686, is the oldest Japanese book and the most comprehensive collection of Japanese Shinto myths.

The *Nihongi (Chronicles of Japan)*, written in A.D. 720, is twice as long as the *Kojiki* and contains many variations of the same myths.

MESOAMERICA

The Popul Vuh (Book of Counsel) is the sacred book of the Quiche Maya, written sometime in the sixteenth century. The first part deals with the creation of the world, the middle part deals with the adventures of the Hero Twins, Hunahpu and Xbalanque, and the last part contains a legendary history of the Quiche.

The pre-Hispanic codices were screenfold books written in hieroglyphics. Only four of these codices remain: the Madrid, the Paris, and the Grolier Codices, and the Dresden Codex, the most renowned of the four and the best source of astronomical mythology among the Maya.

The most important Aztec sources date from the colonial period and represent the works of sixteenth-century friars, such as Fray Bernadino de Sahagun and Fray Diego Duran. Sahagun's most renowned work is *Historia General de las Cosas de Nueva Espana,* commonly known as the *Florentine Codex.* Duran's most renowned work is *Historia de las Indias de Nueva Espana.* He also published separately *The Book of Gods and Rites* and *The Ancient Calendar.* These works describe Aztec deities and recount myths.

MESOPOTAMIA

Enuma Elish, or the *Epic of Creation,* is one of the world's oldest creation myths, composed in the seventh century B.C. and referred to as the "Babylonian Genesis." In addition to being a creation story, it is a celebration of the high god Marduk, who fashioned order from chaos.

The *Epic of Gilgamesh* recounts the myths and legends of the hero Gilgamesh and includes the story of the flood. The epic was composed in the second millennium B.C. and survives in twelve tablets, written in Akkadian.

Some of the shorter myths from Mesopotamia were also recorded on clay tablets and preserved. Among them are *Atrahasis, The Descent of Ishtar, Nergal and Ereshkigal,* and *The Epic of Anzu.*

PERSIA

The Avesta, the sacred book of the Zoroastrians, contains most of the myths of ancient Persia. It contains historical information about the people, their gods, and the creation of the world. The primary myths of both Zoroastrian and pre-Zoroastrian times appear in a section of hymns called Yasht.

The *Shahnameh,* or the *Book of Kings,* an epic poem written by Firdowsi in A.D. 1010, contains many Persian myths and legends.

SCANDINAVIA

The *Poetic Edda* is a collection of poems about the pagan Germanic gods and heroes, written by numerous singers and poets of the Viking world beginning around A.D. 900. Among the thirty-four poems, "Voluspa" is the most well known. The *Poetic Edda* is sometimes referred to as the Elder Edda.

The *Prose Edda,* written by Snorri Sturluson in Iceland in the twelfth and thirteenth centuries, is a summary of the pagan Germanic myths. It comprises three parts, the first of which recounts the myths of the Norse gods. Snorri's work is sometimes referred to as the Younger Edda.

BIBLIOGRAPHY

Albanese, Catherine L. *Nature Religion in America.* Chicago: University of Chicago Press, 1990.

Alexander, Hartley Burr. *Latin America.* Vol. 11, Mythology of All Races. Boston: Marshall Jones, 1964a.

———. *North America.* Vol. 10, Mythology of All Races. Boston: Marshall Jones, 1964b.

Allen, Richard Hinkley. *Star Names: Their Lore and Meaning.* New York: Dover, 1963.

Alpers, Anthony. *Legends of the South Seas: The World of the Polynesians Seen through Their Myths and Legends.* New York: Thomas Y. Crowell, 1970.

———. *Maori Myths and Tribal Legends.* Boston: Houghton Mifflin, 1966.

Ames, Delano. *Egyptian Mythology.* London: Paul Hamlyn, 1965.

Andersen, Johannes C. *Myths and Legends of the Polynesians.* New York: Dover, 1995. Reprint.

Andrews, Tamra. "Tapping the Sunstick: The Chumash Solstice Ceremony." *Star Date* 23 (5), 1995a, p. 14.

———. "Universal Harmony and the Legend of Yin and Yang." *Star Date* 23 (4), 1995b, p. 14.

———. "Harvest Moon." *Star Date* 22 (5), 1994a, p. 14.

———. "Pawnee Earth Lodges." *Star Date* 22 (3), 1994b, p. 14.

———. "The Navajo Sky People." *Star Date* 21 (5), 1993, pp. 4–7.

———. "Snake Rattle Star." *Star Date* 20 (6), 1992, pp. 17–18.

Anesaki, Masaharu. *Japanese Mythology.* Vol. 8, Mythology of All Races. Boston: Marshall Jones, 1964.

Ann, Martha, and Dorothy Imel. *Goddesses in World Mythology.* Santa Barbara, Calif.: ABC-CLIO, 1993.

Ashe, Geoffrey. *Mythology of the British Isles.* London: Trafalgar Square, 1990.

Austin, Alfredo Lopez. *The Rabbit on the Face of the Moon: Mythology in the Mesoamerican Tradition.* Salt Lake City: University of Utah Press, 1996.

Aveni, Anthony. "Mediators in a Universal Discourse." *Archeology* 46, July/August 1993, p. 31.

———. *Empires of Time: Calendars, Clocks and Cultures.* New York: Basic Books, 1989.

———. *Skywatchers of Ancient Mexico.* Austin: University of Texas Press, 1980.

———. *Archeoastronomy in Pre-Columbian America.* Austin: University of Texas Press, 1978.

———. *Native American Astronomy.* Austin: University of Texas Press, 1977.

Baker, Margaret. *Folklore of the Sea.* London: David and Charles, 1979.

Baring-Gould, Sabine. *Curious Myths of the Middle Ages.* London: Rivingtons, 1897.

Bassett, Fletchers. *Legends and Superstitions of the Sea and of Sailors in All Lands and at All Times.* Detroit: Singing Tree Press, 1971.

Beck, Horace. *Folklore of the Sea.* Mystic, Conn.: Marine Historical Foundation, 1979.

Beckwith, Martha. *Hawaiian Mythology.* Honolulu: University of Hawaii Press, 1970.

Bell, Robert E. *Women of Classical Mythology: A Biographical Dictionary.* Santa Barbara, Calif.: ABC-CLIO, 1991.

Bellamy, H. S. *Moons, Myths, and Man.* Ann Arbor, Mich.: University Microfilms International, 1959.

Benwell, Gwen. *Sea Enchantress: The Tale of the Mermaid and Her Kin.* New York: Citadel Press, 1965.

Bernbaum, Edwin. *Sacred Mountains of the World.* San Francisco: Sierra Club, 1990.

Biedermann, Hans. *Dictionary of Symbolism.* New York: Facts on File, 1992.

Bierhorst, John, ed. *Mythology of Mexico and Central America.* New York: William Morrow, 1990.

———. *Gods and Heroes of the New World: The Mythology of South America.* New York: William Morrow, 1988.

———. *The Mythology of North America.* New York: William Morrow, 1985.

———. *Black Rainbow: Legends of the Incas and Myths of Ancient Peru.* New York: Farrar, Straus and Giroux, 1976.

Bierlin, J. F. *Parallel Myths.* New York: Ballantine, 1994.

Black, Jeremy, and Anthony Green. *Gods, Demons and*

Symbols of Ancient Mesopotamia. Austin: University of Texas Press, 1992.

Bonnefoy, Yves. *Mythologies.* 2 vols. Chicago: University of Chicago Press, 1991.

Bonnerjea, Biren. *A Dictionary of Superstitions and Mythology.* London: Folk Press, 1927.

Bord, Janet, and Colin Bord. *Sacred Waters: Holy Wells and Water Lore in Britain and Ireland.* New York: Granada, 1985.

Boyer, Carl B. *The Rainbow: From Myth to Mathematics.* Princeton, N.J.: Princeton University Press, 1987.

Brecher, Kenneth, and Michael Friertag. *Astronomy of the Ancients.* Cambridge, Mass.: MIT Press, 1979.

Breeden, Stanley. "The First Australians." *National Geographic,* February 1988, pp. 266–289.

Brinton, Daniel G. *Myths of the New World: The Symbolism and Mythology of the Indians of the Americas.* Reprint. New York: Multimedia Publishing, 1976.

Brown, Raymond Lamont. *Phantoms of the Sea: Legends, Customs and Superstitions.* New York: Taplinger, 1972.

Brueton, Diana. *Many Moons.* New York: Prentice-Hall, 1991.

Brundage, Burr Cartwright. *The Jade Steps: A Ritual Life of the Aztecs.* Salt Lake City: University of Utah Press, 1985.

———. *The Phoenix of the Western World: Quetzalcoatl and the Sky Religion.* Norman: University of Oklahoma Press, 1982.

———. *The Fifth Sun: Aztec Gods, Aztec World.* Austin: University of Texas Press, 1979.

Bryant, Page. *The Aquarian Guide to Native American Mythology.* New York: Aquarian Press, 1991.

Budge, A. Wallace. *Legends of the Egyptian Gods: Hieroglyphic Texts and Translations.* Reprint. New York: Dover, 1994.

———. *The Gods of the Egyptians.* 2 vols. New York: Dover, 1969.

Bullard, Fred M. *Volcanoes: In History, in Theory, in Eruption.* Austin: University of Texas Press, 1962.

Bullfinch's Mythology. New York: Avenel Books, 1979.

Bunson, Margaret R., and Stephen M. Bunson. *Encyclopedia of Ancient Mesoamerica.* New York: Facts on File, 1996.

Burckhardt, Titus. "The Primary Qualities." *Parabola* 20 (1), 1995, pp. 12–14.

Burland, Cottie. *North American Indian Mythology.* New York: Peter Bedrick Books, 1985.

———. *The Gods of Mexico.* London: Eyre & Spottiswoode, 1967.

Burn, Lucilla. *Greek Myths.* Austin: University of Texas Press, 1990.

Cain, Kathleen. *Luna: Myth and Mystery.* Boulder, Colo.: Johnson Printing, 1991.

Campbell, Joseph. *Historical Atlas of World Mythology.* 2 vols. San Francisco: Harper and Row, 1988a.

———. *The Power of Myth.* New York: Doubleday, 1988b.

———. *The Masks of God.* 4 vols. Harmondsworth, England: Penguin Books, 1977.

———. *The Mythic Image.* Princeton, N.J.: Princeton University Press, 1974.

———. *Hero with a Thousand Faces.* Princeton, N.J.: Princeton University Press, 1968.

Carlson, John B. "America's Ancient Skywatchers." *National Geographic,* March 1990, pp. 76–107.

Carpenter, E. *Eskimo Realities.* New York: Holt, Rinehart and Winston, 1973.

Carrasco, David. *Religions of Mesoamerica.* San Francisco: Harper and Row, 1990.

Caso, Alfonso. *The Aztecs: People of the Sun.* Norman: University of Oklahoma Press, 1958.

Cavendish, Richard, ed. *Man, Myth and Magic: An Illustrated Encyclopedia of the Supernatural.* 21 vols. New York: Marshall Cavendish, 1994.

———. *Legends of the World.* London: Orbis Publishing, 1982.

———. *An Illustrated Encyclopedia of Mythology.* New York: Crescent Books, 1980.

Cerveny, Randy. "Power of the Gods: Ancient Cultures Grounded on a Fear of Lightning." *Weatherwise* 47, April/May 1994, p. 20.

Chamberlain, Von Del. *When Stars Came Down to Earth.* Los Altos, Calif.: Ballena Press, 1982.

Chevalier, Jean, and Alain Gheerbrant. *The Penguin Dictionary of Symbols.* New York: Penguin, 1996.

Ching, Valerie. "Fire and Ice: Influence of Geology on Beliefs." *Earth Science* 43, Summer 1990, pp. 18–21.

Christie, Anthony. *Chinese Mythology.* New York: Peter Bedrick Books, 1985.

Cirlot, J. E. *Dictionary of Symbols.* London: Routledge and K. Paul, 1971.

Cobo, Father Bernabe. *Inca Religion and Customs.* Translated and edited by Roland Hamilton. Austin: University of Texas Press, 1990.

Coe, Michael. *The Maya.* London: Thames and Hudson, 1987.

Coles, Bryony, and John Coles. *People of the Wetlands: Bogs, Bodies and Lake Dwellers.* London: Thames and Hudson, 1989.

Cooper, J. C. *An Illustrated Encyclopedia of Traditional Symbols.* London: Thames and Hudson, 1978.

Cornell, James. *The First Stargazers.* New York: Scribners, 1981.

Cotterell, Arthur. *The Macmillan Illustrated Encyclopedia of Myths and Legends.* New York: Macmillan, 1989.

———. *A Dictionary of World Mythology.* New York: G. P. Putnam's Sons, 1979.

Courlander, Harold. *Tales of Yoruba Gods and Heroes.* New York: Crown, 1973.

Cox, George W. *The Mythology of the Aryan Nations.* 2 vols. London: Longmans, Green, 1887.

Crossley-Holland, Kevin. *The Norse Myths.* New York: Pantheon Books, 1980.

Curtis, Vesta Sarkhosh. *Persian Myths.* Austin: University of Texas Press, 1993.

Davidson, H. R. Ellis. *The Lost Beliefs of Northern Europe.* New York: Routledge, 1993.

———. *Scandinavian Mythology.* New York: Peter Bedrick Books, 1986.

———. *Gods and Myths of Northern Europe.* Baltimore: Penguin, 1964.

Davis, F. Hadland. *Myths and Legends of Japan.* New York: Dover, 1992.

de la Rue, E. Aubert. *Man and the Winds.* New York: Hutchinson, 1955.

Dennis, Jerry. *It's Raining Frogs and Fishes: Four Seasons of Natural Phenomena and Oddities of the Sky.* New York: Harper Collins, 1992.

Dixon, Roland Burrage. *Oceanic Mythology.* Vol. 9, Mythology of All Races. Boston: Marshall Jones, 1964.

Donnan, John A., and Marcia Donnan. *Rain Dance to Research.* New York: David McKay, 1977.

Dorsey, George A. *The Pawnee Mythology.* Reprint. Lincoln: University of Nebraska Press, 1997.

Dumezil, Georges. *Gods of the Ancient Norsemen.* Berkeley: University of California Press, 1973.

Dundes, Alan. *The Flood Myth.* Berkeley: University of California Press, 1988.

Duran, Fray Diego. *Book of Gods and Rites and the Ancient Calendar.* Norman: University of Oklahoma Press, 1971.

Durkheim, Emile. *Elementary Forms of Religious Life.* Reprint. New York: Free Press, 1995.

Edmonds, Margot, and Ella E. Clark. *Voices of the Winds.* New York: Facts on File, 1989.

Eels, E. "The Thunderbird." *American Anthropologist.* Old Series, vol. 2, 1889, pp. 329–336.

Elder, John, and Hertha D. Wong. *Family of Earth and Sky.* Boston: Beacon Press, 1994.

Eliade, Mircea. "Observing Sacred Time." *Parabola* 15 (1), 1990, pp. 21–28.

———, ed. *Encyclopedia of Religion.* 16 vols. New York: Macmillan, 1987.

———. *Myths, Rites, Symbols.* 2 vols. New York: Harper and Row, 1976.

———. *Australian Religions: An Introduction.* Ithaca, N.Y.: Cornell University Press, 1973.

———. *Shamanism: Archaic Techniques of Ecstasy.* New York: Pantheon Books, 1964.

———. *Myth and Reality.* New York: Harper and Row, 1963.

———. *Images and Symbols: Studies in Religious Symbolism.* London: Harvill Press, 1961.

———. *The Sacred and the Profane: The Nature of Religion.* New York: Harcourt Brace, 1959.

———. *Patterns in Comparative Religion.* New York: Sheed & Ward, 1958.

Elliot, Alexander. *Universal Myths: Heroes, Gods, Tricksters and Others.* New York: Penguin, 1976.

Ellis, Peter Berresford. *A Dictionary of Celtic Mythology.* Santa Barbara, Calif.: ABC-CLIO, 1992.

Ellis, Richard. *Monsters of the Sea: The History, Natural History and Mythology of the Ocean's Most Fantastic Creatures.* New York: Knopf, 1994.

The Enchanted World: Water Spirits. Alexandria, Va.: Time-Life, 1985.

Evslin, Bernard. *Gods, Demigods and Demons: An Encyclopedia of Greek Mythology.* New York: Scholastic, 1975.

Farrington, Oliver C. "The Worship and Folklore of Meteorites. *Journal of American Folklore* 13, 1900, pp. 199–208.

Ferguson, Gary. *Spirits of the Wild: The World's Great Nature Myths.* New York: Clarkson Potter, 1996.

Ferguson, John Calvin. *Chinese Mythology.* Vol. 8, Mythology of All Races. Boston: Marshall Jones, 1964.

Fiske, John. *Myths and Mythmakers.* Reprint. New York: Random House, 1996.

Flatow, Ira. *Rainbows, Curve Balls and Other Wonders of the Natural World Explained.* New York: William Morrow, 1988.

Fletcher, Alice C. "Pawnee Star Lore." *Journal of American Folklore* 16, 1916, pp. 10–15.

———. "Star Cult among the Pawnee." *American Anthropologist* 4 (4), 1902, pp. 730–736.

Forde, D. *African Worlds. Studies in the Cosmological Ideas and Social Values of African Peoples.* London: Oxford University Press, 1954.

Foster, Jerry. "Varieties of Sea Lore." *Western Folklore* 28, 1969, pp. 260–66.

Fox, William Sherwood, ed. *Mythology of All Races.* 13 vols. New York: Cooper Square, 1964. (Individual volumes listed by author.)

Frazer, James George. *Myths of the Origin of Fire.* Reprint. New York: Barnes and Noble, 1996.

———. *The Golden Bough: A Study in Magic and Religion.* New York: Macmillan, 1950.

———. *The Worship of Nature.* London: Macmillan, 1926.

Freeman, Mara. "Sacred Waters, Holy Wells." *Parabola,* Spring 1995, pp. 52–57.

Freund, Philip. *Myths of Creation.* New York: Washington Square Press, 1965.

Frey, Rodney. *The World of the Crow Indians.* Norman: University of Oklahoma Press, 1987.

Frierson, Pamela. *The Burning Island: A Journey through Myth and History in the Volcanic Country, Hawaii.* San Francisco: Sierra Club Books, 1991.

Gallant, Roy A. *The Constellations: How They Came to Be.* New York: Four Winds Press, 1979.

Gardner, Jane F. *Roman Myths.* Austin: University of Texas Press, 1993.

Gelling, Peter. *Chariot of the Sun, and Other Rites and Symbols of the Northern Bronze Age.* New York: Praeger, 1969.

Gerhardt, Mia I. *Old Men of the Sea, from Neptunus to Old French Luiton: Ancestor and Character of a Water-spirit.* Amsterdam: Polak & Van Gennep, 1967.

Getty, Alice. *The Gods of Northern Buddhism.* Rutland, Vt.: C. E. Tuttle, 1962.

Gill, Sam D., and Irene G. Sullivan. *Dictionary of Native American Mythology.* Santa Barbara, Calif.: ABC-CLIO, 1992.

Gimbutas, Marija. *The Gods and Goddess of Old Europe, 7000–3500 B.C.: Myths, Legends and Cult Images.* Berkeley: University of California Press, 1974.

———. *The Slavs.* New York: Praeger, 1971.

Gould, Charles. *Mythical Monsters.* Reprint. New York: Bracken Books, 1989.

Graham, F. Lanier. *The Rainbow Book.* Revised Edition. New York: Vintage Books, 1979.

Graves, Robert. *The Greek Myths.* Mt. Kisco, N.Y.: Penguin, 1988.

———. *The White Goddess.* New York: Farrar, Straus and Giroux, 1966.

———. *Greek Gods and Heroes.* New York: Dell, 1960.

Gray, John. *Near Eastern Mythology.* New York: Peter Bedrick Books, 1982.

Green, Matthew. "The Sacred Sky of the Navajo and Pueblo." *Griffith Observer* 60 (1), 1996, pp. 2–16.

Green, Miranda J. *Celtic Myths.* Austin: University of Texas Press, 1993.

———. *Dictionary of Celtic Myth and Legend.* London: Thames and Hudson, 1992.

———. *The Sun Gods of Ancient Europe.* London: B. T. Batsford, 1991.

———. *Gods of the Celts.* New York: Barnes and Noble, 1986.

Greenler, Robert. *Rainbows, Halos, and Glories.* New York: Cambridge University Press, 1980.

Gregory, K. J., ed. *The Earth's Natural Forces.* New York: Oxford University Press, 1990.

Greimas, Algirdas H. *Of Gods and Men: Studies in Lithuanian Mythology.* Bloomington: Indiana University Press, 1992.

Grey, George. *Polynesian Mythology.* London: Whitcombe and Tombs, 1956.

Griavle, Marcel. "Gifts from the Celestial Granary." *Parabola* 16 (3), 1991, pp. 39–45.

Griffin-Pierce, Trudy. *Earth Is My Mother, Sky Is My Father: SPACE, Time and Astronomy in Navajo Sandpainting.* Albuquerque: University of New Mexico Press, 1992.

Griffiths, J. Gwyn. *The Conflict of Horus and Seth.* Liverpool: Liverpool University Press, 1960.

Grimal, Pierre. *Dictionary of Classical Mythology.* New York: Blackwell, 1986.

Grimm, Jacob. *Teutonic Mythology.* 4 vols. Reprint. New York: Dover, 1966.

Gubernatis, Angelo de. *Zoological Mythology.* London: Trubner, 1872.

Guerber, H. A. *Greece and Rome.* Reprint. London: Bracken Books, 1992.

———. *Myths of the Northern Lands.* Reprint. New York: American Book, 1980.

Guirand, Felix. *Greek Mythology.* Translated by Delano Ames. London: Hamlyn, 1963.

Guthrie, W. K. C. *The Greeks and Their Gods.* London: Methuen, 1950.

Hackin, J., et al. *Asiatic Mythology.* New York: Thomas J. Crowell, 1963.

Hadingham, Evan. *Early Man and the Cosmos.* Norman: University of Oklahoma Press, 1984.

Haile, Father Berard. *Star Lore among the Navajo.* Santa Fe: Museum of Navajo Ceremonial Art, 1947.

Hardin, Terri. *Legends and Lore of the American Indians.* New York: Barnes and Noble, 1993.

Harley, Timothy. *Moon Lore.* Reprint. Detroit: Singing Tree Press, 1969.

Harrison, Jane Ellen. *Ancient Art and Ritual.* New York: Henry Holt, 1913.

Hart, George. *Egyptian Myths.* Austin: British Museum Press and University of Texas Press, 1990.

Harva, U. "Finno-Ugric Mythology" in *Mythology of All Races.* New York: Cooper Square, 1964.

Hastings, James, ed. *Encyclopedia of Religion and Ethics.* Edinburgh: T. and T. Clark, 1925.

Heller, Julek. *Giants.* New York: H. N. Abrams, 1979.

Herbert, Jean. *Shinto.* London: George Allen and Unwin, 1967.

Herskovits, Melville J. *Dahomey: An Ancient West African Kingdom.* New York: J. J. Augustin, 1938.

Hicks, Clive. *Green Man: The Archetype of Our Oneness with the Earth.* San Francisco: Harper Collins, 1990.

Hinnels, John R. *Persian Myth.* London: Hamlyn, 1973.

Holm, Jean, ed. *Attitudes to Nature.* New York: Pinter, 1994.

Holmberg, Uno. *Siberian Mythology.* Vol. 4, Mythology of All Races. Boston: Marshall Jones, 1964.

Hooke, Samuel H. *Babylonian and Assyrian Religion.* Norman: University of Oklahoma Press, 1963.

Hope, Robert Charles. *The Legendary Lore of the Holy*

Wells of England, Including Rivers, Lakes, Fountains and Springs. London: Paternoster, Row, 1893.

Hopfe, Lewis M. *Religions of the World.* Englewood Cliffs, N.J.: Prentice-Hall, 1994.

Hori, Ichiro. "Mountains and Their Importance for the Idea of the Other World." *History of Religions* 6 (1), 1966, pp. 1–23.

Howey, M. Oldfield. *The Encircled Serpent: A Study of Serpent Symbolism in All Countries and Ages.* New York: Arthur Richmond, 1955.

———. *The Horse in Magic and Myth.* London: W. Rider, 1923.

Hubbs, Joanna. *Mother Russia: The Feminine Myth in Russian Culture.* Bloomington: Indiana University Press, 1988.

Hultkrantz, Ake. *Belief and Worship in Native North America.* Syracuse, N.Y.: Syracruse University Press, 1981.

———. *The Religions of the American Indians.* Berkeley: University of California Press, 1967.

———. "The Indians and the Wonders of Yellowstone." *Ethnos* 19, 1954, pp. 34–68.

Huxley, Francis. *The Dragon.* New York: Collier Books, 1979.

Ingersoll, Ernest. *Dragons and Dragon Lore.* New York: Payson and Clark, 1928.

———. *Birds in Legend, Fable and Folklore.* New York: Longmans, Green, 1923.

Inwards, Richard. *Weather Lore: The Unique Bedside Book.* New York: Rider, 1950.

Ions, Veronica. *Indian Mythology.* New York: Peter Bedrick Books, 1984.

———. *Egyptian Mythology.* New York: Peter Bedrick Books, 1983.

Jacobsen, Thorkild. *The Treasures of Darkness: A History of Mesopotamian Religion.* New Haven, Conn.: Yale University Press, 1976.

Jahner, Elaine. "The Spiritual Landscape." *Parabola* 5 (3), 1977, pp. 32–38.

James, E. O. *The Ancient Gods.* London: Weidenfeld and Nicolson, 1960.

———. *Myth and Ritual in the Ancient Near East.* London: Thames and Hudson, 1958.

James, T. G. H. *Myths and Legends of Ancient Egypt.* New York: University Books, 1969.

Jayne, Walter Adison. *The Healing Gods of Ancient Civilizations.* New York: University Books, 1962.

Jobes, Gertrude. *Dictionary of Mythology, Folklore and Symbols.* 2 vols. New York: Scarecrow Press, 1962.

Jordan, Michael. *Myths of the World: A Thematic Encyclopedia.* London: Kyle Cathie, 1993.

Judson, Katharine Berry. *Myths and Legends of Alaska.* Chicago: A. C. McClurg, 1911.

Jung, C. *Man and His Symbols.* London: New York: Doubleday, 1964.

Kato, Genchi. *A Study of Shinto.* Tokyo: Meiji Japan Society, 1926.

Keith, A. Berriedale. *Indian Mythology.* Vol. 6, Mythology of All Races. Boston: Marshall Jones, 1964.

Kirk, G. S. *The Nature of Greek Myths.* New York: Penguin, 1974.

Klein, Cecilia. "Who Was Tlaloc?" *Journal of Latin American Lore* 6(2), 1980, pp. 155–204.

Klepa, Lilian. "Gods and the Sky in Ancient Scandinavia." *Griffith Observer* 49 (6), 1985, pp. 2–11.

Knappert, Jan. *African Mythology: An Encyclopedia of Myth and Legend.* London: Diamond Books, 1995a.

———. *Indian Mythology: An Encyclopedia of Myth and Legend.* London: Diamond Books, 1995b.

———. *Pacific Mythology: An Encyclopedia of Myth and Legend.* London: Diamond Books, 1995c.

Knipe, Rita. *The Water of Life: A Jungian Journey through Hawaiian Myth.* Honolulu: University of Hawaii Press, 1989.

Kramer, Samuel Noah. *Mythologies of the Ancient World.* New York: Doubleday/Anchor Books, 1961.

Krupp, Ed. "Climbing the Cosmic Axis." *Griffith Observer* 61 (1), 1997a, pp. 2–8.

———. *Skywatchers, Shamans, and Kings.* New York: John Wiley, 1997b.

———. "The Thread of Time." *Sky and Telescope* 91, January 1996a, p. 60.

———. "The Top of the Sky, the Center of the World, and the Road Between." *Griffith Observer* 60 (12), 1996b, pp. 2–18.

———. "Negotiating the Highwire of Heaven." *Vistas in Astronomy* 39, 1995a, pp. 405–430.

———. "Partners in Time." *Sky and Telescope* 89 (3), 1995b, p. 64.

———. "The Long Shadow of Winter." *Sky and Telescope* 88(6), 1994, p. 64.

———. "The Midautumn Moon Goddess." *Sky and Telescope* 86 (3), 1993a, pp. 59–60.

———. "Migrating Birds of the Milky Way." *Sky and Telescope* 86 (4), 1993b, p. 58.

———. "Spilled Milk." *Griffith Observer* 57 (12), 1993c, pp. 2–18

———. "Phases of Venus." *Griffith Observer* 56 (12), 1992, pp. 2–18.

———. *Beyond the Blue Horizon: Myths and Legends of the Sun, Moon, Stars and Planets.* New York: Oxford University Press, 1991a.

———. "Seven Sisters." *Griffith Observer* 55 (1), 1991b, pp. 2–16.

———. "Facing the Sun." *Griffith Observer* 54 (1), 1990, pp. 2–13.

———. "Moon Maids." *Griffith Observer* 52 (12), 1988, pp. 2–15.

———. *Echoes of Ancient Skies.* New York: Harper and Row, 1983.

————. "The Serpent Descending." *Griffith Observer* 46 (9), 1982, pp. 10–20.

————. "An Aztec 'Calendar' Stone: and Its Celestial Seal of Approval." *Griffith Observer,* July 1981, pp. 2–7.

————. *In Search of Ancient Astronomies.* New York: Doubleday, 1977.

Kurtz, Seymour. *A World Guide to Antiquities.* New York: Crown, 1975.

Lang, Andrew. *Myth, Ritual and Religion.* 2 vols. Reprint. New York: Random House, 1996.

Larousse, 1968. See *New Larousse Encyclopedia of Mythology.*

Leach, Maria. *Guide to the Gods.* Santa Barbara, Calif.: ABC-CLIO, 1992.

————, ed. *Funk and Wagnalls Standard Dictionary of Folklore, Mythology and Legend.* New York: Harper and Row, 1984.

Leeming, David Adams. *Encyclopedia of Creation Myths.* Santa Barbara, Calif.: ABC-CLIO, 1994.

————. *The World of Myth.* New York: Oxford University Press, 1990.

Lehner, Ernst, and Johanna Lehner. *Folklore and Symbolism of Flowers, Plants and Trees.* New York: Tudor, 1960.

Levi-Strauss, Claude. *The Naked Man.* New York: Harper and Row, 1971.

————. *The Raw and the Cooked.* New York: Harper and Row, 1964.

————. *Totemism.* Boston: Beacon Press, 1963.

Lienhardt, Godfrey. *Divinity and Experience.* Oxford: Clarendon Press, 1961.

Lockhart, Gary. *The Weather Companion: An Album of Meteorological History, Science, Legend, and Folklore.* New York: John Wiley & Sons, 1988.

Lockyer, Joseph Norman. *The Dawn of Astronomy.* Reprint. Cambridge, Mass.: MIT Press, 1964.

Logan, Doug. "The Known and Unknown Wind." *Parabola* 20 (1), 1995, p. 34.

Lopez, Barry Holstun. *Giving Birth to Thunder, Sleeping with His Daughter.* New York: Avon, 1977.

Lovi, George. "The Mists of Antiquity." *Sky and Telescope* 79, April 1990, p. 407.

Luomala, Katherine. *Voices on the Wind: Polynesian Myths and Chants.* Revised Ed. Bishop Museum Special Publication 75. Honolulu: Bishop Museum Press, 1986.

Lurker, Manfred. *The Gods and Symbols of Ancient Egypt.* New York: Thames and Hudson, 1980.

Mabbett, I. W. "The Symbolism of Mount Meru." *History of Religions* 23 (1), 1983, pp. 64–83.

McAlpine, Helen, and William McAlpine. *Japanese Tales and Legends.* Oxford: Oxford University Press, 1958.

McCall, Henrietta. *Mesopotamian Myths.* Austin: British Museum Press and University of Texas Press, 1990.

MacCana, Proinsias. *Celtic Mythology.* New York: Peter Bedrick Books, 1985.

McCartney, E. S. "Greek and Roman Weather Lore of the Sea." *Classical Weekly* 27, 1933, pp. 1, 9, 17, 25.

————. "Classical Weather Lore of Thunder and Lightning." *Classical Weekly* 25, 1932, pp. 183, 200, 212.

————. "Greek and Roman Weather Lore of the Winds." *Classical Weekly* 24, 1930, pp. 11, 18, 25.

————. "Clouds, Rainbows, Weather Galls, Comets and Earthquakes as Weather Prophets in Greek and Latin Writers." *Classical Weekly* 23, 1929, pp. 2, 11.

McCrickard, Janet. *Eclipse of the Sun.* Glastonbury, Somerset: Gothic Image, 1990.

MacCullough, John A. *Eddic Mythology.* Vol. 2, Mythology of All Races. Boston: Marshall Jones, 1964.

McDonald, Marianne. *Tales of the Constellations: The Myths and Legends of the Night Sky.* New York: Smithmark, 1996.

Mackenzie, Donald A. *Mythology of the Babylonian People.* Reprint. London: Bracken Books, 1996.

————. *Myths of China and Japan.* Reprint. New York: Random House, 1994.

————. *Indian Myths and Legends.* New Delhi: Sona, 1971.

————. *The Migration of Symbols.* New York: AMS Press, 1970.

————. *Myths of Pre-Columbian America.* London: Gresham, 1924.

Mackinlay, James M. *Folklore of Scottish Lochs and Springs.* Glasgow: William Hodge, 1893.

McLeish, Kenneth. *Myth: Myths and Legends of the World Explored.* New York: Facts on File, 1996.

McLuhan, T. C. *The Way of the Earth: Native America and Environment.* New York: Simon & Schuster, 1994.

Makemson, Maud Worcester. *The Morning Star Rises: An Account of Polynesian Astronomy.* New Haven, Conn.: Yale University Press, 1941.

Manley, Seon, and Robert Manley. *Islands: Their Lives, Legends and Lore.* New York: Chilton, 1970.

Markham, Clements. *The Incas of Peru.* Reprint. New York: AMS Press, 1969.

Markman, Roberta H., and Peter T. Markman. *The Flayed God: The Mythology of Mesoamerica.* San Francisco: Harper, 1992.

Marriott, Alice, and Carol K. Rachlin. *American Indian Mythology.* New York: Thomas Y. Crowell, 1968.

Marshak, Alexander. *The Roots of Civilization.* Reprint. Mt. Kisco, N.Y.: Moyer-Bell, 1991.

Marshall, Peter. *Nature's Web: Rethinking Our Past on Earth.* New York: Paragon House, 1994.

Matthews, John, and Caitlin Matthews. *British and Irish Mythology.* London: Diamond Books, 1995.

Mayo, Gretchen Will. *Earthmaker's Tales: North American Indian Stories about Earth Happenings.* New York: Walker, 1989.

Mbiti, John S. *Concepts of God in Africa.* New York: Praeger, 1970.

Mercatante, Anthony S. *The Facts on File Encyclopedia of World Mythology and Legend.* New York: Facts on File, 1988.

———. *Who's Who in Egyptian Mythology.* New York: Clarkson N. Potter, 1978.

———. *Zoo of the Gods.* New York: Harper and Row, 1974.

Metzner, Ralph. *The Well of Remembrance: Rediscovering the Earth Wisdom Myths of Northern Europe.* Boston: Shambhala, 1994.

Michell, John. *The Earth Spirit: Its Ways, Shrines and Mysteries.* New York: Crossroads, 1975.

Miller, Mary, and Karl Taube. *Gods and Symbols of Ancient Mexico and the Maya.* London: Thames and Hudson, 1993.

Mishkin, Bernard. "Cosmological Ideas among the Indians of the Southern Andes." *Journal of American Folklore* 53, 1940, pp. 225–241.

Moor, Edward. *The Hindu Pantheon.* Reprint. New York: Garland, 1984.

Moore, Patrick. *Sun, Myths and Men.* New York: W. W. Norton, 1968.

Morrison, Tony. *Pathways to the Gods: The Mystery of the Andes Lines.* New York: Harper and Row, 1978.

Mountford, Charles Pearcy. *The Dreamtime: Australian Aboriginal Myths.* Sydney: Rigby, 1970.

Mudrooroo. *Aboriginal Mythology.* New York: Thirsas, 1994.

Muller, Friedrich Max. *Contributions to the Science of Mythology.* 2 vols. New York: Longmans, Green, 1897.

Muller, Wilhelm Max. *Egyptian Mythology.* Vol. 12, Mythology of All Races. Boston: Marshall Jones, 1964.

Murray, Alexander S. *Who's Who in Mythology: A Classical Guide to the Ancient World.* New York: Bonanza Books, 1988.

———. *Manual of Mythology.* New York: Tudor, 1935.

Muser, Curt. *Facts and Artifacts of Ancient Middle America.* New York: Dutton, 1978.

New Larousse Encyclopedia of Mythology. New York: Prometheus Press, 1968.

Nicholson, Irene. *Mexican and Central American Mythology.* New York: Hamlyn, 1985.

Nimmo, H. Arlo. "Pele, Ancient Goddess of Contemporary Hawaii." *Pacific Studies* 9 (2), 1986, pp. 121–179.

Norman, Howard. *Northern Tales: Traditional Stories of Eskimo and Indian Peoples.* New York: Pantheon, 1990.

Olcott, William Tyler. *Myths of the Sun.* Reprint. New York: Capricorn Books, 1967.

———. *Star Lore of All Ages.* New York: G. P. Putnam, 1911.

O'Neill, John. *Time and the Calendars.* Sydney: Sydney University Press, 1975.

Ono, Sokyo. *Shinto: The Kami Way.* Rutland, Vt.: Charles E. Tuttle, 1962.

Orbell, Margaret. *Illustrated Encyclopedia of Maori Myth and Legend.* Sydney: University of New South Wales Press, 1996.

———. *The Natural World of the Maori.* Auckland: Collins/Bateman, 1985.

Osbourne, Harold. *South American Mythology.* New York: Peter Bedrick Books, 1986.

Page, R. I. *Norse Myths.* Austin: University of Texas Press, 1990.

Pandit, Bansi. *Hindu Dharma.* (Publication of the Hindu Temple of San Antonio.) Glen Ellyn, Ill.: B & V Enterprises, 1996.

Parabola. 20(1), Spring 1995 (thematic issue on earth, air, fire, and water).

Parabola. 4, February, 1979 (thematic issue on tricksters).

Parrinder, Geoffrey. *African Mythology.* New York: Peter Bedrick Books, 1986.

———, ed. *Man and His Gods.* London: Hamlyn, 1971.

———. *West African Religion.* New York: Barnes and Noble, 1961.

Parsons, E. C. *Pueblo Indian Religion.* Reprint. Lincoln: University of Nebraska Press, 1996.

Pelton, Robert D. *The Trickster in West Africa: A Study of Mythic Irony and Sacred Delight.* Berkeley: University of California Press, 1980.

Pennick, Nigel. *Celtic Sacred Landscapes.* London: Thames and Hudson, 1996.

Perowe, Stewart. *Roman Mythology.* New York: Hamlyn, 1969.

Phillpotts, Beatrice. *Mermaids.* New York: Ballantine Books, 1980.

Philpot, J. H. *The Sacred Tree.* New York: Macmillan, 1897.

Picken, Stuart D. B. *Shinto: Japan's Spiritual Roots.* New York: Harper and Row, 1980.

Piggott, Juliet. *Japanese Mythology.* New York: Peter Bedrick Books, 1983.

Pinch, Geraldine. *Magic in Ancient Egypt.* Austin: University of Texas Press, 1994.

Pinsent, John. *Greek Mythology.* New York: Peter Bedrick Books, 1985.

Poignant, Roslyn. *Oceanic Mythology.* London: Hamlyn, 1967.

Porteous, Alexander. *Forest Folklore, Mythology, and Romance.* Detroit: Singing Tree Press, 1968.

Proctor, Mary. *Legends of the Sun and Moon.* London: George G. Garrip, 1926.

Radin, Paul. *The Trickster: A Study in American Indian Mythology.* London: Routledge & Paul, 1955.

Ralston, W. R. S. *Russian Folk-Tales.* London: Smith, Elder, 1873.

———. *The Songs of the Russian People.* London: Ellis & Green, 1872.

Ramage, Edwin S. *Atlantis: Fact or Fiction.* Bloomington: Indiana University Press, 1978.

Rappoport, Angelo S. *The Sea.* Reprint. London: Senate, 1995.

Reed, A. W. *Myths and Legends of Australia.* New York: Taplinger, 1965.

Reed, Mary. "When Animals Roosted in Trees." *Weatherwise* 47 (2), April/May 1994, p. 36.

———. "Demon Gates and Devils Doors." *Weatherwise* 46, December/January 1993, p. 38.

Reichard, Gladys A. *Navaho Religion: A Study of Symbolism.* Tucson: University of Arizona Press, 1983.

Ridpath, Ian. *Star Tales.* New York: Universe Books, 1988.

Rink, D. Henry. *Tales and Traditions of the Eskimo.* London: Wm. Blackwood and Sons, n.d.

Roberts, Ainslie. *The Dreamtime: Australian Aboriginal Myths.* Sydney: Rigby, 1970.

Rolleston, T. W. *Celtic Mythology.* London: Bracken Books, 1990.

Rosalie, David. *Cult of the Sun: Myth and Magic in Ancient Egypt.* London: J. M. Dent & Sons, 1980.

Rose, H. J. *A Handbook of Greek Mythology.* New York: E. P. Dutton, 1959.

Russell, William Clark. *The Father of the Sea and Other Legends of the Deep.* London: S. Low, Marston, 1911.

Sakurai, Dorna S. "The Immortal Sun." *Griffith Observer* 48 (11), November 1984, pp. 11–19.

Sanders, Scott Russell. "Ancient Quartet." *Parabola* 20 (1), Spring 1995, pp. 6–11.

Sanders, Tao Tao Liu. *Dragons, Gods, and Spirits from Chinese Mythology.* New York: Schocken Books, 1980.

Schonland, Basil. *The Flight of Thunderbolts.* London: Oxford University Press, 1964.

Shepard, Paul. *The Sacred Paw: The Bear in Nature, Myth, and Literature.* New York: Viking, 1985.

Simonov, Pyotr. *Essential Russian Mythology: Stories that Change the World.* New York: Thirsis, 1997.

Skinner, Charles M. *Myths and Legends beyond Our Borders.* Philadelphia: J. B. Lippincott, 1899.

———. *Myths and Legends of Our Own Land.* Philadelphia: J. B. Lippincott, 1896.

Smith, Edwin. *African Ideas of God.* London: Edinburgh House, 1950.

Smith, William Ramsay. *Aborigine Myths and Legends.* Reprint. New York: Senate, 1996.

Smithsonian Institution. *Fire of Life: Smithsonian Book of the Sun.* Washington D.C.: Smithsonian Books, 1981.

Snodgrass, Mary Ellen. *Voyages in Classical Mythology.* Santa Barbara, Calif.: ABC-CLIO, 1994.

South, Malcolm. *Mythical and Fabulous Creatures: A Source Book and Research Guide.* New York: Greenwood Press, 1987.

Spence, Lewis. *Ancient Egyptian Myths and Legends.* New York: Dover, 1990.

———. *Myths and Legends of the North American Indians.* New York: Dover, 1989.

———. *Egypt.* Bracken Books, 1986.

———. *Myths of Mexico and Peru.* Reprint. Boston: Longwood Press, 1977.

———. *Magic and Mysteries of Mexico.* London: Rider, 1930.

———. *Myths and Legends of Babylonia and Assyria.* New York: Farrar and Rinehart, n.d.

Squire, Charles. *Celtic Myth and Legend.* San Bernadino, Calif.: Newcastle, 1975.

Staal, Julius D. W. *The New Patterns in the Sky: Myths and Legends of the Stars.* Blacksburg, Va.: McDonald & Woodward, 1988.

———. *Stars of Jade: Astronomy and Star Lore of the Very Ancient Imperial China.* Decatur, Ga.: Writ Press, 1984.

Starr, Frederick. *Fujiyama: The Sacred Mountain of Japan.* Chicago: Covici-McGee, 1924.

Steward, Julian Haynes, ed. *Handbook of South American Indians.* New York: Cooper Square, 1963.

Stewart, R. J. *Celtic Gods, Celtic Goddesses.* London: Blandford, 1990.

Sturtevart, William C., ed. *Handbook of North American Indians.* Washington, D.C.: Smithsonian Institution, 1978.

Suzuki, David, and Peter Knudtson. *Wisdom of the Elders: Honoring Sacred Native Visions of Nature.* New York: Bantam Books, 1992.

Talbot, P. Amaury. *Some Nigerian Fertility Cults.* London: Frank Cass, 1967.

Taube, Karl. *Aztec and Mayan Myths.* Austin: University of Texas Press, 1993.

Tedlock, Dennis. "A Mayan Reading of the Story of the Stars." *Archaeology* 46, July/August 1993, p. 33.

Teich, Howard. "Sun and Moon." *Parabola* 14 (2), Summer 1994, pp. 55–58.

Tenenbaum, Barbara A., ed. *Encyclopedia of Latin American History and Culture.* New York: Scribner's Sons, 1996.

Thomas, P. *Epics, Myths, and Legends of India.* Reprint. Bombay: D. B. Taraporevala and Sons, 1980.

BIBLIOGRAPHY

Thompson, J. Eric A. *Maya History and Religion.* Norman: University of Oklahoma Press, 1970.

Thompson, Stith. *Tales of the North American Indians.* Cambridge, Mass.: Harvard University Press, 1929.

Thompson, Vivian L. *Hawaiian Myths of Earth, Sea and Sky.* Honolulu: University of Hawaii Press, 1988.

Thorpe, Cora Wells. *In the Path of the Trade Winds.* New York: G. P. Putnam's Sons, 1924.

Tierney, Patrick. *The Highest Altar: Unveiling the Mystery of Human Sacrifice.* New York: Penguin Books, 1990.

Time-Life. *Book of Beginnings.* Alexandria, Va.: Time-Life, 1986.

————. *Giants and Ogres.* Alexandria, Va.: Time-Life, 1985.

Tyler, Hamilton A. *Pueblo Gods and Myths.* Norman: University of Oklahoma Press, 1964.

Tylor, Edward. *Researches into the Early History of Mankind.* Reprint. Chicago: University of Chicago Press, 1964.

————. *Primitive Culture.* 2 vols. Reprint. New York: Harper and Brothers, 1958.

Uchendu, Victor C. *The Igbo of Southeast Nigeria.* New York: Holt, Rinehart and Winston, 1965.

Urton, Gary. *At the Crossroads of Earth and Sky.* Austin: University of Texas Press, 1981.

Urton, Gary, ed. *Animal Myths and Metaphors in South America.* Salt Lake City: University of Utah Press, 1985.

Vaillant, George C. *Aztecs of Mexico.* Baltimore: Penguin, 1965.

Van Over, Raymond. *Sun Songs: Creation Myths from around the World.* New York: New American Library/Mentor, 1980.

Verdet, Jean-Pierre. *The Sky: Mystery, Magic and Myth.* New York: Harry N. Abrams, 1992.

Vitaliano, Dorothy B. *Legends of the Earth.* Bloomington: Indiana University Press, 1973.

Wainwright, G. A. *The Sky-Religion in Egypt.* Cambridge: Cambridge University Press, 1938.

Walker, Barbara G. *A Woman's Encyclopedia of Myths and Secrets.* San Francisco: Harper, 1983.

Walker, James R. *Lakota Belief and Ritual.* Lincoln: University of Nebraska Press, 1980.

Watson, Lyall. *Heaven's Breath: A Natural History of the Wind.* New York: William Morrow, 1984.

Werner, Alice. *African Mythology.* Vol. 7, Mythology of All Races. Boston: Marshall Jones, 1964.

Werner, Edward T. C. *Ancient Tales and Folklore of China.* Reprint. London: George Harap, 1995.

Wertime, Richard A., and Angela M. H. Schuster. "Written in the Stars: Celestial Origin of Maya Creation Myth." *Archeology* 46, July/August 1993, pp. 26–32.

Wesler, Allan. *Images Encyclopedia.* Surfside, Fla.: Enterprises, 1990.

Westervelt, William. *Hawaiian Legends of Volcanoes.* Rutland, Vt.: Charles E. Tuttle, 1963.

Williamson, Ray A. *Living the Sky: The Cosmos of the American Indian.* Norman: University of Oklahoma Press, 1984.

Williamson, Ray A., and Clair R. Farrer, eds. *Earth and Sky: Myth and Cosmos in North American Folklore.* Albuquerque: University of New Mexico Press, 1992.

Williamson, Robert W. *Religious and Cosmic Beliefs of Central Polynesia.* 2 vols. Cambridge: Cambridge University Press, 1933.

Willis, Roy, ed. *World Mythology.* New York: Henry Holt, 1993.

Wilson, Colin. *Starseekers.* New York: Doubleday, 1980.

Wood, Marion. *Spirits, Heroes and Hunters from North American Indian Mythology.* New York: Schocken Books, 1982.

Worthen, Thomas D. *The Myth of Replacement.* Tucson: University of Arizona Press, 1991.

Wright, B. *Kachinas: A Hopi Artist's Documentary.* Flagstaff, Ariz.: Northland Press, 1973.

Wright, Hamilton, and Helen Wright, eds. *To the Moon: A Distillation of the Great Writings from Ancient Legend to Space Exploration.* New York: Meredith Press, 1968.

Yeomans, Donald E. *Comets: A Chronological History of Observation, Science, Myth and Folklore.* New York: John Wiley and Sons, 1991.

Zimmer, Heinrich. *Myths and Symbols in Indian Art and Civilization.* Reprint. New York: Harper Torchbooks, 1962.

Zimmerman, J. E. *Dictionary of Classical Mythology.* New York: Harper Row, 1964.

Znayenko, Myroslava. *Gods of the Ancient Slavs.* Columbus, Ohio: Slavica, 1980.

ILLUSTRATION CREDITS

CULTURE INDEX

The terms listed under each geographical area include entries for gods and goddesses worshipped solely in those areas as well as entries that contain a significant amount of material relating to those areas. Additional information on myths from each area appear in the multicultural entries as well. Common alternate names for some of the gods and goddesses appear in parentheses next to their names.

AFRICA
Agbe
Ala
Amma
Deng
Deserts
Great Spirit
Lightning Bird
Mason-Wasp
Mawu-Leza
Mujaji
Rain and Rain Gods
Rainbow Snake
Shango
Tilo
Tsui'goab
Volcanoes

BALTIC AND SLAVIC LANDS
Auszrine
Forests
Frost and Ice
Moist Mother Earth
Moroz
Myesyats
Perun/Perkunas
Rusalka
Saule
Svarog
Ukko
Vikhor

CELTIC LANDS
Bogs

Brigit (Danu)
Dragon Slaying
Grannos (Apollo Grannos)
Lugh (Lug)
Manannan (Manawydan)
Springs and Wells
Stoorworm
Sulis
Taranus
Water Horses
Waves

CHINA
Chhih Sung-tzu (Yu Shih)
Dragon-Kings
Dragons
Eclipses
Feng Po (Fei Lien)
Feng Shui
Harvest Moon
Heng O (Chang O)
Lei Kung
Monsoons
P'an Ku
Shang di (Tien)
T'ien Mu

EGYPT
Amon
Apep (Apophis)
Aten
Bast (Bastet)
Clocks and Calendars
Crocodile
Deserts
Geb
Hathor

Horus
Isis
Nile River
Nut
Osiris
Pyramids
Ra (Re)
Scarab Beetle
Shu (Tefnut)
Thoth (Tahuti)

GREECE AND ROME
Achelous
Aeolus (Hippotades)
Aetna
Amphitrite (Salacia)
Andromeda
Apollo
Aquarius, the Water Carrier
Aries, the Ram
Artemis (Diana)
Cancer, the Crab
Capricorn, the Goat
Circumpolar Stars
Clouds
Cyclopes
Demeter (Ceres)
Gaia (Tellus)
Gemini, the Twins
Giants
Harpies
Helios (Sol)
Hephaestus (Vulcan)
Horae
Hyades
Iris
Leo, the Lion

CULTURE INDEX

CULTURE INDEX

Leo, the Lion
Libra, the Scales
Lightning
Lotus
Marshes and Swamps
Mermaids
Meteors and Meteorites
Milky Way
Mirage
Mirrors
Monsoons
Mountains
Music
Night
North Star
Phosphorescence
Pisces, the Fishes
Planets
Pleiades
Primordial Sea
Pyramids
Rain and Rain Gods
Rainbows and Rainbow Gods
Rivers and Lakes
Rocks and Stones
Sacrifice
Sagittarius, the Archer
St. Elmo's Fire
Scorpio, the Scorpion
Sea and Sea Gods
Sea Foam
Sea Monsters
Seasons
Serpents and Snakes
Shamanism
Sheep and Cattle
Ships
Sirius
Sky and Sky Gods
Snow
Solstices
Spinning and Weaving
Springs and Wells
Stars and Star Gods
Storms and Tempests
Sun and Sun Gods
Sunbeams and Moonbeams
Swan Maidens
Taurus, the Bull
Tears
Thunder and Thunder Gods
Thunderbirds
Tides
Tortoise
Totemism

Trees
Typhoons
Virgo, the Virgin
Volcanoes
Water and Water Spirits
Waterfalls
Waterspouts
Waves
Well of Life
Whirlpools
Whirlwinds
Winds and Wind Gods
World Axis
Zodiac

NORTH AMERICA and ARCTIC LANDS
Canyons, Gorges, and River Valleys
Cloud People
Constellations
Cosmic Order
Ga-oh
Geysers
Glaciers
Glooskap
Great Spirit
Hino (Hinun)
Inyan
Kachinas
Medicine Wheels
Michabo (Manabozho, Nanabush)
Sedna (Avilayoq, Niliajuk, Nerrivik, Arnarquagssaq)
Shamanism
Snow
Solstices
Sun Dance
Sunbeams and Moonbeams
Tate
Tirawahat (Tirawa)
Tortoise
Tricksters
Volcanoes
Waterfalls

OCEANIA
Adaro
Ayers Rock
Canyons, Gorges, and River Valleys
Clouds
Dreamtime
Glaciers
Hina

Kamapua'a
Magellanic Clouds
Marshes and Swamps
Pele
Rainbow Snake
Tane
Tangaroa
Taniwha
Tawhiri-matea
Volcanoes
Wondjina

PERSIA
Atar
Duality
Mithra
Tishtrya
Vayu

SCANDINAVIA
Aegir
Balder
Bifrost
Fenrir
Frey
Freya
Frigg
Frost and Ice
Frost Giants
Hjuki and Bil
Njord
Odin
Skidbladnir
Storms and Tempests
Thor (Donar)
Yggdrasil
Ymir

SOUTH AMERICA
Cuycha
Dark Cloud Constellations
Huacas
Illapa (Apocatequil, Catequil)
Inti
Jaguar
Mama Kilya (Mama Quilla)
Pachacamac
Pillan
Sacrifice
Thunderbirds
Totemism
Tupan
Viracocha

SUBJECT INDEX

SUBJECT INDEX